Social Media
for Journalists
principles & practice

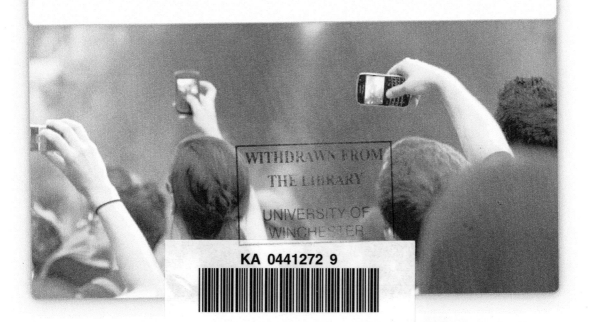

Megan Knight
and Clare Cook

Social Media
for Journalists
principles & practice

SAGE

Los Angeles | London | New Delh
Singapore | Washington DC

Los Angeles | London | New Delhi
Singapore | Washington DC

SAGE Publications Ltd
1 Oliver's Yard
55 City Road
London EC1Y 1SP

SAGE Publications Inc.
2455 Teller Road
Thousand Oaks, California 91320

SAGE Publications India Pvt Ltd
B 1/I 1 Mohan Cooperative Industrial Area
Mathura Road
New Delhi 110 044

SAGE Publications Asia-Pacific Pte Ltd
3 Church Street
#10-04 Samsung Hub
Singapore 049483

Editor: Mila Steele
Editorial assistant: James Piper
Production editor: Imogen Roome
Copyeditor: Neil Dowden
Proofreader: Kate Harrison
Indexer: Indexing Specialists Ltd
Marketing manager: Michael Ainsley
Cover design: Francis Kenney
Typeset by: C&M Digitals (P) Ltd, Chennai, India
Printed in Great Britain by Ashford Colour Press
Ltd

© Megan Knight and Clare Cook 2013

First published 2013

Library of Congress Control Number: 2012951707

British Library Cataloguing in Publication data

A catalogue record for this book is available from the British Library

ISBN 978-1-4462-1112-0
ISBN 978-1-4462-1113-7 (pbk)

For Martin, and for my father, Steve, and in memory of my mother, Shirley
For Michael and Harriet without whom I would be lost

CONTENTS

ACKNOWLEDGEMENTS

The authors would like to thank the following people for their help and support in producing this book:

Nigel Barlow, Robert Beers, Daniel Bentley, Chris Blackhurst, Paul Bradshaw, Nick Brett, Martin Bryant, Dan Burnett, Natasha Courtenay-Smith, Andy Dickinson, Julie Freer, Chris Frost, Anthea Garman, Alison Gow, Mary Hamilton, David Hayward, Graham Holliday, Nicola Hughes, Isabelle Mandraud, Craig McGinty, Jason Mills, François Nel, Meg Pickard, Grzegorz Piechota, Jean Quatremer, Miranda Richardson, George Riley, Mark Rock, Esa Sirkkunen, Jon Snow, Joseph Stashko, Fiona Steggles, John Thompson, Adam Tinworth, Sabine Torres, the team at Scraperwiki, and our colleagues and students at the School of Journalism and Digital Communication at the University of Central Lancashire.

>>Chapter 1<<

INTRODUCTION: NETWORKED JOURNALISM

Overview

The media are changing. This is obvious to anyone who has been paying attention, but over the last decade the pace of change has increased beyond even the ability of the language we use to describe it or the rules we use to govern it. Who is a blogger, really? What is citizen journalism? Who operates under what privileges? A new media ecology has emerged, one that is social and fluid, and trades on connections and collaborative relations. This shift is fundamental to everything we do as journalists and journalism trainers. This is the ecology of the new media environment. This book proposes a new way of examining the practical skills that are necessary to thrive as a journalist, and the principles governing the new media ecology for those working within it, consuming it and researching it.

Key concepts

- Citizen journalism
- Connections
- Media landscape
- Networks
- New media ecology
- Relationships
- Reporting
- Social media
- Traditional media
- User-generated content

Introduction

An ecology is an interdependent network of living things, each fulfilling its own function within the system, but with no one thing dominating or monopolising it. You do not control it, or master it: you find your niche, your relationships, your dependencies and you thrive – as long as the system thrives.

This book is a guide on how to find – or create – your niche in the ecology of new media, and how to understand and nurture the connections that will allow you to thrive. Throughout this book, you will be encouraged to think about relationships, to think about the rest of the system – the other players and participants (not only other producers, but audiences and advertisers as well) – and to work with them, not against them, to create great journalism.

We propose a new way of talking about and operating within the news environment, a new way of examining and defining the media landscape for those working within it, consuming it and researching it. We are not hoping to pin down the definition of what the news landscape now is, but to describe its trajectory in a way that is flexible and dynamic enough to explain both the contemporary ways of reporting, and to illuminate the changes we know will come, although we don't yet know what they are.

A broken model

As the news environment has expanded and fragmented, coalesced and converged, the meanings of terms like 'newspaper' and 'television channel' have become harder and harder to pin down, and more organisations exist for which we have no simple definition. The dichotomy of 'old' and 'new' media is likewise becoming meaningless – talking to a room full of students who were not yet born when the World Wide Web was invented and referring to it as 'new' makes one realise how meaningless 'new' actually is in this context. What is 'online' in a world where those of us who have physical 'lines' to connect to the internet are increasingly in the minority, and where more people have smartphones, tablets and laptop computers than have television sets?

And this change and confusion is not just on the institutional level – individuals working within (and outside) these organisations have found themselves increasingly unable to define what they do in a single sentence, although they know what they are doing, and are doing it well.

Traditionally, news organisations were constructed and determined by their output mechanism, and hence by their technology. Once the printing press was invented, the newspaper was an almost inevitable consequence; and radio and television engendered the news broadcast. Since the technology was both the prerequisite for production, and the locus of a substantial financial investment, we named these organisations for their technology, not their content. We still speak of 'the press' as though the hulking steel machinery in the basements of Fleet Street was the soul of the news media, and the broadcast towers have only recently vanished from the logos of television stations worldwide – as they are vanishing from the physical landscape.

The internet was the agent of this change. We used to measure the importance of a news outlet by the speed of their presses, or a radio station by the power of its antenna, which were themselves functions of the size of their capital investment. We can't measure these new outlets by the clock speed of their servers, or the size of their disk array, although the servers perform the same function the presses and towers did for newspapers and broadcasting. We don't do this because, relatively speaking, a server costs a pittance compared with the cost of a printing press or, and much more importantly, compared with the cost of the people who make the content that is distributed by mechanisms new and old. Almost anyone can set up a site, anyone can create a blog, a Twitter account, a Facebook wall, a platform from which to spread a message – the technology is no longer the stumbling block; the content and connectivity are.

Just as the technology determined the nature of the enterprise, it also had a huge influence on the content that was produced. News organisations produced news in recognisable shapes and formats for recognisable outlets consumed by recognisable consumers in predictable ways. As the technology changed, more and more sources of news became available online and competed with other sources of information and news, in myriad new shapes and sizes. You can still find the third-person-objective inverted pyramid news story and the traditional 'package' for broadcast on the internet, but you also find live blogs and Twitter feeds from people on the ground and in the office, satirical animations of news events on YouTube, and first-person reports, Twitpics, blogs, alternative news sites, aggregators and discussion forums, in all sorts of voices and styles all mixed in together, linked, referenced and cross-posted to a range of places and formats. In this environment, the traditional definitions of what journalism is have inevitably shifted, as have the skills and techniques required to participate in it.

Social media

These changes have created a more social way of doing journalism. More people can be heard. More voices can be included. The focus is less on what platforms to use or what products to produce, and more on whom to speak to and connect with, and how to go about doing that. Everyone steers their way through the network via connections and exchanges, making sense of the content they encounter or use. Journalists are no different.

Relationships emerge as a key unit of currency. These relationships exist at many different levels, but without these voices the web would be nothing more than a structure of portable pieces of code lacking any meaning. News organisations are re-evaluating how they interact with 'the people formerly known as the audience' (Rosen, 2006). They have moved towards curated or humanised approaches to distribution rather than automated feeds and abstract 'packages' of news. Strangers help us find content through recommendations or reviews. Friends contribute to making that journey more relevant and real (Pickard and Catt, 2011).

Out of these relationships grow communities. Journalists have to appreciate how to act within a community, and take an active part in growing and developing them. In this ecology, journalism trades on participation and connections rather than a top-down approach. It is no longer the case that the moment you signal your need you are given everything you desire. This is a culture of collaboration, not co-optation. There's a wealth of information in the crowd, but journalists need to understand how to collaborate with users, not simply take from them. Talking, interacting, thanking and crediting all become key. There are new skills and rules to consider if you are to become a trusted and respected part of the online network.

And the crowd – not journalists – are in control. The crowd can seek out imposters and regulate itself, just as they can amplify and ring out changes. The web community expects transparency, even as identities ebb and flow in different spaces. Journalists have to tell people what they are doing and how they are doing it. This new culture of social media in which journalists operate has to be understood if you, as a participant, are to thrive.

A word about terminology

The terms that define this new landscape are by no means set, and there is considerable confusion regarding what they mean. For this book, we take 'social media' to mean all forms of new media production whose primary function is interaction – not simply presentation of information. Any news product or piece of information that is presented in order to be commented on, discussed, circulated and used within a network of social interaction is, for us, 'social' media. This includes what are increasingly thought of as the 'social media' applications – Twitter and Facebook – but also stories presented for comment online, television panel shows that incorporate audience commentary, live blogs that curate and collect material from multiple sources, and myriad other ways (some not yet invented) in which the audience and the producers meet and talk.

The new media ecology

In this landscape, there's more than one way to define media organisations and individual journalists. Traditionally, newsmaking was a process that took events and turned them into recognisable reports or news packages, using the 'third-person-objective' voice of authority that we have come to associate with news. This voice still exists, and plays an important role in conveying events to people. These are the shaped, formatted and edited packages that we most easily recognise as journalism. After all, we can't all physically attend news or events; neither would we want to. We rely, inevitably, on reporters to reach out and expand our worlds, our discovery, our understanding.

But in the social media ecology, this is not the only version of events that exists. Social media have allowed for a vast expansion of voices and participants, sites and streams. We may watch edited news, but we may also listen, watch or participate in the loose, unedited, stream-of-consciousness voice of social media: the personal blogger or tweeter, or the chaotic and unedited video footage taken by a participant in a protest. The news products here are more divergent, incorporating multiple voices and channels, but creating an environment where one user may need to have access to hundreds of sources to provide an understanding of events.

This brings us to the question of gatekeeping. In the past, edited and polished news products were traditionally closed off to the public; professional journalists in the traditional sense constructed the news product based only on their sources and research, and presented a sealed and finite news product to a passive audience. But social media allows for those gates to open, and the public are given potential access to the news production process, more opportunities to participate in and guide the news agenda. In social spaces, the distinction between journalist and audience has vanished completely: the gates have crumbled away.

From our perspective, the news landscape is becoming more and more social, requiring new perspectives on the interplay between the voice and intent of journalists and media outlets. Even the most traditional news organisations have set out an agenda to become more engaged; they are including live blogs of events on their websites, incorporating amateur video into their feeds, and encouraging user comments and feedback in formal and informal ways.

Journalist by definition

The opening up of the new media ecology to include an infinite array of news producers and providers leaves us with plenty to ponder. What is journalism, anyway, and what makes one news organisation different from another?

First, not everyone working in journalism has the same intentions. The intent of a news organisation varies tremendously from the traditional, mainstream, commercial and industrialised mass media to organisations whose production of news is entirely secondary, or even accidental, to their main goals. News producers may be registered professionals, subject to the oversight typical of their national context, which sets rules on the dissemination of news and the behaviour of news outlets, or they may be activist journalists dedicated to spreading the truth in aid of a political or social cause, or they may be accidental journalists – passersby caught up in events, whose stories and pictures become part of the narrative. All of these people, and the institutions in which they may or may not work, have different ideas on what they do, what they should do and what it means in the greater scheme of things.

As an example, consider the uprisings that racked Egypt in 2011, and dominated the news around the world, as Tahrir Square in Cairo became the focus of the frustrations and hopes of not only the Egyptian people, but people all over the world. A wide variety of reporters and journalists descended on the square to tell the story.

Purely journalistic institutions – the BBC, CNN, New York Times – would cover Tahrir Square because it fulfils a traditional idea of what news is, and claim to do so in an 'objective' way. They would refer to President Mubarak and protestors in the most neutral way possible. Then there are the news organisations that have overt social or political goals. A newspaper with a clearly stated belief in social justice would cover the same events, referring to Mubarak as a dictator or despot and the protestors as campaigners or activists. There are also organisations in which the journalistic goals are less important than the political or social goals. Groups and related blogs may provide reports from Cairo relating directly to the action of the people of Egypt against state repression. At the far extreme, there are organisations whose journalistic goals are incidental to other goals. WikiLeaks's release of diplomatic cables relating to Egypt, and other documents, are not simply journalistic, but include an element of anarchy, of subversion of power on the principle of it.

In this new media landscape news outlets have to carve out a space and identity alongside all these other forms of news. They find themselves having to coexist with blogs and aggregators online, or reports from people and organisations that have goals other than becoming a formal, commercial news organisation, such as 'zines, radical news outlets and activist groups online.

There is also a changing relationship between producers and consumers. It is a rare news organisation or journalist who does not invite contributions from the public, feedback or sharing. In its broadest form this has sparked a range of discussions relating to where the boundary lies between journalists and non-journalists, users and producers, curators and sense-makers.

As a result of this cacophony of competing voices and ideas, it is little wonder that traditional journalists have felt under threat from the fact that anyone can and does produce content and distribute it. Citizen journalists (the very meaning of which is debatable) have been seen as stepping into the terrain previously guarded as the professional journalistic field, but that is not strictly accurate – their goals are different, so how do they fit into this new media ecology? And what is citizen journalism or user-generated content, anyway? Language and terminology struggle to cope with the multitude of ways in which the traditional barriers of the journalistic profession are breaking down as a result of the changes in technology brought on by social media.

Although many definitions exist, and there is no consensus on meaning, in this book we distinguish citizen journalism from user-generated content based on the final product: citizen journalism is its own discrete product, while user-generated content exists within and forms part of a mainstream news product. This can be a complex distinction, especially where commercial news organisations construct their own news sites for the contribution of user-generated content – which can exist both as a discrete product and provide material for the main site.

Individual journalists

These questions have sparked a re-evaluation of what a journalist actually is and what makes us different from anybody else. For almost as long as there have been journalists there has been a struggle over journalistic identity. What, exactly, are we? As actors in society, newsmakers have laid claim to being culturally or socially more significant than plain citizens or even other professions. The role of finding out what is going on and reporting it to others is deemed to have a certain significance, a certain privilege.

The individual journalist has become more visible as the traditional media landscape has exploded and fragmented. In a social-media landscape, the voice of the individual becomes clearer. Journalists working within (and outside) media organisations find themselves in direct contact with audiences and with more options than ever as to where they source or output their work. They are increasingly unable to define what they do or slot their role and interactions under neat labels. They exist in an evolving network of connectivity, across sources and outputs.

Many people have framed this debate as being about the conflict between bloggers and journalists, a perceived standoff between formal and informal journalism. In the new media ecology, however, neither the products journalists produce nor the resources on which they draw are fixed. As a result, the meaning of the word 'journalist' has dissipated. There are lots of people operating as journalists, but they may be bloggers, freelancers, tweeters, YouTube commentators or mainstream reporters – or any combination of these. The waters have become increasingly muddied because amateur journalists can publish material and aggregate content as much as anyone bestowed with a press pass, salary or academic qualification (Knight and Cook, 2011).

The fluidity across these spaces may also spark legal and ethical considerations – if the law or the state recognises 'journalist' as a specific class of person, with differing privileges and obligations to those of the general public, then who can be a journalist becomes a legal, as well as a personal, question.

In both practice and principle, journalists have much to acknowledge and synthesise if they are to thrive in this new media ecology. They need different skills as they move around networked spaces. It is important for a journalist to understand the rules of engagement when sourcing content from the crowd, just as they need to know how best to verify information, avoid being hoaxed, or how to operate fairly. We need to have a clearer sense of what legal and ethical implications our decisions have. Similarly, there's a vast scope of considerations in how best to tell and disseminate stories when the range of possible outputs is so vast. Journalists need to understand their choices in social storytelling for networked distribution. When and how should you produce speedy updates compared to immersive packages in rich media? In terms of practical journalism skills, this book advocates that social-media activities run concurrent to the core principles of traditional reporting.

As journalism re-boots itself within these new parameters, there can be a wealth of exciting opportunities to define great journalism anew. This is a time for innovation. Journalists are looking for ways to reinvent their careers, and are flexing their muscles launching dynamic sites, services and products. We recognise the valid place in the new media ecology for such media entities, which may exist in a more structured way to a freelance journalist, and the increasing likelihood for journalists to work within, alongside or indeed launch such organisations.

This book frames a clearer understanding of a journalist's work as a matter of connections, expectations and reporting norms. Journalists must carve out a new relationship between sources and output, aware of the much wider culture of social media. How you navigate this space is up to you. The amount of time, energy and interest you show in the different sourcing and output practices help you understand what works for you as a journalist. This allows individual reconfiguration of defined roles based more on connections and relationships than saying you are a 'blogger' or a 'local newspaper reporter'. A journalist defined by connections and networks can occupy more than one space within this fragmented media ecology.

Conclusion

As you read through this book, a number of themes and ideas will become apparent. We have, as much as possible, tried to blend discussion of practice and principles together. We have, however, broken the book up into four sections, some more practical, some more theoretical. Throughout the book you will find cross-references to more detailed discussions in other sections, as well as boxes defining terms, giving further reading and discussion, relevant quotes and definitions of terms. The links to further readings, technical information and resources are then included at the end of each chapter, and a complete glossary of all defined terms is found at the end of the book.

The first section of the book, The Networked Journalists' Toolkit, deals with the finding, creating and distributing of news and information, which is what journalists, fundamentally, do. In this section you will find concrete advice on how social media has affected the practice of journalism – the changing relationships with sources and the changing forms of output that penetrate all aspects of life as a contemporary journalist. It looks at how stories are sourced, and then packaged and distributed in an iterative cycle, offering both practical guidance and a way to frame an understanding of how sourcing practices influence doing journalism.

The next section, The Networked Ecology, takes this process wider, and examines the new contexts and environments in which journalists work, and the newer (and older) entities and ideas which now operate within these spaces. This is the most theoretical section of the book, giving as it does the underlying concepts and ideas of this new landscape, as well as practical advice on working within it.

The New Rules of Engagement discusses the conduct in a space that is not quite public, not quite private. It delineates guidelines and best practice for working ethically and morally in the connected new media ecology. Issues of authenticity and verification in the virtual world, pivotal to the function of a journalist, are also tackled.

The New Economics of Journalism then examines the all-important question of money – how to make enough to keep going, to expand, and to make your name and fortune. It acknowledges that media entrepreneurs are finding new and innovative ways to take their place in this landscape, reinventing what it means to do news.

The concluding chapter lays out a typology and mechanism for understanding the landscape of this new media environment: we provide a pair of matrices that examine and define the macro (institutional) and micro (individual) levels of this new ecosystem.

The book is intended both as a primer on how to become a journalist in this new ecosystem, as a guide to navigating the space for experienced journalists, and as an introduction to the theoretical and philosophical ideas which both underpin and rise out of this new landscape. Each chapter and section can be read separately as a guide to the specific issues raised within it, but the book as a whole should serve as a guide to the entire system – the one book which the new, social, connected journalist should

Part 1

THE NETWORKED JOURNALISTS' TOOLKIT

Part 1

>>Chapter 2<<

FINDING THE STORY

Overview

The way journalists source stories has become increasingly complex due to social media because the process of sourcing is non-linear and there is no finite point at which it is done. Indeed, where each story, and each story idea, comes from is hard to quantify. However, as the general network of communication moves more online, the more likely it is for journalists to draw on social networks and online communities as a resource. Many of the traditional methods of finding contacts remain intact, but social media offer a complementary way to generate information.

Key concepts

- Crowdsourcing
- Finding people
- Interviewing
- Off diary
- On diary
- Social-beat reporting
- Sources
- The invisible web
- Tip-offs

Springboard

- *Be observant*: find the best stories by keeping your eyes and ears open. Be on the lookout for ideas and contacts at all times.
- *News sense*: sourcing good stories is cognate with honing your nose for news. You need to sense when something you see or hear will 'make a great story'.
- *Beat reporting*: a patch can be anything from a topic such as education or politics, a breaking news story or a geographical area or theme. Learn how to find information beyond the surface, organise primary sources and explore.
- *Contacts book*: journalism is all about whom you know. Understand that social networks are an invaluable place to widen your contacts, not an add-on. The way you interact with people can move seamlessly between online and offline spaces.
- *Exclusivity*: one constant is the value of exclusive information. Be ready for tip-offs and know how best to move stories forward.

Introduction

Talk to any journalist and the one way they will say social media have changed the way they do their job is in sourcing stories. Getting information can take minutes rather than days. Finding case studies and gauging opinions are but a click away. Put simply, social media help you gather more, and sometimes better, material, more quickly.

Journalism is about digging for things worth talking about. (Philip Trippenbach, producer and game designer)

However, the advice on using social media to source stories has, to date, been somewhat contradictory: rely on the same old processes and contacts that you have been using for years (police, officials, fixers, institutions) – or locate yourself exclusively online, where you can find everything you need to represent the world around you. The protests surrounding the Iranian election in 2009 and the so-called Arab Spring uprisings of 2011, for example, led the world's media to proclaim that the way in which a journalist's work is done would be for ever altered with the emergence of an ever more complex social ecology. (Gow, 2011; Knight, 2012).

If you didn't read the BMDs and announcements it didn't mean you were a poor journalist, just one who wasn't exploiting your sources to the full potential. Same goes for social networks now – you are missing out, even if you don't know it. (Alison Gow, editor (Gow, 2011))

This chapter takes a fresh approach by showing how to combine social media into all manner of sourcing stories. Sources involve people, so it is a simple recognition that journalists have to be where those people – whistleblowers, friends, fixers, friends of friends, experts, institutes, eyewitnesses – may be found. There is a vast range of touchpoints between journalists and contacts, and how you navigate this space can be fluid. How do you connect with social networks as a source? Do you rely on a contacts book of trusted professionals, or do you send out tweets for story ideas? Where do you get your tip-offs?

Can your reputation be enough to get you an exclusive interview, or do you draw on thousands of voices to question politicians? The way in which you interact with these sources plays a key part in framing your identity as a journalist (Quinn, 1998; Pavlik, 1999).

Story ideas

There is pressure to dig out good stories and exclusives. The definition of a good story varies. In commercial journalism it's about getting a scoop to generate sales and be better than the competition. There are also dozens of press agents trading on exclusivity. Natasha Courtenay-Smith secured a lucrative deal when her agency Talk to the Press 'got supergran' – a grandmother who foiled an attempted robbery at a jeweller's (Courtenay-Smith, 2011). Good journalism can relate to a notion of public good, one that has implications for democracy (Keane, 1991; Rosen, 1993; Gans, 2003; Curran and Gurevitch, 2005; Schudson, 2008). Overall, a journalist will need to source a wide range of stories, from campaigns that expose inequalities, to human-interest stories that inspire and amuse. None of this is possible unless you can hone your nose for news, to sense what makes a good story. This is difficult to teach and will also depend on the intent of your journalistic output and your audience (what makes a good story for one newspaper may not be the same for another, for example).

Whether you are live blogging a conference with a series of instant updates or trawling masses of data, journalists have to be able to identify what is newsworthy. For each element consider its value in terms of scale. What's new about this? Who will it affect, how and to what extent? Will it interest my audience, and why? What will be the repercussions of this? Is it strong enough to keep people hooked or get people talking? Would it be shared in social networks? Can I pull out statistics or curate this with something else to add value? Which part will audiences be most informed or entertained by?

There are an infinite number of start points for stories: a chat with friends in a cafe, trawling meeting minutes, an update on Twitter, someone phoning you, or checking with the emergency services. The important thing is to keep your ear to the ground and your eyes open, both online and off.

 When I became a reporter, almost 20 years ago, my job was to dig up scarce, precious facts and deliver them to a passive audience. Today, scarcity has been replaced by an unimaginable surplus and that audience is actively building its own newsroom ... now we're the managers of overabundance. (Mark Little, Storyful (Little, 2011))

Curation

Curation is the process of gathering sources, interviews, comments and facts into a collection, and publishing that online as a finished product. Curation is a way for journalists to add value by adding context or filtering information. Curation is discussed in practical terms in Chapter 5 and in theoretical terms in Chapter 7.

While it would be impossible to compile – or even identify – every story beginning, this list combines traditional perspectives on finding stories (Sissons, 2006; Quinn and Lamble, 2007; Harcup, 2009; Randall, 2011) with social media sourcing practice. Consider the following people and places for a story starting point:

- *people*: comments or experiences from friends, friends of friends, colleagues, parents, acquaintances, followers on Twitter and discussions in networks like Google+ or LinkedIn, contributors to the blogosphere;
- *human interest*: achievements, rewards, success, adversity, adventures, accolades;
- *notice boards*: village and town notice boards, supermarket notice boards, groups, forums, notice boards online;

- *status updates*: births, marriages and deaths, social network status updates, classified advertising;
- *updates*: organisation feeds on Twitter, automated feeds, newsletters, Really Simple Syndication (RSS) readers, alerts;
- *diary events*: anniversaries, birthdays, births, follow-ups, visits, use monitor.bbc.co.uk;
- *debates and issues*: editor and letters pages, broadcast debate shows, trending topics, analysis, discussions, ideas, talks, seminars, academic journals or research;
- *decisions*: planning, closures, launches, redundancies, investments;
- *authorities*: public meetings, councils, councillors and politicians, courts, inquests, inquiries, pressure groups, unions, health authorities, international organisations, charities, solicitors, transport bodies, government and non-government agencies, think-tanks;
- *institutes*: universities and research centres, places of worship, heritage centres, libraries, post offices, pubs, schools, scouts, theatres, clubs, galleries, museums;
- *emergency services*: police, fire, ambulance, armed forces via routine calls, press releases or Twitter feeds and social network pages;
- *observations*: seeing what is going on, following hashtags, spotting anomalies, statistics or data, putting two and two together, archives, investigations;
- *campaigns*: online petitions, community groups, challenges, competitions, crowdfunding sites, appeals;
- *celebrities*: updates or blunders on sites such as Twitter, MySpace or Facebook;
- *press events*: other news organisations, press agencies, wires, curated feeds such as @breakingnews, press releases, press conferences.

On diary and off diary

On diary refers to any stories whose start point is scheduled (birthdays, anniversaries, press releases, embargoes, visits, strikes). Off diary are stories that are sparked by unpredictable events (accidents, crime, crisis, reaction, comments). This includes observations or stories sparked by the journalist's news sense.

Follow-ups

Most stories have a basic trigger – the reason it is being reported now. The follow-up is the story that moves the issue on. Follow-ups can be dealt with in layers (see Chapter 3) and are often a development of story angles. They could involve diarying an event for future reference.

Sourcing stories

The interplay between journalists and sources is a significant factor in affecting what and who makes the news. A study of American journalists found that 89 per cent said they turn to blogs for story research, 65 per cent to social-media sites such as Facebook and LinkedIn, and 52 per cent to microblogging services such as Twitter. 'It's also clear that, while social media is supplementing the research done by journalists, it is not replacing editors' and reporters' reliance on primary sources, fact-checking and other traditional best practices in journalism' (George Washington University, 2010).

The way journalists source stories has become increasingly complex now that social networks and traditional methods are both good resources on which to draw. In order to visualise the range of practices open to a journalist, imagine them on the matrix shown in Figure 2.1. The bottom half of this matrix attempts to show the range of sources open to journalists. The range of outputs a journalist might have are marked on the top half of the matrix, and will be discussed in Chapter 3. How you

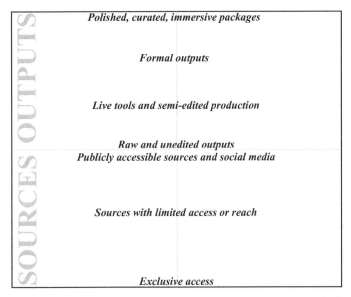

FIGURE 2.1 Individual journalists combine a range of sources (on the lower half of this matrix) and a range of outputs (marked on the top half). Social-media activities dominate the centre space around the horizontal line.

navigate this space is up to you. The amount of time, energy and interest you show in the different sourcing and outputs helps you understand what works for you as a journalist.

Each journalist commands an area of space below and above the line. As such, a journalist's identity is defined by two fields of influence: sources and outputs. This allows journalists to reconfigure a definition of their role based more on the relationship between sources and outputs than saying they are a 'blogger' or a 'local newspaper reporter'. The central horizontal line represents social media and the stories that have been sourced largely from networks. The distance down the vertical line represents access to exclusive contacts, most associated with traditional journalistic practice.

A detailed analysis of the sourcing options open to journalists is presented with examples in Figure 2.2. Journalists who are most comfortable in social

Primary and secondary sources

Primary sources are original reports or documents; secondary sources are those quoting, linking or commenting on something. Increasingly, journalists are expected to gather information from other sources and synthesise or explain it to readers. This is seen as a tertiary source, as it offers a level of service.

 Twitter for newsrooms is a bit redundant for me because Twitter is my newsroom. (Megan McCarthy, Mediagazer founding editor (Tsotsis, 2011))

spaces rely on the network for contacts and sourcing stories. They have many sources, but they are not far below the public surface and are open to everyone. A journalist who can access hundreds or thousands of social network sources, and organise them into a story or narrative, is using the network to their advantage, in a way that is almost completely opposite to the traditional way. They work with public sources but bring skills to this space, making sense of the cacophony of voices. Such journalists are empowered by the reach of their connectivity: scope rather than depth. Here, notions of quantity have their own dimension of defining quality, as networks naturally push and prioritise the best contacts and content to the fore. As their reputation grows, they will be able to access more information and increasingly inaccessible people.

The more exclusive the contacts become, the lower down the vertical axis they are. Towards the middle of the sourcing space you would find public institutions that have their own outputs direct to the public. The European Central Bank or police, for example, now operate live press conferences or Twitter feeds. But the likelihood of these being accessed by the public – without the interpretation or amplification of some other intermediary or journalist – remains relatively small.

At the bottom of the vertical line are a journalist's exclusive contacts. A major tip-off from a well-trusted contact is at the bottom of the vertical: the notion of journalist with the power to open doors.

In a networked media environment, the journalist emerges as a central node trusted to authenticate, interpret, and contextualise information flows on social awareness streams, drawing on a distributed and networked newsroom where knowledge and expertise are fluid, dynamic and hybrid. (Hermida, 2012a)

This may involve trading on your reputation or experience, or your association with major news organisations. The width here is very small, to depict the smaller number of potential sources. At the very bottom are people to whom the general public has very limited access – heads of state, corporate directors, film stars, pop musicians, whistleblowers and trusted contacts.

Publicly accessible sources and social media

The closer the journalist operates to the network, represented on the horizontal line of the matrix in Figure 2.1 the more he may rely on many people getting in touch about small issues. The journalist filters and tracks trends to expose threads and themes, to authenticate, prioritise and corroborate. Here, the journalist's sourcing practice is about connections, engagement and participation.

They're both perfectly valid and useful activities but they perform different roles: curation compiles and collates; journalism adds a layer of narrative, context and analysis. (Matthew Eltringham, 2011b)

It's now increasingly accepted that major stories break in social networks. The Clarence House and Prince of Wales Twitter feeds announced all the details on Prince William and Kate Middleton's wedding in Britain. US presidential candidates used Twitter to announce their 2012 election campaigns. News of protestors being killed in Bahrain was seen by Robert Hernandez when he searched YouTube (Brooks, 2011).

One journalist who is frequently cited for his take on using social media as a source is National Public Radio (NPR) strategist Andy Carvin. As a networked journalist, he draws his authority and identity from that bestowed on him by the crowd. He sources stories from a wide range of contacts,

Breaking news

Journalists refer to breaking news or the act of 'breaking' a story to refer to live information that interrupts the expected flow of news.

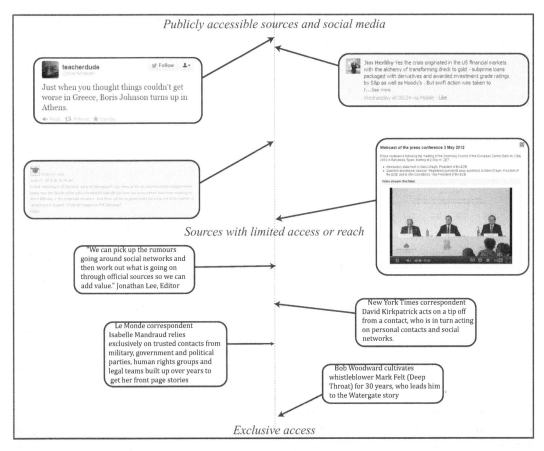

FIGURE 2.2 Shows a range of sources with publicly accessible sources and social media at the top. The more exclusive the source, the lower down the vertical axis you move. From the top: a tweet on the euro crisis; a response on the BBC *World Have Your Say's* Facebook page; a comment on the forum KeepTalkingGreece; a publicly viewable, but not widely publicised press conference by the European Central Bank; adding value to social network and public information to flesh out a story; using tip-offs from contacts and fixers, direct contact with government and institutional officials; using a whistleblower.

often on digital platforms. Carvin finds and connects key people across social media in a way to get added value in the journalistic storytelling process. Through this massive network of individual voices reporting what is going on in their small part of the world, he can create a picture of what is happening that is as valid, and as interesting, as those sourced by traditional mainstream journalists such as David Kirkpatrick or Robert Fisk.

Studies into Carvin's working practice confirm the influence of non-elite sources and the innovative forms of sourcing that can emerge with new communication technologies (Bergman, 2011;

Verification

Knowing the authenticity of information sourced online or from new contacts is a hugely important concern for a journalist. It is discussed in more detail in Chapter 9.

White House, 2011). This is not least through his 'choice of actor types and the frequency of citation' (Hermida, 2012a). His coverage on Twitter during key periods of the 2011 Tunisian and Egyptian uprisings – spanning upwards of 16 hours a day, seven days a week – featured hundreds of tweets per day, making him a 'one-man Twitter news bureau' (Farhi, 2011; see also Gans, 2004; Awad, 2006; Boyce, 2006; Messner and Distaso, 2008; Davis, 2009; Franklin and Carlson, 2011).

Exclusive access

Despite the rhetoric of the importance of social media in alerting the global community to events, journalists themselves do not turn exclusively to that social media for their own information. For the most part they rely on their traditional sourcing practices. This is the deep penetration most associated with the role of a journalist – opening doors, accessing hard-to-access people, and uncovering hidden truths.

Indeed for some newsrooms, the interplay with social media is more opportunistic as social media fill a vacuum that can follow the immediate aftermath of a breaking news event. Nicola Bruno's study of the 2010 Haiti earthquake coverage by the BBC, the Guardian and CNN suggests an opportunistic model at play, rather than a networked spectrum of voices (Bruno, 2011).

Sourcing

The earliest research into sourcing practices characterised the channels of information as informal, routine and enterprising (Sigal, 1973). Since then most research confirms routine sources to be the main way journalists source stories (Gans, 2004; Awad, 2006; Boyce, 2006; Davis, 2009; Messner and Distaso, 2008; Franklin and Carson, 2011). However, studies are beginning to capture the influence of non-elite sources (Lasorsa et al., 2011; Papacharissi, 2011; Poell and Borra, 2011; Hermida, 2012a) and the way sourcing practice is changing (Ahmad, 2010; Nardelli, 2011).

Isabelle Mandraud, senior foreign correspondent at Le Monde, relied on traditional sources while covering events in Tunisia in 2011, both from Paris and on the ground (she was initially denied a visa to travel to Tunisia and did not file a story from there until after the ouster of President Zine El Abidine Ben Ali). She used trusted contacts from the military, the government, political parties, human-rights groups and legal teams that she had built up over the years. 'I don't tweet. I don't Facebook. It is not the source of information for me. I prefer human contact and people with whom I have trust and those who I feel can best analyse the situation' (Mandraud, 2011).

This need for steadfast relationships with sources as friends and trusted contacts was pivotal in one of the most gripping political dramas of the twentieth century: the exposure of the Watergate scandal that forced Richard Nixon's resignation. Mark Felt, operating under the pseudonym 'Deep Throat', secretly guided the Washington Post reporter Bob Woodward who, with colleague Carl Bernstein, pursued the story of the 1972 break-in at the Democratic National Committee's headquarters at the Watergate office building. Felt was instrumental in exposing the Nixon administration's spying and sabotage against its political adversaries. It shows the value of whistleblowers as sources in keeping governments in check. It's also a fascinating story of how a young naval lieutenant cultivated a source over the course of 30 years. 'He showed no interest in striking up a long conversation, but I was intent on it … I believe I encountered him only one more time at the White House. But I had set the hook' (Woodward, 2005).

The price of sourcing sensitive stories can be high, though, not least in the Iraq dossier case in the UK. Dr David Kelly, an employee of the British Ministry of Defence, was found dead after he had been named as the source of quotations used by BBC journalist Andrew Gilligan. These quotations had formed the basis of media reports claiming the then government had knowingly 'sexed up' a report into Iraq and the UK supposed possession of weapons of mass destruction. The Hutton Inquiry was set up to investigate the death and Gilligan later resigned (BBC News, 2004).

New York Times journalist David Kirkpatrick does not use social media extensively, but is aware how people on the ground are using it. A story published on 13 January about the Tunisian uprisings included reportage gathered when he was informed by a taxi driver using a mobile phone that a protest was planned at the French Embassy later that day. He says it was clear the authorities were using the same sources as the protestors because the protest was quickly broken up (Knight, 2013). Another story came about when a colleague – well versed in social networks – tipped him off about a protest in a wealthy suburb of Tunis, allowing him to be the only journalist there. In this way, although journalists may not quote social media directly, their information about what is going on in any given environment is likely to be increasingly informed by social media – at least in so far as the fixers and contacts they use are informed by it (Knight, 2013). Indeed, your most trusted contacts may be someone with whom you have forged relationships on social networks. It is the relationship that counts, not where the relationship exists.

> It's possible that (a student) overlooked Facebook because it has too much power, not too little. He may not see it as an information source because it's so ingrained in his world, such an extension of the self, that he doesn't see it as an external source at all. Like the air around him, it's so essential that it doesn't need to be acknowledged. (Harner, 2011)

Social beat reporting: how to

Any journalist will carve out a patch for themselves. It could be a topic assigned such as health, politics or education. Or it might be a geographical zone or interest. Whatever the patch, you need to be confident that you are covering it well, that you are connected to the right sources both offline and online, and that tip-offs will come to you, not your competitors.

One of the major roles of a social beat is to manage information. As we have seen, social media have added a range of voices, sites, ideas and networks to your in-tray. Picking a way through this to identify story sources of value is a real skill. Clay Shirky (2008) goes so far as to say 'it's not information overload but filter failure'. As Paul Bradshaw points out, journalists tend to worry they'll miss out on something because they're not following the right sources, or they'll miss out on something because they follow too many sources. This leads to two broad approaches: the follow-then-filter approach where people sign up for everything of any interest; the filter-then-follow people are very strict about the number of sources of information to which they listen (Bradshaw and Rohumaa, 2011).

Start by building your contacts book. This is a major tool of the social journalist's trade. Keep a list of all the movers and shakers in your patch: bloggers, experts, charities, clubs – across all different media, both offline and online. Cultivate contacts for hard-to-access stories; you never

Lists, circles, stacks

The social-media version of a contacts book can have many forms: you can group people in circles, stacks or lists, depending on the network and platform.

know when you may need them. When you meet people, make a note of their contact details, when and where you met and what their area of expertise is.

Whether it's lists or circles, stacks or streams, make it easier for yourself to have different networks within networks. It's a good idea to go for an online- or cloud-based contacts book, as these are increasingly geared towards 'access from anywhere'. This is where the social side of your beat can come alive. There's no need to rely on the same case studies, the same tired old quotes every story. You'll be heard when you put out an appeal for information or case study if you have the right network. Remember, there are different social networks popular in different countries or interest areas – such as the medical profession's DoctorsHangout.com, Weibo in China or Blacknet for the Afro-Caribbean community – so don't presume where people will be online.

The cloud

Cloud-based applications are ones that store data on a central server, making them accessible to you from any internet connection as well as on multiple devices. This makes your contacts or files accessible even if you have lost your laptop or mobile phone.

Social bookmarking

This is the way for you to organise and store all the information you read socially. It acts like a favourites or bookmarks bar but, instead of being for an entire site, it lets you save individual web pages and share them.

Journalist Jake Tapper from ABC News has used social networks to get case studies. 'When a health insurance company raised its premiums in California and it affected thousands of people, I didn't know how to reach any of them. So I sent a tweet out to my followers. @lemoneyes tweeted me that she had (been affected) and so I followed her. I got her information through DM and then emailed her, we verified her situation and then we sent a camera crew to her. The next morning she was on ABC's *Good Morning America*. There is no way I could have done that before.' (Twitter Developers, 2012)

Deciding in which networks to be active is important. 'The key is who to follow – I choose a small number of experts in my field who filter their news for all of us in a way they never used to' (Keegan in Bradshaw, 2011: 18). Journalist Joseph Stashko focuses on people, not institutes. 'Out of around 800 Twitter accounts I follow, only about 50 are news organisations, because I want to see opinions and analysis, not articles; I have a reader for that. I want the personality from social media' (Stashko, 2012). These networks then allow you to source and connect in a shallow but vast sphere. Journalist Daniel Bentley used beat reporting to build a football community site from #nonaynever. 'It started off as five or six fans who found each other through social networks and we basically grew a community around the hashtag, which then became a blog' (Bentley, 2012).

Build routines and patches into your day-to-day work. Most digital native journalists feel comfortable being wired to social networks for several hours a day. Make sure information comes to you via RSS feeds, alerts or emails. Some search engines such as Technorati, YouTube or Google Alerts allow you to subscribe to results from a particular search or a specific tag. It's about creating a one-stop page that you check every day that gathers together any new stories since you last checked. Social bookmarking sites like Delicious or Diigo are a goldmine of information and leads. As well as being searchable, most offer RSS feeds of tags and users.

Take time to organise yourself in a way that works for you: put different connections together, use tags and social bookmarking, have updates going where you want them, maximise 'read later' options or personal filter tools. Widen your world as much as possible to avoid missing anything, or have the confidence to know you are connected to everyone you need.

Smart searching

Sourcing stories online is as much a skill as finding pages, people and answers online. Most people don't make use of even a small percentage of available content. There are several search engines to help you: Yahoo!, Google, Wolfram Alpha and Bing, to name but a few. Meta search engines such as Yippy, Ixquick and Dogpile differ in that they piggyback their searches on the back of other search engines. They can increase the likelihood of finding information because they search several different engines at the same time.

If you want to search the blogosphere, then use a specific search engine such as Google Blogs, Technorati or Icerocket. It is worth getting to know Google Advanced Search. You can filter by dates, times and locations as well as for news or images only. Soople also offers advanced Google searching. Tools for searching social networks are evolving constantly. It's worth experimenting with new software as and when it comes out to see if it can make your journalistic work easier.

Be aware that most major government, university and public corporation sites must be entered and searched through a portal. The bulk of the information, and the pages they contain, are not accessible from a straight search. Similarly for historical information, Internet Archive Wayback Machine stores different versions of a large number of web pages.

Blogosphere

It is possible to communally refer to all blogs as the blogosphere to reflect the interconnections that exist between the various blogging communities.

You can use aggregating news services as part of your one-stop-shop newsgathering portfolio. Sites such as Thepaperboy.com and Actualidad.com let you see which newspapers and stories are available in regions around the world. Aggregators like NewsNow and The Huffington Post scrape news, blogs, research, audio, video and other digital media content from global news, shared, user-generated and open-access sources. Newser, Popurls, Paper.li and Summify allow you to create personal feeds. Along with mobile-only sites such as Flipboard and Topheadlin. es, which aggregate editorial news judgements, aggregating services are becoming increasingly sophisticated.

Interviewing

There are several books which deal with interviewing techniques (Pape and Featherstone, 2006; Harcup, 2009; Randall, 2011). It is worth noting here, though, that you won't source a good story or produce a good package without the right quotes. Make sure you have quotes that focus on the drama or newsworthiness, as these are likely to be pulled out as a graphic, bullet point or even sent out to social networks shortly after or during the interview. It is important to be proactive and to have in mind what the top news line seems to be. You can summarise quotes in indirect speech, but be careful when using quotation marks. There are plenty of recording devices to help if you don't have shorthand.

Look up work from some of the great journalists such as Michael Parkinson, Gilbert Noble, John Sergeant and Vikram Chandra. Know when to use open questions (using words such as how and what that will invite the interviewee to share thoughts) and closed ones (when the only possible answer is yes or no – good for challenging people in authority). Interviewing is an exercise in finding answers. You need to think on your feet at the same time as responses come in, taking each thread of the questioning to its absolute conclusion. Remember to check the basics: name spellings, titles, marital status, ages, contact details.

Try to consider where the interview will fit in the overall package. If it is set to be written as a question-and-answer session to complement a different piece then ask questions accordingly; similarly, if you need the interview to sit alone as a module (as discussed in Chapter 3) you may want to record responses about a specific part rather than the whole. Remember to thank the interviewee appropriately: a socially-networked contact will appreciate an @mention; others may want discretion.

Conclusion

This chapter takes a fresh approach to sourcing stories by showing how to combine social media into all manner of ways of finding and researching journalistically. The way journalists source stories has become increasingly complex because the process of sourcing is non-linear and there is no finite point at which it is done. Sources involve people so we recognise that journalists have to be where those people – whistleblowers, friends, fixers, friends of friends, experts, institutes, eyewitnesses – may be found. In this way, sourcing good stories is more about finding and building relationships, and less about where those relationships happen.

The chapter sets out a range of different sourcing practices and the validity of them all. We acknowledge the difference of sourcing the 'old way' and the 'social way', but present the diversity and scope as fundamental to the iterative process of journalism rather than something to choose between. There are more options than ever to source stories, and how you navigate this space is up to you.

Journalists who are most comfortable in social spaces rely on the network for contacts and sourcing stories. Their area of influence around social media involves many sources, but they are not far below the public surface and are open to everyone. A journalist who can access hundreds or thousands of social-network sources and organise them into a story or narrative is using the network to their advantage, in a way that is almost completely opposite to the traditional way. Here, reach and connectivity are important.

The more exclusive the contacts become, the more you move towards traditional journalistic practices. A major tip-off from a well-trusted contact plays to the notion of the journalist with the power to open doors. This may involve trading on your reputation or experience, or your association with major news organisations. Here, the journalist has access to people to whom the general public do not – heads of state, corporate directors, film stars, pop musicians, whistleblowers, trusted contacts.

This chapter argues that social media are a constant rather than an extra. For sourcing stories it avoids journalists getting stuck in a rut, citing the same representatives, panels or experts. It can be a rich source: whether that is a shout-out for story ideas before a news conference (Turner 2012), or appeals for information and feedback, or an entirely new way of reporting. But the traditional expertise of developing and protecting longstanding and trusted contacts is far from being replaced and, moreover, can still represent an important avenue to cut through the noise of social media. How you negotiate a fluid place within this space will frame your journalistic identity.

> # BBC North West Tonight

BBC North West Tonight broadcasts the latest news, sport and weather for the North West of England. The 40-strong team work to cover breaking news and investigations, drawing on an 'ever-more sophisticated' range of resources to source stories.

Fiona Steggles, former producer of BBC North West Tonight, says social media are a valuable addition to a journalist's sourcing toolkit, but one that should not be relied on in isolation. 'It's hard to pin down where we get stories from because the sources are so huge and so wide: it could be a press release, a tweet, a briefing from a spokesperson, a letter in a newspaper, a local MPs campaign, a conversation in a bar, a court case – and that was always the case. It's just that social media has added a few more things to that. The range of sources journalists now deal with is much wider. You have to be plugged in to as many things as possible and the uses are becoming ever more sophisticated.

'You can't watch everything, though, and that is the danger with social media because you watch the new, fashionable tools more, and maybe there is a pile of post on your desk that you don't open but there's something really good in there. There are so many sources now that it is very difficult to be across everything all the time. That is the good thing about social media: if you haven't seen it, someone else has and will be sharing it.

'We receive hundreds of press releases sent to email accounts, we also pick up things from radio, local newspapers and competitors, and other departments who are making hourly calls to the emergency services. There are ideas from viewers and listeners contacting us by phone and email, Facebook especially and Twitter @BBCNWT. Social media has definitely increased the contact with viewers in that presenters can have a conversation, and you get a lot more back.

'Original journalism comes from someone you know, conversations, tip-offs, constantly being wired to know what makes a good story. Sometimes it can be in recognising that a story is worth more than a few small news pieces. We had a row over fracking, a type of drilling in Lancashire for shale gas, so we sent a correspondent over to America to investigate and develop it.'

Laura Yates is the health correspondent, specialising in off-diary. Her main story ideas come from contacts and tip-offs, building up good relationships with press officers so they trust her with the best stories, and social media for case studies and audience reaction.

'We did a great piece about a patient contracting Hepatitis B at Aintree Hospital. We got a tip-off that the hospital were going to test another 40 patients but still hadn't sent out the letters warning the other patients. Social media is interesting for what people think: audience reaction. I got a great case study from Twitter when someone had been caught up in an appointments fiasco. I follow the people who do a similar job to me, and my rivals, then see who they are following. Keep your profile up to date so people know you are the person to contact for particular stories, then look who follows you and see if it is interesting to follow them back.'

Correspondent Stuart Flinders used a Freedom of Information (FOI) request to uncover emails and photographs relating to the then British Culture Secretary James Purnell, who had been invited to the opening of a hospital wing in Tameside but arrived late. Photos of the opening dignitaries were doctored to add in his picture.

'A local photo desk gave us the tip-off that they realised they didn't look right. We did an FOI for emails between the health trust and local MPs to uncover how the decision to doctor the pictures had unravelled. We also got more photos and the personal details of the photographer who had been involved in it so I was able to contact him. It was a good story, taken up nationally and internationally. We won an award for it.'

Key reflections

- This chapter has depicted a continuum of sourcing practices, moving from publicly accessible sources and social media to exclusive access. Where do you think the future potential lies?
- Consider how your sourcing practices would differ for a breaking story compared with an ongoing investigation. How would your conduct change?
- In what ways is Twitter a newsroom?
- Practise your online research skills. See how search results differ depending on which search engines and Boolean terms you use, and explore trending topics. Explore RSS and social-bookmarking sites to see how best to use them for social beat reporting.
- Founding UGC hub editor at the BBC Matthew Eltringham suggests that curation and journalism have different roles. To what extent do you agree with his definitions and what impact does this have on sourcing?

 TOOLKIT

Tips and tools

Trending topics: there are dozens of tools for watching what is hot across social media such as Twitter Advanced Search, Kurrently, Topsy and Social Mention. Addict-o-matic lets you create a custom page with the latest buzz on any topic. Sites such as Rippla.com in the UK tell you which stories are being talked about.

Manage your contacts: as your contacts book expands to include social networks, you'll need a more sophisticated content management system to keep people efficiently grouped. TweetDeck and HootSuite are user-friendly interfaces for Twitter. You can build your own social network with sites such as Ning. Tools such as Muck Rack, Klout and Plaxo help you search and navigate contacts.

Tagging: this is the method used to categorise content in detail by adding key words. It allows story elements, multimedia or URLs to be easily filed and then repurposed or searched. Users build up a bank of tags that help navigate feeds and archives.

Social bookmarking: this key way for you to organise all the information you read, and then want to find again. It acts like a favourites or bookmarks bar but, instead of being for an entire site, it lets you save individual web pages and share them. Try Delicious, Digg, Diigo, StumbleUpon or Reddit. You can search other people's lists and tags too.

Really Simple Syndication: RSS is the way of publishing site updates via a feed. Subscribing to a feed allows you to receive those updates, rather than having to check sites manually. It is a fundamental building block of managing navigation of the web. If sites don't have RSS enabled, most easily identified by the orange RSS logo, you can create your own feed with Page2rss.com. Yahoo! Pipes, Dapper and Spundge are more advanced tools for organising feeds.

RSS readers: you need an RSS reader to manage your feeds. Spundge, Bloglines and Netvibes are a good place to start.

Alerts: several social-networking sites allow you to subscribe for updates based on tags or key words. For example you can set up a Google Alert or Google News Scraper on names such as celebrities, criminals, places or topics. They make sure you don't miss story follow-ups or ideas.

Find multimedia: sourcing stories is increasingly about sourcing multimedia. The range of hosting sites is changing all the time. Find pictures on Flickr, Google Images, Twitpic or Photobucket and videos on YouTube, Vimeo or Google Video. Slideshare lets you share presentations, galleries or slideshows. Specific searches based on copyright restrictions such as search.creativecommons.org can help.

Civic-interest sites: there are several bespoke sites to help search or source stories based on common matters of concern or freedom of information. Explore sites such as They Work For You, Planning Finder, Help Me Investigate, What Do They Know and Fix My Street.

Recording: tools for recording interviews are increasingly sophisticated. There is a range of Voice over Internet Protocol (VoIP) facilities such as Skype, as well as voice-recognition pens and automated scribing tools.

Finding sources: Help a Reporter Out (HARO) and PR Newswire's Profnet offer connection services between experts and journalists. Don't overlook universities, though, such as New York University's Global Beat Syndicate, and professional social networks, such as LinkedIn. Whois. net offers advanced people searching.

Find answers: There are several databases for answering specific questions but refdesk.com and Wikipedia can offer a starting point.

Finding people: where once a journalist was limited to a phone book, there are now myriad online directories to help find people combining social networks. Try 123people, yoName, Wink.com, Zoominfo or yell.com for general searches and then focus on niche interest such as Couchsurfing, a volunteer-based worldwide network connecting travellers with members of local communities.

Social networks: the important thing here is to remember there are millions of social networks so don't think the social networking world begins and ends with one or two brand names. Just as popular nightclubs come and go, so too will social networks. Sina Weibo, QQ and RenRen are wildly popular among young Chinese just as Hi5 or Second Life appeal to others.

Find groups and forums: you can search Google and Yahoo groups or find forums with dedicated search engines such as Google+ forum, Boardreader or Omgili.

Location-based sourcing: you may need to source contacts based on locality. These tools are increasingly sophisticated thanks to the Global Positioning System (GPS). You can use location-based networks such as Foursquare, or search Twitter using near:place and within:10mi, use Trendsmap to locate Twitter trends geographically and Google Maps for a wide range of information or contacts.

Readings and resources

Advice and tools: with social-media sites launching daily it's really useful to draw on the latest tips which are pooled together on sites such as Scoop.it. Social Media and Journalists, Social Media Kitbag and Social Media Pronto are useful: www.scoop.it/t/social-media-and-journalists; www.scoop.it/t/social-media-kitbag; www.scoop.it/t/social-media-pronto.

Twitter Fan Wiki: this PB Works site pools a range of apps and tools which can help widen your exploration of Twitter. It's available at: http://twitter.pbworks.com/w/page/1779796/FrontPage.

Search Engine Society: this book by Alexander Halavais explores research around how people use search engines and navigate the virtual world (Halavais, 2009).

Great interviews: to be inspired about interviewing techniques you can browse this archive of some great interviewing moments in audio, multimedia and text: www.guardian.co.uk/theguardian/series/greatinterviews.

Online Newsgathering: Research and Reporting for Journalism: includes plenty of golden rules and tips which still apply (Quinn and Lamble, 2007).

Daniel M. Russell: discusses search, search skills, teaching search, learning how to search and learning how to use Google effectively in his personal blog: http://searchresearch1.blogspot.co.uk/.

Reuters guide to sourcing: there are valuable insights and best practice in this online handbook available at: http://handbook.reuters.com/index.php/The_Essentials_of_Reuters_sourcing.

>>Chapter 3<<

PRODUCING CONTENT IN A SOCIAL LANDSCAPE

Overview

This chapter looks at how instant, interactive and freely available production processes are evolving the way news is written and broadcast within an iterative cycle of sourcing and distribution. It builds on the understanding that outputs change in their voice and construction depending on the intent and objective of the producer. It sets out best practice for harnessing the power of social media in storytelling and how to think creatively about news production by integrating a much broader portfolio of voices and tools.

Key concepts

- Blogging
- Interactivity
- Microblogging
- Multimedia
- Producing packages
- Social-media storytelling
- Speed
- Voice
- Writing for the web

Springboard

- *Make the right choice*: the fundamental shift in producing for social media is that journalists have unbridled choice. They can combine myriad tools for production with a vast range of voices and platforms.
- *Infrastructure*: storytelling has always been about bringing together pieces of content and ordering them to be easily understood, whether that is quotes, statistics or the 'Five Ws': the who, what, where, when, why of a story. Now storytelling is even more creative. Stories are constructed with a range of elements known as units, chunks or modules.
- *Inform*: journalists have to constantly negotiate the environment of being right or being fast – and the meaning of 'inform' changes depending on your journalistic intent.
- *Immerse*: some users want to read and go; others want a rich media experience. Understanding the level of immersion is pivotal to good storytelling for social media.
- *Interest*: it's a journalist's responsibility to prepare their work to generate as much interest in it as possible.
- *Interact*: gone are the days of one- or even two-way modes of communication. Whether it is through comments, contributions or actions, there needs to be a deep understanding of how stories are built within an 'active' process.
- *Experiment*: tools and technology are changing daily – don't look for an excuse to avoid change but look for a reason to try it.

Introduction

Media content is produced in an always-on news stream within a cycle of sourcing and distribution. Journalists have to produce for mobile and blogs, forums and social networks, TV, print and radio. New and social-media technologies have changed the format and shape of news – from rigid conventions of pyramid-shaped stories and television journalists expounding direct to camera, to multiple shapes and forms. As such, producers need to adapt to the changing expectations of function in the news environment.

Technology toolkit

Once upon a time, a journalist covering an event was likely to be accompanied by a photographer, a cameraman or both. Nowadays you are often expected to file text, photos and video yourself. Consider your kit bag accordingly.

In this ecology, there is one underpinning theme: choice. The journalist's modern-day toolkit is not about using everything all the time or shouting to everyone every minute. It is about adapting to the culture of social media and selecting the right tool at the right time for the right audience. Stories can be conveyed using text, video, audio, images, blogs, microblogs, maps, infographics, games and links – and the whole process is evolving continually.

Choice is also pivotal to integrate a range of voices. Where once journalists were the sole voice 'telling' the story, social media and online or mobile production allows limitless possibilities for inclusion. To whom they should speak is as important as to whom they should listen. Eyewitness or audience comments sit alongside expert discussions or more edited packages. Journalists need to know how best to combine these elements to best tell the story. The tools and methods for communicating, as well as the tone and style for varying audiences, can be fluid.

As such, journalists have to think about the production process more creatively. They must understand the difference between live news coverage, the place and value of speedy short updates such as microblogs compared with drafts or short-form journalism, and long-form content or in-depth packages. It's important to grasp the context that has changed, and the skills needed to survive in this landscape. This chapter will focus on fine-tuning journalists' ability to work in all contexts of social-news production.

> ## Nicknames
>
> Media professionals develop nicknames for everything: from products such as red tops and Berliners, to top lines, death knocks and colour pieces. Social-media parlance simply adds to the range. Reading social-media forums will help, but if you hear a word you don't understand it's likely to be a quirk: just ask.

Storytelling for social media

Storytelling in social spaces has several characteristics that need to be considered. Single outputs have become multitudinous, built from a range of multimedia multi-voice elements. The founding skills of a journalist's work are as important as ever, however, and authors have given much attention to the building blocks of journalism practice (Hennessy, 2006; McKane, 2006; Phillips, 2006; Boyd et al., 2008; Hicks et al., 2008; Harcup, 2009; Randall, 2011). But social media add another dimension, another value – and one which journalists must grasp if they are to survive in the new-media landscape. This section sets out the 'Five Is' of social-media storytelling which embrace the non-linear nature of content creation:

- infrastructure
- inform
- immerse
- interest
- interact

Infrastructure

It's essential to conceptualise journalism as a process, not a product. The flow of sourcing, making and distributing content is so fluid as to blur many of the boundaries once accepted as start points in storytelling. You are dealing with non-linear con-

> ## Internet
>
> The internet is the infrastructure which connects computers around the world. Your internet service provider hooks you up to this. The World Wide Web is the technology which interlinks hypertext documents. To access a website you use a software application called a browser from where you can navigate unique resource locators – specific site addresses.

sumption, and therefore production. Put simply, that means you cannot presume a starting point for your audience or their needs in terms of what they want from that storytelling experience. Users consume as much or as little as they like; they begin where they want and discover the parts they

The digital world ... can instantly rearrange itself for each person and each person's current task. (Weinberger, 2007)

Layering content

The term 'layering' refers to the way stories can be built on the web. The story being read is the top layer, but each time a link is added it acts like another layer of content underneath. Understanding layering is key to social storytelling, as it acknowledges the user has different start points and needs, and the journalist has a wide range of content on which to draw.

Chunking

Chunking is the technique used to produce stories in a non-linear way. It means splitting a story into specific chunks of material that each tackle a different aspect of the issue being covered (the who as an image, the analysis as a graphic, the where as a map). It also serves to avoid long blocks of text. Stories are created by building units together: bullet points, side bars, break-outs, pull quotes, subheadings, images, maps, graphs, audio, comments, video – there are infinite possibilities.

Motion tracking

One of many interactive elements being used in broadcast news production, motion tracking allows tags as words or numbers to float against video footage to make content easier to understand and retain.

consider to have value. And each piece of content has its own unique journey around the web (as discussed in Chapter 4).

However, there is still a heart, a trigger, a top line. Whether it is analysis, breaking news, comment or colour, there will always be a reason why you are talking about something now. This is known as the peg. And your writing will often include some if not all of the classic who, what, when, where, why and how questions.

All this has an impact on the way stories are built. Journalists increasingly have to think about 'chunking' a story into units, often described as modules.

The news story from the BBC shown in Figure 3.1 is typical of a chunking approach to storytelling. In building this story, the journalist has made decisions about how to chunk and layer the content. They have considered in which ways to best tell the Five Ws. There is the trigger (in this case the fresh talks), and then the journey of explaining that story by constructing and combining from the grassroots with follow-ups and backgrounders, analysis and commentary. This process is likely to be highly collaborative across departments and teams as well as users, but it is the journalist who needs to make informed choices about how best to tell the story.

- who may be a profile story, picture or gallery;
- what may be quotes, polls, timelines, interviews, links to documents, pictures or fact box;
- when may be a calendar, curated feed or bullet points;
- where might be a graphic or map;
- why may be features, background, question and answer format, history, interviews or analysis;
- how might be analysis, interactivity or a step-by-step explainer.

Inform

Inform refers to the core reporting process of communicating to people what is going on. This is a cornerstone of a journalist's role, yet it is one that is becoming more complex in social spaces.

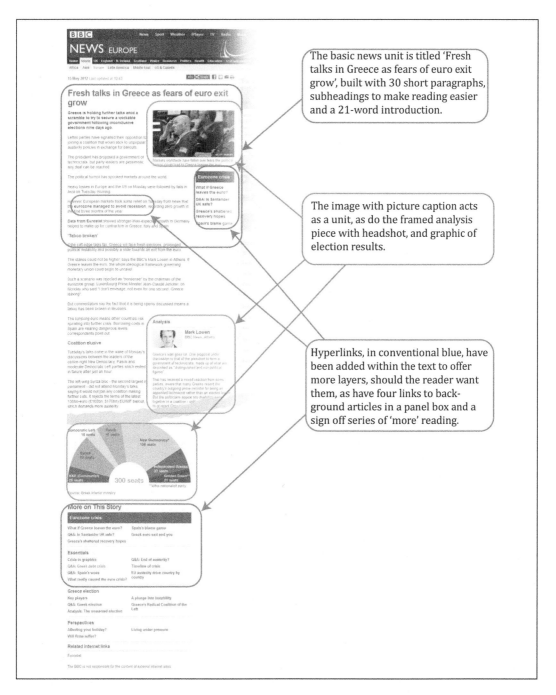

The basic news unit is titled 'Fresh talks in Greece as fears of euro exit grow', built with 30 short paragraphs, subheadings to make reading easier and a 21-word introduction.

The image with picture caption acts as a unit, as do the framed analysis piece with headshot, and graphic of election results.

Hyperlinks, in conventional blue, have been added within the text to offer more layers, should the reader want them, as have four links to back-ground articles in a panel box and a sign off series of 'more' reading.

FIGURE 3.1 An example of how a composite story is made up of units, each of which works on its own, as well as part of the whole piece, and could be reused in other composite stories.

Source: www.bbc.co.uk/news/world-europe-18068189.

Social or splash?

It used to be that writing a news splash – a front-page news story – was the ambition of most aspiring journalists. Now success is as likely to be gauged by how 'viral' a story goes on social networks or the level of engagement or traction it creates between audiences.

Rich media

This is a term used to describe content which contains a broad range of digital interactive media.

Talk to any journalist and they will express the need to constantly negotiate the environment of being right or being fast. There is a pressure from iterative reporting that you want to inform and connect as quickly as possible. Think of the sinking of the MS Costa Concordia in January 2012 off the Tuscan island of Giglio: pictures were distributed as it was sinking, whereas in the past you would have had to wait hours. Yet accuracy cannot be compromised for speed. 'Journalists of the future have to be faster than the ones we have now but just as reliable' (Blackhurst, 2012).

If you are posting to social networks to inform or crowdsource, but are unsure of verification, then say so. NPR journalist Andy Carvin has built a reputation for doing just that. It may be that verification is the raison d'être for the output, as with a Google map created by a team at the Guardian to highlight verified and unverified areas affected by riots in the UK in August 2011. If your intention, on the other hand, is to produce objective journalistic output, make sure it is balanced.

Accuracy is non-negotiable. In larger organisations there is scope for teams to edit and revise content. However, most journalists write directly into templates, and the existence of subeditors for checking and editing is becoming increasingly rare. Be sure to preview or reread everything you produce before you press upload or send. In a matter of seconds that content may have been redistributed – and it's not always possible to backtrack. Check spelling, grammar and punctuation as well as the keywords and tags. Be mindful of the legal or ethical implications (as discussed in Part 3) and make sure you have attributed where necessary.

Immerse

It's essential to acknowledge that audiences want different experiences from storytelling. Some people are looking for a full immersion complemented by an ever-increasing sophistication of rich media. Others want the surface news fast. As such, understanding the needs of your target audience is crucial to 'do' journalism effectively. There's also more potential to offer deep and broad storytelling experiences because of the unlimited space of the internet. On what device is this story likely to be consumed? Do you want to stimulate debate and reaction? Is your content aimed at the rush-hour commuter or to afford someone leisure reading?

Delivering an immersive news experience is likely to involve a different combination of infrastructure: more links, rich media, graphics, gaming and interactivity. The vocabulary, phrasing or length of your package will also change because of the time dedicated to it. Readers and viewers may also want to be active rather than passive. They may be expecting to participate, comment or discuss ideas, so address them accordingly. They may be happy to offer footage or an image from the ground, and want to be acknowledged. Understand what user-generated content is and how it affects how you produce stories (as discussed in Chapter 6).

Other people want to read and go. These are the people who haven't got time to decipher or battle with puns and heavy-going prose. They are consuming information 'peripherally', probably at the workplace (Boyd, 2010; Bradshaw, 2012). Users also read much more slowly online, as the screen resolution is lower than print. Clear, unambiguous headlines help users decide quickly if content is relevant to them. Think function over fluff. Introductions may be the only sentence users skim if they have come to the story from a reader or aggregator.

Gamification

Gamification is the integration of game mechanics into any customer-facing element. It is being increasingly used by news providers to offer a more immersive storytelling experience. See Chapter 4 for more.

Interest

Interest in your content is expressed in many different ways, but here we are thinking hits. Consider how users are going to find your story from social media or search, and how to adapt your writing and production accordingly. Stories are also rated through web analytics. The onus is on journalists to understand how to drive search and social traffic by optimising their articles with keywords, and allowing them to be readily shared and recommended on services such as Digg, Twitter, Google+, Tumblr, Posterous, Audioboo, Pinterest, Facebook, Instagram, CoveritLive and Vimeo.

Keywords are specific words or phrases that best sum up your content. They need to be used in headlines, picture captions, subheadings and the introduction. Think about what a reader would be searching for with which words, and remember that an online or mobile audience is a global one. Don't be afraid of repetition or using a colon. For example, a headline that says 'Greece debt crisis: Far left Syriza pulls out of talks' has keywords and nouns such as crisis and talks, but 'Papoulias fears future' may be lower down in the long-term results because it relies on remembering a name and the word future does not retain meaning out of context.

Social traffic

This refers to the way social networks have contributed to someone finding or sharing your content. It comprises a range of analytics.

Tagging is the technique of categorising content with keywords. Most blogs, social bookmarking and networking sites or content-management systems will let you add keyword tags. These help you, and others, order and sort content in a way that suits you. It helps to deliver content effectively across emails, mobile, social networks and search. Categories tend to be broad topics such as Greece, Eurozone or economy but tags would be specific subsets within this such as key people,

Tagging

Tags are the metadata that describe, categorise and label content. When you click on a tag it will navigate you to all the content that has been filed under that term. A tag cloud is the list of tags commonly used on a site. You can also create alerts or RSS feeds on tag terms.

places, dates or organisations. Hashtags are a crucial part of the social media ecology, as they create links around a group of threads and themes such as #greece, #euro and #eurozone.

Interact

Interactivity is ubiquitous to social storytelling. It is an acceptance of journalism as a two-way process. How you interact with the audience depends on you, but interactivity is open to you at every turn: surveys, polls and questionnaires, rating tools, comments and feedback, asking for story ideas on Facebook, responding to comments on stories or blog posts, replying and promoting other people's tweets, delivering a service and user experience, and producing for two and three screeners.

Two screeners

The trend is increasingly for users to have more than one device in use at any one time (using a smart phone while watching a TV and surfing on a tablet), also dubbed 'belly vision'. It is worth considering how this can be harnessed for better interaction.

It's second nature for producers to cite activity on social networks and drive users seamlessly between platforms. Perhaps you post planning applications on Slideshare, do a video-taste test when a new restaurant chain opens, or expand the debate of a letters page in social networks. Channel 4 sparked major online buzz when it flashed the #ticketscandal hashtag on the screen during the broadcast of a documentary on underhand practices in the music industry. The show racked up almost 12,000 tweets in 24 hours, and featured as three of the top trending topics on the night that it aired (Macmillan, 2012). And it is not just interactivity for editorial: the advertising campaign for the film *Prometheus* in 2012 was the first to combine nearly live tweets in a commercial. Think about who you can connect with, who cares about the story being told, and what related events are going on and where.

Interactive media

This includes products and services on digital computer-based systems that are open to be modified or respond to a user's actions.

Example

You are working for a city newspaper when news of protests in Greece over the euro crisis starts to come in on social networks. From this example, you can see that social media are woven entirely into the production process – it is integral to your choices about how to do good reporting. You may not use all these steps, but this demonstrates the range of activities that could go into telling a story:

- Instant updates appear in raw feeds across social and multimedia networks. You focus on searching, trend-spotting and verification.
- Liaise with newsdesk and your team, and put out calls to your best contacts both offline and online.
- Short-form breaking news updates are produced on social networks or tickers sharing information, outstanding questions and updates.
- As your jigsaw begins to come together, consider the news value of the story and how best to visualise it. What does it need to best tell the story? How best can you report on it?
- Continue to source and verify information and multimedia via all your available sources.

- Start a live blog pulling in #feeds and draft a post answering the Five Ws on an appropriate platform.
- What story modules does this story need? What chunks and layers? How can you go about getting them done efficiently? Liaise with other teams or producers.
- Develop your curation of links to other content or stories. Consider polls, surveys and responding to comments.
- Set up a live Q&A with an expert and users.
- Create depth by researching and pulling in a variety of perspectives and voices.
- Refresh draft posts with more detail and information.
- Produce your in-depth packages or features. Offer insight and analysis.
- Create lists, forums or groups for more focused discussions and thank anyone who has helped you.
- Develop your curation. Consider how your content will be best distributed.

Communicating the story

The way journalists bring stories to life demands a variety of production techniques. It is now common journalistic practice for instant updates to be followed by short-form draft storytelling and then edited packages in a non-linear way. So far, much attention has been given to the different stages of content production from the theoretical and mapping perspective (Bradshaw, 2007; Canavilhas, 2009; Mishra and Bradshaw, 2010). Building on this, we now explore not only what these stages are but how best to produce the different story elements: instant updates and raw news coverage; live reporting; draft posts and blogs; basic news units; and then in-depth packages both in text and broadcast. Visualising it in this way allows us to show that different stages of content production can be written and constructed in very different ways.

Angles and pegs

The angle of the story is your unique approach or 'take' on it. It's what makes your report original and interesting. The peg is why a story is being written or why it is relevant now.

We draw on examples pertaining to one topic: the Greek debt crisis of 2012 which threatened the country towards bankrupcy and a forced exit from the euro. This in no way purports to represent a complete list. The possibilities are near endless and changing all the time. But it does attempt to highlight the vast opportunities and range in terms of how stories can be told in different ways, combining different voices and levels of formality. It depicts the reporting process as being less about platforms, and more about how content and connections are drawn together.

Building on Chapter 2, Figure 2.1, where we visualised the sourcing practices open to journalists on the bottom half of a matrix, this chapter sets out the range of outputs on the top half. The space closest to the horizontal represents outputs to the crowd that may be more informal, raw and unedited dominated again by publicly accessible and social media. As you move up the vertical axis, outputs become more polished and formal. The middle space is dominated by draft updates and live reporting tools. At the top of the vertical are edited, often well-researched outputs that are more recognisable journalistically, and that offer exploration and customisation to the user with a rich combination of media. A journalist may find themselves producing a range of different story elements, moving fluidly around this space.

Take instant updates as an example. A journalist may write chatty speedy updates to Twitter (depicted close to the horizontal, as these are relatively raw) as well as short-form instant updates like a ticker or text message alert (higher up the vertical, as they are more formal, but away from the very top, as their brevity prevents them from offering context and immersion). These are both instant draft-form updates but are written with different levels of formality and polish.

Similarly with live reporting: a hashtag feed of updates from a social network being pulled onto a site would be close to the horizontal (this remains raw, but it is more edited than the original outpouring because the hashtag acts as a nominal filter). An hourly bulletin update from a reporter standing in Athens, which is live and unedited, is higher up the vertical (it is often rehearsed and the journalist is adding a layer of interpretation within defined formats and expected forms of address). A live blog that pulls in carefully selected video, comments and analysis is very near the top of the vertical (it constructs a much more cohesive narrative and immersive experience for the user as an in-depth package). The writing styles and production techniques change as you move through the different stages, from instant updates right through to edited packages.

Instant updates and raw news coverage

Instant updates have become popularised by the rise of microblogging site Twitter and its 140-character updates; they are used across a range of outputs: tickers which appear as a rolling feed across broadcasts, text messages, status updates, alert emails and feeds. These are visualised in Figure 3.2. You may be dealing with a raw feed of an event or conversation as it happens, typically across social platforms. At this level, the news is simply the outpouring of data and material of events, unedited, unverified and utterly raw. Here, immediacy and audience participation are key, but the level of editing and formality are low.

For a journalist, being active in this space shows you are 'on it', and that you have the awareness and reactions to be part of the conversation. Instant updates on social media are also a great way to add extra behind-the-scenes information, personality or colour. Interpretations of how to use networks like Twitter are vast: from using it as a fourth broadcasting wire service, crowdsourcing and curating, to drawing out journalistic stories around themes as they ebb and flow. It's quite a personal decision as to what works best for you (and potentially your employer).

Brevity and simplicity are key, as you are writing for an audience that wants information quickly and succinctly. Writing for this type of output requires a keen sense of self-editing. If you are using instant updates on social platforms, be active towards your audience by using direct messages and retweets. This is the space where audiences may be able to

Twitter jargon

A post to Twitter is known as a tweet. RT is a re-posting of someone else's tweet. To direct a tweet to someone, you use the @mention functionality. A DM is a private message exchange between two people who follow each other. Following people means their updates will appear in your feed. #ff is a recommendation of someone worth following.

News in brief

A news in brief (NIB) is a story written in two to four paragraphs. A top is slightly longer.

help by responding to questions. Check you have included the @name of users in the conversation, the #hashtag or a link, as well as famous people and places where appropriate.

But be aware of pitfalls: it's distracting and time-consuming to produce constant short updates, and you need to be careful not to miss important points at events or conferences by updating your status. It's also important to be aware that mistakes can be permanently snapshot. In terms of the wider use of instant updates by journalists, consider to what extent conduct in this space needs to reflect objectivity and balance. For more on the legality and ethical implications, see Part 3.

Reporting live

There are more options than ever for live reporting, which is effectively publishing in real time. A range of live reports are visualised in Figure 3.3. It can be streaming of video or audio, a Q&A session, an interview or webonair, a reporter on the scene or coverage of an event, all published live as they occur. They can vary in their relative scale of editing and cohesiveness, but they all trade in some way on bringing information together in an unpredictable stream. This may not function as a cohesive narrative or story, but will still maintain some of the elements of journalistic practice: verification, mixing of sources and some consistency of expression.

Live reporting is the right choice when immediacy is key. There's plenty of scope for offering up-to-the-minute reporting that's in touch with on-the-ground experiences. It has always been a popular way of covering events for broadcasters, but social media let you incorporate a much wider range of voices and material. Several short updates can be combined to form a flowing commentary, perhaps of court proceedings, an event, a press conference or a crisis. Live reporting through social media allows for content curation – the act of finding, grouping, organising or sharing the best and most relevant content on a specific issue. It allows people to participate remotely, adding an interactive dimension.

The skill is to select only the most interesting and relevant updates, which will test your news sense and your ability to identify what would be of most interest to your audience (you may be talking to more than one audience at any one time on different platforms). Pull out key points and statistics rather than opt for a chronological approach in your updates or broadcast. Check you have linked to source information, where appropriate, and be transparent about the level of verification being presented. If you are dealing with a live feed or a breaking news story, this could be crucial.

Attribution

Getting people's names and acknowledgements right is pivotal. Remember to clarify someone's title so that you can refer to them after first name mention as Mr, Dr, Mrs or Miss, and so on, and check if sources want to be referred to as their real name or their avatar, such as @cecook (they may prefer the social recognition).

Hyperlinks

Hyperlinks allow us to navigate around the web. There are two variables with links – the words highlighted and the destination content to which you link. The words you choose will become blue and underlined so choose them carefully to maximise scannability (as well as search-engine optimisation – SEO) and to give an obvious indication of what the hyperlinked page contains. The link should add context and transparency, so consider who or what you need to credit, and what information the reader would find useful.

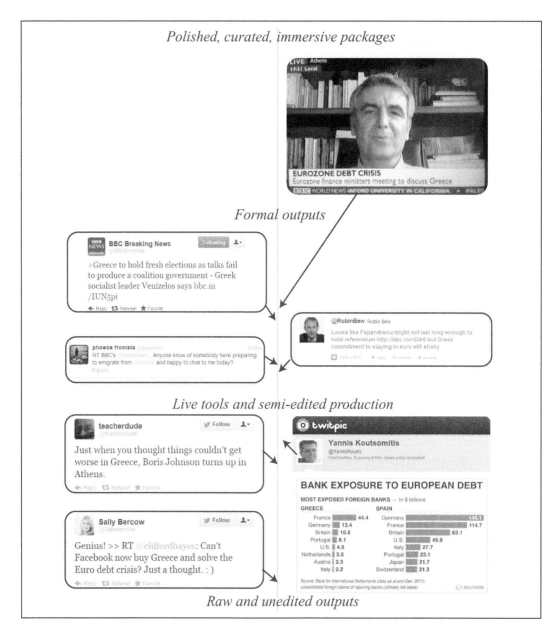

FIGURE 3.2 The various kinds of raw news coverage, showing their relative scale of editing and cohesiveness. The tone gets more informal and conversational the lower down the line you go. From the top: News of more Greek uncertainty as it was announced on the BBC ticker; the @BBCbreaking News Twitter feed announcing the failure of coalition talks; The Economist's Intelligence Unit Robin Bew adds context and a link in his Twitter feed; BBC Athens correspondent Mark Lowen asks the crowd for sources for a later story; Yannis Koutsomitis, who lives in Athens, shares a graph on Twitter; @teacherdude adds a touch of levity; @sallybercow retweets a comment from @cliffordhayes.

If you want to live blog an event, prepare in advance, including the options for internet connections. It's unavoidable that some mistakes or errors will creep in if you're trying to report in as close to real time as possible, but watch for them and correct them as soon as possible. If you are working on breaking news and feel comfortable with networking on social media, you can use the crowd to help you. Asking questions and building connections will help your reporting. It has been suggested that journalists can add value to this space by restricting the information they repeat to that which is verified – it avoids adding grist to the rumour mill. It is about making sense rather than adding more noise (Bhargava, 2011). If you do see something that is incorrect, suggest corrections or updates.

Live blogging

A live blog, at its simplest, is a record of an event, published live as it occurs. It is a written commentary online, the textual equivalent of a radio report. A single, automatically refreshing web page is created, with material added to a running narrative with a time stamp attached. It allows any user seeing the page to see the entire narrative, but with the latest material at the top. The journalist can then add to the page as events progress, incorporating material from other sites or news organisations, comments, links, audio and video. See Chapter 7 for more.

Draft posts and blogs

There is a multitude of social media and blogging sites – from Facebook to Boing Boing – where you can write in draft form. They all include posts, much like articles or entries, and pages. There are literally thousands of options in terms of where you can publish draft posts, but at this point in the content production we are specifying output that has moved on from raw or short-form updates. At this stage, the update offers a

Blogs

Blog is an abbreviation of 'weblog', originally a log of daily life, information and material collected online. Blogs are made up of posts which include links and comments. The homepage of a blog will typically show the most recent post at the top.

development from unedited flows of information but lacks the formal structure of the news package. It's worth noting that the draft article or blog post is becoming increasingly sophisticated, with users bringing in a range of content from elsewhere, including multimedia. Options are visualised in Figure 3.4.

This may be the first time you have enough content to offer an overview or first reflection on something that has happened. They can be somewhere to write up an interview, cover an event, reflect, review or summarise. It is usually a snapshot of incomplete or open discussions, or open thoughts. It's also the place to form a closer connection with a specific group of readers, ask questions or source ideas. The possibilities are endless, but your choice of platform will depend on what you are writing and how you want it to

 Can we agree to a new accepted wisdom: that the most precious resource in news is reporting and so maximising the acquisition of facts and answers is what we need? So what is an article? An article can be a byproduct of the process. When digital comes first and print last, then the article is something you need to put together to fill the paper; it's not the goal of the entire process. The process is the goal of the process: keeping the public constantly informed. (Jarvis, 2011)

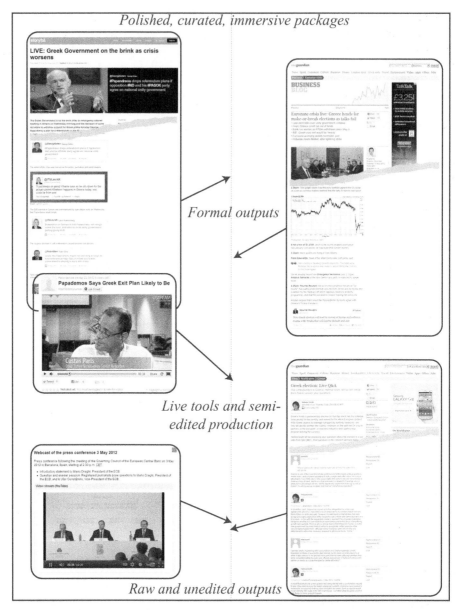

FIGURE 3.3 Live reports and their relative scale of editing and cohesiveness. From the top: this Storyful curates a 'follow live' feed plus quotes from social networks, text and an official quote and hyperlink to the European Central Bank, as well as two broadcast packages from Reuters and Euronews, both under two minutes. Note that times are placed in zones for context; Graeme Wearden runs a live blog for the Guardian on 15 May 2012, filing four paragraphs every few minutes; the WSJ runs a live video feed on Ustream, drawing on interviews, clips and comment; the Guardian hosts a live text-based Q&A session with their correspondent in Greece; the press conference following the meeting of the Governing Council of the European Central Bank on 3 May 2012, in Barcelona, Spain, is streamed live.

be available in the future (Facebook, for example, tends to lend itself to short-term ongoing links and more controversial material, while blogging software has evolved to incorporate comments and discussions). Blogs are an effective place for a virtual clippings file, as well as somewhere to practise and extend your work.

Draft updates can be a place to inject more personality compared with the objectivity of official news outputs, so a chattier tone works well. The tone and style of your writing will vary immensely, depending on what you are using the draft for and your audience. The Washington Post's Ian Shapira and the New York Times's Nicholas Kristof have both used Facebook pages for compelling storytelling. Don't be afraid to clearly mark 'updates' if you edit or make changes, as this is a big part of the transparency and authenticity which dictates the space.

NCTJ guidelines suggest 'a blog can be regarded in a similar way to a newspaper column or leader'. However, printed opinion columns typify a communication closed to response, whereas blogging encourages debate and collaboration. Be transparent about who you are and in what capacity you are reporting at a given time. It's highly likely you will be running, or at least active, on lots of blogs and platforms at once.

The news unit

There comes a point when you need an interim report of what has happened, via print, audio or broadcast. Basic news writing is about delivering information clearly and in a way that can be easily understood. This may be the first time in the content production cycle that you have compiled output that answers all of the Five Ws. Here the production has moved into the traditional journalistic domain. It is likely to form the central building block of your storytelling infrastructure. It may be an on-the-hour bulletin from a reporter standing in Athens, a webcam review of events or a written news story of around a dozen paragraphs, as visualised in Figure 3.5.

Writing a news unit is the right choice when the voice has become more formal; the journalist is acting as interpreter of events for the public, working within defined formats and expected forms of address. That is not to say that social media are removed from this space, or that this is the first time the journalistic voice may have been used, but the level of editing has shifted towards the balance and objectivity associated with recognisable, professional reporting. It is worth noting that many news consumers still rely on formal news articles to help them understand what is 'newsworthy'. In this way, the editorial decision to make a more formal output has value to users, as it distinguishes the topic from the infinity of the internet.

There is a degree of rehearsal and preparation in writing a news piece, regardless of the platform. First check that the overall piece is balanced and accurate. That means verifying the sources and making sure you offer both sides of the story. In any well-written report, the most important information is summarised in the first paragraph. There's lots of advice available about how to write a good introduction but it's worth remembering that you are aiming to hook the reader in – and make them want to read more or

Cues

As well as an introduction, some stories have a lead in, either verbally as a cue or in text as a sell. For example: 'Voters throughout Europe are rebuking leaders who have promoted austerity measures. Will the new guard do any better? Our chief reporter has the details ...'

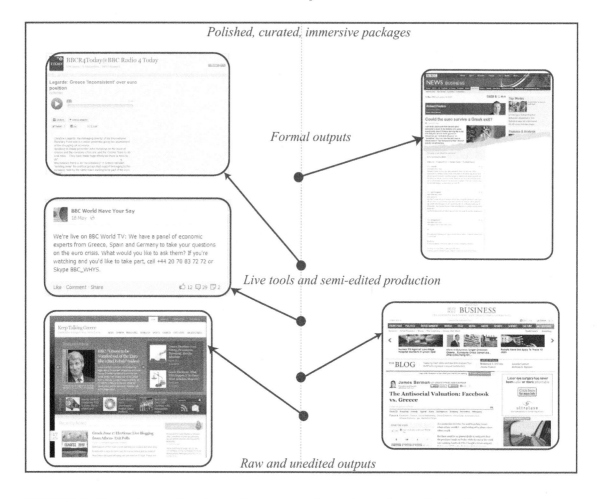

FIGURE 3.4 The various options for draft posts, showing their relative scale of editing and cohesiveness. Note how items fall towards the lower half of the scale, being relatively unedited. From the top: three BBC News items: Robert Peston's blog had more than 800 comments on this post within a day; a BBC Radio Four Audioboo; BBC World Have Your Say calls for comments on Facebook;a personal opinion piece on the Huffington Post from a non-journalist; Keeptalkinggreece is a blog created in 2010 to share with international audiences the 'real' Greeks, their personal stories, comments, fears and anger about the hopeless situation they find themselves in – news with a personal angle.

keep listening. Move on to construct the story with names and details, backed up with short quotes that are carefully selected to back up both sides. If you are writing for the web, a 12-paragraph story should have four good-quality links. You are likely to be speaking in the third-person-objective voice

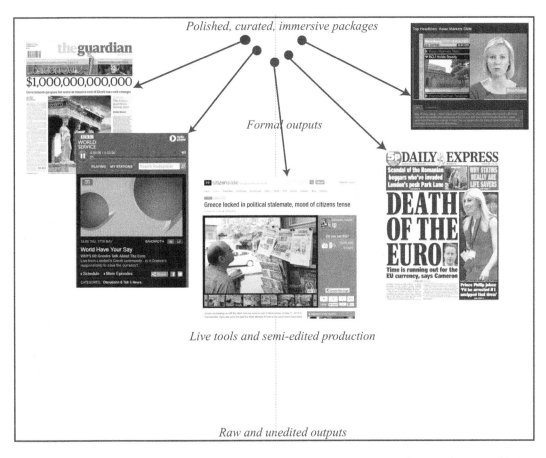

FIGURE 3.5 The various types of basic news unit. Note that all items are close to the top, all being relatively edited and packaged. From the left: the front page of the Guardian showing a numeric headline; the BBC World Service's World Have Your Say programme produces a radio package in a Greek restaurant in London; a post on Citizenside gives a conversational, on-the-ground perspective; the Express with a more 'folksy', tabloid-style headline; Bloomberg TV, with a straight report featuring a fact-laden, neutral 'cue' or intro.

rather than the more informal personal. Use short sentences that people can easily understand. To sustain a level of interactivity where appropriate, add contact details (emails or avatars) as part of the byline or recording to encourage interactivity.

Keep the writing of scripts or articles tight. This usually involves avoiding adjectives and bombarding the audience with too much detail or information too soon. Where links are included,

Introductions

In crowded social spaces, it is more important than ever to grab a reader's attention and hold on to them. A good introduction for news blurts out the main information and angle of the story as if you were telling a friend what has happened.

Box-outs

Pulling out highlights from your packages works to break up the content, make it easy to scan or understand at a glance and drive the reader through the story. It's great for things like quotes, best of, top ten, timelines, how to, at a glance, maps and images.

avoid 'click here' or 'more information', as this is a wasted chance to guide the reader. Remember that links are a service and should offer a resource in terms of good navigation around the web as well as added transparency. The link should be for a specific page, picture or document rather than Wikipedia or random sites.

In-depth text features and packages

These are fully researched and scripted stories detailing exactly what has happened, with comments and interviews from experts and bystanders carefully woven into a cohesive narrative. They are often referred to as long-form journalism, features or packages, and take time to do, as they pull in a much wider range of voices and analytics. The aim of the in-depth package is usually to offer a formal, objective journalistic voice, or a combination of voices, which explains as much as it analyses. Here, there may be more scope to offer immersion or interactivity in the production process (as detailed in Figure 3.6).

> Always grab the reader by the throat in the first paragraph, sink your thumbs into his wind pipe the second, and hold him against the wall until the tag line. (O'Neil in Randall, 2011)

A broadcast package is a report combining multiple broadcasting techniques, usually a voice-over, images, a piece to camera, interviews and graphics. You have to plan what you need to shoot, based on a script, and map out the story elements much like for written packages. The level of editing has now shifted towards the most professional reporting and editing. Audio can be used by journalists in a number of ways: as a stand-alone story element such as an interview; as a live vox pop; as embedded clips to liven up or chunk text-based stories, or as part of a package. Podcasts are audio files that can be distributed over the internet and downloaded.

Platforms

The jury's out on what the term 'platform' really means. Even back in 2007 the concept of platforms was 'the focus of a swirling vortex of confusion' (Musser, 2007). Early on, it was often a synonym for an operating system, one that can be programmed and therefore customised by outside developers. As such it is a software program that gives everyone the power to create what they want. But lately it is used more fluidly. To most internet users, it's just another buzzword that doesn't mean much of anything (Scenable, 2012). It has been used freely for the last five years, especially in relation to multiplatform journalism. In this sense it refers to the production of content across output channels: a platform is the website, the mobile phone or the print product.

Consider an in-depth feature when a basic news story would seem too simplistic for the complexity or depth of the issue. Take time to do a package when you want to add more creativity to the writing as a genre or show off your craftsmanship with more advanced writing techniques, such as a delayed drop intro or thematic vocabulary. You may want to combine facts, quotes, description, anecdotes, opinions and analysis. This is the time to offer exploration and customisation to the user, with a rich combination of media and storytelling experiences. It's likely you will find yourself liaising with other members of the team in a newsroom who may be able to help bring the story to life with graphics, images or multimedia.

Broadcast news packages work well to combine the visual stimulation and immediacy of video in a polished, more formal journalistic output. The technique is writing to pictures – you need to add information and context to what the viewer can already see, not repeat it. This can take time to master.

Alternatively, a slideshow of images combined with text can also provide a compelling story.

It works best if you construct or map the package from the beginning with a range of storytelling elements in mind. In this way, the modules of content and the inclusion of multimedia happen organically in a much more authentic way and the overall package is of better quality. Each module of content should stand alone as a start and end point as well as work alongside other elements as part of a more immersive experience. Consider the options for developing the who, what, where, when, why and how questions as set out earlier. Where is your package destined to be published? If it is for a mainstream news organisation, you have to match their voice and style. You also need to consider images and multimedia from the outset. Individual elements may need to be reused or linked to as the story develops over time.

Features

There are a range of specific writing techniques for reviews, travel, comment and long-form features. A colour piece documents what an experience was like, with a specific focus on the senses (what could you see, smell, hear, taste?). A backgrounder develops the basic news units with more insight and analysis (what are the other angles, the areas of interest, the questions that need more reflection or synthesis?).

Broadcast packages are traditionally the most closed-off kind of reporting, most commonly associated with the one-way voice, as there was little or no way to interact with a prime-time news broadcast. As such, news presenters and reporters are having to be more innovative in the way they incorporate social media. Sky News, for example, during the one-day strike in the UK in November 2011, pulled Twitter content in from around the country on #righttostrike and #wrongtostrike and used it to update a graphic for broadcast every 30 seconds. News anchors are increasingly referring to their social-networking accounts during or at the end of broadcasts to encourage conversation and interactivity in multiple spaces. In terms of the filming and editing, more polished broadcast packages tend to combine wide-angle shots of the scenery or setting, mid-close-ups of people or action and close-ups. Videos have to 'sit' on the first frame when they are posted online to make sure the opening and closing shots are strong, and tell the story as well as possible.

Good feature writing takes time to master, as does good writing for the web and scripting. Reading and analysing other good articles will help, especially as the capacity for social and iterative storytelling changes so quickly. One of the easiest traps to fall into is to map the feature when you get home from researching it – rather than before. This will make constructing your feature or package for social audiences more

Usability

Usability refers to the ease with which your content can be consumed on different platforms. You may consider breaking up an article every few paragraphs with bold subheadings, bullet points or breakouts to make it easier to view on print, mobile phones, tablets or screens, for example.

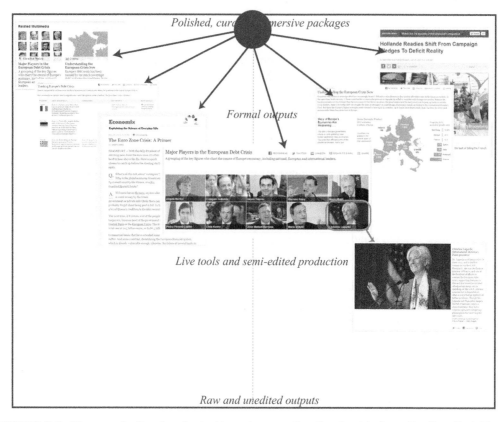

FIGURE 3.6 The complexity of an in-depth package on the Greek crisis from the *New York Times* in July 2012. It is almost impossible to define a start or end point to the reporting. The user can navigate between images, interactive graphics, video, stories, backgrounders, blogs and Q&As. These have been designed to work together as well as being stand-alone elements.

The echo chamber

This is when the same vocabulary is repeated in different story elements. It's bad practice for both a caption and sell to begin with 'the Eurozone crisis', for example. Story elements should be made to complement one another across platforms, not repeat themselves.

difficult, as the story elements are less likely to sit well together. Mind map all the angles, questions and possible resources on which you can draw.

There's a wealth of expert advice on producing broadcast packages for television, radio and the web – more detailed than can be presented here. It is worth noting, though, that shorter videos work best for social-networked distribution. The guide is three spoken words per second, and any video destined for online distribution should be less than two minutes long. Write scripts in a conver-sational style using 'it's' instead of 'it is', and avoid complex writing such as subordinate clauses and conjunctions.

Conclusion

Social media have opened up the production process and allowed it to become more creative in terms of who and what can be included. As such, the journalist's modern-day toolkit is about understanding the range of tools open to them and the culture of social media. Good reporting will often involve adapting choices to best communicate events: it's about selecting the right tool at the right time for the right audience. Stories can be conveyed using short-form updates, drafts and packages, text, video, audio, images, blogs, microblogs, maps, infographics, games, and links – and the whole process is evolving continually.

Social media and online or mobile production allows limitless possibilities for inclusion in storytelling. The new expertise that is emerging for journalists is how best to navigate these new relationships and opportunities. Eyewitness or audience comments sit alongside expert discussions or more edited packages. Citizen journalism may offer a rich and diverse addition to work previously ringfenced to a profession. Journalists need to know how best to combine these elements to best tell the story and how to add value along the way.

The founding skills of a journalist's work are as important as ever; however, social media add another dimension, another value – and one which journalists must grasp if they are to survive in the new media landscape. The Five Is of social-media storytelling help embrace the non-linear nature of content creation: infrastructure, inform, immerse, interact and interest.

These recognise that reporting now happens in a non-linear way, which means you cannot presume a start point for your audience or what they want from the storytelling experience. Users consume as much or as little as they like. They contribute with different motivations and for different purposes. The core role of communicating what is going on to people is also shifting. This is a cornerstone of a journalist's role. Yet it is one that is becoming more complex in social spaces and an awareness of the negotiations that takes place is essential.

Sky newsroom

Sky News was the UK's first dedicated 24-hour news channel and launched its iPad app in March 2011. It is an integrated newsroom, producing content for a range of platforms simultaneously. At each stage of the production process, journalists liaise across teams to consider how best to present information in the most accessible way. Pieces of content, such as an article, video clip or image, are defined as modules by the digital teams. Journalists are expected to make editorial decisions on how best to combine modules, and to judge which module type would be best used when.

For broadcast, graphics are combined with interviews, stills, voice-overs, live broadcasting and pieces to camera. There is also scope for producing social-media content for broadcast. Miranda Richardson, head of social media at Sky News, says: 'We don't include social media content for no reason; there always has to be a genuine editorial reason as to why it adds value to the storytelling.'

FIGURE 3.7

For the web, templates are built throughout the day to enable the easy combination of agency material and embed videos, pictures and galleries with captions, graphics and tables, stylised maps, bullet points, and more. A typical story would consist of an image or aggregated images from the wires, picture captions, text and hyperlinks (both to other sites around the web and correspondent pages). Live blogs or chats are also used to pull in a correspondent's Twitter feed or open up discussions for comments and interaction. Curating social-media services, such as ScribbleLive, showcase relevant tweets and pictures of user-generated content. Phil Thomas, online producer at Sky News, says: 'To a great extent we want to be joined up: online, iPad and broadcast, so we want to reflect and complement what the main channel is doing. It is about creating the fullest user experience possible. We can give people much more information and choice about how they want to consume it.'

Best-practice writing for digital platforms takes into consideration the balance of a story, adherence to house style, accurate spelling and fact checking. An average story might have 12 paragraphs, built with front-loaded sentences and around four hyperlinks to other pieces of content on the web. Those links are to primary sources either as an acknowledgement of the source (a council press release or charity statement, for example) or to add value to the reader in terms of continuing their understanding of a topic. As with most news organisations, journalists write directly into templates, with the first three words of a headline being the most crucial. Typical page furniture includes pull quotes and fact boxes.

For online video modules, staff work to ensure the correct attribution and distribution rights are in place as well as the content's verification and authenticity. Attention is placed on the first frame, as the content sits on this first still, and to make the content work as a stand-alone as well as within the context of an article.

The same is true for more substantial infographics, which are labour intensive and have more longevity. Hugh Westbrook, product-development producer at Sky News, says: 'Infographics might not always get the page impressions but it is about how you improve the storytelling experience. It is about quality – making really good stories sing – as well as seeing the news in a different way. Websites can give you text, images and videos, and the interactivity gives you the fourth dimension. Imagination here is key: graphics need to be useable and add value by letting you see stories in a new way.'

Content production is heavily influenced by performance metrics on a module by module basis. Journalists are expected to be aware of how stories and modules are performing in terms of search and social optimisation. Peaks in web traffic usually occur at 9 a.m. and lunchtime in the UK. Niche content can often gain more traction than anything else, but aggregated content by sites such as the Drudge Report can generate spikes in traffic. User experience is also a prime concern. For example, the iPad team members select content for commuters or viewers with more leisure time. Stories are built with full consideration for multiplatform (creating both HTML5 and Flash options, as well as varied graphic sizes for mobile use). Most importantly, as the executive producer for the iPad Rob Owers says: 'This is not just chopped up bits of telly; we are highlighting the best content we have and adding value. This is about creating premium products which deepen the user experience.'

Key reflections

- What is real-time and instantaneous journalism? What does it mean for the new norms of storytelling?
- Which of the Five Is of social storytelling do you consider will have the most impact on the future of news production?
- To what extent does a journalist still need to be objective and balanced in short-form updates? How can they be?
- Practice live blogging an event. This will test your ability to sense the news top lines on a rolling basis, use links, interact, thank and communicate. Try curating content together to build a news piece at the end of the day. What is the difference between chunking and layering?
- What is best practice for linking? Research the debates surrounding the BBC's linking strategy and discuss whether mainstream news organisations have a responsibility to link to a more diverse range of sources.

Tips and tools

Technology: journalists need a grasp of technology, what it can do and how it can make life easier. Your audience know how to upload pictures, video and audio in minutes – or indeed live stream – and so must you. The quality of tools and devices is improving all the time, so enjoy exploring what is on offer.

Links: these are the fundamental building blocks of any web-based storytelling. You can include shortened hyperlinks using software such as Tinyurl or Bit.ly on social networks and blogrolls.

Slideshows and galleries: combining audio to images can be a compelling way to story tell and takes less editing than video or packages. They work best with a series of unique and compelling images. Keep it under two minutes. Try Soundslides, Slideshare, Animoto or Vuvox.

Website builders: there are dozens of free website builders but Google Sites, Moonfruit, Yola, Weebly and Bravenet all offer a range of services, from your own domain name, to customised design and search-optimised pages.

Embed video: an embedded video (often in mp4) is placed within a text article to enhance the story, hosted on sites such as Vimeo, Viddler, Seismic or Spreecast (click on 'Share' for the embed code).

Piece to camera (PTC): whether talking into a webcam or handheld video, the PTC is used when you want to give genuine insight and provide a sense of immediacy, watching events as they unfold. It is you talking into the camera. You can record information when there is no footage or pictures available. Make sure there is nothing embarrassing or distracting in the background.

Live blogging: add-on services such as CoveritLive or ScribbleLive produce a module that embeds into any content-management system to give a blog-like interface. Users can ask questions, comment or participate in polls in real time as well as pulling in feeds and content. Curating tools such as Storify and Tumblr can make it easier to create a social-media package combing multimedia.

Moblogging: mobile blogging has emerged as a further convenience for bloggers who want to update their readers instantly from their smart phones. It brings the blogging experience as close to real time as possible. Try services such as ShoZu and Moblog, but the possibilities are endless.

Live broadcasting: several sites and apps offer live streaming, but you do need a solid internet connection. Try Twitcasting, Ustream, Bambuser, Qik, Livestream or Justin.tv.

Images: there are two main types of photography, posed (when you have time to frame) and grabbed (rushed shots in a live situation). If you are working on a breaking story such as a riot, forget about being clever and use your automatic settings (for shutter speeds and exposures). The main file types are jpeg or gif. Sites such as Demotix or Citizenside allow you to sell images to newsdesks all over the world. Experiment with GifBoom for animated images.

Audio: once an audio file has been created it needs to be compressed for online use, usually when you press save and export. The mp3 format is the most popular. Tools such as Audioboo and SoundCloud lend themselves perfectly to short interviews, aural accounts from the ground and personal reflections. If you want to use audio for slideshows, remember to ask the subject to include the question in their answer. For example, 'The hardest part of living in Greece now is ...'

Video: make sure you have enough set-up shots and cutaways to edit successfully. Keep fancy zooms and dissolves to a minimum. Always keep the camera still. Remember the rule of thirds: if someone is being interviewed they should be off-centre and their head below the top line

Polls: you can sound out public opinion quickly and easily with online surveys. Try SurveyMonkey, Google Surveys and PollDaddy. Check embed options before starting if you want the outcome to be portable.

Analytics: Google Analytics and Trends as well as data from Bit.ly and your content-management system or blog would give a good picture of the keywords and distribution you need to focus on.

Word and tag clouds: for easy visualisations that bring an added dimension to words and themes try Many Eyes or Wordle.

Presentation tools: try Prezi for an alternative to PowerPoint. Blurb, HP MagCloud and Lulu allow a range of self publishing.

Readings and resources

The Online Journalism Handbook by Paul Bradshaw and Liisa Rohumaa (2011) is essential reading for anyone needing a springboard into writing for the web, data journalism, producing blogs, audio and multimedia.

Alison Gow: newspaper editor Alison Gow includes a great range of posts on storytelling for the web. She blogs here: www.alisongow.com/

The Stream: Al Jazeera English produce a daily television programme about social-media communities: http://stream.aljazeera.com.

Podcasts: there are more than you could listen to in a week but start with Matt Wells's Media Talk, BBC Radio 4's *The Media Show*, or The Social Geeks.

Tech talk: there are plenty of great tech and tool blogs. Try 10,000 Words (www.10000words.net) and AllTwitter (www.mediabistro.com/alltwitter/), both good places to keep abreast of changes to journalism and technology, and The Next Web (http://thenextweb.com/).

People to follow: Cindy Green and Andy Dickinson are a good starting point to find out more about online video. Mindy McAdams has run the Teaching Online Journalism blog since 2005 (http://mindymcadams.com/tojou/). Tony Harcup is credited with one of the best all-round introductions to journalism with his book *Journalism: Principles & Practice* (2009).

Meta-journalism sites: Journalism.co.uk, Lost Remote, Poynter.org, the BBC College of Journalism and Reportr.net offer a wide range of practical tips and tools for good storytelling.

Conceptual texts: to frame the culture of social media these books are all well worth a read: *Mediactive* by Dan Gillmor (2010), *Connected* by Nicholas Christakis and James Fowler (2009), *Everything is Miscellaneous* by Dave Weinberger (2007).

>>Chapter 4<<

DATA JOURNALISM AND CROWDSOURCING

Overview

As advances in communication technology and changes in legislation worldwide make more and more information available in mass and in electronic formats, journalists increasingly need to be able to make sense of this information for their audience. From words to maps and moving graphics, to video and interactive features, journalism is increasingly about the collection and presentation of data in a collaborative and interpretative way. This social dimension of data journalism, of finding material, of sharing it and collaborating with the public, puts the new practice of data journalism well within the realm of social journalism.

Key concepts

- Data journalism
- Design
- Interactivity
- Leaks
- Narrative
- Transparency
- Visualisation
- Whistleblowers

Springboard

- *Remember the story*: journalism is about stories; data can be used to tell those stories in more interesting, interactive and comprehensive ways, but data without the story can be dry and off-putting. Always ask yourself: what is this adding to my story?
- *Interaction*: data allows your readers to interact with the story in ways that traditional narratives don't. Think about the ways your readers can use the data, manipulate their views, add to and comment on the data, and keep the channels open for them to feed back to you.
- *Transparency*: give the data back to the public. Making the raw data available to your users can add immeasurably to your story, people can interact, suggest angles or views, and correct any errors you might make. In addition to this, being transparent makes you more trustworthy.
- *Don't fear the technology*: data journalism doesn't need the most sophisticated software or the most qualified programmers. Technology is getting easier and easier to use, and the stories are getting better and better. Online communities are very helpful with technology as well – as long as you give something back, you can get all sorts of help.
- *Cultivate your community*: the more you do, the more open you are with your stories and data, the more you engage with the community of users and journalists, the more you will get back, and the greater your impact and influence within that community will be.

Introduction

Data journalism has become something of a buzzword in journalistic circles recently and, although conceptually it is not new, changes in both technology and the law have made the acquisition and presentation of data by journalists far more common.

The world is full of data, and modern government and society revels in gathering, storing and analysing that data – from the traffic patterns and accident rates at a local intersection to the movement of troops in a war zone; from broadband access to election results. The world is increasingly explained (and obscured) for us through data.

Financial data is probably the oldest form of data journalism – every newspaper of sufficient size runs graphs of stock movements and pages of fine-printed numbers, but these are intended primarily for expert use. Any person who has ever decided they needed to know more about finance and has picked up the stock-market pages of a major daily in the hopes of learning something can attest to the difficulty of making sense of columns and pages of numbers, codes and names.

Data

Data just means information, nothing more. In the common usage, however, it refers to large amounts of information, often numeric, which can be presented by use of graphs, maps and other illustrative means.

Although the stocks pages are an important kind of journalism, most news that uses data does so in the service of telling a story, not simply presenting the numbers for analysis. This storytelling is fundamental to the process of journalism – if the audience can access the raw data for themselves (and, except in the cases of the most exclusive leaks, or data collected specifically by the news organisation, they can), then the journalistic function must be to make sense of that data and to tell stories from it, not simply present it.

It is this narrative function that is essential to the process of data journalism, and distinguishes news outlets from everyone else publishing data.

In the new age of social media, data itself become social. There is a new wealth of data that is being created by the social networks, as well as new sources of information and material from users. The practice of crowdsourcing (discussed in Chapter 7) is also important to data journalism, making the analysis and representation of large bodies of data practical for smaller news organisations.

> ## Narrative function
>
> The function of journalists is to tell stories and make sense of raw information. This is particularly evident in data journalism, where the difference between the raw information and the final story is apparent.

Finding data

Data is really just a modern word for information and, in that sense, all journalism is data journalism, since all journalism trades in information of one sort or another. In its common usage, however, the phrase 'data journalism' is usually taken to refer to numeric or digital data, or information that is given in such bulk as to be difficult to access or understand by average users. Such data is seen as the product of the modern, digital, age, because technology has made the gathering, storing and dissemination of such data far easier than previously.

Although sources of data abound, and anyone with access to the internet can find enough data to tell hundreds of stories, there are a few common sources of data with which any journalist should be familiar.

> ## Reporting numbers
>
> Numbers are hard for journalists; the need to keep the story going, but also to explain complex numerical concepts, often fight with each other. A few key concepts: percentages make sense only when you know the context – a percentage of 'what' total? Don't report percentage changes – report the actual change. A 50 per cent increase in the cancer rate sounds different to an increase from 0.05 per cent to 0.075 per cent. Even better, use the actual numbers – last year 375 people were diagnosed with cancer, out of the population of 500,000, an increase of 125 over the year before.
>
> More advice on using numbers in stories can be found at: the BBC College of Journalism (2012) and the Royal Statistical Society (Marshall, 2012; Royal Statistical Society, 2012).

Commissioned data

Many large news organisations may commission the gathering of data themselves for the purposes of news stories: the most common example of this is commissioned polls, often on political questions. Political polling has been a standby of political coverage for decades, and although it is expensive it is often considered essential for coverage. Occasionally, a news organisation will commission other kinds of data or information for a story, but given the expense and the time involved, this is rare. What is more common is to commission teams and tools to work on ways of collating existing data.

Polling

Polling usually refers to asking the electorate whom they will vote for, but in principle it simply means asking a range of people their opinions. Polling can be as formal as that conducted by professional organisations, or as informal as asking people at the bus stop what they think (a vox pop), or asking a question on a website, social network or microblog feed.

In 2004, in the run-up to the national elections, and the local-council elections the following year, the South African Broadcasting Corporation commissioned a team including the Council of Scientific and Economic Research, Tata Technology, and their own journalists and experts to create tools that would collate data from previous elections with economic and housing data, the census, and incoming election results that would then be used to create stories that linked economic and social issues with election outcomes. The subsequent stories included issues around the delivery of basic services to communities (such as plumbing and waste disposal), and have been credited with the ongoing campaigns in South Africa to hold councils to account for lack of delivery (Gerber et al., 2010).

If you are working with a news organisation that is commissioning polling or other data, this is an excellent opportunity to think about what stories you would like to tell, and whether you can request that the data include specific information. If you anticipate a split in voter choices along specific lines (age, geographic location, size of household), you may be able to request that the polling company include those questions when asking. Think creatively about what stories you could find beyond the simple 'Who are you going to vote for?', and try to work with the pollsters to get more out of the time and effort expended in conducting the poll. Also think beyond the election – would any of this information be useful in storytelling then?

Smaller news organisations may not have the resources to commission large-scale studies, but they often have considerable data about the communities they serve, usually in their circulation, advertising and audience departments. Although information about the news organisation's reach and market is not necessarily news (except to other journalists and editors) there may well be information about increases and declines in circulation, or changes in advertising patterns that can be linked to events in the community, and then to stories. It is also possible that these departments have purchased proprietary information such as mapping and business data that could also be used by the newsroom.

Government and institutional data

This is by far the largest source of data for any news organisation. From census data, which in most democratic countries is publicly accessible, to voters' rolls, to company registrations, to crime statistics, the apparatus of government is awash in data that journalists may be able to use in stories.

Most countries will have a government office of statistics which is where much of this information will be made available. A simple search should provide links to this. Although many democratic countries make this information available to the public, others make no information accessible – however, organisations such as the United Nations (and its constituent organisations such as UNICEF, UNESCO and the WFP) have considerable data on many countries around the world (United Nations, 2011b). Large charity and activist groups such as Oxfam (Oxfam, 2011) and Amnesty International (Amnesty International, 2011) may also have material, although you may need to request to see the raw data, rather than their news releases based on it.

Business and financial entities may also have data available – chambers of commerce, or local groups of businesses may be able to provide information on activity and changes within the regions. Stock and share market data (for those who understand it) can provide invaluable insight into patterns and stories.

> # Finding local data
>
> Keep a set of bookmarks of which organisations (government, non-profit and business) maintain and distribute data about your community or beat. Although many organisations will provide media releases when new data is made available, not all will. Make contact with the people who collate and manage this data – they can be very helpful with finding and massaging the data you need.

Depending on the circumstances, differing levels of government may have different information available. In the UK, for example, almost all data is available via the Office for National Statistics, even down to local-council level (Office for National Statistics, 2011). In the USA, on the other hand, each level of government will maintain its own data, and you may need to go through several levels of town, county, state and federal agencies to find what you are looking for. Get into the habit as well of checking in with these organisations regularly to see what new information they have.

Freedom of information

In recent years a number of countries have passed legislation guaranteeing the public's freedom of access to information, often referred to as the Freedom of Information Act (FOIA). This legislation generally allows for any member of the public to request information from the government (FOIAs usually exclude corporations, individuals and private entities) and, provided the information does not violate specific requirements (usually issues of national security and the privacy of individuals will be excluded), the information must be provided.

> # FOIAs
>
> Freedom of Information Acts, or FOIAs, are any legislation that guarantees the legal right of access to government or corporate information – part of the stated democratic goal of transparency. Specific countries may use different titles for the legislation, but they are often referred to as FOIA, and in the USA at least, FOIA is now a verb – journalists talk about 'FOIAing' a government institution.

In November 2011, the BBC's Inside Out programme used data obtained through the Freedom of Information Act to analyse how much money councils raised from parking fees and fines: £186 million over three years. The issue of the cost of parking in London remains a highly contentious one for residents, and this story added considerably to the debate, and may well affect the outcomes of local politics (Good, 2011).

Although Freedom of Information legislation has been enacted in more than 85 countries, and in supranational bodies such as the Council of Europe, the African Union, the Organisation of American States and the United Nations, the implementation of such laws is erratic, and extracting information from the relevant government bodies can be difficult (Banisar, 2006). However, this should not deter journalists from requesting information that they believe is in the public interest to know and, as FOIA legislation is increasingly used by journalists, the likelihood is that governments will become less reluctant to provide such information.

Large news organisations may have staff whose primary role is to assist in FOI requests, who can prove invaluable. However, in many places non-profit and activist groups also exist to assist people with making FOI requests, who can be extremely useful to journalists needing advice. Freedominfo. org (http://freedominfo.org/) and Global Integrity (www.globalintegrity.org/) both maintain archives of information about FOI resources and activists across the globe (Freedominfo, 2011; Global Integrity, 2011).

MPs' expenses

Heather Brooke is an American-British journalist who fought a four-year battle to have the details of Members of Parliament's expenses disclosed under the Freedom of Information Act. She eventually won the case, but the story was pre-empted by the purchase of the data by the Daily Telegraph newspaper in May 2009. The data went on to become the basis of the biggest political story of the year, and has been credited at least in part with the Labour Party's loss in the election in the following year. Although Brooke was not the first person to see the data, it is unlikely any of it would ever have been released or leaked had she not fought and won a series of court cases. The ruling affected not only data collected to that point, but changed the whole principle of parliamentary privilege and access to information, leaving a legacy of transparency and access (Hayes, 2009; Brooke, 2011).

Information wants to be free

In the second half of the twentieth century computing and communications technology developed to the point that their effect on society and culture could be seen. Stewart Brand, writing in 1987 about the developments taking place at the Massachusetts Institute of Technology's New Media Lab, coined the phrase 'information wants to be free', reflecting the idea that the default state of communications technology is accessible. The hacker culture that developed during the late seventies and eighties had been influenced by the social ideas of the sixties and seventies (Stoll 1989; Hafner and Markoff 1991; Barlow 1994), and the concepts of freedom and transparency were to have a profound effect on the development of the internet and new and social media (Battelle and O'Reilly 2004; The Editors, 2011).

The idea that access to information is a cornerstone of democratic society is also embedded in the development of democracy itself. From the Magna Carta to the US Constitution, the idea that government serves the people, and that therefore the people have the right to know what the government is doing runs through political systems. (Katz, 2001)

Other sources

Not all data comes from official sources, or through official channels. Leaky institutions have always been one of the best friends a journalist could have, and leaked information has been used by news organisations throughout their history. Increasingly, what is leaked is data – reports, statistics, numbers, often in large files.

The ethical and legal ramifications of accepting leaked data are complex, and leaks should not be taken lightly. The person providing the data (sometimes called a whistleblower) may have broken the law or a contract in acquiring and distributing it, and the news organisation may be considered an accessory to criminal or civil charges. In addition, it is important to consider that data whose origin you are not entirely certain of may in fact not be valid – spreading disinformation to news organisations. Be very cautious and take legal advice whenever you are approached with confidential or damaging information.

Data dumps

Data dumps are similar to leaks in that they contain information that would otherwise not be made available but, instead of being leaked to a specific journalist or news organisation in a one-to-one basis, the information is dumped in public view on the internet, making it available to anyone to use (WikiLeaks, 2011). WikiLeaks is probably the best known of these organisations, but more and more alternatives are springing up – some created by news organisations, such as the Wall Street Journal's Safehouse, or Al Jazeera's Transparency Unit; others are independent organisations or individuals. They all work essentially the same way – they provide servers and a list of data, as well as a method of sending the data, that makes it impossible (in theory, at least) for the authorities to know its origin (Marks, 2011).

Bear in mind that information dumped in this way can be even harder to verify than material leaked in traditional ways: when the leaker is unknown it is almost impossible to know whether the data is valid or not. Some clearing houses for leaked data will attempt to vouch for the origins of the material, but this is also hard to judge.

Because the data is public, this may mitigate some of the legal consequences of having or accessing the data, but this is by no means certain. Different countries may have different laws regarding the use of such information, and you should be absolutely certain of your legal and ethical standing before producing any content based on such data.

WikiLeaks is undeniably the biggest repository of dumped data at this point, but other organisations have arisen since the Iraq War logs were released in 2010. These logs documented every death in Iraq

Whistleblowers

Whistleblowers are people who reveal (usually) criminal activity on the part of organisations to the government or the press. In many countries, whistleblowers are protected by the law, so even if they have broken copyright or contract law to make the information available they cannot be held liable if the information is in the public interest. However, this is not a judgement a journalist can make. If you are approached by a whistleblower, seek legal advice before proceeding.

Disinformation

Disinformation is the deliberate spreading of false information via the media. Journalists increasingly need to be on their guard for disinformation, especially any information or data that is provided anonymously. This is discussed in Chapter 9.

WikiLeaks and its imitators

At the time of writing this, WikiLeaks is in a somewhat precarious situation, legally and financially. Regardless of what happens to Julian Assange and that organisation, the method of leaking data online will remain, and several competitors have arisen, ranging from anarchist activists to mainstream news organisations.

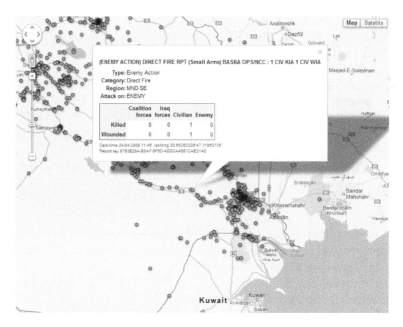

FIGURE 4.1   Detail of one of the 400,000 items of information provided by the leak of the Iraq War logs as visualised by the *Guardian's* data blog team (Rogers, 2011b).

Source: www.guardian.co.uk/world/datablog/interactive/2010/oct/23/wikileaks-iraq-deaths-map.

at the hands of the military in the period 2004 to 2009. The data is painstaking and detailed, logged in military jargon and contained in close to 400,000 records. The data was daunting, and inaccessible in many ways to individual users. The Guardian's team of data journalists set to work, creating maps of every death, and cluster maps of keywords and information (Rogers, 2011a, 2011b; Stray, 2011).

Crowdsourcing

Crowdsourcing data is another way news organisations can acquire information. Crowdsourcing uses the public to gather and share data and information about a community, from littering to transport problems. Getting the local community to report what is happening in their neighbourhoods can provide insight and stories, and with the application of some simple technology can provide a powerful source of data, as well as working to increase your readership's engagement with the news.

Setting up crowdsourced data feeds can be as simple as asking people to email or tweet the newsroom, or as complex as creating a custom application to run on people's computers and smartphones. As with any other kind of custom, or commissioned, data, the important thing is to think through what it is you want or need from the information before you start.

In August 2011 riots broke out in a number of London suburbs, following the shooting of Mark Duggan by the London Metropolitan Police. Over five days, rioting spread to a number of other cities in England and became one of the largest stories of the year. It is difficult to cover events like this: aside from the risk to journalists of being attacked, it can be very hard to know where the action is, or what is happening everywhere. The Guardian's data-journalism team turned to crowdsourcing, requesting their readers to tell them what was going on in their neighbourhoods. The subsequent map of verified events, linked to pictures and video, became one of the best resources on the riots, and was used in setting up the more academic 'Reading the Riots' study which investigated the causes of the riots (Crowdsourcing, 2011; The Guardian et al., 2011, Rogers, 2011a).

Using data

Unfortunately, real life is not like the movies, where the hero's geeky sidekick makes three mouse clicks and suddenly all the data they have just stolen from their arch enemy's mega-computer is presented in glorious three-dimensional moving colour, and the key piece of information is just sitting there, waiting to be used. In the real world data is often messy, it comes in strange file formats (governments that have not fully embraced the spirit of Freedom of Information are notorious for this, often providing journalists with un-editable PDF files of information, rather than the original spreadsheet or database files), with spelling mistakes and strange characters. The first thing to do with any data is to clean it up – known as 'massaging' it, in order to make it usable, and importing it into a usable format.

Formats vary but, in general, data used in data journalism will at some point be stored in some kind of delimited database or spreadsheet file, such as that used in Excel or Calc applications. Data in these kinds of files are organised into columns and rows – each column containing a separate kind of information, and each row containing one set of information. A dataset of crimes, for example might have columns for *date, time, type of crime, location* (often expressed in geographic terms such as latitude and longitude or postal or zip codes) and *outcome*. Each row would contain one event – so one row of this dataset would list: *May 21, 2010; 11:15h; Attempted Robbery; 123 Main Street A1B 2C3, suspect arrested*. The next row might read: *May 21; 11:20h; Jaywalking; Corner Main and High Streets A1B 2C3, suspect cautioned*, and so on.

By organising information in this way, it is easy to present it to make sense of things – you can arrange events by time, so you can see if there are particular times of the day, week or year, when certain crimes are more or less common. You can use the location to make a crime map (if the information is available in the correct format); you could then colour-code the marks on the map by the kinds of crime, or by the outcome, or whatever helps to make sense of the information. Once the information is standardised (making sure all the dates are in the same format, making sure all the postcodes are correct, etc.), you can then use the information to find and make stories, as well as generate graphs, maps, charts and other visualisations.

A relational database adds another dimension to this structure, by allowing the creation of additional tables linked to the original one, so a separate table containing voters' roll information could be linked to the original table of crime reports. Since voters' roll data would include the ages of residents, journalists could then look for links between age and certain types of crime (are the elderly more likely to be victims of crime in your community?), or how often crimes are committed in houses with children resident.

A relational database allows for more complex searches to be performed, and allows for the data to be placed on the web and an interactive interface constructed from it. Relational databases, such as Microsoft's Access software, use a Structured Query Language to allow for complex queries to be made from the data, and generally allow for larger datasets (many spreadsheet applications have a limit of 64,000 rows of data, and battle to process even that much information).

Relational databases are not as scary as they sound, and there are plenty of online tutorials and help available. Once you find yourself wanting to use a database, though, a short course can be very useful in understanding the principles. Journalism training institutions may be able to provide this, but even a course aimed at business management staff would be a good springboard.

Presenting data

Getting your data sorted into the correct format is only the start, rather like transcribing your interviews and pulling all your notes together – an essential part of the process, but not the final result.

Once you have your data, and have started to look at it, move it around and re-arrange it, you will start to see stories in it, and to think about how to use the information. At its simplest, data can be simply a precursor to a story told in a more traditional format – crime statistics may lead you to a part of town where crime is particularly bad, and from there you may find a story. National health statistics may show regional patterns of particular diseases which could lead you into stories about research, or human interest.

What is more likely, though, is that at some point you will want to show your data in a visual way – something known as data visualisation. There are many ways of doing this, but some of the most useful to journalists are listed below.

Timelines

News is about telling a story, and stories are about things happening in sequence. A timeline can be a particularly useful way of showing events, especially when you have a long-running story, and you want to remind your audience of things that happened before without explaining all of it.

Timelines can be as simple as a list of events, with a date and explanation attached to each one, or as complex as a stand-alone application on the web which allows users to zoom in, link to stories (or other media) about each event and customise the view. You could even build a timeline which would allow users to post their own media or information.

The key issue with a timeline, as with any visualisation, is to ensure that it is the appropriate method of telling that story. Timelines work best with a large number of discrete, time-based pieces of information. A story that contains four or five points, each one explained by a paragraph or more, is possibly not the best usage of a timeline. All stories have a chronological element, but timelines work best for stories when the chronology is confused, or is a key element necessary to understanding how events unfolded, and the meaning of those events.

Timelines can be a useful way for a news organisation to use its archive: consider a timeline of stories about a key person to accompany a profile or an obituary. Timelines can also be an excellent way to show a picture collection or archive.

Example

The Guardian's timeline of the events of the Arab Spring in 2011 is an excellent example of how to use the medium to show a range of linked events. The timeline has 17 strands, one for each country

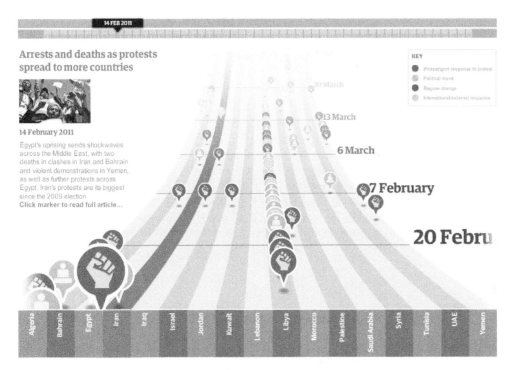

FIGURE 4.2   The *Guardian's* Arab Spring Timeline: www.guardian.co.uk/world/interactive/2011/
mar/22/middle-east-protest-interactive-timeline.

involved in, or affected by, the uprisings. Events are coded with icons indicating protest, political responses, regime change and external responses to events. Scrolling through the timeline one can see how events in Tunisia triggered uprisings and protests elsewhere. Mousing over an icon highlights one strand, and shows a brief explanation of the event concerned. Clicking on it brings up the full story. The whole graphic becomes a way into the entirety of events, and is both comprehensive and accessible (Blight and Pulham, 2011).

Graphs and charts: showing change and comparison

Graphs and charts are the most common form of data visualisation used – everyone is familiar with the visual trope of the line of a graph going up past the edge of the page, or falling off the bottom. Graphs usually show change over time – the horizontal line showing time, the vertical showing an amount of something. Graphs are a kind of visual shorthand – for most of your audience, they can convey the meaning of a set of data far faster than words would but, as with other kinds of shorthand, it's not ideal for presenting complex data that the audience would expect to interrogate or examine closely.

Charts show relationships between elements and numbers, making the relationship between them immediately apparent. A bar chart shows various numbers in side-by-side comparison, a pie chart divides a total number into its sub-elements. Charts can also be a kind of shorthand, and useful, but it is very easy to overload them with figures, making them harder to understand than a written explanation would be. A pie chart with six sections makes sense, while one with 26 is likely to be ignored – either try to group the sections, or consider presenting the data in another way.

Example

The US debt crisis of 2011 is a story that is both important and extremely complex to understand. The New York Times used charts to show key elements of the information, the amount of debt, how it was accumulated, the rise in the ceiling over time, and the potential impact of not raising the debt ceiling. Instead of trying to create one graphic or visual analogy that explained everything, they created a series, each chart or graph explaining one key point, but the series adding up to complex information. This is an excellent example of the importance of simplifying and clarifying information, and not creating something that may look dramatic at first sight, but is too overwhelming for the audience to comprehend (*New York Times*, 2011a).

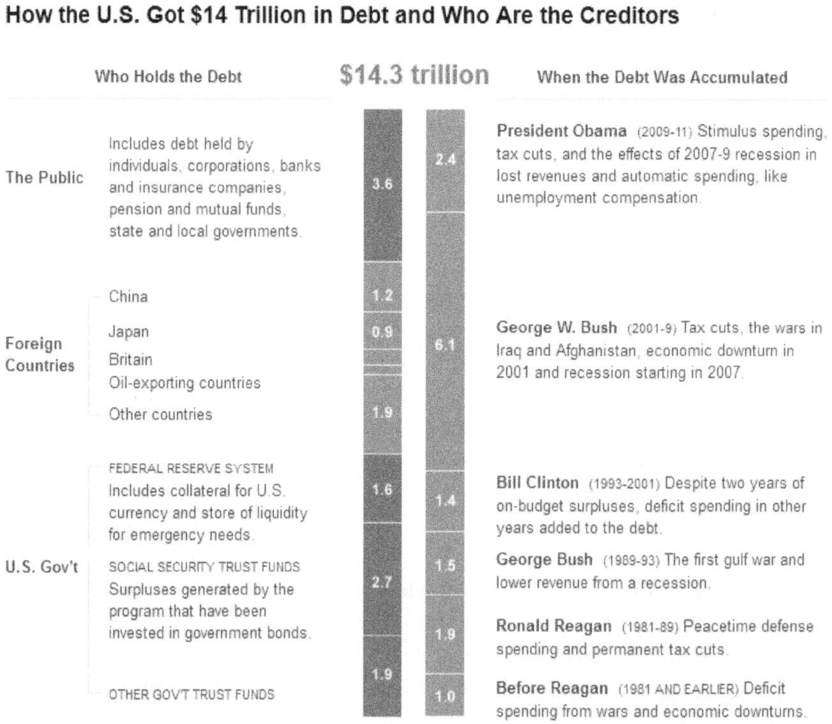

How the U.S. Got $14 Trillion in Debt and Who Are the Creditors

Who Holds the Debt		$14.3 trillion		When the Debt Was Accumulated
The Public	Includes debt held by individuals, corporations, banks and insurance companies, pension and mutual funds, state and local governments.	3.6	2.4	**President Obama** (2009-11) Stimulus spending, tax cuts, and the effects of 2007-9 recession in lost revenues and automatic spending, like unemployment compensation.
Foreign Countries	China	1.2	6.1	**George W. Bush** (2001-9) Tax cuts, the wars in Iraq and Afghanistan, economic downturn in 2001 and recession starting in 2007.
	Japan	0.9		
	Britain			
	Oil-exporting countries			
	Other countries	1.9		
U.S. Gov't	FEDERAL RESERVE SYSTEM Includes collateral for U.S. currency and store of liquidity for emergency needs.	1.6	1.4	**Bill Clinton** (1993-2001) Despite two years of on-budget surpluses, deficit spending in other years added to the debt.
	SOCIAL SECURITY TRUST FUNDS Surpluses generated by the program that have been invested in government bonds.	2.7	1.5	**George Bush** (1989-93) The first gulf war and lower revenue from a recession.
			1.9	**Ronald Reagan** (1981-89) Peacetime defense spending and permanent tax cuts.
	OTHER GOV'T TRUST FUNDS	1.9	1.0	**Before Reagan** (1981 AND EARLIER) Deficit spending from wars and economic downturns.

FIGURE 4.3   The *New York Times'* analysis of the US debt crisis: www.nytimes.com/interactive/2011/07/28/us/charting-the-american-debt-crisis.html.

Sources: Department of the Treasury, Financial Management Service, Bureau of the Public Debt; Federal Reserve Bank of New York; Office of Management and Budget.

Maps

Maps are probably the most useful visualisation tool for journalists. From a map that shows the location of traffic accidents in a town, to one showing troop movements in a war, or one coloured to show the voting patterns in a country, maps work extremely well to show the geographic dimension of information and provide a personal connection to the story.

As with other forms of data visualisation, it is important to focus on the information that is important to the story – a map of the USA or UK showing county-level political-party allegiance is useful and interesting because there is a regional aspect to voting patterns in those countries, and the information will be apparent in the visualisation, and readers will recognise that. It is also important to consider your readers' familiarity with the area being presented – a map of China showing recent pollution incidents may show the regional nature of these, but for an American or British audience, the subtlety might be lost due to a lack of knowledge about China's geography.

Maps can be combined with other visualisations as well – a map showing the GDP of countries as three-dimensional bar charts is an excellent way of showing relative economic and geographic data, since it incorporates physical location and size into the representation while adding visual interest.

Example

During the riots in the UK in August 2011, the Guardian's data team produced a map of reported incidents, based on reports received over the days of the rioting. Using a Google Map, every story

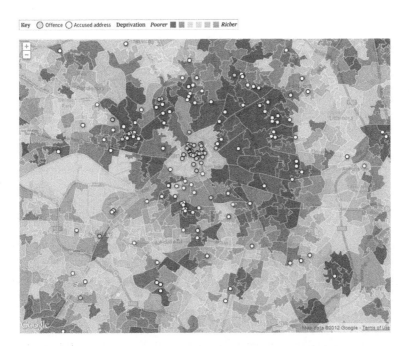

FIGURE 4.4 A map of Greater Manchester, with riot incidents and rioters' addresses mapped to a map of poverty in the area.

Source: www.guardian.co.uk/news/datablog/interactive/2011/aug/16/riots-poverty-map.

was given a geographic tag and, over time, the map built up into a visualisation of events. Readers could click on any incident and be taken to the story reporting that incident. The map provided readers with both an overall understanding of the spread of event and access to information about their own neighbourhoods (Rogers et al., 2011).

When the riots were over, the Guardian team went a step further, and started relating the data they already had with other information. Poverty was raised as an issue early on in the discussion of the riots, so the Guardian team took existing map data showing poverty levels, and layered the incident map with data showing the addresses of suspects arrested over it. Although the actual incidents happened in a range of places, the map clearly shows that the majority of suspects came from the poorest parts of the cities. This visualisation adds a dimension to the story and the reporting that is immensely useful in understanding events – the primary role of any journalist (Rogers, 2011c).

Interactive

The simplest form of interactivity is to allow your audience to download your raw data and invite them to post their own interpretations and visualisations on your site. Provided you have the legal right to offer the data, this can be an excellent strategy – you get story ideas and feedback, your audience feels involved in the story and in your site. On the other hand, it requires a substantial amount of engagement and interest on the part of your audience, so it may only work for some organisations.

Other forms of interactivity allow users to play with the data, to try their hand at solving the problems of the day. This is sometimes known as gamification and, although it is time-consuming and complex to create, it can have very engaging and interesting results. American Public Media's Budget Heroes game, in which you attempt to balance the USA's national budget, is an example of this – it is both informative about the issues of government spending and a fun challenge. Users can also compare their results to others, comment and tweak their budget plans, all using data provided by the Congress of the United States government. The game is playable at: www.marketplace.org/topics/economy/budget-hero.

Gamification

This term refers to bringing elements of interactivity and game-design mechanics into other disciplines to make them more engaging. It can incorporate everything from a simple quiz on current events, to elaborate scenarios in which the user role-plays a general, a president or other leader to try to solve a social, political or economic problem.

In 2010, Sky News produced 'Who should I vote for?', an interactive quiz which advised users on which political party best represented their views (Sky News, 2010). MTV won a Knight News Foundation grant to build a fantasy-football-style game in which users will be able to pick their 'dream team' to win the 2012 US election (Knight Foundation, 2012).

Maps lend themselves well to interactivity – the online audience is increasingly familiar with tools like Google Earth and Google Maps, so the mechanism of interaction is familiar to them. At their simplest level, maps can be resizable, allowing readers to choose the specific area they wish to view. Timelines can also be made this way, which is especially useful when they are large and complex. Adding a search function, or specific zoom function to allow audiences to easily access the area they are interested in, can add to the usability of the map, and allowing people to save their views and post them to social media can also be an excellent way to get people interacting and attracting other users to your site.

If you have the resources, you can also make maps that allow people to add or remove data to the view. Large volumes of data, such as budgets or census information, can be especially effective when presented this way, and a good online application can have people coming back to your site for years. Although the effort to build these tools can be daunting, they can also pay off in future stories, and reuse of information and skills.

Example

A fun example of a large amount of data presented on an interactive graph is the 'Baby Name Voyager'. Taking all the public records of births in the USA, from the 1880s to the present day, the site shows the top ranked 1,000 names for boys and girls in every year. One can separate names by boys and girls, or search for a specific name to see how its popularity has changed in 130 years. The graph is very simple to use and understand, and has become immensely popular (Wattenberg, 2011).

The New York Times's 2010 Census explorer map provides an interactive insight into the population distribution of the USA. Using a simple representation of one dot equalling 200 people, viewers can see both density of population across the chosen area and its racial distribution. Adding colour to the dots to show racial or ethnic groups, income level, education or the cost of housing adds another dimension to the map. Viewers can also zoom down to the area of one city block, or out to view the whole country, and can save, tweet and post their own maps (*New York Times*, 2011b).

Conclusion

This chapter is by no means a comprehensive guide to data journalism: the possibilities and technicalities are too vast and disparate for any one chapter to do that. What we have tried to do is give an introduction to some of the possibilities of incorporating data, visualisations, crowdsourcing and interactivity into your storytelling.

The list of resources and tools at the end of this chapter will give you some guidance on where to learn more, where to hone your skills as a data journalist, and where to find people with whom to collaborate and co-operate.

Channel 4's *Selling Off Britain*

On 7 March 2011, Channel 4 in the UK ran an episode of their current-affairs show *Dispatches* entitled *Selling Off Britain* that asked the question: 'Could the sale of government properties cover the national debt?' How seriously to take the proposal is a matter of opinion (although plans were already under way to sell off some of the national forest lands – an idea since partially scrapped), but the story was a great way to highlight a number of key issues – the debt itself, development of council-owned land, and the sheer scale of government assets.

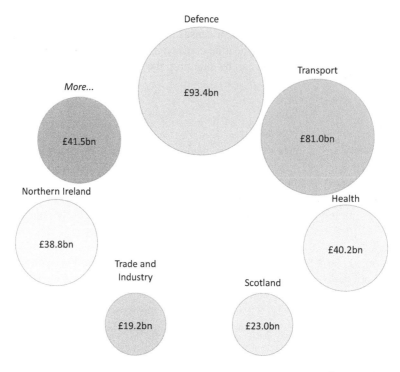

FIGURE 4.5 Picture courtesy Channel 4 and ScraperWiki: http://blog.scraperwiki.com/2011/03/08/600-lines-of-code-748-revisions-a-load-of-bubbles/.

The story itself was based on the National Asset Register, a public tranche of data listing everything that the government owns: fairly standard governmental information, and in fairly standard government style, it is recorded in uneditable PDF files. Channel 4 worked with Scraperwiki to first convert the data, then present it in interesting visual ways.

ScraperWiki's team used both technology and old-fashioned human power to convert the data in the PDF files into a spreadsheet of information, identifying each asset, its value, which government department or structure actually owned it and other information. This spreadsheet was then used to build a visualisation showing 'asset bubbles' – renderings showing the amount of money tied up in the asset by changing the size.

This was turned into an interactive tool – users could see the big picture, or drill down to see what specific assets each department or layer of government owned. In addition, land-based assets had been identified in the original PDFs with postcodes, and this allowed ScraperWiki to create an interactive map showing what assets were owned, and allowing users to zoom in to their local area.

Both data presentations were used in a live debate on the issue on Channel 4 – appearing during the broadcast and in a story on the Channel 4 website. Specific pieces of information were also used as the basis of journalistic stories.

By using data-journalism techniques, the team behind this story used freely available government data to not simply tell the story embedded in the data itself, but another story, that of the national debt, and of council developments. The project provided the basis of a considerable amount of content, and

GARAGE OFFICES AND CAR PARK, SHEEP STREET

Cotswold District Council own this brownfield land.

FIGURE 4.6   Picture courtesy Channel 4 and Scraperwiki: http://blog.scraperwiki.com/2011/03/08/ 600-lines-of-code-748-revisions-a-load-of-bubbles/.

was designed to not only inform, but engage the audience and the public. The map was particularly important to this, and engendered considerable comment and feedback for the team. This was not just a technological exercise, but a fundamentally journalistic one as well (Channel 4 *Dispatches*, 2011; Guru-Murthy, 2011; Hughes, 2011b).

Key reflections

- Keep your eye on the story. Data is fun, but your users want to know what's going on.
- Give and take: let your readers see the data, see where it came from, and listen to their ideas and interpretations.
- Jump right in: technology is not as scary as it looks; try some tools, play around with them, and use the tools and help available online.
- What kinds of government data are most useful in storytelling?
- Is data journalism an essential part of journalism? What kinds of stories can best be told with it or without it?
- How important is it to have access to data?

Tips and tools

Google Fusion Tables: (www.google.com/fusiontables/Home) allows the upload of data using standard formats and the visual display of that data via Google's servers. Advanced users can also create their own interactivity features using Google's Application Programming Interface (API). Users can share data or not, as they choose (Google, 2011a).

Google Maps: (http://maps.google.com/) provides interactive maps of the entire planet (and the moon) along with layers of data. Users can add their own information and data to the base map and publish it online; data can also be solicited from the public, or via photo and location tools like Twitter (Google, 2011b).

ScraperWiki: (https://scraperwiki.com) is an organisation that provides a platform, tools, training and assistance in both finding and presenting data. The platform allows people to create their own visualisations, find people to collaborate with, and use and reuse information provided by other members of the community (all data accessed and published via their platform is public). They conduct training workshops and tutorials, as well as being available for data visualisation commissions (if you need to keep your data and visualisations within copyright) (ScraperWiki, 2011).

Tableau: (www.tableausoftware.com/public) is free data visualisation software that anyone can download and use to publish their data to the web. There are tutorials and forums to help you get started, and they may be available to conduct training. As with ScraperWiki, all data published using their free tool is automatically public: there is a premium service if you need to keep your data private (Tableau, 2011).

A number of online timeline tools exist, such as Dipity (www.dipity.com/) and SIMILE (www.simile-widgets.org/timeline/). ProPublica has its own tool as well, available at: www.propublica.org/tools/.

Mapping: when the story is about where something happened then a map will be the right way to tell it. Mapbuilder.net works with both Google Maps and Yahoo! Maps, or try ZeeMaps, UMapper.com or MapAlist.com.

Event calendars and timelines: these are a great way to compile what's on or present information that is based around the 'when'. Using an external service such as Google Calendars or Local Calendar allows your site to become more collaborative. There are a range of timeline tools which spit out an embeddable graphic: try Tiki-Toki, Dipity, Timeline.js or Timetoast.

Visualisations: Simple editing tools can add interactivity or an impressive dimension to facts and stats. Thinglink or Taggstar allow for information to be laid over images. Try Visual.ly or Infogr.am to bring charts to life.

Readings and resources

The Guardian's data journalism site is both a showcase for the work of their team and an excellent resource of ideas, data and collaboration for other journalists. It's viewable at: www.guardian. co.uk/data. Simon Rogers's book about data journalism at the *Guardian, Facts are Sacred: The Power of Data* (2011b), is also extremely useful.

The Nieman Lab at Harvard University maintains an excellent site of information and stories about the future of journalism. The archive of their stories on data journalism is available at: www. niemanlab.org/tag/data-journalism/ (Nieman Lab, 2011).

Journalism in the Age of Data is a project of the Nieman Foundation: the full report can be read at: http://datajournalism.stanford.edu/ (McGhee, 2010).

Data Miner UK is the blog of Nicola Hughes of ScraperWiki. It's got links to tutorials, projects, ideas and resources. It's at: https://datamineruk.wordpress.com/ (Hughes, 2011).

The Poynter Institute in Florida also maintains an archive of data journalism stories and resources at www.poynter.org/tag/hackshackers/ (Poynter Institute, 2011).

ProPublica is a non-profit investigative news agency that produces stories for syndication as well as training and supporting investigative journalists around the world. They have an excellent set of resources available at: www.propublica.org/tools/ (ProPublica, 2011).

Hacks and Hackers is a group of journalists, geeks and activists who run projects and training and get people involved in and excited about data journalism. The main site is here: http://hackshackers. com/ but there are groups all over the world. They also have an excellent glossary of terms at http:// hackshackers.com/resources/hackshackers-survival-glossary/ (Hacks and Hackers, 2011).

Advice on using numbers in journalism can be found at the BBC College of Journalism (www.bbc. co.uk/academy/collegeofjournalism/how-to/how-to-report/reporting-averages-percentages-and-data) and the Royal Statistical Society's Getstats campaign (www.getstats.org.uk/).

Data-gathering resources

Government agencies are usually the best place to start looking for data – government websites should have links to what data is available. The United Nations and its member organisations are also extremely useful – there is a comprehensive list at: http://data.un.org/Default.aspx (United Nations, 2011b).

For assistance with freedom of information requests, both Global Integrity (www.globalintegrity. org/) and Freedom Info (www.freedominfo.org/) maintain lists of groups and individuals that may be able to provide advice.

For other ways of gathering data, Robert Niles's *Journalist's Guide to Crowdsourcing* can get you started. It's at www.ojr.org/ojr/stories/070731niles/ (Niles, 2007).

Dr Kathleen Woodruft Wickham authors *Math Tools for Journalists* (Marion Street Press, 2003).

>>Chapter 5<<

DISTRIBUTING THE STORY

Overview

Social media have fundamentally shifted the way news producers and users share content. There are myriad ways content can now be distributed to multiple platforms, from feeds to hashtag streams, social networks and links. Distribution strategies form a crucial part of affirming news as a process rather than a finished product, allowing content to 'live' on self-publishing and collaborative platforms way beyond the reach of traditional outputs. This chapter will look at the ways in which new technologies allow users to aggregate, organise and share content, and how this is both a challenge and an opportunity for journalists.

Key concepts

- Aggregation
- Amplification
- Analytics
- Curation
- Filtering
- Referral traffic
- Search
- Search engine optimisation (SEO)
- Sharing
- Social media optimisation (SMO)

Springboard

- *Navigating abundance*: information used to be scarce, expensive, institutionally orientated and designed for consumption. Now it is abundant, cheap, personally orientated and designed for participation. In a landscape of unlimited information, users rarely come to content from a home page. Instead they search for content or have it come to them.
- *Search engine optimisation (SEO)*: having good return results on search engines can improve the performance of content by ensuring it is found by interested audiences.
- *Social media optimisation (SMO)*: more and more users discover news via social media, recommended or passed to them from their network. News sites can use social media to gain traction and are employing increasingly sophisticated strategies to bring traffic to their sites. Effective distribution on social media is facilitated by bridges and hubs – those people who add context to make sense of raw information or pass information on from one small network to another.
- *Strangers and friends*: stories increasingly live on beyond fixed-distribution strategies on social networks through sharing and recommendations. Strangers help us find and prioritise information but friends contribute in making it relevant to us in a way that makes us take note.
- *Themes, not publications*: media can be unbundled and rebundled to create a personal publication. Users can easily aggregate and select content into categories that make sense to them. Native audiences to social media think in themes, not publications.

Introduction

Much of traditional distribution paired well with linear newsgathering because it was a logical sequence of sourcing, producing and then packaging news for defined audiences. If you were in the print business, you printed an edition, bundled it up and sent it out in your delivery van. If you were a broadcaster, you recorded and packaged a broadcast and people watched or listened, as detailed in Figure 5.1. To quote from A.J. Liebling: 'Freedom of the press is guaranteed only to those who own one' (1960). The sheer logistics of the printing or broadcasting process were sufficient barriers to entry to protect news organisations as an industry.

Distribution

How to get content in front of audiences has become more complicated, as content can be pushed, pulled and re-purposed at almost every level of the production process. Distribution strategies play an integral part in rebooting journalism.

But in a networked environment, Big Media have lost their monopoly on distribution as social media offer new and speedier ways to find and discover content. Finite news outputs have become infinite. Now, output to one organisation can become input to another. Distribution happens at a grassroots level as well as at an institutional one.

FIGURE 5.1   Linear newsgathering paired well with linear distribution.

Social media have facilitated a shift towards decentralised news operations. Audiences have the power not only to search, read and write on the web but also to share and distribute content they choose. Anyone can produce, edit and distribute content. There are thousands of tools and sites to upload content, send and share.

In some ways, harnessing the power of the people to act as the distributors is nothing new. People always passed on newspapers (newspaper circulation has always counted both copies sold and copies read, acknowledging that sharing the paper is a fundamental part of the distribution model for that medium), or told friends about a story they have just heard on the radio. The Metro newspapers, published in city centres across Europe, built a successful business model using commuters – their readers – to do the distributing for them. Replicating this process of sharing has simply been made easier and more instant by digital technologies.

> ## Syndication
>
> There are different types of syndication but most trade on how content produced by one organisation is made available to another. It could be individual programmes, articles or feeds. Tweetminster, for example, generate Twitter feeds relating to certain topics and syndicate them.

Users also navigate the social news environment differently and much of the future of good journalism depends on working out how best to predict and respond to multiway consumption. Audiences expect to receive information in a bespoke way at a time that suits them: content on demand. Social media facilitate a place for users in a rolling process of journalism rather than being passive consumers thereof.

As such, distribution strategies have to take into consideration a range of new factors:

- Stories are spread faster than ever and the crowd is in control of what comes to the fore, not the editors.
- Search engines play an important role in users finding and discovering content based on keywords.
- Aggregation, linking and syndication allow for content to be unbundled and rebundled into bespoke packages.
- Curation allows editors to offer added value in the distribution of content: selecting, filtering or prioritising.
- Distribution is increasingly influenced by social media, where friend recommendations and referrals to content come from social networks.
- Individual journalists have their own capacity to distribute content to the network through their expert use of social media.

Journalism is a process, not a product

As social media have become more prolific, content producers have become increasingly aware that distribution has to be built into the very process of doing journalism. You no longer produce and package content up and give it to someone else to deliver; you distribute as you go along. The connections and networks evolve in the same breaths as the story.

Author and academic Paul Bradshaw points out: 'As journalism becomes more networked, the distribution element becomes much more organic and an intuitive part of the news production process. It no longer stands out as an independent element 'after' a news product is deemed complete. The journalist, along with users, is now a distributor. Thanks to networked technologies – and RSS in particular – there is no reason why newsgathering cannot also be news production, or news distribution.' (Bradshaw, 2011)

Ambient journalism

Much scholarly work has been dedicated to the changes in information discovery brought about through instant, online dissemination of content. Hermida (2010) suggests that these asynchronous, always-on systems are enabling citizens to construct a mental picture of events around them known as 'ambient journalism'.

No one piece of content will have the same lifecycle. An entirely unique set of input and output factors mean the journey of content evolves and morphs in response to demand in real time. It is the speed, unpredictability and bespoke aspect to distribution which is keeping content producers on their toes.

In this continual cycle of content being pushed out to social networks, pulled into inboxes or syndication streams, paired with other elements of content or links and then promoted back out to the network, journalism has become less about finished products and more about the process (Karp, 2007; Beckett, 2008; Jarvis, 2009). Comment, reflections, aggregation and curation constantly flow to evolve the interpretation and representation of events.

As detailed in Figure 5.2, journalists who have embraced social media often find distribution sitting along other elements of their workflow. They often report logging on to social networks and sharing content long before any official 'clocking in'. At work, they have story ideas come to them from social networks, microblogging sites or comments on stories (as discussed in Chapter 2). They actively engage with the network, responding and discovering. Blog posts and tweets allow them to open up the production process as they prepare copy and, once stories are filed,

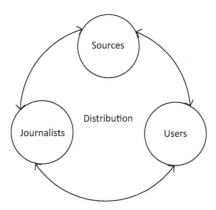

FIGURE 5.2 The networked media landscape leaves it increasingly difficult to determine any clear start and end point to the distribution process.

analyse how their content gets shared, commented on and rebundled across an enormous pyramid of distribution.

In an online and mobile environment, individual pieces of content have unique distribution journeys. As such, content producers have to design story elements to move around freely – and management systems that have the potential to encourage internal and external collaboration. 'News is demand led not supply led' (Bell, 2009). Whether by search or by social, content lives on well beyond the publish button.

 I remember tweeting the video and looking an hour later at the retweets and realising that we had this enormous pyramid of distribution and then three hours later looking at the geographical spread – Brazil, America – and thinking that is an extraordinary thing. (Guardian's Janine Gibson on the video footage of the death of Ian Tomlinson at the G20 protests in 2009, in Newman, 2011)

Distribution can also be a way of reconnecting audiences: 'The great challenge and opportunity at the moment is that we live in an incredibly confusing, complex and uncertain world where people are mostly confused most of the time so it's actually a great opportunity for journalists who can provide accurate information quickly and understandably but then they can connect to people where they are having conversations in their own lives. We have to think about the clever platforms and networks we can be part of.' (Beckett, 2011)

Example

You are working for a city newspaper and find out that there has been a four-car pile-up on the city ring road. From the bullet points below, you can see that the distribution is entirely woven in with the production and consumption – it is almost impossible to extract a clear beginning and end point. The news day never ends; and the news lives on.

- While waiting for a press release from the local police, you see a tweet in your Twitter stream (input) from an eye witness at the scene.
- You RT it (output) with the #traffic asking for verification and more information. Your tweet then gets favourited by someone else (output), covering the same patch.
- A blogger who has set up an alert on #traffic hashtag sees the content in their RSS feed (input) and then writes a blog about it (output).
- You write a blog post for your news website, linking to available content and social-networking pictures. You include Twitter handles and Facebook names where appropriate in your updates. You comment on other people's stories about the incident.
- Both blog posts are scraped by RSS (input) and re-purposed into an aggregator (output) to be delivered to a reader's email.
- They click on a link within the email (input), read it and bookmark it to a social bookmarking site and Facebook, which is automated to send updates to Twitter (output).
- Your final story for the next day's newspaper (output) includes pictures and comments from observers pulling the inputs and outputs together in a package. You ask interviewees to tweet and share it (output).
- The newspaper story on the website gets shared, comments come in from social media (input), a human interest follow-up (output) is sparked by someone involved in the accident seeing comments on Facebook, etc.

Speed

The infrastructure of social media has facilitated a crucial tipping point in the distribution of content: speed. Shortly after news of Steve Jobs's death on 5 October 2011, Twitter was handling a phenomenal 6,049 tweets per second (Gaudin, 2011). The speed with which reports can be picked up and disseminated via text messages, updates, alerts, live blogs and microblogs led professionals at first to talk about the deadline as always 'now'. But the heightened sense of connectivity that is becoming normalised through technology is shifting distribution to be less about any end point at all. As content lives on through real-time reporting, constantly evolving and shifting 'the deadline isn't now because there is no deadline' (Gow, 2008).

Guardian editor-in-chief Alan Rusbridger makes it clear why Twitter matters so much to news producers: 'It's a highly effective way of spreading ideas, information and content. A lot of the best tweets are links. It's instantaneous. Its reach can be immensely far and wide. Why does this matter? Because we do distribution too. We're now competing with a medium that can do many things incomparably faster than we can. The life expectancy of much exclusive information can now be measured in minutes, if not in seconds.' (Rusbridger, 2010). The speed element comes from the infrastructure of social media allowing for a one-to-one connection to become a one-to-many. In the world of social media, it is very difficult to keep a media blackout. Hubs and networks, whether they are individual journalists, commentators or well-connected users, can amplify small snippets into much larger breaking stories.

The reporting of Osama bin Laden's death is one such case study. As Black Hawk helicopters swooped down on a Pakistani compound, IT consultant Sohaib Athar in Abbottabad tweeted his experiences (albeit without knowing exactly what he was listening to): the worry that it could be the start of something nasty; a window shaking and a blast that could be heard 6km away. At that moment @ReallyVirtual was 'inadvertently' live tweeting the raid on the compound and the death of one of the world's most wanted terrorists.

His observations would have been limited to his followers had it not been for a couple of RTs by journalists and a Google Realtime search by Chris Applegate (2011). In the US, the story also broke on Twitter as the communications director at the White House tweeted that the President was about to make a TV announcement. Keith Urbahn, chief of staff for Donald Rumsfeld, a former Defense Secretary, had a call from a well-connected television news producer. Urbahn tweeted: 'So I'm told

Semantic web

There is growing reflection on how best to capitalise on the power of distribution capacities: is it through the automated referrals of 'machines' or is it through social media and the power of the crowd? Tim Berners-Lee set out his vision for a semantic web in 1999 and how machines would understand the information on the web in a way as to become 'intelligent agents'. British mathematician Conrad Wolfram, creator of search engine Wolfram Alpha, believes the future of effective distribution is through computers creating answers (Kobie, 2010).

There is increasing recognition, however, that content is distributed among social connections far more virally than by any set distribution strategy. Social syndication denotes the capacity for content to 'live' well beyond any single set output. This trend is known as 'Really Social Syndication' (Böhringer, 2009), where the social nature of spreading content can be as valuable – if not more so – as automated feeds. Much work has been dedicated to Facebook and how connections are built and information exchanged (Ellison et al., 2011).

by a reputable person they have killed Osama bin Laden. Hot damn.' The post went viral within minutes with the help of influential well-connected journalist Brian Stelter of the New York Times (Economist, 2011).

Of course reporting as it unfolds in real time has its dangers, though. *Brokeback Mountain* actor Heath Ledger's naked body was neither scattered with sleeping pills nor found at Mary-Kate Olsen's New York apartment but both had air time on mainstream sites in the scramble to be first with the news (worldmag.com 2008). See Chapter 11 for more.

Search engines

For publishers, making sure pages are well represented in searches is a fundamental building block of distribution. A site's architecture, usability, speed and keywords make pages easy to be 'read' by the spiders and therefore easily found and ranked. Search engines work by sending out spiders to trawl the web for pages which they then index. Complex algorithms determine the scale or relative weight of a web page to best respond to an inputted search request. The search engines here are filtering news: finding quality represented in quantity.

Search engines

Search engines are good at looking through large sets of data and returning results based on keywords. For publishers, making sure pages are well represented in searches is a fundamental building block of distribution.

Search-engine optimisation

This is done by content producers to make their site pages easy to find by search engines. There are hundreds of factors which affect performance – getting content to appear at the top of search results – but links, tags, keywords and metadata within the HTML can help.

In the 40 per cent of traffic that comes to top news sites from outside referrals, one player emerges as more important than all others. Together, Google Search and, to a lesser extent, Google News remain the biggest single driver of traffic to top news sites, at least in the USA. On average the search engine was responsible for 30 per cent of the traffic to these sites and was the lead referring site for 17 of them (Project for Excellence in Journalism, 2011a). In the UK, survey evidence shows that 61 per cent of respondents use search as their main way to look for information (OxIs, 2011).

There is a balance to be struck in attracting traffic to sites through an SEO strategy and making the site easy to use. Many news organisations do this by modifying layers of the code and wording, to suit both humans and algorithms. Stories online can be built with multiple pointers. The first is at the top of the story, with many news organisations following a 'keywords: headline' style to get searched-for terms at the front of their headlines. But Google does not actually show the on-page headline in its web results: it ranks the HTML title instead which is the data hidden in the page structure. The HTML title and the page title do not have to match. Short versions of headlines can be written for navigation within the site's pages, as picture captions and with different tags again for social media distribution.

The award-winning MailOnline, the world's most popular English-language newspaper website, briefly maximised its story to the high-volume searches of 'Pippa Middleton's arse' after Prince William's wedding to her sister in 2011, with one version of their headline in their HTML title shown in Google's web results and news sitemap, but the version of the headline on their page using the less potentially offensive word 'bum' (Coles, 2011). This shows how distribution can be manipulated to push certain content higher up search engines and in front of consumers.

A range of ever-more sophisticated analytical tools are being devised to reveal how users find and publish content for themselves, and show what is going on behind the scenes. If overlaps, anomalies, rankings and the pulse of the most popular stories are exposed then reader recommendations can be improved.

Understanding referral traffic is big business. It enables writers and news organisations to more fully understand where readers are coming from, given they rarely arrive through the home page. Measurement indexes engage journalists in the wider ecosystem. 'You quickly realise with social media you have to move from a world of counting to a world of context. So you have to set goals all the time. Numbers are everything in our business. Numbers are real people. We do a lot of search engine optimisation (SEO) training and tweaking metadata to give bits of evidence to make journalists realise the value in what they are doing. If they get that part right then we link it to their ego: more readers will see their work.' (Narisetti in McAthy, 2011).

> # Metadata
>
> Metadata describes pieces of content in terms of what is 'behind the scenes'. The metadata of a picture may include its size or when it was created. The metadata of a news unit may include keywords, tags, the author's name and its length.

> # Referral traffic
>
> A sophisticated range of metrics and analytical tools are being constantly developed to better understand how stories are distributed online – both at organisational level and through social media. Referral traffic maps where users have come from.

Adding the aggregators

Aggregation is a key building block in distributing content around the internet. Almost all news sites practise some form of aggregation by linking to material that appears elsewhere, or acknowledging stories were first reported by other journalists.

There are several different types of aggregation. In their most automated form, aggregators use RSS based on keywords (translated into code) to scrape content together. Search aggregation happens in readers, such as Omea Reader, FeedDemon, NewzCrawler or NewsGator. The user subscribes to RSS feeds, or sets up search-based feeds, which are brought together in an 'inbox' creating their own personal reading stream. Sites which create your own newspaper, such as Paper.li or Flipboard, are doing a similar 'pull' by bringing content to you.

News aggregation works in a similar way by scraping available news content on the web and bundling it together. Google News belongs to the most basic type of aggregation as it is entirely automatic, using algorithms which carry out contextual analysis which sort news by source topic or story

Search aggregation

Content can easily be delivered to you, either on a home page or reader, via RSS, so you automatically know when a site has been updated with something new.

News aggregators

News aggregation scrapes available news content on the web and bundles it together. These services are becoming increasingly sophisticated and personalised.

and display the headline, a link and sometimes a few lines of the story. It aggregates headlines from news sources worldwide.

Yahoo! News is an enhanced aggregation feed as it adds some degree of editorial management by preferencing content from the media companies from which it licenses content such as wires like Associated Press and Reuters. But news aggregation, facilitated by the free structures of the web, is becoming increasingly intuitive (Grueskin et al., 2011).

News aggregators first gained global recognition in 1998 during the Clinton presidency for posting insider information about the Monica Lewinsky scandal (Williams and Delli Carpini, 2000). Two decades later, while the Drudge Report is still a small-scale operation and compendium of links, it has become an influential driver of traffic to top news sites. Drudgereport.com provided more than 30 per cent of the traffic to MailOnline, 19 per cent of the traffic to the NYPost.com, 15 per cent to Washingtonpost.com and 11 per cent to Boston.com and FoxNews.com – far more than Facebook and Twitter (Project for Excellence in Journalism, 2011).

Adding the editor

Automated searches can tell you the potential scale or relative weight of search results, and aggregation can follow 'rules' but both struggle with humanised interpretations of importance. As humans get involved with the distribution process, they can filter and display information to reflect added context. Machines left alone to make decisions are not as smart as people – yet.

And therein lies the irony with many media organisations' attitude to social media and distribution: control. Despite the realisation among many that social spaces are largely governed by the crowd – with users having a far greater say in what comes to the fore – there remains an irresistible chance to master and influence how content is distributed in order to maximise content performance. Great content, after all, is worthless if no one knows about it.

Seeding

This is a technique used to kick-start the viral dissemination of content. It counteracts the effects of a potential low pass-along rate between users, by using paid placements, syndication, sponsorships – or even just tapping into known hubs – to grow the initial number of users exposed to a piece of content.

Social-media optimisation has become a new buzzword in media circles to reflect strategies aimed at maximising traction in social distribution. It is a type of content marketing to publicise and draw attention to content across social platforms, creating interest and the potential viral exchange of links and stories. Al Jazeera used this effectively during the Arab Spring when they bought prominent placements on key hashtags with links to a live broadcast stream (Minty in Newman, 2011). Any type of seeding aims to capture the viral capacity of social distribution.

The Huffington Post is possibly the master of this balance between social and editorial control – having fine-tuned automation with social media, comments from readers and some original content to form an effective response to what its public wants. The site demonstrates the appeal of edited aggregation: bringing together content with minimal costs and giving prominence to otherwise unheard voices. It scrapes original stories available on the internet, gauges their audience relevance against internal traffic analysis, compresses the story, compiles links around it and adds an environment for commenting and sharing. Former editor-in-chief of CNET Dan Farber coined the term 'aggrefilter' to reflect this hybrid of adding editorial filtering to automated aggregation (Farber, 2008).

As an aggrefilter, Techmeme is similar: it fine-tunes a crawl of sources and applies a clever algorithm using 600 parameters then adds a human editing layer to provide a comprehensive round-up of the tech sector. Founder Gabe Riviera told ReadWriteWeb: 'I believe human editing plus automation have always been and will always be needed for top-notch aggregation. Until editors arrived, Techmeme would often make questionable choices – like spotlighting too many redundant stories, keeping obsolete stories on the page, and overemphasising odd topics only introspective bloggers care about. Significant stories would often take much too long to appear. In the age of Twitter and hyper competitive news bloggers, even a 15 minute delay on big news is inexcusable.' (MacManus, 2010).

Large media companies such as the New York Times and Washington Post and independent companies like Flipboard are developing programs that can recommend content based on a user's previous choices. This is a highly complex process because of the range of topics and enormous volume of stories posted.

Aggrefilters

These combine automated feeds with some editorial control. Adding a layer of human 'decision making' to aggregation is an added filter to make results more bespoke.

Linking Strategy

The 2010 BBC Strategy Review by then Director-General Mark Thompson set as one of its goals a major increase in outbound links from the BBC website – a doubling of the number of 'click-throughs' to external sites from 10 to 20 million a month by 2013 (Herrman, 2010). There is also popular thinking that, true to a genuinely open networked environment, offering external links that will not damage your traffic. In fact, some would go as far as to say that links to trusted sites show you have nothing to hide, have confidence in your site and that this helps visitors place your site in a wider context (Voget and Selbach, 2006).

A hybrid of automation and curation works especially well for distribution on microblogs. Wales' Daily Post editor Alison Gow warns that automation can turn readers off: 'Automated feeds can quickly look like spam' (Gow, 2011). Former social media editor at the New York Times Liz Heron led their @nytimes account to a fully human experience without automated headlines in 2011 following a move from the Wall Street Journal the year before. 'Human-powered feeds do much, much better than automated ones, by any relevant metric' (Sonderman, 2011c).

The Guardian uses humans and robots. For example the Guardian Technology feed is plumbed in to be automated and comes out at any time of the day; it's just an RSS feed which works well for an audience who are used to the feed mentality. But Guardian Books, which is another branded feed, is hand-crafted and timed, depending on time zones and target audiences. 'The ones with more pacing and human input seem to get more followers. Automated ones drive traffic but they don't necessarily grow audiences. Distribution is about not always pushing the same monolith forward' (Pickard, 2011).

Newsroom staff

The social distribution of stories, and the desire to add an editorial layer, has necessitated new roles being created in newsrooms. SEO sub-editors spot what's hot on trending sites so they can maximise the potential reach of stories on the web. Headlines are optimised with search words, looking to see how they sit within clusters, and that they work 'out of context', as an independent element of content that makes sense to the reader. Keywords are tweaked depending on whether the story is being filed for search over the short or longer term. 'SEO is not so much about serving algorithms as it is knowing what will make the audience want to click. Every story is different. The art in writing a web headline is small wording changes can make a big difference but it needs to make sense' (Hamilton, 2011).

Community editors

Several posts are being created in newsrooms to maximise the distribution of content across the social-media landscape. SEO sub-editors maximise content distribution via keywords and headlines, while community coordinators manage relationships on social platforms and drive traffic.

The role of community coordinators or digital editors has evolved in many newsrooms to assist in bridging the gap between automation and humanising distribution so as to improve the quality of conversations between producers and audiences. Their job description is nebulous but incorporates elements of steering and improving conversations both on and off news platforms, and responding to concerns. By monitoring live blogs, Twitter hashtags and lists, and comments or trends on social platforms they can encourage best practice in social-media conversion. They are often involved in live Q&A and assisting with promoting content on multi-platforms such as Tumblr: signalling and connecting.

News correspondents and reporters are also gaining an important role in the distribution of content to their individual networks, sometimes attracting audiences to rival that of their parent brands. The one-to-one, many-to-many nature of social platforms allow for them to distribute content directly to users. This is discussed in more detail in Chapter 11.

Distribution: pulling traffic in

If facilitating simple searching for news was a pivotal development of the last decade, sharing news across social platforms may be among the most important of the next. We have so far discussed how content can be pushed out via search, aggregation and by adding a level of editorial influence. But in its truest form, social media can bring traffic to sites from the grassroots as users share, bookmark and recommend. Senior research analyst at Hitwise, James Murray, told the 2011 World Newspaper

Congress, 'Far from cannibalising news and media traffic, social media is helping drive traffic to news sites' (in Newman, 2011).

Social-referral traffic

With roughly 800 million users worldwide (Ostrow, 2011), Facebook is the largest social network in terms of referrals to news sites – it is vastly larger than any single news organisation. The site's role has evolved from a friends' network sharing trivia and personal updates to a way for people to share, link information, recommend and consume news.

The Daily Mail's Martin Clarke says that 10 per cent of their website's UK traffic is generated by referrals from Facebook, a 'gigantic free marketing engine' (in Robinson, 2010). Facebook itself says that the average news organisation has increased referrals by 300 per cent in the year to June 2011 by the introduction of the sharing button Facebook Like. Vadim Lavrusik, Facebook's journalist programme manager, said: 'They are discovering news via their friends – it finds them' (Lavrusik, in Marshall, 2011).

> # Social-media optimisation
>
> Content producers are increasingly sensitive to the performance of stories on social platforms. Optimising how content is shared and discovered across social media can increase a story's reach.

> # Upstream and downstream traffic
>
> Upstream refers to the incoming traffic to your site. If someone arrives at your site from a link on a blogroll, for example, that is upstream to you. Downstream is the traffic that is sent out from your site – if someone leaves your site by clicking on a link. Downstream was considered something to be avoided, as it meant users were leaving your site. But now it is a more commonly accepted part of web navigation.

In 2010, a study of detailed audience statistics of the top 25 most popular news websites in the USA found that Facebook ranked as the second or third most popular driver to their content for five of them (Project for Excellence in Journalism, 2011). Facebook is an influential and probably growing force. Along with social bookmarking sites, and multimedia communities such as YouTube, social media play an integral part in distribution.

Strangers and acquaintances

Across social media, there are different relationships to which we respond. Strangers and acquaintances play a part as do friends and colleagues – all with different levels of influence (Pickard and Catt, 2011). Many of us get travel advice on sites such as TripAdvisor, Google Maps or Lonely Planet. Just as when we search for references on Wikipedia, we are drawing on the knowledge of an anonymous fraternity of contributors to provide us with information. When we follow the indicator of quality from 'most read', 'most commented' and 'most shared' columns found on the websites of most mainstream news websites we are letting the crowd act as distributor to us.

In this way, we are looking to leverage our decisions on other people's experiences. This level of recommendation cannot be controlled by editors or directors but is an important part of how content gets passed on, spread and put in front of other potential readers. In this way, strangers can offer signals on filtering content and answering our questions.

Friend recommendations

In order to capitalise on the connections between friends for distributing content, media organisations have worked with major social networks either to bring apps onto their site, or take their content onto social networks.

Social plugins

Where strangers are good at making things come to the fore, friends and voices we trust add value in making content relevant to us – or adding a dimension of importance. As such, social networks are proving to have increasing influence in the distribution of content. The search giant's social-networking platform Google+ brought this into focus when it introduced Circles, in which it acknowledged the different levels of influence corresponding to networks in which we operate.

The rise of social media as a distribution tool may also result in a loss of serendipity. There are concerns that the filtering of news through friends results in a narrowing of consumption, potentially reinforcing prejudices (Zillman and Bryan, 1985; Sunstein, 2011) while others argue social media broaden horizons (Dutton, 2007; Garrett, 2009).

Editors have increasingly taken to the idea that amplifying the scope and dissemination of content will happen if they can get a closer relationship with their audiences. Some publishers have taken it literally: Bauer Media's Grazia moved their offices into the centre of a London shopping centre for a week in 2008 (Gallagher, 2008). Walesonline encourages comments and interaction by hosting planning applications and appeals on Slideshare (St Clears Times, 2010). The Liverpool Echo and the Guardian newspapers have broadcast news conferences live. Some news desks post their news lists on Facebook prior to conference, to solicit ideas and updates.

 We would be shooting ourselves in the foot to see social media as an institution or something separate; we need to see how it affects the way we behave and the way we use modern tools to say who we are. It is just part of the wave. Social distribution is when stories come alive. I wanted to democratise the Muslim identity so it could be fluid and evolve through participation. Social media is a new way of immersive information consumption. (Mohamed El-Fatatry, former CEO and founder of Muxlim)

Social-gaming giant Zynga, producers of Farmville and Cityville, has been hugely successful by putting priority on understanding human connections. The company's chief game designer, Brian Reynolds, told the 2011 Engage digital-gaming conference in New York that its runaway success was about 'keeping in touch with people you care about' (Jackson, 2011).

News organisations wanting to tap into the power of friend recommendations are negotiating a range of functionalities with the major social networking sites. Broadly speaking, strategies fall into two camps: those who want to bring the social experience onto their sites, like Yahoo! News and the Independent; and those who want the social-news experience on Facebook, like the Guardian. The Washington Post integrated Facebook Platform to create social experience across the site with Network News. It saw a more than 280 per cent increase in referral traffic year-over-year, as news becomes instantly relevant and as readers respond to what their friends have liked or what piece of today's news is most recommended (Osofsky, 2010).

Karla Geci, Head of International Media, Strategic Partner Development, Facebook, says publishers still hold the discretion as to whether to make the social-networking site the end destination or an added distribution strategy: 'It is not Facebook's objective to become a media product. Facebook want to be a part of bringing users back to a destination where they can enjoy the content in the way that it was intended. We value all these connections but we also value all the things we love such as music or films. Facebook is horizontal.' (Geci, in Nel, 2011).

For the Independent.co.uk, integration of the plugin Facepile was successful in driving users to click the Like button, and engage with stories under a genuine identity. In a function that head of Digital Audience & Content Development Jack Riley likened to walking into a bar and seeing your friends, Facepile displays the Facebook profile pictures of users who have liked your page or have signed up for your site. The Independent has also successfully embraced Facebook as a way of promoting links for videos and podcasts, for polling audiences and connecting journalists with audiences. In all, Riley told the Digital Editors Network in 2011 there had been 430 per cent growth in Facebook referrals in a year, contributing to 35 per cent growth in daily unique users (Riley, in Nel, 2011).

Vanity Fair, from Condé Nast Publications, uses Facebook as a place for exclusive content, video and giveaways. Not only was Justin Bieber the subject of a coveted cover story in Vanity Fair's January 2011 issue, the teenage pop superstar was tapped to be the first guest editor of the magazine's Facebook page (Vena, 2011).

Sentiment analysis

Knowing how a follower feels about a brand or product can reveal more than a simple Like or Follow. Sentiment analysis focuses on the comments and suggestions left on social media, using the wording, tone, context and emotion to paint a full picture.

Innovation

Distribution is one of the fastest moving sectors of social media as technology and social shifts affect how we consume media. Trinity Mirror's Liverpool Echo have experimented with Bluetooth as a way of distributing crime stories and alerts, which are sent to enabled phones (*Liverpool Echo*, 2008). News organisations are also increasingly using QR codes, quick-response scannable grids, that can add interactivity to content or to quickly facilitate a

QR codes

Quick Response (QR) codes are a two-dimensional matrix barcode that can be read by an appropriate app on smart phones. It allows users to access information such as web pages or special offers. They are used effectively to drive users between offline and online spaces.

reader moving from a print format to digital alternative. Geotagging and location-based services such as Foursquare offer content based on locality. We are also seeing myriad organisational tie-ups which facilitate content being distributed, such as newswire Agence France-Presse with online video network ClipSyndicate to distribute its video service, AFPTV, virally to thousands of blogs and websites (Luft, 2007).

Projects concerning media distribution are also moving into the sphere of sentiment analysis. Analysts in Hewlett Packard labs in Palo Alto have patented a way to crunch the Twitter effect to perfectly correlate box-office ratings of films, while media firms are using it for real-time marketing feedback (Talbot, 2011).

Open API

Open Application Programming Interface (API) refers to the sets of technologies that enable websites to interact with each other. It has formed an integral part of distribution, as it allows programmers to move content from site to site.

Open API is proving a pivotal way of developing news organisations for more open distribution. Meg Pickard, former Head of Digital Engagement at the Guardian, says: 'Our API is a big part of our distribution strategy, as you can create relationships with us as an organisation and as a developer to take our content and have it on your site. This is about how we make our content more readily accessible and more 'encounterable' and malleable within the reasonable terms of control considering legal, technical and brand responsibilities.'

Conclusion

As it may not seem to directly impact on the way stories are sourced or written, the evolution of non-linear distribution in the new media ecology is not always the first thing journalists think of when wanting to understand social media. However, this chapter argues how understanding the distribution of journalism is fundamental. Social media has shifted the way news producers and users share content in a way to directly impact on the process of journalism. There are myriad ways content can now be distributed to multiple platforms, from feeds to hashtag streams, social networks and links. Distribution strategies form a crucial part of allowing content to 'live' on self-publishing and collaborative platforms way beyond the reach of traditional outputs. New technologies allow users to aggregate, organise and share content, in a way that is both a challenge and an opportunity for journalists and media organisations.

Journalism is a process, not a complete product. As such, distribution strategies have to take into consideration a range of new factors. Stories are spread faster than ever and the crowd is in control of what comes to the fore, not the editors. Search engines play an important role in users finding and discovering content based on keywords, but social media is also playing an increasingly powerful role in terms of how users find and make sense of otherwise individuated modules of content.

Aggregation, linking and syndication allow for content to be unbundled and rebundled into bespoke packages in an ever-flowing cycle. Journalists are carving out a new sense-making role in this distributed space: one that focuses on curation. Attention is turning to the capacity of editors and journalists to add value in the distribution of content: selecting, filtering or prioritising news. Journalists themselves need to master an ever richer portfolio of possibilities to distribute and share content to the network through their expert use of social media.

 **The Guardian**

Guardian News & Media was the first British national newspaper to offer a web-first strategy in 2006, arranging content as a series of channels rather than a broad newsroom to create distribution and activity in targeted areas. It was one of the first to launch a news app alongside the social-networking giant Facebook in 2011 and has developed Zeitgeist, an innovative algorithm to monitor 'interesting-ness'. Meg Pickard was the Head of Digital Engagement.

'As an open organisation and our open digital strategy we want to think about how we can create audiences off our sites as well as on and that might be creating new audiences that never come to our site. It is all about growing social attention, new audiences, thinking about the social attention that we do get, recording it and using it alongside other metrics. The way that our architect is put together, everything has its own feed, true to the semantic web. You can put RSS on the end of any Guardian URL and create a feed for that, which might be a topic, section, comments or articles. We have made feeds part of everything we do instead of trying to guess what people would want. Users are in control when it comes to distribution.

'Stories are available on mobile, Facebook and on the site but it would not be actively pushed unless a human intervenes – and that might be a coordinator, an editor of the network front or it might be a reporter wanting to reach a wider audience. We try to support organic distribution so content will be put to the right places and distributed to the people who want to receive it, but also to support journalists, editors and subs [subeditors] who want to distribute themselves and feed their own communities.

'This was especially true with our Facebook app – the audience belongs and like being there so why try to persuade them to come somewhere else? We have used our open API with Facebook's Open Graphs to put our content core with their social widgets so you get an experience that lives in between the two. We get to count page views, serve the advertising and cookies but with the widgets on the site they get to know who that person is through the social graph. So the user gets the best of both worlds, Facebook gets the data they need and we get the data we need – but we also get engagement. Around 6 per cent of our traffic was coming from Facebook and those people were looking at a link and going straight back out again. So what does that tell us? The answer is people are addicted to their friends. There is something very addictive about your friends being the signal of what is interesting or relevant or where to go. So we wanted to see how friends could become part of your discovery experience and embrace that.

'We also wanted to make something that is native to that environment so that as a user you don't have to think about how it works: familiarity and user education and privacy. In Facebook you know the rules and local norms of what is being recorded because you are within those frameworks where things are viral and shared. It makes people more relaxed about distributing the Guardian because they understand the norms of that platform. Doing things and having them recorded and then shared is going to become a lot less scary over time.

'Zeitgeist is about recording distribution. It is primarily back end with a front, visible layer. It sits in between 'most read, most because it shows interestingness'. It shows not just that someone has shown up or that someone has left a comment, but activity on Twitter or Facebook and shares – it shows the correlation between views and activity which is a way of gauging engagement. It makes sense of the difference between a story being viewed by 1,000 people and two people leaving a comment, or 1,000 people viewing and 200 comments, and if those comments were just between two people, or if someone stayed for long enough to read comments even if they didn't write anything. It tells you what is interesting and engaging to small or large audiences, breadth and distribution. It is not just what happened to you but what happened next. A good day for Charlie Brooker is millions

of comments and retweets so for him to have a really good day would be billions – he only shows up there when he has outpaced himself. It is likely he will be in the most commented and most viewed sections on a Monday but maybe not Zeitgeist. This is emotion agnostic; it wants to know what the numbers are and what the behaviour patterns are and, like a well-trained robot, wants to see patterns and say what is behaving compared to similar benchmark items. It is related measurement not universal'.

Key reflections

- What is importance? Distribution strategies have to grapple with an increasingly complex definition of importance. Algorithms can tell us scale or relative weight but personalised recommendations from search engines, strangers, editors, or friends can effect what we deem to be important.
- Consider how news organisations feel increasingly uncomfortable with the growing influence of social media on distribution. Who is in control of this space and why?
- Aggregators versus aggrefilters: the goodies or the baddies?
- To what extent have news organisations shaped their news lists to maximise their performance on social and search criteria, and what implications does this have?
- Consider the difference between information and news. How do your definitions change in light of how content is discovered?

TOOLKIT

Tips and tools

Bookmarklets: sharing icons, either in the toolbar as a bookmarklet or near stories, is a way to facilitate and promote social bookmarking. There are a number of off-the-shelf solutions such as Mediafed, ShareThis or Gregarious, all of which contain the most popular cloud services. The addition of social networking 'share' tools to the margins of nearly every news story seems to have paid off in terms of driving traffic. While these are technically clicks away from the site, they are positive in that they potentially multiply additional readers to that story.

Email: exchanging digital messages in the traditional format of electronic mail or newsletters is still a trusted way of targeting content in a way that audiences of all ages understand. They now seem old-fashioned, but remain a useful part of any distribution strategy and can be tailored and streamed.

Embedding: when publishers provide the hyperlink or code required to put multimedia content into other people's websites it facilitates how that media can be used. The BBC began allowing some of its video content to be embeddable from 2009 (BBC News, 2011).

Hyperlinks: usually underlined or highlighted, these links under hypertext are references that readers can directly follow, either to other documents or URLs. In this way, each individual page of any newspaper, blog or forum can be distributed. Stories can be multilayered by putting links within or to the side of text to offer additional resources or references. It is also an efficient way of building up additional writer recommendations, such as a blogroll. Links can either be of related stories within your own site, or outside your site.

Linkbacks: there are three main types: trackbacks, pingbacks and refbacks. They are a way for sites to communicate with one another to automatically signal when updates have taken place on a specific page.

Link shortening: services such as Tiny.url or Bitly automatically shorten hyperlinks, making them easier to share. The links do expire, though, so this is not a long-term strategy for maintaining a web.

Really Simple Syndication: fast and efficient way to send out updates of interest. These standardised feed formats are used to publish any updated works in an automated way that is read by an RSS reader, either web, desktop or mobile based. Feeds benefit publishers by letting them syndicate content automatically, and the more RSS feeds being offered, the better. At a basic level, there are often feeds for traditional sections or subsections of media organisations. You can also customise feeds based on submitted keywords, Twitter feeds, tag words on photo sharing sites, particular users on YouTube and more.

Social bookmarking: a key way for content to come 'alive' after it has been published is through social bookmarking, where users choose to share content with friends, colleagues and groups. Having content posted, republished and then tagged in this way means several users act as the disseminators, potentially ad infinitum. Popular sites allow any web page to be referenced, tagged, highlighted and bookmarked to shared spaces. Social bookmarking is a massive way of organising what you read, connecting and sharing. Martin Stabe from the Financial Times recommends logging everything you read obsessively (BBC College of Journalism, 2010a).

Social networking: as we will see, publishers are increasingly aware that teaming up with social networks helps disseminate content virally. Facebook, for example, has moved increasingly towards allowing third-party developers to build social spaces within the platform, thanks to services such as Facebook Connect and Open Graph.

Widgets: also known as a gadget, badge, module or snippet, these portable pieces of dynamic HTML code can be installed on users' blogs or social-network pages. They republish content and, as such, are a further opportunity for reaching new audiences, with blogging platforms such as Blogger or Wordpress offering a wide range of customable feeds (removing the need for high-tech expertise). The content creator retains authorship of the content.

Readings and resources

Robots, Editors, Strangers & Friends by Meg Pickard and Dan Catt is a conference presentation exploring some of the ways that attention and social patterns influence the way we discover, consume and curate content online. It is available on Vimeo http://topsy.com/vimeo.com/25621341.

Reuters Institute for the Study of Journalism has commissioned several papers including *Mainstream Media and the Distribution of News in the Age of Social Discovery*: http://reutersinstitute.politics. ox.ac.uk/ (Newman, 2011).

Experian Hitwise offers a range of data insights and analytics about distribution and user behaviour online: www.hitwise.com/

Mashable is a comprehensive guide and round-up of technical tips and social media news: http://mashable.com/

Juliette De Maeyer has studied hyperlinks and their effect on journalism. See http://juliettedm.wordpress.com/ to source her work.

Malcolm Coles is a content strategist and SEO consultant based in London. His blog maintains a good range of examples on mainstream news using SEO, for better or worse: www.malcolmcoles.co.uk/blog/ (Coles, 2011).

Project for Excellence in Journalism has produced several reports documenting the fundamental changes in the news industry and the way news is distributed: www.journalism.org/

Charlie Beckett is founding director of Polis, the media think-tank at the London School of Economics. He runs an informative blog – http://blogs.lse.ac.uk/polis/

Part 2
THE NETWORKED ECOLOGY

>>Chapter 6<<

CITIZEN JOURNALISM AND
THE PUBLIC SPHERE

Overview

This chapter introduces the concept of 'citizen journalism' and examines some of the key ideas that inform this new movement: the public sphere; the network society; and public or civic journalism. In comparison with other chapters this contains more of the 'why we do things', and less of the 'what we are doing'. Although this chapter may appear more abstract than others, an understanding of the ideas and motives of the players in the field of social media, as well a grounding in the philosophy of the internet and of journalism, is important in order to be able to understand and prepare for the changes that have already happened, and the ones that are still coming.

Key concepts

- Citizen journalism
- Fourth estate
- Industrial journalism
- Network society
- Non-profit journalism
- Online activism
- Public sphere
- Social capital

Springboard

- *Activist, citizen and public journalism*: this collection of terms refers generally to journalism that has an agenda other than the production of news as a commodity to be sold. Conceived in part as a response to the perceived hyper-commercialism of the news industry in the last part of the twentieth century, these new forms of journalism also hark back to the early days of the news media, to the pamphleteers and campaigners of the eighteenth century.
- *Public sphere*: the public sphere is envisioned as the space, whether real or virtual, in which the citizens of a society discuss and negotiate the ways in which that society will be constructed. The internet, the World Wide Web and social media are often presented as the new form of the public sphere.
- *Social capital*: this is the idea that one's value within a community or network can be measured in the impact one's ideas or reputation has, rather than simply in monetary terms.
- *Fourth estate*: in Anglo-Saxon countries, the fourth estate is the media, the watchdog that guards and represents the interests of the public against the activities of the other three estates: the church, the aristocracy and the commons. Nowadays, the phrase is used to refer to the news media in its function as watchdog and protector of the public interest.
- *Online activism*: the internet has become a locus for organising of political and social activism. Online activism may refer specifically to activities conducted online, such as virtual protests, or to activities conducted in all spheres, but planned and organised online.

Introduction

At the beginning of the twenty-first century, a new phrase 'citizen journalism' began to be circulated. Two documents started this discussion: Dan Gillmor's book *We The Media* (2004), and Bowman and Willis's *We Media* report for the American Press Institute (2003). Both works owe something to a seminal article by Jay Rosen, 'Beyond Objectivity' (1993), in which he exhorted the American news media to reinvent itself in a voice and manner that was more engaged with the audience, more subjective, and would create a closer relationship. Although Rosen's article was written before the World Wide Web became the phenomenon it now is, the web was quickly lept on as the catalyst and location of these possible new forms of journalism: collectively (and loosely) named citizen journalism.

It is important to understand that the citizen journalism movement as it started in the USA was a response to a specific set of circumstances: the rise of corporate news media in the last decade of the twentieth century, and the overall lack of trust in journalists that was prevalent in the USA at the time (some would say as a consequence of the corporatisation). Rosen's call for more subjective, engaged journalism is a response to the American journalistic ideal of objectivity, something that European thinkers had already rejected as impossible and possibly meaningless. However, the corporatisation and commercialisation of the industrial news media remains an issue in many countries, as does the control of the media by political interests in many others.

However, despite the specificity of the circumstances, the phrase citizen journalism caught on and was presented as both a threat to, and possible saviour of, mainstream, commercial, professional journalism. This also tied in with the considerable activist and alternative news organisations which had existed alongside mainstream news for hundreds of years, but which were starting to undergo something of a revival, thanks to the internet.

Traditional news media organisations need to be large industrialised organisations. The cost of printing presses, of broadcast towers (and broadcast licences) means that an organisation needs to have a minimum size and revenue in order to be viable. The nature of advertising revenue also tends to favour larger organisations – the more audience you can reach and the more efficient that reach, the more the advertisers will be interested in your product. Corporatisation – the process of bringing small companies together into a single networked organisation – also helps to increase the profits of news organisations, by allowing them to save costs on duplicated services and functions.

Technology has broken the stranglehold that news organisations used to have by virtue of their ownership of the means of production and distribution, and made it more possible for smaller news organisations to compete: freedom of the press belonged to those who had one. Now everyone has one, or access to one. In this new landscape, news organisations are competing and collaborating not only with each other, but with organisations and individuals who provide news content and information, but do not adhere to the techniques, intents and principle of the mainstream.

New forms of activist and engaged journalism are not necessarily functions of new technologies, and some of them clearly predate the changes brought by the World Wide Web, but they are greatly enhanced by the lower barriers to entry and ease of distribution that technological changes have provided. These forms of journalism are then themselves informed by ideas about the network and how it functions, while the network is also informed by ideas about communication and politics. It is these interlinking ideas that inform this chapter, and its discussion of the highly confused terms of citizen, public, activist and new journalism.

Citizen journalism

The key ideas that underpin grassroots media and citizen journalism are outlined in Dan Gillmor's 2006 book *We the Media: Grassroots Journalism by the People, for the People*, and in the *We Media* report, published by the American Press Institute (Bowman and Willis, 2003). Both documents are informed by the call to arms for a journalism that moves 'Beyond Obectivity' published by Jay Rosen in 1993.

The phrase 'citizen journalism' is both widely circulated and inconsistently defined. Jay Rosen refers to 'the people formerly known as the audience' as 'citizen journalists', but that definition is too loose for some commenters, including as it does all forms of public engagement and response to the news (Rosen, 2006). Mark Deuze characterises citizen journalists as 'news-producing consumers', but also in opposition to professional journalists – as 'competitor-colleagues' (Deuze 2007: 122). Neither of these definitions go as far as to explain what citizen journalists do, and whether that is different from other forms of journalism.

Citizen journalism

Citizen journalism as a term has been used to signify many different things and ideas over the last two decades. In its original form it was taken to refer to groups of citizens using the internet to report on events in their own communities, something the increasingly corporatised and commercialised press was failing to do. It has also been used to refer to people providing media content to other, more formal, outlets, such as the provision of video footage of events although this is more commonly distinguished as user-generated content.

Stuart Allan and Einar Thorsen do not attempt to define citizen journalism in their book of the same name, but they do discuss the forms of citizen journalism: blogs, citizen newsgathering and, implicitly, something other than 'corporate' news ventures (Allan and Thorsen, 2009).

What is clear from the literature is that the term embraces everything from people commenting on stories or responding to polls (Lewis et al., 2010), to news material provided by the public to mainstream news organisations (Allan and Thorsen, 2009), to personal blogs, to fully fledged, professionally run news organisations that exist in parallel to the mainstream news (Bowman and Willis, 2003).

It is this last definition, that of the *We Media* manifesto, that is used in this chapter. As they put it: 'The act of a citizen, or group of citizens, playing an active role in the process of collecting, reporting, analysing and disseminating news and information. The intent of this participation is to provide independent, reliable, accurate, wide-ranging and relevant information that a democracy requires.' (Bowman and Willis, 2003). This locates citizen journalism firmly within the field of activism, and within the roles not only of collecting (what we would call user-generated content), but also of producing and distributing the news they have collected: there is a degree of motivation to act in some way journalistically. This narrows down the scope of this chapter, but still leaves a fairly wide range of possibilities to be considered, and two main sub-fields of citizen journalism: public and activist journalism, which inform the citizen journalism movement.

Public journalism

At the time of writing, public journalism as a phrase is almost uniquely American, although the ideas and practices that underpin it are not. Public, or civic, journalism is journalism that has explicitly abandoned the ideology of objectivity or neutrality and has become engaged in civic life, and especially in the defence of democracy. As with other forms of citizen and activist journalism, public journalism is responding to a specific set of circumstances: the corporatisation of the media, and its perceived subsequent move away from the communities it serves (Friedland, 2010).

Public journalism has been advocated by the Kettering Foundation, and its President, David Mathews, as well as by organisations like the Pew Center for Civic Journalism, the Knight Foundation and others. Public journalism is similar to Dan Gillmor's grassroots journalism in conception: the move away from dispassionate observation and reporting to engagement and activism is key to both ideas, and there are considerable overlaps in these ideas, at least in the USA. In some instances, public journalism is constructed as a deliberate alternative to commercial or corporate forms of journalism, but this is not universal to the movement. In contrast to the more radical form of activist citizen journalism (discussed below), public journalism seeks more to inform and improve existing journalistic forms and outlets than to overthrow them (Rosenberry and St John III, 2010).

ProPublica was launched in 2008 as a non-profit organisation dedicated to investigative journalism in the public interest. Working collaboratively with a number of professional news organisations, and with funding from donations and philanthropic foundations, it provides stories both on its own site and in syndication to its partners: 'In the best traditions of American journalism in the public service, we seek to stimulate positive change. We uncover unsavory practices in order to stimulate reform. We do this in an entirely non-partisan and non-ideological manner, adhering to the strictest standards of journalistic impartiality. We won't lobby. We won't ally with politicians or advocacy groups. We look hard at the critical functions of business and of government, the two biggest centers of power, in areas ranging from product safety to securities fraud, from flaws in our system of criminal justice to practices that undermine fair elections.' (ProPublica, n.d.).

ProPublica is not a citizen-journalist organisation: it is staffed by experienced and professional investigative journalists, but in its ideals it has much in common with forms of journalism that are called citizen journalism, and it is clearly intent on enhancing and supporting the civic public sphere.

Alternative and activist journalism

Alternative news sources (pirate and community radio, underground or alternative newspapers and magazines) have been around for as long as there has been a mainstream press, with a greater or lesser presence, depending on the circumstances. In western societies, these outlets have been largely tolerated; some have even become mainstream themselves over time. The Village Voice in New York has gone from scrappy newsletter presenting the ideas of the beats and hippies to being a an entertainment and lifestyle guide for the city; the original Manchester Guardian newspaper founded after the Peterloo Massacre is now firmly part of the British media establishment, although with its original ideals intact (Atton, 2002).

In non-western societies, especially repressive ones, alternative news sources remain(ed) important, although often repressed. Technology made a massive difference to these alternative sources of information. Prior to the development of the internet, these outlets were limited by their access to printing or broadcasting technology and distribution mechanisms. These are expensive, and fairly easily disrupted by the interests of the state. Even in democratic societies, where alternative sources of news were tolerated, they were limited by financial constraints (the number of papers published, the footprint of the broadcast tower). The internet suddenly changed all of that, and alternative and mainstream sources of news were now competing on the relatively level playing field of the internet.

These two ideals, of a new movement of amateur journalism based on the internet, and the existing activist movements that had been using old media forms moving onto the internet, have been joined in the minds of many as a movement of citizen journalists, one that is part of a new, revived, public sphere.

Citizen journalism, inasmuch as it exists, poses a theoretical challenge to the professional identity of journalists, and the boundaries of the journalistic field. Much of the discourse within the commercialised mainstream media regarding social media and citizen journalism constructs it as this – a threat to the very existence of professional news practitioners.

Theoretical understandings

This section introduces some of the key theoretical concepts that underpin this new practice of journalism. In usual practice, traditional journalism has simple motives: for commercial organisations – making money; for public and state-funded organisations – fulfilling social and political requirements. New forms of journalism have more complex varied motives: social engagement, political activism and abstract pursuits of 'truth' or 'justice'. This is not to say that the people working within traditional news structures do not have altruistic or world-changing motives, or that activist and citizen journalists may not be concerned with money, but that as institutions, these organisations tend to concern themselves primarily with these goals.

Citizen, public, activist and non-industrialised journalism locates itself firmly within the context of democratisation and activism, rather than a purely neutral activity, or one located only within economic or technological concerns. The theory of journalism practice has always considered journalism within its context of political, social and economic factors. Journalism must always negotiate its relations with the power elites in a society and, within the new, computer-networked environment, all of those considerations remain.

There is a library of works that discuss and analyse the role of journalism and its function within society, but within this chapter we aim to set out some of the key ideas which we believe are most useful in understanding this new media environment. We then show how these ideas can be seen as influencing journalism, especially within the new (or newly rediscovered) forms of citizen and activist journalism.

The public sphere

The public sphere is the space, whether physical or conceptual, in which citizens engage with the broader society, and in which consensus is reached as to the nature of that society. It is not necessarily the explicit spaces in which issues are debated, such as parliaments and congresses, but also includes the media and other areas of public engagement, the places where public, as opposed to private, life is carried out.

Although his is not the first use of the phrase, 'public sphere' is most often associated with Jürgen Habermas's *Strukturwandel der Öffentlicheit:Untersuchungen zu einer Kategorie der bürgerlichen Gesellschaft*, originally published in 1962, and translated into English in 1989 as *The Structural Transformation of the Public Sphere*. It is a difficult but extremely rewarding book. Craig Calhoun's 1993 book *Habermas and the Public Sphere* provides an excellent introduction to Habermas's ideas, and to their impact on specific areas of theory, including the media.

Habermas's book is famously dense, and spans history, economics, politics, sociology and philosophy, dealing only peripherally with the media, but the key idea for media and journalism theorists is the way in which the media functioned as an enabler of the public sphere (through the first literary products, newspapers and books, in the eighteenth century), and that the modern mass media then served to replace the original 'authentic' public sphere with an illusory one: one in which the 'public' is replaced by the illusion of participation. Critical engagement with society via the public sphere is replaced by mindless consumption (Habermas, 1989; Calhoun, 1993a; Calhoun, 1993b; Garnham, 1993).

Jürgen Habermas is usually considered a member, or at least the inheritor, of the Frankfurt School – a group of Marxist social theorists based first at Frankfurt University, and then in the USA after the Nazis came to power in Germany. The Frankfurt School has had a great impact on almost all areas of thought in the twentieth century, including media studies.

The network society

The publication of *The Structural Transformation of the Public Sphere* in English coincided with the rise of the new internet-enabled 'networked' society. The 'Network Society' was described by Jan van Dijk and Manuel Castells as one in which society was structured through electronic networks of relationships. Drawing on theories of the information society, as well as on the technological mechanisms used in the construction of computer networks, both argue that communication technology has fundamentally changed society. Castells argues that this new, electronically mediated form of relationship is entirely constructed by computer networks; van Dijk holds that other social relationships still have weight, although they may be mediated by electronic, rather than organic, communication networks; but they both agree that the nature of engagement and communication within society has been changed by networked communications (Castells, 2000; van Dijk, 2006).

Computer networks such as the internet are not necessarily hierarchical. Egalitarian ones are generally more stable than hierarchical ones – for technical reasons. The internet was largely developed as a collaborative research tool among universities, and it is a legacy of this that access to the network is largely open to the public, and the legacy of collaboration and transparency has persisted into the new social networks. Unlike other mass-media technologies, the differential between the cost of production and that of consumption (compare the cost of a printing press and the cost of a newspaper) is minimal, although not entirely vanished – a server and a web-hosting agreement to run a blog does not cost that much more than a home computer and internet access. Social media, even more so, erase this strictly financial barrier to entry, although other barriers remain.

The matrix discussed in Chapter 1 of this book lays out the landscape as one in which technology, financial capital and infrastructure are less important than reach, intent and voice. Intent and voice are choices, not constraints, and, although reach is something that can be increased through financial investment, money is not a prerequisite. Andy Carvin's reach through Twitter is substantial, and costs only the investment of social relationships and time.

The network, therefore, that makes up the backbone of the network society is one which does not place a huge amount of emphasis on one's status or role within the network (or at least, on the status of the node with which one connects to the network), or the wider community. To the network, you are simply an Internet Protocol (IP) address, just like every other IP address. Unlike the traditional mass media, there is no technological or structural differential between producers and consumers.

This is something of a fantasy, though: although the technology cannot see the difference between a student in a high school in Nairobi and the president of the United States, the internet is still made up of people and as soon as one's identity is known, status can usually be inferred. The fact remains that although the technological barriers to entry are much lower than for other mass media, the content and recognition barriers are not, and it is the best-known organisations that have the largest audiences.

The internet

The internet was originally designed as a robust communication network that would function well in times of war and disaster. Unlike other networks, such as broadcasting or telephone networks, it has no central hub that can be easily damaged. Instead, each node on the network connects to multiple other nodes, providing redundancy, and meaning that, even if nodes are destroyed, communication will continue to flow around the gaps. In practice, this is not always the case; many parts of the world are connected to the network by a single cable, and entire countries and regions have spent days and weeks cut off when that cable has failed.

Commodification

Commodification refers to the process of turning something into an object that can be traded, and that has economic value. The commodification of information is a fundamental aspect of the practice of media – information is what is being traded. Habermas and others believe that this commodification is damaging to society as a whole – moving knowledge from a public good to a scarce commodity.

The original structure and concept of the network, though, was one which does not recognise or credit importance or wealth to messages, but one which allowed free communication to all parties.

It is this that has led thinkers to posit the network as the salvation of the public sphere. Where Habermas saw that commodification of information (through the commercial mass media) and the rise of consumerism had transformed the public sphere from an open forum for discourse and engagement into one in which the mass media simply reinforced the ideas of the dominant elites in society, that is capitalism, proponents saw in the internet the potential for the revival of the original, supposedly egalitarian, public sphere, one in which rational discourse among equals was paramount (Boeder, 2005; Jan, 2011).

The way online interaction is structured and substantially different from other forms of communication is discussed in the works of Manuel Castells (2000) and Jan van Dijk (2006) on network theory, the new, engaged form of computer-aided communication and interaction that informs online lives. Both of these thinkers are informed by Stewart Brand's (1987) discussion of the way the network works. Another internet theorist, Henry Jenkins (2006a, 2006b), discusses participatory and fan cultures online, which although not specific to journalism, have a lot to say about all kinds of online cultures.

Social capital and the journalistic field

Another theorist whose ideas have contributed to our understanding of the communication and human networks in which we are all engaged is Pierre Bourdieu. Bourdieu was a French sociologist and philosopher whose work spanned a wide range of disciplines, but the concept that is most often applied to these discussions is that of social capital.

Capital can be defined as the base resource one brings to society, and it usually refers to financial capital. Financial or economic capital is the main source of power in capitalist societies, but Bourdieu and others posited different kinds of capital to the simply financial. Human capital is the resources an individual commands – time and skills – and for most people it is this that they use to engage in the economic marketplace, and gain power in society, but there are still other forms of capital. Cultural capital consists of the knowledge, skills and information one can access and use – one's education; social capital derives from one's relationships – memberships of groups and networks within society; and symbolic capital is capital one accrues through status or prestige (Jenkins, 2002).

Bourdieu and others argue that capital of all kinds can be traded or negotiated for power within society, or within the social network and community one operates within. In structured societies,

Social capital

Social capital may be a relatively new concept for English speakers, but in many societies it is a clearly recognised and structured part of society. Known in Arabic as Wasta and in Chinese as Guanxi, for example, influence is simply part and parcel of all social interactions. The fact that there is no English-word equivalent does not mean that social capital has less influence within western society, simply that we are perhaps less likely to acknowledge it.

Objectivity

Objectivity has often been held up as the ideal of journalistic practice – the completely disinterested and uninvolved commentator, presenting all sides of an argument 'without fear or favor' (Allan, 2010). More recent thinkers, influenced by postmodernism's contention that objective truth is an impossibility, maintain that objectivity is also an impossible goal.

the ability to gain and use the various forms of capital may be constrained by other factors (access to education may be limited to those with economic means, group membership may be limited on the basis of gender, or race), and people's ability to advance within the system may be limited (Bourdieu, 1993; Jenkins, 2002; Benson, 2005).

Social capital is usually constructed within a field of endeavour or expertise, so journalists accrue social capital through their status and links within the field of journalism. This is a key idea for students of media, especially of journalism, because despite the importance of the audience to the industry as a whole, journalists look most often to their peers for affirmation, and for judgement on their work (Bourdieu, 1993b).

The rigid hierarchy and boundaries of the field are challenged by the network society, in that the technology of the internet allows access to all newcomers, without the requirement of prior membership of the field itself. In the mid-nineties, shortly after the development of the World Wide Web, theorists and activists began to posit the idea that this meant the end of professional (commercial) journalism; that the field would be dismantled by the network society and replaced by alternative forms of journalism (Rosen, 1993; Bowman and Willis, 2003; Gillmor, 2004).

This projected death of professional journalism led to the development of the concept of citizen journalism.

Profession or trade?

The question of whether journalism is a profession or a trade is a complex one. In Anglo-Saxon societies, professional status has certain rights, such as the formal right to regulate access to the profession through accreditation, and the right to maintain standards and discipline within the profession (as through medical or legal councils). This grants the professions considerable status within these societies. Journalism is not legally a profession, but it has pretensions to being one, through training councils and self-regulation. The internet, and social media specifically, presents a considerable challenge to the professional identity of journalists. These issues are further discussed in Chapter 10, especially in terms of legal and ethical constraints.

Citizen journalism in practice

Although citizen journalism may or may not exist in the form which Gillmor, Rosen, Bowman and Willis envisioned, it is repeatedly invoked by both professional journalists and the public as an entity, sometimes even a monolithic one. The fear of citizen journalism is evident in much of the public discourse around it, and far in excess of the actual prevalence of citizen journalism in practice.

Sites and practices identified as examples of 'citizen journalism' generally take one of the following forms: user-generated content, blogs, hyperlocal community sites, and activist or alternative sites.

User-generated content is discussed more extensively in the following chapter, but it refers to either raw news material (images, footage, audio recordings or information) that is provided

Sites, pages, blogs, channels, feeds

As technology and social media change, the specifics of what people do online changes. Although initially the website was the common denominator of web-based content and for citizen-journalism activities, increasingly the activities may be centred around a Facebook page, a YouTube channel, a Twitter feed or an actual site that aggregates all of the above. However, it is impossible to refer to a list of sites, pages, blogs, channels or feeds every time one mentions them, so the term site is being used to incorporate all of these things.

to a news organisation by the public for use within their own edited, constructed news product, or to the comments, discussion and interaction which is created around a formal news product. User-generated content always exists within the constructed news product of a formal outlet, and is mediated by them.

In this book we distinguish citizen journalism from user-generated content, based on the final product: citizen journalism is its own discrete product; user-generated content exists within and forms part of a mainstream news product. This can be a complex distinction, especially where commercial news organisations construct their own sites for the contribution of user-generated content which can both exist as discrete product and provide material for the main site.

Citizen-journalism projects

It is tempting to refer to these, unironically, as 'true' or 'traditional' citizen-journalism projects, so much has the phrase been borrowed, changed, adapted and abused. We won't do that, but there are citizen-journalism projects that best embody the principles of citizen journalism, inasmuch as there are concrete principles. There is, however, no one way to do citizen journalism, no one ideal perfect site.

OhMyNews, launched in 2000, in South Korea, is often considered the original citizen-journalism site. The site uses material provided by some 20,000 volunteer reporters, which is posted to the site after being checked by the team of professional journalists. OhMyNews is often held up as the ideal of a successful citizen-journalism project; it is also a commercial enterprise, selling advertising to the same organisations as the mainstream media (Gillmor, 2004).

Although OhMyNews's contributors are encouraged to cover stories not included in the mainstream press, the process of publication is similar to any news organisation using a network of freelancers: material is edited and placed on the page by the professional staff. Citizen reporters working for OhMyNews are paid according to how important and useful the professional editors consider their contributions, creating the possibility that the site's content will eventually reflect not the interests of the contributors but the professionally paid staff (Kim and Hamilton, 2006).

WikiNews is based on the model of Wikipedia, and is one of the projects run by Wikipedia's parent organisation, the Wikimedia foundation. WikiNews is a collaborative, citizen-led news site, with contributions from anyone who registers and chooses to upload content. Unlike other citizen-journalism sites, the site does not mimic a news site, but instead follows the structure of Wikipedia, with links and references, the ability of any user to edit the story, and no bylines. The identification of journalists through bylines is one of the hallmarks of traditional journalism, and the lack of bylines makes WikiNews possibly unique among citizen-journalism projects (Wikinews, n.d.).

> # Wikiwhat
>
> 'Wiki' is a Hawaiian word meaning quick, but in internet culture it is a kind of shorthand for an open-source, collaborative publishing project such as Wikipedia, the open-source encyclopaedia, WikiLeaks and WikiNews. A wiki can also refer to any site using an interlinked and collaborative structure, as exemplified by Wikipedia.

The site does not impose a news diary or structure on its contributors, but work is reviewed by more experienced volunteers, and rated on a number of key points including newsworthiness, verifiability and a neutral point of view – all traditional journalistic goals. The neutral point of view is key to the Wikimedia Foundation's goals, but is uncommon among citizen-journalism projects, which tend to embrace opinion and subjectivity (Thorsen, 2008).

Mainstream media's citizen journalism

CNN's iReport, Bild's (Germany) Leserreporter and Avusa's (South Africa) Reporter.co.za are examples. These sites appear(ed) as separate entities from the parent site, but exist as a way for the main news organisation to attract aspiring citizen journalists who will post stories and videos (especially in the case of Bild) which can then be used as a resource by the parent organisation to attract audience, sell advertising and provide content for the main product (Knight, 2010).

As an example of this, CNN's iReport was launched in 2006 to allow non-journalists to upload images, stories and video to a website, www.ireport.com. Stories and material can be viewed on the iReport site, but can also be incorporated into CNN's own coverage. Despite the rhetoric of being a truly independent and collaborative site, and one which attempts to 'expand the current definition of news' (CNN, n.d.), CNN maintains editorial control, suggesting assignments, vetting stories and content, and controlling the news agenda. Although it is true that any citizen can contribute to the site, the overall feel is very much that of a formal news organisation, and the news values and angles that are presented are hardly different from that of the parent organisation.

This form of citizen journalism has been criticised for co-opting the voice and ideas of true citizen journalism, but these sites remain a substantive forum for citizen journalism and contribution (Kperogi, 2010).

Hyperlocal

Hyperlocal news sites are small news organisations, whether commercial, amateur or a mix of both, which represent a community and its interests. First posited (albeit indirectly, since he does not use the term) by John Pavlik in *Journalism and New Media* (Pavlik, 2001), hyperlocal sites are constructed as an alternative to the increasing corporatisation of news outlets within the western world, and the ensuing lack of news available for citizens of smaller communities and towns. Thanks to the increasing financial pressure on news organisations in the twenty-first century, more and more towns and cities in the developed world have no local news outlet, it having been closed or merged with a larger news outlet; hyperlocal sites are arising to fill this gap (Kurpius et al., 2010).

Hyperlocal sites provide an imitation of the norms and behaviours of professional and commercial news production, often using the same funding models and being staffed by professionally trained journalists. Hyperlocal sites in many ways are the strongest evidence of new forms of journalism posing a financial and cultural threat to the entrenched professional and commercial news interests, except for the fact that they tend to thrive best in communities that have been abandoned by those very same interests.

Blogpreston (http://blogpreston.co.uk/) is a hyperlocal site, covering the small city of Preston in northern England. The site was launched in January 2009 as 'a hub of news, views and information about the city' (Blog Preston, n.d.), and contains a range of content from professionally written news stories to citizen-submitted photos of the city, to reports on social events organised by the team of volunteers. The site runs advertisements and has also received funding to train local people as community journalists – combining the goals of hyperlocal and public journalism. The site is a challenge to the local corporate newspaper in many ways – covering the same ground, in the same ways, and even, to some extent, going after the same advertising.

Activist citizen journalism

Activist citizen-journalism sites are probably the most common form of the medium worldwide, being the direct inheritors of the tradition of activist and alternative news sources that has remained intact through technological and social change. The number of sites and projects have increased, however, since the internet substantially lowers the technological and financial barriers to entry for would-be activists and journalists, and provides considerable sanctuary for sites and projects that would otherwise have been shut down by authorities. The increased dispersion of social media as well has meant that more individual channels exist for people to express their opinions: individual blogs, Twitter feeds and Facebook pages abound, some more 'journalistic' than others.

The speed with which these new forms of online publishing can be launched and start functioning is also a factor in their favour. It takes only a minute to create a new feed or channel and, provided the information is newsworthy enough, it will be picked up and circulated immediately. The events of the so-called Arab Spring were publicised in this way, and the speed of the network directly fed into the events, bringing them to the fore much faster than would have happened in the days of samizdat printing presses and pirate radio (Hermida, 2012a).

In addition, a number of projects exist which provide frameworks, expertise, training and infrastructure for those wishing to set up a citizen-journalism site, or wishing to participate in one. Allvoices (www.allvoices.com), Global Voices Online (globalvoices.org), the Guerrilla News Network (GNN.tv – now defunct) and Indymedia (www.indymedia.org) all provide a locus for gathering disparate groups of citizen journalists into a single identifiable framework. Most of these projects are explicitly activist, and many receive funding through charitable organisations and political groups. These kinds of projects are of interest to mainstream journalists primarily because of the insight and information they can provide to reporters and researchers, and their primary journalistic impact is on the news agendas of the world's media. The events of the so-called Arab Spring of 2011 were heavily discussed and reported on within these networks of activists, social media users, bloggers, citizen journalists and the like, and this did filter its way through to the agenda of the mainstream media (Akinfemisoye, 2011; Knight, 2012, 2013).

Issues in citizen journalism

These forms of citizen journalism are important, at least for the communities in which they function, and interesting, but the questions remain as to their role in relationship to mainstream forms of news media. Whether they pose genuine challenges to mainstream commercial news is hard to quantify, but in specific areas and sectors they may prove to do so.

Financial constraints

The main constraint facing these kinds of projects is financial. Although the barriers to entry are lower than for mainstream media, financial clout (capital, in Bourdieu's words) is still important. Web hosting and development are also expensive, although these costs can be mitigated against with the use of freely available services. Free services tend to make it difficult to generate revenue, though, since control of the linked advertising may remain with the hosting company, and once sites begin to generate enough traffic for the linked revenue to be more than negligible, the hosting costs can become prohibitive.

It is, however, the cost of content that remains the substantive barrier. Journalists need to be paid and, simply put, the more you pay, the better the journalism you get (up to a point). Some citizen journalism sites are run entirely with volunteers, but this can create its own problems, especially with consistency and range of product, and with issues of overall control. Left to their own devices, most people would rather write opinion or columns. Several citizen-journalism projects such as Reporter. co.za, Demotix, Blottr and Global Voices Online tend(ed) to be repositories of comment pieces and photography, all interesting, but it is unclear how they can form a replacement for the mainstream or commercial news sector (Knight, 2010).

Consistency

Audiences expect and want a consistent and predictable news product: a certain amount of hard news, a certain amount of comment, some entertainment or light news, sport, a weather report and, in a printed product, the horoscope, the TV guide and a crossword. This is a reductive list of the content of mainstream news products, yes, but there is considerable truth in it. Citizen or activist journalism products that are looking to become the comprehensive news source for a community may find it hard to provide this kind of range. Many sites at best form a counterpoint to or commentary on the news provided in other contexts and forms.

Sites also need to provide enough material on a regular enough schedule that readers will return consistently. Random updates don't drive audience or advertising. The consistent product which drives loyal readers also drives advertisers – it is difficult to make revenue from advertising unless you can show that you have a consistent product (automatically served Google ads have limited revenue-generating possibility).

For activist projects, one assumes that money is less relevant, or that money is being provided through other means to maintain the project. In addition, in an activist context, the drive and motivation to maintain the project and its content is rooted in something other than the product itself. Most projects function either until the aim is achieved, or the movement that inspired them burns out entirely.

Accusations of bias

One of the main criticisms of amateur journalism from the mainstream media is that it is biased. This bias, whether perceived or real, forms much of the debate around amateur-journalism sites, at least in the way it is presented in professional-journalism contexts. There is considerable doubt as to whether this matters at all to either the audience or the advertisers. Certainly, some of the most popular blogs, forums and information sites on the internet are informed by very clear political aims and points of view (from all parts of the spectrum), and, if anything, the readership is more loyal than that of more middle-of-the-road sites. It is apparent that despite the stated need of communities for unbiased information provided to the audience in a neutral space (a key tenet of democratisation, as reiterated in documents from the American Constitution to the UN Charter of Rights and Freedoms), the desire of people is for news and information that reinforces their pre-existing beliefs. The popularity of news organisations that hold specific and clear political views – from Fox News in the USA to the more extreme of the British tabloids – shows that giving the people what they want often means giving them biased and prejudicial information.

But neutrality and freedom from bias is a key part of the ideology of professional journalism (Allan, 2010). The construction of a journalistic identity is built on the bedrock of 'objectivity', which in western democratic societies is clearly linked to the independence of the media from political interference or regulation. It is this supposed objectivity that is the magic that transforms ordinary writing into journalism, and then grants it specific legal protections, such as the right to protect ones sources, and the defence of public interest against other possible charges (discussed further in Chapter 10).

The myth of objectivity, which has been thoroughly unpicked and discredited among the media theorists, at least remains firmly entrenched in the professional practice of journalism, and the more the profession comes under fire, the more objectivity is defended as a necessary part of the contribution that news organisations make to society as a whole. Even in countries like the UK, where it is accepted that newspapers, at least, have clear political-party allegiances, the ideal of objectivity is upheld. The UK's Leveson Inquiry into press standards and phone hacking was more concerned with issues of corruption and illegal behaviour, but the journalists and editors who appeared before it roared their defence of the importance of the free press, on the grounds that professional, objective, neutral journalism is an essential part of a democratic society. Whether any citizens of that democratic society are paying any attention, or whether this, and numerous other, similar, debates that occupy the media pages of the newspapers, or the academic textbooks, are of any interest to the public whose interests we are supposedly so concerned with is an open debate.

Conclusion

The question remains as to whether any of the supposed conflict between citizen or amateur journalism and the more traditional, mainstream journalism is genuine, or whether there is, in fact, any serious threat to the mainstream or commercial news sector posed by these projects.

Certainly, activist news organisations may pose a structural or political threat to the state-backed news organisations that control the free flow of information in undemocratic societies. These contexts, however, move journalism clearly into the realm of politics, and the conflict is inherently political, not journalistic. In societies where there has been a transition of power, the activist news organisations either closed down, or became simply the news media of the new society, in a relationship with the political power of the society that is mirrored across democratic societies worldwide.

In other contexts, however, activist news organisations are a valuable resource for other journalists – every foreign correspondent needs to know the sites and projects that offer an alternative take on events to the state-controlled media.

Other forms of citizen journalism, hyperlocal sites, social-aggregation projects like the Huffington Post and community alternative sites either remain too small and focused on the interests of a specific community (whether geographic, cultural, political or sub-cultural) to be of interest to a larger organisation (although they may well be completely viable as projects in and of themselves), or they are large enough to compete with the mainstream organisations, in which case the distinction between them is irrelevant – media pundits may go on at length about the structural, economic and philosophical differences between the Huffington Post and USA Today, but readers and advertisers don't often care. The fact remains that, despite the constructed tension between 'professional' and 'amateur' journalism, in practice, and to the audience, there is little to be found between them.

Less-constructed forms of 'citizen' information sharing, Twitter feeds, Facebook pages, Google+ circles, may well be part of the public sphere that Habermas envisioned, and for a social theorist they are fascinating. It seems unlikely, however, that they would pose any kind of threat to the existence of more traditional, constructed and managed forms of news (if anything, the managed product that news organisations are now moving into these spaces is more of a threat to the amateur efforts than the other way round).

However, it is important to remember that news is an ecosystem, and the effect of amateur, activist and alternative news sites on other sites within that ecosystem is noticeable. Social media might not have provided the perfect public sphere, but the existence of these projects within the same landscape as the more traditional news media can be seen to have an effect. The higher level of engagement with the audience, the greater proportion of opinion to hard news, and the lowered formality of language are all hallmarks of amateur journalism that are increasingly visible within the mainstream. The network has changed everyone within it, not simply the newcomers.

CASE STUDY 'Netizen' journalism in China

In July 2011 two high-speed trains running through the eastern city of Wenzhou, China, collided while crossing a viaduct. Four cars were derailed and 40 people died. The accident, as well as being a tragedy, was a great embarrassment for China's much-publicised high-speed rail programme, and the government moved to limit the public-relations damage by issuing media directives, limiting access to the site and clearing away the wreckage as soon as possible (Blanchard and Wee, 2011).

Media directives are a common way for the Chinese authorities to control a news story: instructions are given to news editors as to what angles to use, and how to construct the story. In the case of the train crash, directives instructed that: 'Reporting of the accident is to use "in the face of great tragedy, there's great love" as the major theme. Do not question. Do not elaborate. Do not associate. No re-posting on micro-blogs will be allowed!' (Hernandez, 2011).

Three years earlier, the Wenchuan earthquake had provoked a similar response from the government, but the prevalence of mobile phones and internet access had resulted in images, news and information being spread across social networks, embarrassing the Chinese authorities and undermining their control of information (Nip, 2009).

In the time between the Wenchuan earthquake and the Wenzhou train crash, Chinese use of the internet rose to some 450 million users (China Internet Watch, 2011), known as 'netizens' in China, many of them using microblogging and discussion platforms such as Weibo (a Chinese version of Twitter), Tianye and QQ.

This growing online public was horrified by the news of the train crash, and reports began to appear on the social-media networks in China, reports that contradicted the official version as to the time of the accident, and that began to create a picture not just of 'in the face of great tragedy, there's great love', but of a disaster being covered up because it did not tally with the government's desires and plans. As the story unfolded, the demands by the families for explanation and compensation was highlighted on the networks, something the directives had not wanted discussed (Chen, 2011).

The mainstream Chinese media became caught between the official version of events, and the version they could see unfolding online, faster than the online censors could erase it. Many news organisations began to report what was happening on social media, a move that at least one senior editor believed would be seminal in changing the Chinese media: 'Thanks to micro-blogs, it was providing a convenient platform for people to collect variety information together. Micro-blog can make people get their power together and foster citizen consciousness to help people who need to help, also can supervise our government and society. It's seems like that micro-blog offer a microphone to everyone, If you got 10 million followers, then what you post on your micro-blog will be concerned by your followers. I think it can be an individual media and everyone can be a journalist in the future. It will make the media in China become more freedom and be responsibility to expose the truth.' (Liu Xiang, quoted in Chen, 2011)

Whether or not the Chinese media is more free, it is certainly more subject to scrutiny by the new networked and connected educated population, who do use social media as a way to hold the mainstream media to account. The more activist news organisations, the ones that chafed against central government controls, have been emboldened by online activism, and many took the opportunity of repeating and amplifying what was being said online, taking their news agenda guidance from the public, rather than from the state.

Social-media and citizen-media activism in China is still evolving. Certainly there are changes, and the ways in which social media can influence public opinion, and possibly public activism, can be seen. The rising influence of social media can be evidenced in the new guidelines on their use issued by the Beijing government in December 2011. These controls, which include a prohibition against 'rumour-mongering' and a ban on accounts not linked to a genuine name, are clearly designed to prevent similar responses to events like the Wenzhou train crash (Bandurski, 2011).

Note: Thanks to Chen Dan Qi, for her assistance with this case study.

Key reflections

- Within this new, fluid environment it is possible for ideas and individuals that do not have access to the elite power structures to be heard, but it is not a given: access must still be fought for.
- Can commercial journalism still maintain the goals of public journalism while serving business interests?
- Is the online space more egalitarian and accessible for people left isolated and ignored by mainstream media, or does it simply reflect the rest of the media?
- Is non-professional journalism still journalism? Does it matter if the people doing it are not trained or certified?
- What can mainstream commercial journalism learn from citizen journalism and community engagement?
- Is social capital in the new media space more useful than financial capital? Why?

Readings and resources

Jürgen Habermas's *The Structural Transformation of the Public Sphere* (1989) is a key text for this chapter. Craig Calhoun's 1993 book *Habermas and the Public Sphere* (1993a) is a slightly more accessible introduction to the original text, and Pieter Boeder's essay 'Habermas' heritage: the future of the public sphere in a network society' (2005) is a good starting point for the subject.

The network society is discussed primarily by Manuel Castells in *The Rise of the Network Society* (2000) and by Jan van Dijk in *The Network Society* (2006). Henry Jenkins is the leading thinker on fan and participatory culture. His main works are the books *Convergence Culture* (2006a) and *Fans, Bloggers and Gamers* (2006b), and he maintains a blog at http://henryjenkins.org/.

Dan Gillmor's book *We the Media: Grassroots Journalism by the People for the People* (2004) can almost be considered the manifesto of the citizen-journalism movement. This book, along with Bowman and Willis's 2003 report *We Media*, is core reading for anyone interested in the subject. Dan Gillmor maintains a blog at http://dangillmor.com/.

The main works on alternative and activist media are Chris Atton's books *Alternative Media* (2002) and *An Alternative Internet* (2004).

Einar Thorsen writes about citizen journalism in the book *Citizen Journalism: Global Perspectives* (co-edited with Stuart Allan), and in journal articles and other works. He maintains a website at http://multimediajournalism.info/ and tweets as @einarthorsen.

Indymedia (www.indymedia.org/en/index.shtml) and Global Voices Online (http://globalvoicesonline. org/) both provide technology, training and support for citizen journalists, as well as hosting news and material from citizen journalists around the world. Indymedia maintains local organisations in a number of countries as well.

A number of initiatives exist to promote public journalism, including the Knight Community News Network, which is part of the John S. and James L. Knight foundation, and provides a wealth of information and services for aspiring community and public journalists.

The Center for Investigative Reporting (http://centerforinvestigativereporting.org/) and ProPublica (www.propublica.org/) both do independent investigative journalism, and provide tools and support for journalists as well.

For a development of alternative media since the 1970s see Tony Harcup's *Alternative Journalism, Alternative Voices* (Routledge, 2012).

>>Chapter 7<<

COLLABORATIVE JOURNALISM AND USER-GENERATED CONTENT

Overview

In this chapter we discuss the increasing openness and transparency of news organisations to content and users from outside the newsroom. We call this form of journalism 'collaborative' because it incorporates the audience and the public in a collaborative effort to create news. User-generated content, participatory journalism and community creation are key ways in which news organisations can connect with, and make use of, their users as producers. The increasing dependence and community relationship between users and producers is discussed, as well as some of the concerns and limits of the practice.

Key concepts

- Comments and conversations
- Communities
- Crowdsourcing
- Curation
- Live blogging
- Participatory journalism
- Trolls
- Using user-generated content

Springboard

- *Collaboration, not co-optation*: there's a wealth of information in the crowd, but you need to collaborate with your users, not simply take from them. Talk back, communicate with them, thank them and credit them.
- *Maintain your community*: don't wait until there is a breaking news story to look for people who can contribute: work on finding and maintaining a community of users and contributors from day one. They'll be there when you need them, and, if they know you, they'll trust you (and you will be able to trust them).
- *Be open, but cautious*: online hoaxes do happen, and news organisations do get fooled. Don't let go of your journalistic instincts when you enter the social-media pool – corroborate, check back and, if something smells fishy, consider that it may in fact be bait.
- *Your users are family*: there are thousands of places for people to discuss the news online: you want them to do it at your site. Consider the user experience, the interface and the systems, and listen to your users' comments about it.
- *Be transparent*: the web community expects transparency; tell people what you are doing, tell them how you are doing it, and listen to them. The more of your process and ideas you open up, the more you will get back from the audience.

Introduction

This chapter will discuss the changing relationship between producers and consumers, and the increasing number of ways in which the public (or audience) contribute to news content. It is a rare news organisation these days which does not invite contributions from its consumers, in the form of comments on stories or in a linked forum, feedback to journalists, or following them on Twitter, sharing on Facebook or other social-media sites, or sending original content (especially video and images) direct to the organisation. This practice is sometimes included under the heading of citizen journalism but, as was discussed in Chapter 6, this is an increasingly problematic concept, and a term which no longer adequately covers the multitude of ways in which the traditional barriers of the journalistic profession are breaking down as a result of changes in technology.

The theory of participatory, user-generated and collaborative journalism is discussed in a number of ways. Mark Deuze places these new kinds of collaborative work within the field of sociology of work, and the changes in society which are rendering work a more fluid and flexible part of life: a phenomenon called 'casualisation' (2007, 2011). He then links this to Manuel Castells's theory of the Network Society (discussed in Chapter 6), to generate a theory of networked and collaborative journalism.

Participatory journalism

In their 2011 book, Jane Singer and her co-authors coined the term 'participatory journalism' in order to cover the gap between professional journalists and the people who contribute to the news in ways that are increasingly visible in the end product.

Jane Singer and her co-authors argue for the term 'participatory journalism' because they feel it captures the idea of collaborative and collective – not simply parallel – action'. They describe the activities of participatory journalists as engaged in the 'ongoing process of creating a news website and building a multi-faceted community' (2011).

This process of collaboratively creating news is not new – Alfred Hermida describes newspapers in the seventeenth century that included blank pages for the reader to write their own news on before being passed on to someone else to read: one imagines people adding family or local news, or commenting on something in the paper, something that evokes the modern phenomenon of reading an article and then posting it on Facebook, with a commentary (Singer et al., 2011).

However, this charming practice rapidly fell out of favour and was replaced by the news product of the twentieth century: constructed by professionals, it was a closed, discrete, packaged product, distinguished clearly from other forms of discourse by its boundaries, access to which was controlled by the requirements of the profession. Contributions from people not members of the journalism trade (or profession) were limited to letters to the editor, whose publication remained firmly within the control of the news organisation itself (and, controversially, were sometimes written by the journalists themselves) (Allan, 1999; Hermida, 2011a).

Despite the continued presence of alternative news organisations (see Chapter 6), the boundaries of this industry only began to be eroded at the very end of the twentieth century, when online news sites began to allow comments on stories posted on the web, and to solicit contributions of images and news stories from the general public. This erosion of professional and product boundaries is considered one of the main ways in which the practice of journalism has changed since the creation of the World Wide Web in 1993.

Although comments are probably the most common means of engaging readers in the production of content, the boundaries between the original story and the comments below it remain as clear as the boundaries between the letters to the editor's page and the rest of the newspaper. More flexible are the boundaries between professionally acquired news material (especially photographs and video footage) and those created by amateurs and passed on to the professional news organisations (often for money), although most news organisations still go to considerable lengths to ensure that the consumer is aware that the material was 'non-traditionally acquired' (O'Sullivan and Heinonen, 2008; Wardle and Williams, 2010; Knight, 2012, 2013).

The ways in which fans and participants influence and collaborate with popular media is discussed by Henry Jenkins, and, although he does not discuss journalism directly, there are valuable insights in his work (2006a, 2006b). Fans of TV shows such as *Star Trek* have always found the internet a valuable space in which to discuss their ideas and reactions to events in the fictional world. Savvy producers and directors, such as Joss Whedon (of *Buffy the Vampire Slayer*), have used these communities as a sounding board and a resource of ideas.

Breaking news and the accidental journalist

It is important to note that news organisations have always used material, especially visual material, provided by witnesses and passers-by who happened to have cameras. In 1963, Abraham Zapruder happened to have a home-movie camera with him while watching the president visit Dallas, Texas. The film he shot of the assassination of John F. Kennedy was handed over to the Secret Service, but was also sold to Life magazine, which used stills from the film in its next issue (*Life Magazine*, 1963).

Twenty-nine years later, George Holliday caught the beating of Rodney King by five officers of the Los Angeles Police Department on a video camera. He gave the video tape to a local television station, which broadcast it on its news show. The content of that tape set off some of the worst riots the US has ever seen (Goldstein, 2006). These instances, of a passer-by happening to have a camera to hand at the moment a dramatic event was unfolding, are notable, but fairly uncommon – what Paul Bradshaw refers to as 'accidental journalists' (Bradshaw and Rohumaa, 2011). When it did happen, however, news organisations displayed no qualms about using the footage.

However, the use of this kind of footage on the news was rare until recently, not necessarily because of any particular reticence on the part of the news organisations, but because until the advent of mobile-phone cameras only a minority of people had access to a camera at any given point in time – many events went unrecorded and unnoticed. Technology changed this: by December 2004, when a tsunami ripped through the Indian Ocean, destroying coastal communities from the Seychelles to Indonesia, news organisations were overwhelmed by amateur footage and stills of the event, and the use of 'user-generated content' by news organisations has since then been the norm for any major unexpected and public event (Allan et al., 2007).

For on-diary events (still a large part of professional news content), news organisations still tend to rely on professional footage, especially in terms of broadcast material. For off-diary events such as the Haiti earthquake, amateur pictures are becoming increasingly common in news usage. Nicola Bruno's 2011 study found, however, that although news organisations rely on user-generated content at first, they tend to move to professionally sourced material as the story unfolds (and they are able to get their staff in place).

Active citizens and active sources

Although commentators and researchers tend to frame the use of this kind of material as the expansion of the practice of journalism into the broader community, it could also be seen not so much as the changing practice of journalism, but the changing practice of sourcing, and the evolution of the relationship between journalists and sources.

Traditionally, a source for a news story, especially an unexpected one, is either a bystander or witness to events, or a participant in those events (sourcing is discussed in Chapter 2). The journalist then approaches the source and, after asking a few questions, reframes the person's experience for inclusion in the constructed news narrative. The source is a passive participant in the story which is actively created by the journalist. It is that passivity which has changed: increasingly, the news organisation will be contacted directly by someone with information or news material, whether via traditional means or through the increasing numbers of portals and channels which social-media outlets provide, and, increasingly, the source will already have published their own version of events, their own footage, their own narrative, which then lives alongside the journalistically constructed one (Jönsson and Örnebring, 2011).

In January 2009 US Airways flight 1549 ran into a flock of geese and had to make an emergency ditching in the Hudson River, in New York City. People both on the plane and in the densely populated area, began posting tweets and pictures to the recently popularised social networking services. Users on Twitter were among the first to know about the event, and to see pictures of the plane floating on the river and people crowded on the wings awaiting rescue. Janis Krums, who broke the story online with 'There's a plane in the Hudson. I'm on the ferry going to pick up the people. Crazy' (Krums, 2009), took a picture of the plane on his phone which became briefly famous and was reproduced in media all over the world. This event was hailed as the vanguard of a revolution in reporting the news (Beaumont, 2009).

Later that year, in June, Iran erupted in street demonstrations and protests after the result of the election was declared in favour of the incumbent, Mahmoud Ahmedinejad. These protests were widely planned, discussed and reported in both social media and the mainstream media in the west. The uprising came to a head with the death of music student Neda Agha-Soltan on 20 June, apparently at the hands of the state militia. Footage shot on a mobile phone was sent to a friend of the owner in the Netherlands, and then uploaded to YouTube. News organisations leapt on the footage, and it was picked up and shown on news websites and TV channels (often edited, with voiceover and captions added); stills were printed in the newspapers. However, unlike with earlier amateur footage that was used in this way, the original footage remained online, the raw material living alongside the constructed and negotiated use of it, and interaction and comments on that footage expanded the story and filled in the details, in a way that the mainstream news organisations, by that point forbidden to leave their hotel rooms in Tehran, could not (Mortensen, 2011; Knight, 2012).

In a traditional context, the source is a passive tool in the construction of journalism, simply part of the raw material used to construct news. As the sources and the audience become more active in the construction, and the feedback loop tightens, the pool of potential sources gets larger, and the relationship between the source and the journalist gets closer.

Mark Deuze characterises this as the 'opening' of the newsroom, and typifies news organisations as 'open' or 'closed', depending on the extent to which they engage with the public, and allow the public to engage with them (2007, 2011).

Ways and means of opening the gates

Gatekeeping theory is a fundamental part of the study of the practice of journalism. David White's 1953 study focused on the implicit reasons why events were included or not in the daily newspaper.

Gatekeeping

The ways in which news organisations maintain control of the news agenda by deciding which stories will be published has been referred to as 'gatekeeping' since David White used the term in 1950. The image of the gates of news being guarded by journalists is an enduring one, and one that writers from Jane Singer and Axel Bruns to Mark Deuze have all invoked.

'News values', a phrase created by Galtung and Ruge in 1965, refers to the criteria that journalists and editors use to decided what is newsworthy (Harcup and O'Neill, 2011). Both of these concepts remain fundamental to journalism theory – how journalists decide what is news. The new social media have challenged the journalist's right to decide for the public what news is: this process of opening the gates is discussed by Axel Bruns in his 2005 book *Gatewatching*.

There are a number of ways in which news organisations allow 'the people formerly known as the audience' (Rosen, 2006) into the news-production process. These are all things that move an organisation down the macro matrix (see page 234), into the realm of engaged and collaborative media production.

Comments

Commenting is the simplest form of user contribution, and an extension of the more traditional letters to the editor, which have been a part of print news for more than 100 years. Commenting systems allow readers to express their point of view on a story, and comments are then listed below the story, forming an adjunct to the primary narrative of the news. Comments are an important part of the appeal of the news for a notable proportion of the audience, and a robust commenting system forms a substantial part of the online strategy for a number of news organisations. The UK's MailOnline, which has among the largest readerships of any English-language news organisation in the world (Ponsford, 2011), relies on the comments system to drive participation and interaction, and to make the site 'sticky', that is to bring people back to the site. A good and interesting (or an outrageous and infuriating) comments thread on a story will bring readers back to the same story repeatedly, as the comments and conversation grow. A robust comment thread will keep a story on the main page of the site, even when the event that precipitated the story is well over (Pickard and Catt, 2011).

The downside of this strategy is that focusing too heavily on stories that will generate comments and traffic at the expense of news can downgrade the credibility of your brand as a serious news organisation, and encourage trolling, but it does create page impressions and drive advertising revenue (Pickard and Catt, 2011).

It is also interesting to note that editors and journalists still control comments, both in the moderation process, and in the decision to allow or disallow commenting on specific stories. Court stories, and ones on controversial topics (such as race), may not have comments permitted, out of fear of legal or social ramifications.

In addition to having comments on the page below the story, news organisations have also created separately branded websites and forums, where debates and conversation can continue without being specifically linked to the original news story (Quandt, 2008). Discussion forums were one of the first ways in which news organisations encouraged participation, and they still persist, albeit in changed form, in such sites as the Guardian's Comment is Free, the Daily Mail's RightMinds and Salon.com's Open Salon (although Salon recently closed their original discussion forum, Table Talk). These sites tend to consist of a combination of blogs and posts by journalists, as well as content created by trusted users and bloggers. The content on these sites is usually explicitly opinion-based and unedited but the discussion is generally linked to current events and news (some might say parasitic upon it), and the material is often extensively cross-linked.

Trolling

The word 'trolling', which has its origins in a fishing technique, refers to participants in an online community who seem to be there simply to create conflict and generate outrage. Trolls can drive initial traffic as people react to their presence with denouncements and outrage, but persistent trolling will also drive people away from a site.

Moderation and post-moderation

Moderation refers to the process of checking comments that users have posted. Depending on the story, and the news organisation, comments may be moderated prior to publication (which is the cautious, but expensive and time-consuming approach) or after (referred to as post-moderation). Moderation may change your legal responsibility for the comments posted, and any company policy should be carefully checked with the legal team.

Identity and anonymity

Identity and anonymity are constant issues for any site that solicits comments and contributions from the public. It is a sad fact that anonymity brings out the worst in people, and maintaining a balance

Persistent identity

The development of a mechanism to allow users a single persistent identity across websites probably dates to Microsoft's Passport (now Windows LiveId), which was launched in 1999 as a single sign-on service (SSO). Since then a number of competing services have arisen, including OpenId and Disqus. Although an SSO is convenient for users, it can create concerns about privacy and security.

between an open discussion and a free-for-all is a constant battle for site managers. There are a number of strategies that can be used: one is registration (with or without payment required) and the use of verified names and email addresses; another is moderation: the checking of comments before publication. Identity is problematic and, as even Facebook and Google have seen, the web community can be very resistant to the idea of 'real-name' usage (Boyd, 2011; Doctorow, 2011). Moderation is time-consuming and expensive, and the delay in seeing their comments appear may deter users. 'Somebody spending 10 minutes writing a comment that will almost certainly not even be read let alone published, and if it is published won't make any difference anyway, is a waste of that somebody's time' (Anonymous, cited in Wardle and Williams, 2010).

The creation of social-network plugins for news sites which allow users to use a persistent identity across sites is becoming increasingly popular. Facepile – a plugin that uses people's Facebook identity and allows users to comment on and recommend stories to their friends online – is being used by a number of news organisations, including the Independent. The application allows for both the verification of identity online, thereby obviating some of the worst trolling and spamming, and the tracking of users and their friends through the network. Similarly, other social-media networks increasingly provide plugins and extensions that allow news organisations to encourage users to comment using persistent identities, and to continue the discussion in other spaces. Although it is not difficult to create a false Facebook identity simply in order to comment, the extra steps involved in that process and the fact that Facebook itself does some basic checks on identity when an account is created are themselves a deterrent to random trolling. The use of social-media plugins, especially as a means of creating traffic, is discussed in more detail in Chapter 4.

Spam

Spam originally referred to unsolicited advertising emails, but now refers to any kind of content that is advertising-based and irrelevant to the original intent. Comment spam is increasingly a problem for any site which does not require registration to use, and even for those which do.

Comment ratings

Allowing users to rate other participants' comments on a site is one of the simplest ways to both build community engagement and maintain some control of the discourse on the site. Rating systems vary from a simple up/down click, to more complex algorithms based on a sliding scale, and on the ratings of the users themselves.

The thinking behind these applications is that if people comment using identities that are also used for broader social interactions, the worst of online behaviour can be reduced – if your grandmother or boss could easily see what you are posting, would you still post it? In addition, since more and more people maintain a social-network presence, and are consistently logged in to those sites, the need for users to remember and manage logins and passwords for multiple sites is removed, making it much easier and simpler for people to comment. There are concerns, of course, the main ones being the same concerns people have about social networks: the loss of privacy, the use of their information and identity for marketing purposes, and the close integration of systems and information with a third party.

Moderation

Moderation, the management of comments to ensure that they aren't advertising, offensive or legally damaging (for more discussion of the legal and ethical issues, see Chapter 10), remains one of the main concerns regarding news sites' use of commenting systems. The decision to moderate or not is a hard one: it can be very time-consuming, but the benefit to the community can be great.

Technology has helped with this, especially the use of ratings and rankings. Sophisticated algorithms exist that allow site managers to work with records of users' interactions, and with other users' comments and ratings, to identify trusted users and commenters. Using a mechanism first implemented by Slashdot.org, but now common in discussion forums and online communities, a new user's posts will be marked for oversight by a moderator, but after a number of posts being approved without changes, the user's status can be updated to allow them to post without moderation – encouraging users to participate more until they achieve trusted status on the site (Bruns, 2005; Poor, 2005).

In December 2011, the New York Times revamped their newspaper's commenting system. Introduced at that time were a number of new features, including threaded comments, readers' picks (the most popular comments according to the users) and the creation of 'trusted' users whose comments do not require moderation. Users must use a Facebook account on the site in order to become 'trusted' (Ingram, 2011; Sonderman, 2011a, 2011b).

Threaded comments

The simplest way to display comments on a story is to order them chronologically. However, creating a threaded conversation, in which responses to a specific comment are displayed linked to that comment, create more of a conversational dynamic, which in turn creates more engagement and discussion. Systems can also be set up to inform a user when someone responds to them directly, bringing them back to the site to contribute again.

Real-name policy

In July 2011, Google introduced its 'real-name' policy which stated that users of its Google+ service would need to use their 'real' names, which is similar to Facebook's requirement that users have only one identity on the site, and that that be linked to their 'real' identity. Both organisations claim that real-name policies result in more civil discourse and discourage anti-social behaviours such as trolling on the networks. However, the policy was criticised heavily: for the heavy-handedness of its execution (some Google users had their accounts suspended with no warning); for their insistence that names follow specifically western-style rubrics of given and family names; their rejection of pseudonyms, even when they had been in use for years; and their failure to understand that anonymity can be a matter of security as much as choice. The fact that real names also makes it easier for trackers to follow and tag individuals, and to customise the marketing of products, did not escape the critics' notice, either. The policy has been relaxed since its initial introduction, but the question of online anonymity remains a controversial one, as it has since the early days of the web (Boyd, 2011; Doctorow, 2011).

Speaking to the Poynter Institute, the New York Times's Marc Frons said of the changes: 'It has to do with increasing the sense of identity and reputation on the site, making it easier to find your social actions and follow others. That is the main thrust of it.' He added: 'At the same time, we want to be smarter about encouraging our best commenters, our best contributors, and figuring out how to recognise them on the website' (Frons, cited in Sonderman, 2011b)

Comments, while an important part of generating an online community and creating a space in which users interact not only with the content and its creators but also with each other, remains, in the minds of many journalists, something of a fringe activity to the practice of journalism. Journalists, especially at news organisations still focused on newsprint and broadcast, still tend to treat comments as something after the fact, not relevant to their practice, and tend not to engage with the commenting systems or the users (Singer and Ashman, 2009; Lewis et al., 2010).

News organisations that do engage more with their readers, where journalists respond to comments and get involved in the discussion, tend to report a more robust and respectful online community (Binns, 2012). However, despite some of the rhetoric, it remains a rare comment or user that has any impact on the story directly, or on the news agenda.

User-generated content and audience-sourced news material

Although the phrase 'user-generated content' can be used as a comprehensive term denoting any form of interaction, collaborative production or engagement between the professional news producers and the 'people formerly known as the audience', within this chapter it is used to refer to raw news material that has been acquired by someone not normally employed as a journalist.

> # Trounced by amateurs
>
> 'Never before has there been a major international story where television news crews have been so emphatically trounced in their coverage by amateurs wielding their own cameras' (Anonymous in Allan et al., 2007).

As is discussed above, the use of material (especially images and footage) that has been gathered by non-journalists is not new, but what is new is the sheer volume of such material that is now available to news organisations. If the events of 11 September 2001 became the catalyst for a new kind of community journalism, one in which people harnessed the power of the web to share the kinds of information that they had access to, and that they needed (Zelizer and Allan, 2003), then the South Asian tsunami of 2004 showed an even greater development in the power of individuals to share and collaborate on news stories, especially stories where the news organisations had been caught flat-footed, with few correspondents in place. However, the region's popularity as a holiday destination, coupled with the season, meant that there was a large number of tourists well equipped with cameras in place. 'Never before has there been a major international story where television news crews have been so emphatically trounced in their coverage by amateurs wielding their own cameras,' observed one British newspaper: 'Producers and professional news cameramen often found themselves being sent not to the scenes of disaster to capture footage of its aftermath, but to the airports where holiday-makers were returning home with footage of the catastrophe as it happened.' (Allan et al., 2007)

This footage became the basis of a large number of news reports and was reprinted in newspapers, shown on air and became thoroughly integrated into the coverage, although not without the usual concerns expressed about the quality of the material, or the wisdom of using material not created by trusted sources (Outing, 2005).

However, despite these reservations, things had changed. Writing in 2007, Stuart Allan concludes: 'From today's perspective, the ways in which ordinary members of the public – 'accidental journalists' in the view of some – engaged in impromptu newsgathering can be interpreted as signifying a tipping-point for online news, not least by opening up for redefinition what counts as 'news' and who can be a 'journalist' in ways which continue to reverberate today.' (Allan et al., 2007).

The forms of user-generated content

In 2005, the BBC set up its User-Generated-Content Hub, a centralised mechanism for receiving, sorting, processing and distributing material received from the audience. Currently employing a staff of 23 journalists, the hub processes thousands of bits of information every day, verifying and cataloguing images, videos, audio and text before adding them to the website, or passing them on to news editors across the organisation (Eltringham, 2011a).

The BBC is the most studied example of the use of user-generated content: due to its size, reach and reputation as a benchmark for good journalism. The sheer volume of material the organisation creates and uses, the respect with which its journalism is viewed, its status as a public broadcaster and its resource base make it the industry standard for the use of user-generated content.

Several attempts have been made to categorise or formalise our understanding of how news organisations find, manage and use user-generated content. Wardle and Williams categorised five kinds of user-generated content at the BBC: comments, networked journalism, collaborative content, non-news content and audience content, which they broke down further into footage, experiences and stories (Wardle and Williams, 2010). Jackie Harrison, also studying the BBC, broke contributions down into four types: unsolicited news stories, solicited content linked to an existing story, content solicited as forward planning for a story and watchdog content (i.e. complaints about existing coverage) (Harrison, 2010). Working with both of these typologies, it is possible to see user-generated content as fitting within one of three forms in a newsroom: ideas or suggestions for stories which are then picked up by the newsroom; material sent in to an existing story, whether solicited by the newsroom or not; and unsolicited material not attached to a specific existing story, thereby combining both elements of raw news material and a story idea.

Story ideas are one of the key ways in which users contribute to the news diary. Users contact the newsroom in order to inform journalists of what is going on in their area – whether an unexpected event or an ongoing issue. As with other forms of user-generated content, this is not new (news organisations have always made a phone number or contact details available for users to contact them), but the volume and channel in which these contacts are made is changing. Social media, comments and discussions all add to the more traditional direct forms of contact (letters, email and telephone) that individuals and organisations can use to alert the newsroom to events and issues.

The closer a journalist or news organisation is to their community of readers, the easier it is to link up with that community in order to find and tell stories. The more journalists connect with and communicate with their users, the more users will come to the journalists with stories – part of the culture of being an open newsroom is that it will encourage contributions.

In their study of citizen journalism in local newspapers in Texas, Seth Lewis and his co-authors interviewed an editor who agreed: 'I think we're very involved in it (citizen journalism). I think we

Explore sources

'We look forward to finding new ways to … make our reporting process more transparent and accountable, and when we can we'll open source the code so other newsrooms can show their work, too' (Shaw, 2011).

do a good job of letting people participate in the paper, in the content of the paper … I think any time you get input from your readers, it's good … We don't really make much of an effort to get citizens involved, but we get it anyway. I think it's hard to explain. Every newspaper has its own personality and people have always had ease submitting things to us, and we pretty well take most of their information.' (Hawkins, in Lewis et al., 2010).

Contributions to existing stories are probably the most publicly visible form of user-generated content. The BBC has a clear policy on this, and ends many stories on the web and on air with an invitation to contribute experiences, data and footage to the organisation. One of the most public occurrences of this was in November 2008, after the attacks on Mumbai that saw almost 200 people killed and a number taken hostage in one of the city's luxury hotels. Mark Abell, a British citizen, was one of those hostages. He contacted the BBC directly after the attacks, and provided updates and information to the newsdesk, who responded by using interviews with him across the coverage. Abell became both source and contributor and, in the words of the BBC's UGC hub editor: 'Hearing the stories directly from the people involved in them changed the way we reported events' (Eltringham, 2011a).

To pay or not to pay

Should you pay for user-generated content? Some news organisations, such as the BBC, never pay for content or sources, but others may. Paying for images or footage may grant exclusivity, which can bring traffic, but it can be an expensive proposition, and not worth the investment unless you are certain that your source is the only one (and is genuine).

Many other news organisations make use of social media in a similar way to that of the BBC, several even having their own 'citizen journalism' sites which present the user-generated content within a discrete site, not simply incorporating the content into their own narratives. Sites like Bild's Leserreporter, CNN's IReport and Avusa's Reporter.co.za are examples; these are discussed in more detail in Chapter 6.

Opening up the news process, crowdsourcing

Crowdsourcing is also discussed in Chapter 8, in the context of data journalism, but it is not necessarily exclusive to data journalism. Crowdsourcing, like many of the terms used in this book, is still open to interpretation but, in general, it refers to soliciting raw material from the users – the crowd – prior to completing, or sometimes even starting, a story.

Crowdsourcing

Crowdsourcing refers to the practice of asking the public for input. This can be anything from soliciting pictures to asking for help in the reporting process.

In October 2011, the Guardian newspaper did something that possibly no other news organisation had ever done before: it made its newslist public. The editors were clear about why they were doing this – they wanted the readers to contribute to the process: 'The idea is to publish a carefully selected portion of the national, international and business newslists on this daily blog and encourage people to get in touch with reporters and editors via Twitter if they have ideas. ... If readers can see that we've got a reporter looking into the police killing of someone with a Taser – to use a recent example – they might be able to direct us to other recent deaths or the definitive report on their safety risks.' (Roberts, 2011).

Another way of making journalism transparent is to be explicit about the origin of information, linking back to the original source. Journalists have always negotiated the tension between being absolutely clear about the origin of information and constructing a story that flows and is well written. ProPublica, the non-profit US-based investigative-journalism organisation, recently launched a new web feature which they call 'Explore Sources'. This creates links throughout the text, referring the reader to the origin of that piece of information in the text: 'While "Explore Sources" is just an experiment, we look forward to finding new ways to use it to make our reporting process more transparent and accountable, and when we can we'll open source the code so other newsrooms can show their work, too.' (Shaw, 2011).

The interview is the heart of journalistic practice, and it is access to interviewees (as well as the skill of conducting the interview, discussed in Chapter 2) that comes with the status of being a professional journalist. Opening up the interview

> # Newslist and diaries
>
> The newslist, or diary, is the news organisation's plan of what they are working on, what stories are building, what the plan for the next edition will be. It has traditionally been very jealously guarded. Increasingly, however, news organisations publicise their newslists online in order to solicit ideas, comments and sources prior to production.

process to the public can feel like opening the doors of the inner sanctum of journalism, but those that do use open-source interviews find the level of engagement and participation is heightened.

There are two main strategies for opening up the interview to a public process: making the raw material available, and soliciting questions from the public, often live, online. An online question and answer session, such as that used by the Guardian's Greece correspondent, Helena Smith, can be an excellent source of ideas, as well as a news product in and of itself (Smith, 2012). Writing up an interview is of necessity a process of editing, reworking quotes and ideas into a complete narrative. Posting the original interview alongside the final edited story can assist with transparency, and provide greater access and information for the users.

Verification

One of the most often raised concerns with regard to user-generated content is verification – online hoaxes are rife, from the easily refutable 2011 reports that Kanye West was dead, to the provision of faked images to news organisations, which can be harder to establish. Although there are only a few noted cases of faked material being provided to news organisations, it remains a concern: the embarrassment of having made a public mistake of that nature can be unpleasant.

The BBC College of Journalism provides some guidance on how they verify sources, chief among them being the ability to contact the source yourself, independently (2010b, 2010c). Authenticity and verification are discussed in more detail in Chapter 9.

Curation and live blogging

Curation is both a research method providing the basis for more complete finished stories and a product in itself. Any collection of public online sources for a story (video, images, tweets, blog posts, comments and the like) could be called curation. Publishing this collection online turns a journalist's personal resource collection into a public one, and opens up the possibility of greater contribution and input from the public.

Some writers have likened curation to the traditional journalistic practice of copytasting – selecting the best stories for publication from the wire services – but, although it has something in common with that process, requiring similar skills in news judgements, it also has skills in common with source finding and newsgathering, especially within the social web. Finding sources and ideas within the social web is discussed in Chapter 2.

Curation leads almost directly to live blogging, one of the newest forms of online journalism. One of the earliest examples was the coverage of the Haiti earthquake at the beginning of 2010, although the practice of attending a live event and providing updates and comments on a live format has been around for some time longer, especially in sports coverage (Beckett, 2010). At the We Media conference in London in May 2006, the live conference was accompanied by an open live chatroom (referred to as the 'backchannel chat' – this predates Twitter) participated in by members of the audience and the wider public – the channel contained both reports of what people were saying at the conference, as well as comments and discussion from the audience. People participating in the channel then contributed questions and comments that were relayed to the panel. The chat logs remained as a record of the event, and formed a kind of precursor to the live blog.

A live blog, at its simplest, is a record of an event, published live as it occurs. A journalist attending a football match, for example, would provide a written commentary online: the textual equivalent of a live radio or television report. A single, automatically refreshing web page, with material added to a running narrative with a time

Curation

Curation is the process of gathering sources, interviews, comments and facts into a collection, and publishing that online as a finished product (and possibly also as a preliminary to another piece of journalism). Curation is different from aggregation in that it contains at least some of the journalist's own voice, and cannot be automatically generated. Curation is discussed in practical terms in Chapter 5.

Live blogging

Live blogging is the online equivalent of rolling news. While an event unfolds, a journalist collects and presents information as it comes into the newsroom, curating clips, quotes and other information into a constantly updated stream of information with the latest news at the top.

Aggregation

Aggregation is a more or less automated collection of information, tweets, facts and reports from the web, collected into a single area. It differs from curation and live blogging in that the editorial input by the journalist is minimal.

stamp attached, is created, allowing any user seeing the page to see the entire narrative, but with the latest material at the top.

The journalist can then add to the page as events progress, incorporating comments from users (often tweeted, using a specific hashtag – this is discussed further in Chapter 4), material from other sites or news organisations, comments, links, audio and video. The final live blog then stands as a curated, recorded narrative of events – not a finished news product, packaged and edited into a single narrative, but a comprehensive record, somewhat akin to the notes and research a journalist would have done prior to creating the finished product.

Live blogs can be a vibrant, engaging way of bringing traffic to your site (one report had live blogs providing nine per cent of the Guardian's hits in a month (Wells, 2011)), of providing rolling news in a format that has both the immediacy of a live broadcast and the record of a more formal piece of journalism. On the other hand, they can be confusing and anarchic, and some users may find them frustrating when what they would prefer is a simpler, more familiar, narrative.

 There is no structure and therefore no sense, and the effect is of being in the middle of a room full of loud, shouty and excitable people all yelling at once with all the phones ringing, the fire alarm going off and a drunken old boy slurring in your ear about 'what it all means'. (Morpork, 2011)

Robert Mackay of the New York Times agrees that live blogs are not a substitute for a finished news product: 'You are more or less providing readers with raw material rather than telling them a story. You also tend to get swept up in the rush of events, and don't have nearly as much time as you'd like to think about what's happening and make connections, or write any sort of news analysis.' (Mackay, quoted in (Wells, 2011)).

Live blogging can bring out the best in the new forms of journalism – transparency, immediacy and interaction – but they are not the only form of news available, and are not a direct substitute for the traditional summative, authoritative, structured news report. They are also not suited to all stories, and careful consideration needs to be given to the question of whether a specific incident or event is worth the effort of creating and running a live blog, and whether there is sufficient audience or content to make it worthwhile (Anderson, cited in Wells, 2011).

Conclusion

User-generated content is frequently cited as both the death and the saviour of traditional journalism. For news organisations, facing increasing competition for both readers and amateurs, the thought of free content can be very tempting; for the professional journalists employed by that news organisation to see all this material being created by amateurs can be a worrying development. Ironically, it is the sheer volume of amateur content that makes the journalist's job so important. It is possible to follow the hashtag of a news event on Twitter and get some idea of what is happening, but anyone who has done that knows that the sheer volume of tweets can be intimidating and overwhelming to anyone trying to find out the information that is relevant to them. Once you filter out the tweets that reference professional news content, you are left with a haphazard and chaotic collection of comment, observation and unverified eyewitness reports,

and that's assuming the hashtag hasn't been hijacked by a fringe interest. The journalist is needed to create order out of that chaos, to select and verify information, to structure it into a cohesive whole, to link it with other research and other information provided by professional and institutional sources, and to make sense of it.

The journalist's role has changed, yes, especially becoming more transparent, but their function within society, that of making sense of the events that happen, of selecting, sorting and making meaningful the chaos of life, has not.

Ushahidi, the Australian Broadcasting Corporation and the Queensland floods

When the rivers began to rise in the Australian state of Queensland in December 2010, journalists at the Australian Broadcasting Corporation were faced with the challenge of reporting events, and of working with the public and emergency services to gather and provide information and resources that could be used to save lives and rebuild the community.

ABC turned to Kenya, and to technology company Ushahidi, to provide assistance with mapping, using and distributing the massive amount of social media and other forms of information that were being generated as the floodwaters headed towards the urbanised coastline of the state (Bruns, 2011; Gosier, 2011).

Ushahidi, or 'Witness' in Swahili, was originally set up to map texted reports of violence in the wake of the Kenyan elections in 2007. Since then it has developed into a comprehensive suite of disaster- and crisis-reporting tools, including mapping, scraping social networks and interaction. Since its launch, Ushahidi's software has been used to report on and assist with a large number of events, including events in the Arab Spring, and the Haitian and Christchurch earthquakes.

Using a range of tools from Ushahidi, staff at ABC created a number of products, including a crowdsourced map of reports of electricity and road outages, evacuations, hazards, help and services, volunteer efforts, and places where assistance was needed (see Figure 7.1). The map was continuously updated over 24 days, using verified data, eyewitness reports and social media data.

The Corporation solicited information from the public via their own web page, on email and on Twitter, as well as via Ushahidi's own iPhone application. Reports were verified before publishing. By the time the project was archived, at the end of January 2011, 1,500 verified reports had been published, and the site had generated more than 230,000 hits, bringing down the original servers and necessitating emergency backups (Gosier, 2011).

Since then, the ABC has reinforced its commitment to using and harnessing social media as a reporting and community tool, launching several similar projects. Their commitment to community

The ABC launched an interactive map of the Queensland floods in January 2011. This was an experiment in gathering information from the community. We are no longer accepting details or new incidents to the map but encourage you to view the existing reports and information posted up to 31 January, 2011.

FIGURE 7.1   Picture courtesy of the Australian Broadcasting Corporation and Crowdmap. http://queenslandfloods.crowdmap.com/.

engagement, social media and reporting their communities remains clear. Ping Lo, an information analyst and journalist, highlighted these issues in a blog post for the BBC College of Journalism: 'The ABC's experience piloting Ushahidi during the Queensland floods sharpened some questions for the Corporation; in particular, around verification and moderation load, defining its key purpose in using the platform, training (of both staff and the public), and managing expectations' (Lo, 2011).

   Broadcasters (and, by extension, all journalists) need to think about their relationship to their communities in times of crisis: is it simply a reporting role, or is it important to become involved in activism? Should companies manage crowdsourcing and newsgathering themselves, or work with other community organisations? How does one do this without compromising one's reputation and relationships? But, most importantly: 'How can all organisations, community groups and individuals combine to produce the clearest, most reliable content possible – that is, minimising duplication and inaccuracy – at a time when people need it most?' (Lo, 2011).

Key reflections

- The lines between the journalists, the users and sources have been blurred, if not completely erased.
- Cultivate your community: they are both the source of your news and the audience for it.
- Maintain control of your product, and keep your voice and identity intact within the communal noise.
- What can a journalist learn from the comments on their stories? Should they participate in the discussion?
- Is opening up the news diary and conference to the users (as the Guardian has done) useful, or just a gimmick?
- How can you best prevent malicious users from abusing your community?

TOOLKIT

Readings and resources

BBC College of Journalism: an invaluable training resource for student and practising journalists alike. The section on citizen journalism, which contains discussion of user-generated content and the UGC hub, is particularly useful, even if you do not have the reach and resources of the BBC. The College's website is at: www.bbc.co.uk/journalism/ and the citizen journalism section is at: www.bbc.co.uk/journalism/skills/citizen-journalism/citizen-journalism-guide/.

Axel Bruns: Axel Bruns's 2005 book *Gatewatching: Collaborative Online News Production* is one of the first studies of collaborative journalism. His ongoing work is discussed on his blog, http://snurb.info/, and his twitter feed, @snurb_dot_info.

Mark Deuze: Mark Deuze's books *Media Work* (2007) and *Managing Media Work* are key to the changing newsroom. He blogs and discusses his work at http://deuze.blogspot.com/ and at http://indiana.academia.edu/MarkDeuze.

Participatory Journalism: *Participatory Journalism* by Jane Singer et al. (2011) is a comprehensive and seminal study of both the theories and forms of this new kind of journalism.

Alf Hermida: Alf Hermida, former BBC journalist and now Professor of Journalism at the University of British Columbia, maintains an excellent blog at www.reportr.net/ which showcases work and projects in social media. A more formal website listing his academic research is at http://alfredhermida.com/.

The Poynter Institute: the institute, based in St Petersburg, Florida, has been researching and training 'future journalism' since 1975. The website at www.poynter.org/ contains resources on a range of journalism-related material, including information about training courses and resources. The section of the website on social media (www.poynter.org/category/latest-news/media-lab/social-media/) is particularly useful.

Guardian: like the BBC, the London-based *Guardian* newspaper (www.guardian.co.uk) is considered a world leader in open and participatory journalism. The media section of the site (www.guardian.co.uk/media), the digital subsection of that and the PDA Digital Content Blog (www.guardian.co.uk/media/pda) are all excellent resources on the changes facing the news industry.

Pressthink: Jay Rosen's Pressthink blog contains a wealth of information and material by him and other contributors on the subjects of collaborative and open news media. It can be found at http://pressthink.org/. Jay Rosen also tweets as @jayrosen_nyu.

News Rewired: Journalism.co.uk's recurring conference, News Rewired, covers issues in new and breaking news. The site at www.newsrewired.com remains an astounding repository of presentations, papers, discussions and ideas on the future of journalism.

Part 3

THE NEW RULES OF ENGAGEMENT

>>Chapter 8<<

ETHICS AND THE CODE OF CONDUCT

Overview

The change in social relationships and networks that new technology has brought has also altered the way in which journalists are perceived by the public. This has put journalistic practice under far greater scrutiny. In addition, the ways in which private life is increasingly on display on the internet has meant that journalists have a greater resource of material to gather and use in stories, but also a far greater obligation to ensure that they use this material both fairly and ethically. This chapter deals with the fair use of content and information, and with the ethics of participating in these new social spaces as journalists and as people. Open journalism is also discussed, as an ideological stance and, to a lesser extent, as a practice.

Key concepts

- Code of ethics
- Fairness
- Honesty
- Open journalism
- Privacy
- Respect
- Secrecy
- Transparency

Springboard

- *Respect*: respect people, and their content: you are an equal player in this environment, and what goes around comes around. Imagine yourself not only as a journalist, but as the subject of a story. Always remember your sources and subjects are people as well as material.
- *Impact*: consider the impact your words are having: on you, your colleagues, your sources and the wider public. You not only work in this community, you live here too. Could you face your neighbours, your family, your friends if they were the subject of your story?
- *Privacy*: people have a right to some privacy, even online. People have a right to know things that are in their interest. Journalism is a balancing act between the rights of the public to privacy and their right to know.
- *Backlash*: in this new media landscape, sources and audience are one and the same. Treating sources badly, invading their privacy or abusing their trust can have serious consequences in the form of boycotts and backlash.
- *Open up*: let people know what you are doing. People are not only interested in the journalistic process (make public your progress on a story content in and of itself), but can also contribute ideas, feedback and information to the story.

Introduction

The change in social relationships and networks that new technology has brought has also altered the way in which journalists are perceived by the public. This has brought all public figures under far greater scrutiny, journalists included. In addition, the ways in which private life is increasingly on display on the internet has meant that journalists have a greater resource of material to gather and use in stories, but also a far greater obligation to ensure that they use this material both fairly and ethically.

This chapter grapples with the space between ethics and the law, the new rules of engagement in a new sphere that is not quite public, not quite private. It delineates guidelines and best practices for working within the new media ecology. The authors, however, are not legal experts or lawyers, or experts in the regulation of the news media in any of the countries in which this book is being published, and none of the advice given should be taken as overriding, or more definitive than, the advice of a local and experienced media lawyer or expert. We have tried to provide here, not a set of absolute rules, but a tool for understanding the processes and ideas and, through that, the mechanisms for creating your own set of ethical and social guidelines by which to operate.

Professional ethics

Journalistic ethics vary considerably across global and organisational constraints; however, in most countries there are professional associations, journalism trade unions, industry associations and other institutional structures which provide guidance and standards for that specific context. Individual news organisations very often will have their own ethical codes to which journalists are expected to subscribe (and adherence to which is usually a condition of continued employment); smaller organisations would do well to adopt one of the codes available.

Ethics and the internet

Traditional ethical guidelines for journalists tend to assume a level of real-time face-to-face interaction between journalist and source that is increasingly not the case. It is currently accepted that journalists should always identify themselves in any interaction with a potential source or story. This becomes problematic when that interaction takes place within the boundaries of a Facebook group or Twitter feed. The requirement (in many countries a legal requirement, rather than simply an ethical guideline) that both parties agree that a conversation can be recorded is difficult to police when the 'conversation' is an online chat, or a series of comments and responses on a blog or website, and the recording may constitute a log file stored on a third party's server.

Legally, the principle that any information posted online is in the public domain (for the purposes of quoting) may hold but, in practice, members of the public are often outraged or appalled when they find themselves pictured or quoted in the local news after an interaction that they may well have considered to be, if not completely private, at least not fully public. A journalist who uses words or images posted online in a story may have the legal right on their side (note the 'may'), but if you have offended a member of your audience, or find yourselves on the receiving end of a social-media protest campaign, the legal right becomes a nicety, and may be moot.

Privacy

Privacy is an important legal principle, enshrined in the United Nations declaration of Human Rights (United Nations, 2011a), but it is not an absolute. A world where privacy was absolute would have no journalism in it – the rights of journalists (and, by extension, the public which those journalists serve) are always weighed against the right of privacy – sometimes in the journalist's favour, sometimes not. This balancing act between the public's right to know (and the attached rights of the journalist to investigate and reveal on the public's behalf) and the individual's right to privacy is where media law and ethics come into play.

Open ethics

Journalistic ethical codes have traditionally been set by elites within journalism, although there are increasing movements to creating ethics by social consensus, something described as 'open ethics' (Ward and Wasserman, 2010).

Public domain

'Public domain' most commonly refers to the copyright status of an artefact (see Chapter 10), but it can also refer to material that is not private, i.e. that can be quoted or reproduced for journalistic purposes, and therefore roughly equivalent to 'on the record' in traditional journalistic parlance.

Journalistic privilege

Theory regarding journalism ethics tends (at least in the Anglo-Saxon world) to start from issues around the liberal theory of the press, the 'fourth estate' and the ideology of objectivity which is closely linked to these ideas. What underpins all of these debates is the fundamental question: What is journalism for? How does it balance its commitment to inform with the requirements of making money and its own continuing survival? How do we, as journalists, balance the human desire for gossip with the need to protect individuals' privacy? (Merrill, 1997; Friend and Singer, 2007; D.M. Berry, 2008; Ess, 2009; Ward and Wasserman, 2010; Whitehouse, 2010)

None of this changed when the internet was invented. The overriding legal and ethical principles of journalism (or of life in general) were not altered when we began to interact online, but the fundamental nature of our social interactions did begin to change, in ways we couldn't predict, or even, really, control.

In one of the earliest books published on this new social space, *Life on the Screen*, psychologist Sherry Turkle explores the ways in which people construct 'windows' for their lives online, separating activities in online environments such as chatrooms and game spaces – known as MUDs (or multi-user dungeons) and MOOs (or MUD, object-oriented) – from real life, or 'RL'. This separation is important for the participants, and people are often surprised or shocked when their various lives and personas clash (Turkle, 1995).

Turkle's insights into human behaviour online are important to journalists, because understanding how the public perceives an interaction is necessary in order to behave ethically. Although she was writing in the early days of the internet and the World Wide Web, well before the invention of Facebook and other social media, her insights into human interaction online still have value. The question does remain as to how much, in the age of social media, people still distinguish between 'real life' and online interaction, and whether the two are merging into one, and further research is needed into these assumptions.

Privacy on social media

Social media moved online interaction from something participated in by a small minority of the population (largely those involved in the computer industry in one form or another), and often focused around specific subjects, into something that a substantial portion of the population in developed countries, at least, participate in on a regular basis, in all aspects of their lives. It is notoriously difficult to gauge the actual size of the online community, but reliable sources indicate that Facebook penetration in North America and Europe is near 50 per cent of the population (Socialbakers.com, 2012). Regardless of the extent of penetration, it is increasingly clear that online identity is a key part of life for people in the industrialised world, and in the globalised sectors of the developing world.

Muds, Moos, Usenet and BBs (BO)

In its early days, many of the participants and contributors to the internet were attached to universities or the computing industry. Despite the stereotype, many of the functions of the early internet were communication tools. Online text-based gaming environments, the massive discussion forums known as Usenet and smaller, private Bulletin Boards (BBs) were all the precursors to the modern social network: places where communication, identity and interaction were primary.

As social media grow, concerns about users' privacy are increasingly being discussed and related issues are now often raised in public forums. Initially, much of the publicity around social media's imposition on people's privacy was based on concerns regarding children online, and specifically their targeting by sexual predators. Books such as Katie.com (Tarbox, 2001), published in 2001 and widely discussed on chat shows and in the news, were the beginning of awareness of the danger a life online can present, but as the online community grew, further concerns regarding the boundaries of social media arose. Users became aware that the information they posted on the network was not as private as they thought, and as the broader social institutions began to be aware of social networks, the ramifications of posting all of one's thoughts and information online began to be apparent (Margulis, 2003; Viegas, 2005; Barnes, 2006; Boyd and Hargittai, 2010).

In 2002, the issue erupted both online and offline when blogger Heather Armstrong (better known as 'dooce') was fired from her job as a web developer for making satirical posts about her work environment on her personal blog. The word 'dooced' has now become slang for being fired from one's job for posting online (Armstrong, 2011).

Despite the lessons learned by Armstrong and others, and despite the discussion of the boundaries between online and offline personas and identities that permeates sectors of the online community, people are still often startled to find that what they post on a social network can be publicly viewed and used. Social networks, which make it easier to participate online, and which have far greater penetration than blogs and personal websites do, make it more likely that people will be caught unawares by the revelation of personal details.

In 2011, a student of ours was offended and angry that we knew that she had lied about being unable to attend class because we had seen her comments on Facebook thanking her friends for covering for her. It was pointed out to the students concerned that if this were a work situation, rather than a university one, she (and also possibly the friends who had lied) would have been fired. She insisted that we had invaded her privacy by reading the post on her 'wall', despite the fact that she had 'friended' us voluntarily. Even after the argument, she did not 'unfriend' either of us, or make any further attempts to block access to information about her social and private life. This naïveté regarding the limits of privacy on social networks remains prevalent, and something an unscrupulous journalist can easily take advantage of.

By 2012, the question of social privacy online had become mainstream, with the debate focusing on three main areas: the use of social data by companies for targeted marketing (see the furore around the various changes and updates to user licence agreements by Google and Facebook); the protection of identity online (particularly that of children); and the question of whether information (words and pictures) posted online can be truly said to be private or confidential.

Use of social-media source material

It is the third point above that most concerns journalists – how much of what is said online can be said to be usable by the media? If traditional ethical and sometimes legal guidelines say that a journalist must always identify themselves when interacting with a potential source, how is that to be interpreted online? Journalists are not only journalists, they are citizens, social actors and individuals within this world as well as being reporters.

Note on social and publishing platforms

Although in this book we have tried to avoid using specific sites or applications' names too much, choosing instead to focus on the functions and uses of social media, it is important to distinguish between various kinds of social media, because the ethics and norms of using material from them will vary according to the functions and expectations of the user.

Material posted on social-media networks that are primarily publishing platforms, such as Twitter (and other microblogging services) and blogging platforms (Blogger, Blogspot, Wordpress, Tumblr), can probably be considered to be on the record, and in the public domain for quoting purposes: the default setting for those systems is public, and material published on them can usually be considered to have already been published. Photographs posted on these networks may, however, have copyright attached to them (see Chapter 10), and should not be used without permission. Pinterest, particularly, whose main intent is the collection and republishing of material posted elsewhere, is particularly risky in terms of copyright.

Networks whose primary function is not publishing, but forging social connections, such as Facebook and LinkedIn, are a more problematic area: users tend to characterise their interaction on these sites in terms of friendships or relationships, and may well believe that communication on them is private, or at least not fully public. If the material is publicly visible to any internet user (as in an unsecured Facebook profile, or a public page on LinkedIn), then it is probably fair to use, but if you need to 'friend' or 'connect to' a person, or make some kind of social connection before seeing the material, then the ethical boundaries become blurred. Are they aware you are a journalist? Are you lying or deceiving them in order to gain access to the material? Just as you wouldn't walk up to someone in the street and ask them questions without first identifying yourself as a journalist, it is probably good practice to identify yourself as a journalist in search of a story when 'friending' or 'connecting' to someone on a social network, if that act will give you access to more information than that which is publicly available.

In a book published in 2012, in the wake of the phone-hacking scandal that racked British journalism, a number of journalists were interviewed regarding their views on the use of Facebook for information and sources in the wake of a story. Although a number of incidents had already occurred in which the press had been criticised by the Press Complaints Commission (PCC) for the use of photographs published on Facebook and elsewhere online, journalists persisted in their belief that anything published online was 'fair game', free to be used by the press (Fletcher, 2007; Cooper, 2012; Newton and Duncan, 2012).

Whether material lifted from social media can be used by journalists is not an absolute rule: the specifics of the story and the circumstances will have a bearing on whether the practice is acceptable. The ethical principle of identifying yourself as a journalist, and of warning people that their words are being recorded, should probably still apply and, at the very least, the people concerned should be contacted to confirm that they agree to have their words used.

The death knock, or 'pickup'

Journalism often reports on death, and one of the tasks of a journalist covering a death is to visit the family and friends in search of quotes, pictures and other usable information. Visiting people at their most vulnerable is emotionally taxing for journalists, and requires a fine social sense, as well as nerves of steel. Every journalist remembers their first death knock, and although some find it a very rewarding task, many still find it harrowing (Cornies, 2010).

Death knock

The 'death knock', or 'pickup', is considered one of the most hated tasks in journalism. The cold call or visit to a bereaved family in search of pictures or a quote is one of the hardest things to do and, despite the bravado of old hacks, it doesn't get easier. Small wonder, then, that journalists have looked for ways to make this less invasive, less harrowing for all concerned, and social media are moving into that gap. Facebook has naturally become a focal point for grieving families, and the creation of memorial pages for a dead friend or relative has become common (Moore, 2009; Cooper, 2012). Journalists may be increasingly tempted to lift quotes and images from these pages, in a practice sometimes known as 'Facebook creeping'. Opinions are divided on this: some journalists liken the practice to lifting quotes from cards left at a public site, while others consider it out of bounds for ethical reasons – the people posting those quotes did not intend them for the media. What must also be considered is whether the practice is good journalism – several journalists think not, saying that the lack of face-to-face contact, and not knowing the relationship of the commenter to the deceased, means that the journalist will not get a true sense of the person, or the best possible quote for the story (Fletcher, 2007; Riehl, 2011; Cooper, 2012; Pugh, 2012).

Although some journalists in the studies quoted above expressed concern regarding the use of social-media material in the event of a tragedy, others felt no such qualms. One quoted reporter even felt that social-media material was better to use because: 'A lot of the time you get just as good quotes from a SNS (Social Networking Site) because people are happier to say how they feel when they write it than saying it to someone' (Anonymous, in Newton and Duncan, 2012).

> ## 'Facebook creeping'
>
> 'Creeping' refers to the practice of looking through someone's social-media presence without their knowledge or permission, in pursuit of information. It is considered unethical and is against the terms of use of many social networks, but it is used by journalists in search of quotes, contacts or pictures (Riehl, 2011; Pugh 2012).

In other words, people in social-media settings say and write things that they would not normally tell a journalist. While this may make for better quotes, and a better story, the ethical concerns cannot be dismissed, and the people quoted may rightly feel violated, and that their words were unfairly used.

> To speak to and for real people means you have to meet them and feel what they feel … How can I translate the true pain and emotions of a family if I rely on a picture and some stylised words that capture a moment in time from Twitter or Facebook? (Anonymous, in Cooper, 2012).

One of the concerns regarding the use of material lifted from social-media memorial pages is the risk of offending or hurting the family and friends of the deceased. Journalists should consider the feelings of the wider public, and whether the news value, or public interest, of the story outweighs the potential discomfort or damage to the people involved in the story. In the case of a death story, the concerns of the family and friends should not be outweighed by those of the news organisation; in the words of Larry Cornies: 'If family members ask to be left alone, respect that. Period' (2010).

Criminals and victims

Lifting material from social media as an alternative or supplement to interviewing bereaved family members is probably understandable, and any offence caused can (it is hoped) be assumed to be inadvertent. The same cannot be said for material from social networks used by journalists to add to crime stories. When 27-year-old Rebecca Leighton from Manchester was arrested in connection with the deaths of five patients at the hospital where she worked, the British press, especially the tabloids, went straight to her Facebook account. The pictures lifted from the social network showed her behaving rather typically for someone of her age: hugging her fiancé, drinking with friends, mugging for the camera but which, in the light of the charges she faced, were used by the tabloids as evidence of her debauched lifestyle – she was branded a party girl, and effectively tried in the court of public opinion. She was never charged with any offence, and threatened to sue several papers for defamation (Arscott, 2011; BBC News, 2011; Cooper, 2012).

The same thing had happened to American Amanda Knox, who was at first convicted, then acquitted on appeal, of the 2007 murder of British student Meredith Kercher in Italy. Knox's postings on social networks, including Facebook and MySpace, revealed things that the tabloids took as damning: a violent short story she had written, and a picture of her boyfriend and co-accused dressed up as a butcher for a costume party were particularly emphasised. Even the normally staid and conservative Telegraph newspaper rooted through her online presence, and even after she was acquitted, the tabloids continued to scrutinise her behaviour and lift comments and images from social networks, as well as using the more traditional techniques of hiring paparazzi to follow her (Simpson, 2007; Cooper, 2012).

Copyright and pictures

Copyright is discussed in more detail in the following chapter, but the question of what you can use from a social network does not hinge on privacy alone. Photographs have inherent copyright, and the permission of the photographer (not the person in the picture) is needed to reproduce the image.

Under-age contacts

The law varies, but in many countries it is illegal or against the ethical code to interview or photograph children without their parents' consent. Social networks may also have age restrictions, but these are often improperly enforced. This creates a situation where a journalist looking for a quote online may inadvertently make contact with a child, creating another set of problems.

In many countries, especially ones that follow broadly Anglo-Saxon legal and social codes, the naming of victims of certain kinds of crimes, especially rape, is either illegal or proscribed by tradition. In addition, the police generally do not release the names of people who have died until their family has been informed. Social media, however, are less controlled and in many cases information that has been traditionally kept out of the public eye by tacit agreement between the mainstream media and the authorities, or by legal injunction, can easily be found online.

In 2003, basketball player Kobe Bryant was charged with the rape of a hotel employee. Within days of the charge being made public, the name, address and photograph of the victim were being circulated online. Some news organisations succumbed to competitive pressure and released the same information; others did not. As radio journalist Lee Bailey said: '[T]here are no standards online – it's like the Wild Wild West' (in Friend and Singer, 2007). More recently, the death of a teenager in Canada caused a similar controversy, with one local news organisation deciding to publish the victim's name against the wishes of her family. The editor, Mike Johnston, justified the decision to go against the family's wishes: 'Many in the community already knew the name so we decided to include it. Our readers who don't use Twitter or Facebook would have questioned who the victim was' (Alzner, 2012; Johnston, 2012).

In 2011, the question of whether information posted online can be considered fully public, even when a court order exists against its publication, came to a head in the UK. A series of scandals involving celebrities who had taken out injunctions against the news media to prevent information about their personal lives being spread, caused outrage on social-media networks, and concerted campaigns were launched to make as many people aware of the details as possible. As Jeremy Clarkson, who was trying to prevent his ex-wife from publishing information about his behaviour, put it: '(I)njunctions don't work. You take out an injunction against somebody or some organisation and immediately news of that injunction and the people involved and the story behind the injunction is in a legal-free world on Twitter and the internet. It's pointless' (in Seamark, 2011).

This defence of 'everyone already knows, so we might as well publish' is increasingly common among news organisations. Social networks have increased the publicity of information, and everyone within a community might well 'already know' the details, but that does not mitigate the newspapers' actions in publicising information. The defence that information is readily accessible online is a complicated one: in the case of a legal injunction against publication, the defence might stand as a valid justification for breaking the injunction; but in the case of the name of a victim of a crime, the fact that people on social networks may be discussing the details may not be sufficient justification for the news organisation to break the silence.

The principles and norms by which news organisations decide whether to reveal the name of a victim of a crime (or alleged crime) vary considerably across the world and among news organisations. The rapidly changing online environment has created something of a vacuum in terms of precedent and standards, especially when the relative lawlessness of some social-media environments, such as 4Chan, are considered. However, news organisations which operate within other social constraints (as businesses, as public enterprises, as organisations with access to some level of journalistic privilege) are probably wise to remain within the constraints which have governed their non-online activities. The distinction between online and offline is increasingly blurred, and applying differing sets of standards

4Chan and Anonymous

If the internet is the Wild Wild West, as Lee Bailey would have it, then 4Chan is the rowdiest, drunkest saloon in town. This online community, which is widely considered to be the birthplace of many of the internet's most ubiquitous memes (ideas, including jokes, that become popularly replicated and adapted), such as lolcats (pictures of cats with captions attached), is also known as the home of the online (and offline) hacking and activist group Anonymous, and is an environment in which anything goes.

makes no sense. The internet and social media have brought a new, more personal and engaged, voice to offline news media, but the things that made offline media so valuable to society – fact-checking, integrity, respect and truth-seeking – should not be abandoned.

Although some journalists tend to persist in believing that anything posted online is 'fair game' (Friend and Singer, 2007; Cooper, 2012; Newton and Duncan, 2012), and although preliminary legal opinion (more in the area of employment law than media law) seems to agree, public opinion still seems to hold, in agreement with my student above, that 'what happens on Facebook should stay on Facebook'.

Public interest

Whether material published on social media is open to be reproduced or reported on seems to hinge, at least in the eyes of the UK's Press Complaints Commission (PCC), on whether the material, or the individual, is in the 'public interest'. In 2009, two cases of the use of quotes from Facebook were brought to the attention of the

Public interest

Public interest is a common journalistic defence against accusations of invasion of privacy, or even lawbreaking. It's important to remember that what's interesting to the public is not necessarily in the public interest: public interest requires that the information be necessary for the public's continued participation in civic and political life.

PCC. Comments made by a police officer about the death of Ian Tomlinson during the G20 protests in London on his Facebook page were deemed to be acceptable, despite only being visible to his 'friends' on the site, because of the public interest in the case, and the fact of the man quoted being a law-enforcement official. In a second case, quotes from the Facebook accounts of the survivors of the 1996 Dunblane massacre were deemed not fair use, since the people who posted were not public figures, and there was no public interest in publishing the information (Press Complaints Commission, 2009).

It is worth noting that the PCC did not rule conclusively that material lifted from Facebook was either acceptable or not: it chose instead to focus on the underlying story, and whether it presents a justification for the invasion of privacy. The rulings are different, not because the actions of the journalists were different, but because the stories were different. The behaviour of the survivors of Dunblane were deemed not to be in the public interest; the comments of the police officer were: the matter of Facebook was irrelevant.

> ## Press Complaints Commission (PCC)
>
> In the UK, the PCC is (at the time of writing, at least) an industry body that polices the behaviour of the print press. It has no legal power, but can insist member newspapers apologise or withdraw articles. Its 'Editors' Code of Conduct' is considered to be the ethical standard by which UK newspapers operate.

Backlash

The Dunblane survivors' story still makes an interesting case study, because the response to the story shows another of the dangers of interfering with privacy online: backlash. As Mike Jempson explains, although it took three months for the PCC to rule that the story was 'a serious error of judgement', it had taken only three weeks before 'the newspaper had already removed the offending article from its website and published an apology, in response to an online petition which attracted 11,186 signatures' (Jempson and Powell, 2012).

> ## Anonymous sources
>
> To the public, it may seem that journalists rely extensively on anonymous sources. Strictly speaking, this is not true – the unnamed source is not unknown to the journalist, or the editor, just to the public. Guidelines for major news organisations such as the BBC, Reuters and the New York Times prohibit journalists from using material from sources that they cannot identify. Anonymity is further discussed in Chapter 10.

Social media have a regulatory capacity that is far more powerful than the rules or laws governing its use: in the Dunblane story, it was this social backlash that forced a reaction from the news organisation, not just the regulator. Any news organisation that finds itself on the receiving end of a social-media campaign is likely to learn quickly that the regulatory ethics are not as important as the social ones: being legally in the right doesn't help when your audience and your advertisers are jamming your communication, and abandoning your sites.

Legally, material posted on social-networking sites may be considered to be in the public eye, and therefore usable. In terms of public expectations, however, the risk of offending or causing a backlash is high – especially when it comes to Facebook – and the possibility of being hoist by your own petard, being attacked through the same social-media networks that you used, is extremely high.

Setting professional and personal boundaries

One of the hallmarks of the networked social environment is the loss of the clearly delineated identities and personas people had. When your workplace is defined by the physical boundaries of the building in which you worked, and the times in which you were there, it is easy to determine when you are working, and when you are not. Traditionally, journalists have been held to the professional boundaries of the job, and the identity of journalist held, even when outside the physical newsroom – the public knew when they were speaking to a journalist. Most formal ethical codes of journalistic practice require the journalist to identify themselves as such when engaging with the public, and inform people that they are being quoted. In some countries, it can be considered acceptable to deceive someone in order to get a story, but this is usually only permitted in specific cases (i.e. where there is a public interest that is deemed to be more important).

These guidelines are easy to observe in a face-to-face world: it is easy to preface any interaction with 'I'm a journalist, would you mind answering a few questions?' In the networked social environment, however, this is more problematic.

One issue is deciding when you are a journalist, and when you are not (this is discussed further in Chapter 11). Traditional journalists have also wrestled with this – a good journalist never truly leaves the newsroom, and always has an eye out for a good story. When socialising with friends, for example, it helps to have an ear for news: however, it is a rare circumstance in which you would find yourself hearing something newsworthy in a context in which the person speaking was not aware that you were a journalist. If you do hear such a thing, there is an ethical dilemma which presents itself: can you use material given to you in those circumstances? Eavesdropping may be considered unethical, but in the offline world, eavesdropping that results in useful information is so rare that the point is almost entirely academic. Even if you overhear a comment on a bus, it can't be used without speaking to the person to verify their identity, forcing you to make the person aware of your intention to use their words.

In a social-network environment, where the person may not even be aware you are listening or reading, and may never have met you, but where identity (or some form of it) is immediately apparent to any observer, these issues become more blurred. Do you need to contact the person to ask their permission, or inform them of their use in a story? What do you do if they refuse?

Although the ethical guidelines are not clear on this, many journalists agree that material that is visible to the public may be publicly used in any other medium.

Codes of conduct

Although the law is taking considerable time to catch up with the changes that social media have wrought, news organisations have begun to formalise the ways in which their staff engage on social networks. The concerns addressed in these codes of conduct tend to be two-fold: not bringing the organisation into disrepute through material posted online, and not misleading the public.

Bringing the organisation into disrepute through material posted online is not only a concern for news organisations, but of most modern employers. Social media guidelines for Associated Press, the Wall Street Journal, Sky News and the New York Times all proscribe the posting of opinions, or 'editorialising' (Halliday, 2012): 'Sharing your personal opinions, as well as expressing partisan political views, whether on Dow Jones (the parent company of the Wall Street Journal) sites or on the larger web, could open us to criticism that we have biases and could make a reporter ineligible to cover topics in the future for Dow Jones' (Lasica, 2009a, 2009b, 2009c; Halliday, 2012).

The Washington Post agrees that the reputation of the news organisation is paramount, and that reputation is based primarily on 'objectivity': 'When using these networks, nothing we do must call into question the impartiality of our news judgment.' The guidelines also advise against revealing any information regarding the news production process, and posting any information that has not been cleared by the main editorial team (Hohmann and 2010–11 ASNE Ethics and Values Committee, 2011).

In other words, these policies expect you to behave in the social space the way you would in the professional offline world – as nothing more than a reporter for your organisation, a cog in the wheel, as it were, wearing your branded press card on your sleeve at all times. This may not be a realistic way to expect people to engage with social media (and probably not even in the physical world, either), and, more importantly, it is not the way the social network expects people to engage. The network expects that you will participate and contribute content, as well as using the environment as a source and as a place to gain audience. The danger in formal guidelines presented above is when they assume that the network is like the newsstand: that the traffic is one-way only, and that what matters most is the presentation, not the communication.

Other news organisations such as the Guardian and the BBC have a slightly more progressive approach to the social network. The BBC is concerned with its reputation online, but, first, it advises its staff to: 'participate online: don't "broadcast" messages to users' (BBC, 2011). The Guardian's guidelines, likewise, emphasise contribution and communication over the presentation of a unified brand on social media: the first two guidelines are: 'Participate in conversations …' and 'Focus on the constructive …' (*Guardian*, 2010). These guidelines demonstrate a more network-aware understanding of social-media engagement by big news organisations. As Meg Pickard, the Guardian's former head of digital engagement, puts it: 'It's no coincidence that the first word of the guidelines is "participate". It's a call to action for journalists not just to use digital and social media platforms as a way of broadcasting our work further than ever, but also to engage with readers over contexts of mutual interest, for mutual benefit.' (2010).

Conclusion

What these more progressive guidelines have in common with each other is that there is a greater emphasis on the autonomy of the journalist, and on their ability to make judgements on how they should behave in any given context. A traditional news organisation has a hierarchy, not only of people, but of content, and only content which has gone through the formal processes of commissioning and editing through to final approval is considered good enough to be published. The traditional newsroom has been likened to a factory: the final product is uniform and packaged. Social media has changed that: the identity of the individual journalist can be as important as the institutional identity, and material published on a blog, a Facebook page or a comment can be as important as material that has gone through the formal manufacturing process. In this environment, it is essential to trust journalists to make their own decisions, to act ethically, and to conduct themselves fairly and professionally in all circumstances, even ones we haven't imagined yet. A good code of ethics will reflect this, giving context to the news organisation's engagements with the public, and giving the journalists tools to enable them to act fairly and professionally with the public.

CASE STUDY > # The social-media backlash

The internet may not still be the Wild Wild West that some proclaimed it to be, but it is clear that the regulation, laws and traditions that govern offline media have not yet fully taken hold in the social-media age.

In 2009, the Scottish Sunday Express ran a story purporting to show the bad behaviour and 'shame' of a group of young people who had survived a massacre 13 years earlier (see Figure 8.1). The story was based entirely on material lifted from social-media networks, pictures and posts from a group of mostly young men boasting about the kinds of things young men usually boast about – drinking and having sex, while using bad language.

The outrage was palpable. On the same social media which spawned the story, people shared comments and, more importantly, the contact details of editor Derek Lambie and journalist Paula Murray. People were encouraged to contact the newspaper directly and so many did that, in the words of one reply, 'As you are no doubt aware – thanks to mass bloggers on the internet – we have been inundated with letters and comments. Many of them have been extremely personal' (Lambie in Ireland, 2009; Vowl, 2009).

FIGURE 8.1 The *Scottish Sunday Express* prompts a social media backlash
Picture courtesy of: www.andrewt.net/blog/sunday-express-smash-world-record-for-tabloid-limbo/.

Formal complaints were made to the PCC, and they eventually ruled that the story was an unwarranted invasion of privacy not, it is worth noting, because the use of material from social networks is fundamentally an invasion of privacy, but because there was no public interest in the story, but the social network (those mass bloggers on the internet, as the editor clumsily put it) had already acted. A petition demanding an apology collected some 12,000 signatures, and two weeks after the original story appeared, it was removed from the website and the paper apologised (Jempson and Powell, 2012).

This is a perfect example of the way in which the social network works – a kind of self-regulating ethics system, as it were: the journalists made an error of judgement in plundering a social network, and the network responded in its own defence. That is not to say this is a perfect system – crowds may be wise, but they may also be mad. Anonymous, the anarchic protest movement spawned by the even more anarchic discussion forum 4Chan, show this: although they have brought attention to many injustices, including targeting the Fox News channel in the USA for its biased coverage, they have also engaged in actions that many would consider hostile to the social fabric (Saklofske, 2011; Phillips, 2012).

The social network may be a very useful source of material and stories, but it is also an environment with its own rules, ethics and expectations. You cannot expect to simply take from the network – you need to participate in it and contribute to it, and follow its rules.

Key reflections

- You are both the journalist and potentially the subject of interest. The public are both the audience and the source.
- Ethics haven't changed, but the social network has made punishing news organisations for ethical violations more possible. This can help to regulate the behaviour of journalists, but it can also become bullying and abusive itself.
- The boundaries of what is 'public' have blurred. Information that is findable may not have been intended to be publicly accessible, raising the issue of whether it is ethical to use it.
- The need to find a contact to complete a story can be overwhelming, and it is in those desperate moments that ethical (and sometimes legal) rules are broken. Make sure you know what your guidelines are, and what your personal limits are, before you need to test them.

TOOLKIT

Readings and resources

A number of books give a good overview of modern day journalistic ethics. David Berry's *Journalism, Ethics and Society* (2008) is an excellent introduction to the practice and the underlying philosophical issues, as is John Merrill's *Journalism Ethics: Philosophical Foundations for News Media* (1997). Merrill is American and Berry is British: these books tend to be specific to those contexts.

Friend and Singer's *Online Journalism Ethics: Traditions and Transitions* (2007) and Charles Ess's *Digital Media Ethics* (2009) engage with the changing nature of ethics in this new environment.

A number of media organisations maintain blogs and discussions of the issues that face them. As always, the BBC College of Journalism is an excellent resource on ethics and news productions. The main site is at: www.bbc.co.uk/academy/collegeofjournalism.

The PCC is still in effect at the time of writing, although its future is uncertain. They maintain a set of guidelines at www.pcc.org.uk/cop/practice.html and previous cases and discussion can be seen at: www.pcc.org.uk/cases/index.html.

The American Society of Newspaper Editors' ethics committee publishes regular guidance and advice for news organisations at http://asne.org/Key_Initiatives/Ethics.aspx.

The Poynter Institute in Florida regularly publishes research and advice on ethics. A list of articles on the subject can be found at www.poynter.org/tag/ethics/.

>> Chapter 9 <<

TRUTH AND
VERIFICATION

Overview

This chapter will discuss the importance of information verification in the online age, especially for journalists. Specific issues, such as hoaxes, fake identities, disinformation and astroturfing, as well as broader issues pertaining to authenticity both online and offline, are discussed. In this chapter, guidelines for protecting yourself are given, as well as broader social issues that pertain to questions of authenticity and truth in the online environment.

Key concepts

- Astroturfing
- Authenticity
- Authorship
- Credits
- Hoax
- Sharing
- Trust
- Verification

Springboard

- *Develop your instincts*: trust them. If something is too good to be true, it may well be. Everyone wants something: ask yourself 'Am I being manipulated?' and 'Why'?
- *Crowds are wise*: use them to help you verify information, identify images and keep your contributors honest.
- *Admit when you are wrong*: everyone makes mistakes, but admitting them is essential if you are to maintain your community and support.
- *Be cynical*: always assume someone is lying, until you are certain they aren't. Check all your information, material and facts.
- *Know the landscape*: develop your patch, your contacts and your knowledge. It will stand you in good stead to develop those hunches.

Introduction

On the internet nobody knows you're a dog – or so goes the punch-line to a cartoon published in 1993 (Fleishman, 2000). While it is unlikely that there are any actual canines lurking within the network, the truth is it can be impossible to know for sure whether people are what they claim to be online.

This is not a problem that is unique to the online world, of course, but the lack of face-to-face contact makes it particularly problematic. For the overwhelming majority of history, human beings have developed skills needed to judge whether someone is honest or lying, but these skills are all geared towards face-to-face interaction. Journalists have been caught by hoaxes offline as well, but the skill required to pretend to be someone you are not in a live in-person interview is considerably greater than that needed to create an online presence. The more journalists move away from on-the-ground, face-to-face interaction, the easier it is to be fooled or hoaxed.

This chapter deals with the truth – finding it, verifying it and ensuring that you are reporting the truth, or as close to it as you can get. Various kinds of mistakes, hoaxes, and the practice of astroturfing are discussed in depth, as well as strategies for verifying user-generated content.

Hoaxes, mistakes and lies

In late April 2004, the editor of London's Mirror newspaper was approached by people selling photographs of British soldiers abusing Iraqi prisoners. This was at the height of the second Gulf War, and the Mirror was known for having remained staunchly opposed to the war, and for attracting considerable hostility for that. The pictures were profoundly damaging to the reputation of the British Army and, after they were published on 1 May, dominated the news in the UK for weeks. As the story unfolded, though, it turned from an exposé of abuse by soldiers to a tale of an editor brought down by either his own hubris and lack

Hoax

A hoax is a deliberate attempt to mislead someone, either for financial gain (although this could more rightly be called a 'con'), for attention, or as a prank. A hoax is more than a simple lie – it requires planning and the intent to mislead.

of diligence (Greenslade, 2005), or by a malicious hoax (Mirror, 2004), depending on whom you believe.

The editor of the Mirror at the time, Piers Morgan, was fired for allowing the pictures to be published without first verifying them, and although the damage to his career was debatable (he never worked as a journalist again, but he has done extremely well in television), the fall-out of this story was dramatic.

Frustratingly, nobody involved in the production or publication of the pictures has ever fully confessed the details, so it is impossible to truly analyse the failures in the process that resulted in the pictures being published. Morgan, in his memoirs, claims that the pictures were shown to the Mirror before the publication of similar pictures showing abuse of Iraqi prisoners by American soldiers. The Mirror published their pictures after the Abu Ghraib images had been released, and some imply that the images were faked in response to the Abu Ghraib pictures. Although Morgan remained unconvinced that the paper had been fooled at all (Morgan in Brown, 2005), it seems clear that the images were staged, and that the paper was either deliberately hoaxed, or made a blunder.

Within days of publication, critics began pointing out errors in the pictures – the wrong kind of vehicle, the wrong kind of shoelaces, simple things that most probably could, and should, have been checked. When the paper apologised, they claimed that they had been the victims of a 'calculated and malicious hoax' (Trinity Mirror, in Tryhorn and O'Carroll, 2004), implying that the fault was not theirs. Whether the photos were, in fact, a calculated hoax aimed specifically at the Mirror (in revenge for its position on the Iraq War, as some have implied), a joke gone wrong (pictures posed by soldiers having an incredibly tasteless laugh, and passed off to the papers by someone who thought they were real), or even a money-making scam (the paper apparently paid for the pictures, although nobody has revealed how much), the fact remains that in the eyes of the public, responsibility for ensuring that everything in the newspaper is true lies with the journalists and the editor. Even the Mirror itself agreed, in retrospect, claiming that the responsibility lay with them to prove the photos' authenticity: 'the evidence against them (the people who supplied the pictures) is not strong enough to convict in a court but that is not the burden of proof the Daily Mirror demands of itself' (Mirror, 2004).

But verifying each and every piece of information that comes into a newsroom can be difficult, expensive and extremely time-consuming. In the highly competitive and fast world of a daily newspaper and the even more rapid one of 24-hour rolling news, that time may not be easily available, and the list of embarrassed apologies grows.

The Yes Men

The Yes Men are a pair of self-proclaimed 'culture jammers' who create fake websites, and impersonate people and companies in order to draw attention to social and political issues. Possibly their most famous stunt was the 2004 impersonation of Dow Chemical executives and their announcement of a $12 billion settlement to pay compensation and fund the clean-up of the Bhopal gas disaster. Several news organisations, including the BBC, were taken in by the prank, and later apologised on air (Bichlbaum et al., 2009).

Verification

Verification for a journalist involves not only checking facts, but also ensuring that people are who they say they are, that they could reasonably be expected to know the things they claim to know, and that all images and video are genuine. It is not a small task, but it is this that preserves the public trust in journalists.

Deliberate hoaxes are not the only pitfalls that news organisations fall prey to: it is far more likely that they will be caught by a joke, or a simple misunderstanding. After the Al Qaeda attacks on the USA in 2001, several images circulated online, including one of what appears to be a young man standing on the observation deck of one of the towers as a plane speeds towards him. The picture was fairly rapidly denounced as a fake. It was in fact, a joking photo-editing job, intended only for the subject's friends, but that didn't stop a few newsrooms and large numbers of people from being caught by it (Hickman, 2001).

Likewise, a startling series of images circulated after the Indian Ocean tsunami in 2004 of people running for their lives as giant waves crash over the shore, and then, a few days later, of bizarre sea creatures supposedly washed up by the wave. Both sets were false, cobbled together images from a range of places and circulated on discussion forums and on email. Many newspapers were caught by the pictures and published them: the drama of the event and the timing of the pictures (a few days after the initial wave, at a time when public interest was at its highest, but not much new material was coming through) meant that the temptation to run them won out over journalistic instinct.

> Journalists should test the accuracy of information from all sources and exercise care to avoid inadvertent error. (Society of Professional Journalists' Code of Ethics, 1996)

All of these examples show the risks of acting too quickly, or being caught by too-tempting an image or fact. There is always a risk in competitive journalism. Editors are constantly balancing the risk of being wrong against the risk of being last, or left out. In the online environment, fact-checking and verification are simpler and faster, but so is hoaxing – the technology has changed, but the balancing act remains (Society of Professional Journalists, 1996).

Verify, verify, verify

One of the first rules of journalism is to check and double-check everything someone tells you. This rule applies whether you are talking to people in your local neighbourhood, or collating user-generated images and video from the other side of the world. The online environment changes a lot, but it doesn't change fundamental rules of human nature and information. Sometimes a story can be so powerful, so explosive, so tempting that the thought that it might not be true is dismissed; these are the stories that can damage a news organisation irreparably.

Verification does not necessarily mean that you need to have two separate sources for exactly the same information, although that would be ideal. There are a few key strategies for examining information.

Know who you are talking to

There is no such thing as an anonymous source, only sources whose identities are not revealed to the public. No source should be anonymous to the journalist. If a source won't tell you his or her name and some identifying details, then the information that comes from them should not be trusted, and only used if it can be thoroughly independently verified. It may be acceptable to agree with a source that their name won't be published and in many countries this is legally protected information. But you will need to know who they are, and do some basic fact checking on that information. It's not just about their name. Do they genuinely work where they say they do? Are they someone who would have access to the information they claim to have access to? The internet can make this kind of verification simpler – staff lists on company websites or social-media pages. These things can make checking on a person's identity much easier. On the other hand, they can also make it much easier to create a hoax identity: fake Twitter and Facebook accounts abound. Be wary of any accounts that are recently created, or have limited connections and friends.

If at all possible, arrange to meet in person at some point. Failing that, arrange a phone or Skype conversation, preferably one that you initiate. Information that comes in purely written form is problematic, not only because it is much easier to pretend to be someone you are not when voice and accent are not part of the equation, but because a lot can be told by tone of voice.

Why is this person telling me this?

The truly altruistic whistleblower is extremely rare. Mark Felt, the famous 'Deep Throat' who revealed the Watergate scandal and brought down a president, all for no benefit and considerable risk to himself, is not, despite the popular mythology surrounding these events and the practice of investigative journalism, at all typical. Most people who approach journalists have an agenda: they are attempting to use the news media to get something. This is not to say that they are dishonest or bad people (although some sources can be blatantly and manipulatively dishonest), but that it is important to remember their situation, and to consider how it might be colouring the information you are getting. A whistleblower who comes to you with information about corruption in the local council might be genuinely concerned about the state of local democracy, or they might be a disgruntled ex-employee with an axe to grind. Most likely, they are somewhere in between perfectly altruistic and vengeful; it's the journalist's job to negotiate this line.

Triangulate

Company registers

In most democratic countries, companies and their directors are publicly known through a central register of commercial interests. It should be a matter of course to check on this information for every company you make contact with, and any discrepancies between what is officially listed and what you are told should be thoroughly investigated. Likewise, charities should also be listed in a register.

Does this piece of information fit in with other verified facts? This is not about whether it is likely that the council is corrupt – that is a judgement call – but whether the specific details you have been given tally with what you already know. Can all the parties (people, companies, institutions) be verified to exist? Are their relationships in the public eye? If you are told that the council is giving road-repair contracts to the brother-in-law of the council leader, check on whether the council leader has a brother-in-law, do the contracts exist and does the council award these contracts. Check the facts around the information, not just the information itself. The overall picture should make sense, not just individual elements of it.

Trust your judgement

This is both the hardest and the best way to judge a story. Does it feel right? Experienced journalists will develop an instinct for a story that 'feels right', that follows from what they already know. Journalists will also develop the ability to tell the difference between a story that feels true, and one they feel should be true: in other words, they can separate their own beliefs and desires from the actual information, and make a genuinely dispassionate judgement. If it feels wrong, don't trust it.

Ask another journalist. Competition is tough, and the temptation is great to sit on a story and break it yourself, but ask a journalist you trust, your editor, or a more experienced colleague to take a look at the information you have, and whether it makes sense to them. Sometimes the desire to have a story be true can blind you to the judgement of whether it actually is true.

Verification and social media

User-generated content is a huge boon to newsrooms desperate for material to fill the ever-increasing news hole. Pictures, stories, video and audio sent from the scene of a story to a news organisation can add much-needed material to the coverage. However, user-generated content can also present a huge risk, as the potential to be misled, either deliberately or accidentally, is huge. A number of organisations that use user-generated content mitigate this risk by keeping user-generated content separate from other material, and running disclaimers around it. This may work in terms of ensuring the organisation is not embarrassed by any mistakes, but this two-tier system of news is cumbersome and probably limits users' interest in the material. It may be more time-consuming to verify material coming in, but it can well be worth it in the long run.

> ## User-generated content
>
> This somewhat clunky term is used to describe raw material, especially visual material, photographs and video, which has been produced by 'the public' and submitted to news organisations to be used in their content. It is distinct from citizen journalism in that it does not usually constitute a discrete news item, but is simply an element of one. UGC is discussed extensively in Chapter 7.

The BBC's user-generated-content hub is probably the largest one in the world, has a staff of more than 20 and receives more than 10,000 contributions daily (Eltringham, 2011a). At the BBC, and at other organisations such as Storyful and National Public Radio, verification of material sent in to newsrooms hinges on verifying both the person who contributed the material, and the material itself (Murray, 2011; Browne, 2012; McAthy, 2012; Silverman, 2012).

Verifying the person

- Do you have an existing relationship with the source? This is where record-keeping, or requiring users to register with you to submit material is extremely useful. If you can quickly bring up a list of material they have submitted, and whether you have used it before, you can quickly make a judgement as to how useful the material is likely to be. Citizenside's unique 'social gaming' approach works particularly well here – they award users points, or levels, depending on how much of their material is used, and how trusted it is. The number of points a user has then becomes

> ## Accent verification
>
> During the Arab Spring in 2011, staff working at the BBC user-generated-content hub relied on their colleagues in the Middle East to verify the accents of people in videos and those calling in to report events. Accents are not an absolute measure of someone's location, but a video purporting to have been shot in Bahrain, where the crowd are speaking in voices more typical of Syria, should raise concerns (Murray, 2011; McAthy, 2012).

a simple rubric for how trustworthy the material is. As Philip Trippenbach puts it: 'If we get a picture from a level 35 user, well, it takes a long time to get to level 35 or 45, and the Citizenside editorial team know that user has demonstrated commitment to our values' (in Goodman, 2011).

- Are they working with other organisations? Some of the best sources of news and information are other networks of users, local citizen-journalism sites or groups – provided you know they are trustworthy. This can be especially useful when you are dealing with a story that is geographically remote from you: linking up with a local news organisation in that area, and collaborating with them and their users is a good way to ensure authenticity of the material.
- Do they have a persistent online identity? Be careful of new social-media accounts: yes, they may have been created to avoid punishment or retribution, or in response to a specific event, but they may also have been created to perpetrate a hoax.
- Does the user have a record of uploading material from one location, or do they aggregate material from a variety of sources. Can you make contact with the actual origin of the video?
- Can you verify where they live? Check geotagging on images and posts, ask for a phone number and check its location, look at time zones and other identifying information.
- Can you speak to them? Voice is always better than text; you can learn a lot from someone's voice or accent, and someone who refuses to speak in person is someone to be cautious of.
- Do other people know them? Ask your network: can other people vouch for them? This is where maintaining your contributor base and networks within the community is important even when there is nothing happening right now.

Verifying the information

There are a large number of strategies for verifying material, especially visual material, which is sent through to the newsroom:

- Check the metadata.
  - o Image files have information about when and how they were created stored in the file. In image files, this is called the Exif data, and it can be viewed in many image-editing programmes, on file-sharing sites such as Flickr and with standalone viewers. Exif data is not infallible – it can be edited or deleted, and the wrong time or date in a camera setting can cause problems as well, but if it does not tally with what else you know about the photographer or image, it can be a reason to be suspicious. The camera type, for example, should match what the photographer tells you about their camera. Exif data may also be able to tell you if the image has been edited, which should also raise some concerns.
  - o Amateur videos are usually shot from a single location – if a video has been edited, or spliced together, that is not a reason to reject it, but you should ask to see the original files.
- Check that the view tallies with other sources of information about that location. This is where Google Maps and Street View can prove invaluable. Google can provide a detailed image of the location that the images come from, and you can check that this tallies with what you see in the image. In 2011, when the army began its repression of protests in Syria, news organisations were flooded with video sent in by users from remote towns and villages in Syria – places where no western journalist had been. Storyful used Google Maps to verify geographic and architectural features in the videos it received – noticing distinctive buildings and landscapes that were visible in the video and on Google satellite images, and verifying that the information was correct (Little, 2011).

- Do elements in the video or image match what you already know about the location – are signs in the expected language (and if you don't read that language, you may need someone else who can verify what they say)? Can you see flags or car-licence plates that would show the country or location? Is the sun in the right position for the supposed time and place of the video? Does the weather match reports given?
- Do any voices in the video match what you know about it? Is the language what you would expect from that region? Is the accent right?
- Call an expert. Sometimes the fastest way is to get advice from trusted contacts, professional or academics.

Crowdsourcing verification

Another strategy for verifying the authenticity of user-generated content is crowdsourcing the process. Andy Carvin, of National Public Radio, used this strategy to great effect during the series of uprisings and protests known as the Arab Spring. Carvin was already in a position to act as a kind of clearing house of social media information, having already had contacts with a number of people in the region through his work as a digital divide activist and with Global Voices. His Twitter feed exploded with information from the ground, some of it genuine, some of it not, and @acarvin increasingly became the feed to follow for those who wanted to know what was going on in Tunisia, Egypt, Libya, Bahrain and the whole region (Katz, 2011; Kiss, 2011).

Carvin faced a problem, though – how to verify the pictures and videos he was being sent. He went straight back to the community that was supplying the material – tweeting the images back to his followers, making clear he was not sure of its provenance, and asking for comments and advice. His network proved to be able to do what he (or any one journalist) could not – check everything: from experts on the manufacture of weapons who could identify the origin of a particular mortar shell, to people who can distinguish an Egyptian from a Libyan accent, to people who can provide eyewitness accounts and even identify individuals in the images and footage (Carvin, 2011).

Crowdsourcing verification is not the most efficient strategy, and given the need for a substantial and reliable (or majority reliable) network, not an option for everyone, but it can be an extremely useful method: both in terms of verifying information, but as a way of maintaining and using the network, and operating within an open, transparent system. This transparency is essential to the continued functioning of the network, and the maintenance of your place within that network (Hermida, 2012b).

Verifying information received through social media is as much an art as a science. There is no one technical test that can be used to ensure that the material is genuine, just as there is no one test to prove it is false. A final decision is based on an aggregate of information, a weighing of the pros and cons, and, in the final balance, going with experience and instinct.

If you run with something that you are not sure about, be open with your audience: tell them you aren't certain. If you get it wrong, retract and apologise, and make as sure as possible that your retraction will get as much attention as your initial information.

Astroturf and disinformation

Aside from simple errors and deliberate hoaxes, there is a third kind of fake information being circulated online: astroturfing. The name is a play on the word grassroots, signifying a social or political movement that is based in community support, and the brand name of a kind of artificial turf,

Astroturfing

Astroturfing refers to the process of trying to create the appearance of public support through the manipulation of social-media content and the media. Astroturfing is unethical, but common, and journalists should be careful of being sucked in by it.

used especially in sporting arenas. In the media world, then, astroturf is a manufactured social movement.

Astroturfing is a strategy most commonly used by unethical public-relations firms to create the appearance of public support for a corporate campaign where there is limited interest or appeal, but it is not beyond political parties or even whole governments to create the appearance of support where none exists, or to undermine a popular campaign or movement. When a government engages in these kinds of tactics, it may also be referred to as disinformation – a word that harks back to the KGB's campaigns of 'black propaganda'.

Astroturfing by PR firms is not common, and, when it occurs, tends not to focus on the news media (who are either too cynical to listen to anything coming from PR firms, or all-too-willing to publicise anything given to them by PR firms, with or without the appearance of a public campaign). Disinformation is more of a concern, especially when it comes to covering events in repressive regimes.

Disinformation

Disinformation is the deliberate spreading of false information both in and around the media in order to mislead the public or journalists.

The Chinese government is particularly known for doing this: the so-called '50-Cent Party' of bloggers and commenters that appears online to support any activity or decision by the ruling Communist Party is believed to consist of people who are paid by the party (at the rate of 5 jiao, or 50 cents RMB (around 5 pence), per comment) to ensure that the dominant discourse online is always in favour of the party (Bandurski, 2008; Morozov, 2011: 130).

During the protests that erupted after the 2009 Iranian elections the western media was increasingly reliant on social media for information both from the defeated opposition party and from the streets. The ruling party in Iran appears to have created or motivated its own support online: after a few days of protests both online and offline, accounts sprung up on social media denouncing the opposition candidate, Mousavi, and expressing support for the incumbent, Ahmedinejad. That is not to say that Ahmedinejad did not genuinely have support among Iran's population, or even its online community, but the timing of the support, and the way in which it was expressed, raised concerns about its authenticity (Morozov, 2012: 135).

For journalists, spotting the online disinformation can be tricky – the best defence against being fooled is to be conscious of the environment, its issues and its players. The longer you are immersed in a place or issue, the easier it is to notice when the tone changes: this could be the result of a genuine change in opinion, or it could be part of an orchestrated campaign. The more familiar you are with the political or social landscape, the more likely you are to notice unfamiliar terrain when it appears overnight.

Consider the timing: movements and public opinion grow slowly and exponentially – one, a few, many, and then a cascade. A spontaneous outpouring of one point of view, at a speed too rapid to have spread naturally may not, in fact, be natural. As with verifying user-generated content, be careful of social media and internet accounts that have been too recently created, and that have little other information or connections.

Consider the words and phrases: people being paid or coerced into expressing support for a particular issue rarely have the time or interest to develop their own perspective on things. They will have been given a set of phrases and points to repeat, and will most likely repeat them with little variation. Just as you can spot the mass-manufactured signs at a protest, you can usually tell the pre-written posts and tweets.

This is not to say that every sign of disagreement should be taken as an attempt to manipulate the social-media landscape. People engaged in contentious political campaigns sometimes seem all-too-willing to accuse their opponents of engaging in astroturfing or disinformation, but the fact is that it is rare. It is expensive and time-consuming to construct such a campaign and, in the absence of known political conflicts, it is unlikely. That said, journalists should always approach any outpouring of support for any position with a certain measure of cynicism: not believing it until you've verified it is just good practice.

Verifying Wikipedia

Wikipedia has become somewhat notorious as a source of disinformation and mistakes. The crowdsourced encyclopaedia which anyone can edit has become something of a battleground for competing ideas, not to mention pranksters and hoaxers. Although Wikipedia should not be the primary source for a news story, it can be useful as a way to check facts and supplementary information quickly.

Wikipedia may be vulnerable to malicious disinformation, but the transparency with which Wikipedia is constructed, is invaluable to anyone wishing to use it as a source: all edits and changes to any site can be seen by any visitor to the site.

Wikipedia

Experienced Wikipedia users know they have to be careful. 'which is what good reporting is supposed to be about anyway' (Wales, in Shaw, 2008: 45).

By clicking on the 'View History' link on the top right of any page, you can see a list of changes that have been made to the article, when and by whom. It is easy to see older versions of the page, or even revert the whole article to a previous version. Most articles simply list a series of minor edits (grammar, style, etc.), additions of more information or citations, and occasional back-and-forth additions and deletions of minor points. Any page that has been substantially edited recently should be treated with caution, especially if the edits substantially change the gist of the material, or specific factual information. 'All Wikipedia articles should be fully cited as well, so a simple click to the original source should clarify any concerns' (Shaw, 2008).

Conclusion

Journalists are trusted by the public to find out and report the truth. In traditional newsgathering this may well have involved access to people at the highest levels of government or industry, rare and closely guarded contacts who provided scarce information. In this new social-media environment, information abounds, and the journalist's role has gone from ferreting out tiny pieces of fact to sorting through mountains of information to find the truth.

The nature of the role may have changed, but the point of it has not, and the skills needed have not changed as much as we would think. Technical skills are useful, but this is not about your understanding of networking technology, imaging software or digital maps. This is still, fundamentally, about your understanding of the environment, your contacts, and how well they trust you (and you them), and your instinct for human nature.

The same rules apply: ask everything twice; ask as many people as possible; think carefully about what you have been told and weigh it against the bigger picture, the things you already know. If you smell smoke, there's probably some kind of a fire. If it's too good to be true, it may well be; in the final accounting: be honest. If you don't know, say so; if you were wrong, apologise and correct it. And ask more questions next time.

The kidnapping that wasn't

When a major story breaks in a country in which there is not a substantial foreign media presence, whether because of prior lack of interest, or active repression of the foreign media, it can be difficult to find sources for stories. This is where social media are particularly useful: it is a rare place in which there are not already bloggers, tweeters and activists who can be used as sources, stringers or contacts.

When the violence of the Arab Spring spread to Syria in early 2011, news organisations went straight online to find material that could add colour and human interest to the hard-news reports of protest and retaliation that were coming out of the country. One site they found was a blog, 'A Gay Girl in Damascus', which told the story of a young lesbian who had recently moved back to Syria from the USA, and launched her blog just months before the uprising began. The blog was in English, spoke about her personal life and her passionate interest in activist politics, and, in retrospect, seemed too perfectly tailor-made for the foreign media, which devoured it.

A post in which she described her father facing down the police, who had come to arrest her, had every-thing: drama, heroism and a little bit of titillation, as the policemen discussed in detail the things she sup-posedly did with her girlfriends, proved to be a hit, and was widely reported on and reposted. Then a cousin reported that she had been kidnapped by the state, and the news coverage kicked into high gear. Bloggers, journalists and activists who had made contact with her over the previous months began frantically trying to contact her, or her family, to find out what was happening, to help, to put pressure on the authorities.

And that's where the story began to fall apart. As the social networks began to scramble to find her, it became increasingly clear that nobody had ever met her, or had even heard her voice. A picture of her which had been circulating online gained even more traction in the wake of the kidnapping, and when the person in the picture, a woman from London, came forward and denied having any contact with the blog, it began to be clear that things might not be as they seem.

Andy Carvin was one of the people who began to ask questions, and, despite some hostility from other members of the social network, persisted. Nobody had met her in person, not even her girl-friend, who admitted in an interview with NPR that the relationship had been entirely virtual. Other gay activists in Damascus denied having met her in the very small gay community in that city. The Guardian's undercover journalist in Damascus admitted that she had not spoken to her in person or on the phone, but had conducted the interview on email.

As the questions grew, eventually, on 12 June, a confession was posted on the Gay Girl in Damascus blog: Amina was an American called Tom McMaster, living in Edinburgh (Henry, 2011; Mackey, 2011; Steger, 2011).

In the wake of the hoax, a number of questions have been asked. How did this happen? The blog was extremely well-constructed and written, by a man with a graduate degree in Arab studies and considerable familiarity with the parts of the world discussed on the blog. In retrospect, his unwillingness to speak on the phone, or on Skype, is something of a red flag, but other aspects of the blog ring true. In fact McMaster had been constructing this online persona for some five years, and it was not only the media who had been fooled, unfortunately. Whether McMaster intended to fool the news media is unclear – he claimed to have been working on a work of fiction, and when the attention got too much, decided to wind down the blog by having Amina disappear. If true, this displays considerable lack of insight on his part into how the news media functions (Polymuche, 2011).

Many of the guidelines discussed in this chapter have been codified and articulated as a result of this hoax: the importance of hearing someone's voice; the importance of examining metadata on images; the importance of fact-checking, especially when a story seems too good to be true, too perfect for the news hole. A journalist should always be sceptical, always double-check the facts, and the people, and social media make no difference to that.

Key reflections

- The need for verification hasn't changed, but the mechanisms of it have. The more remote your sources are, the harder they can be to verify.
- Use the network. Crowdsourcing verification can be an excellent strategy, and being transparent about your concerns from the start can help to mitigate damage.
- Everyone wants something: always ask yourself 'Why is this person telling me this?' and consider their information accordingly.
- How much obligation do news organisations have to verify every piece of information that comes in through user-generated content?
- Is it enough to simply mention that the information is unverified, or that the video has not been authenticated? Will users understand?
- Different organisations have different strategies: from full teams of fact-checkers at the New Yorker magazine, to publishing almost anything with disclaimers indicating it has not been checked. What are the advantages and disadvantages of these strategies?

 TOOLKIT

Readings and resources

Craig Silverman runs the news blog www.regrettheerror.com in which he discusses corrections and correction policies. His other writing, including that on internet verification and social media, is at Craigsilverman. ca, and his columns for the Poynter Institute are archived at www.poynter.org/author/craigsilverman/.

Andy Carvin is generally considered the pioneer of crowdsourced verification. He tweets (and retweets, prolifically) at @acarvin. His personal blog is at www.andycarvin.com/ and he maintains an archive of live blogs at http://storify.com/acarvin/.

Storyful is a crowdsourced news operation that has a detailed discussion of its verification processes at http://blog.storyful.com/category/social-journalism-2/verification/.

BBC College of Journalism provides advice on verifying user-generated content at www.bbc.co.uk/journalism/skills/citizen-journalism/bbc-ugc-hub/.

Poynter Institute gives training and advice on a number of areas for journalists. An archive of their material on verifying information and material can be found at www.poynter.org/tag/verification/.

Alfred Hermida at the University of British Columbia researches and blogs about the impact of social media on journalism. His blog, at www.reportr.net/, is an excellent resource of current thinking and research.

>>Chapter 10<<

JOURNALISM AND THE LAW

Overview

This chapter deals with the changes in law that have arisen in response to social-journalism techniques and new-media technologies. It sets out the attempts by the network community to respond both to the changes, and to the law's response. These frame the fundamental questions of what constitutes journalism, and who is a journalist, and what rights and obligations arise from those questions.

Key concepts

- Aggregation
- Codes of conduct
- Copyleft
- Copyright
- Creative Commons
- Curation
- Fair use
- Journalistic identity
- Legal codes
- Regulation

Springboard

- *Privilege*: you have a particular privilege by virtue of being a journalist. Respect the people who grant you that privilege: the public.
- *Be fair*: if you use someone else's ideas or material, give credit and payment where applicable.
- *Honour requests*: if someone asks you to hold off on publishing something, or tells you something off the record, honour that. If you feel it is imperative that you publish, do so knowing you may never be able to use that source again.
- *The web is a public place*: assume that all communication will be made public; assume that everything you do online will remain online for ever.
- *Professional status*: what does it mean to be a 'professional journalist', and who decides whether you are?

What is a journalist?

For almost as long as there have been journalists, there has been struggle over journalistic identity. What, exactly, are we? As actors in society, newsmakers have laid claim to being culturally and socially more significant than other industries, trades and professions. The role of finding out what is going on and reporting it to others is usually deemed socially significant, and important to the function of government, especially in democratic societies, where the news industry is often characterised as a 'fourth estate', a watchdog on the other estates of government, religion and the judiciary.

This claim to importance has resulted in considerable privileges for the news industry and its practitioners – the right to observe the process of government, specific kinds of access to the apparatus of state and to societal elites, rights to free comment, and the power to confer specific rights of anonymity on sources. These rights are not universal, and are granted, abused and taken away in different ways in different countries, but the principle that journalists, because of their important function in society, are somehow different from other people remains in place, and 'journalistic privilege' remains a constant, albeit one under considerable pressure, and open to interpretation.

One of the ways in which journalistic privilege has been created is through specific skills that are believed to be the special domain of journalists: shorthand and objectivity/balance are usually considered key (Allan, 2010: 23). Shorthand is rarely taught these days (except in journalism schools in the UK, where the standing rule against the use of recording devices in courtrooms makes it a necessity), which leaves

Journalistic privilege

The privilege accorded to journalists allows them access to information and people in order to carry out the journalistic function of reportage.

Objectivity

Objectivity is the supposed completely neutral and balanced perspective that only a trained journalist has. Although the term is heavily contested, and many academics and journalists deny its relevance, it remains a key part of the ideology of journalism in the public discourse.

the ability to present information from multiple sources as an objective and balanced 'truth' as the main skill which journalists have that makes them different from society.

Journalistic identity, then, traditionally arises from three areas: the process of journalistic production (interviewing, access to sources, aggregation of information); the forms of journalistic output (the traditional pyramid – or inverted pyramid, depending on which side of the Atlantic you are – story form, the neutral stance, the absence of the subjective voice); and identity, which derives from access to the formal and industrialised news industry.

New technologies changed all of this: regulation, and the prohibitive cost of distribution, were the first to go. These effectively removed the formal news sector's monopoly on the distribution of news. The next barriers to fall were the formal voice and structure of news stories: new voices arose in the form of bloggers and forum posters. It can be argued that the process of sourcing was the last to go: it was not until large amounts of public information began to coalesce online that the possibility existed for people not attached to the news industry to aggregate information and create news.

This is not to say, of course, that traditional news outlets, forms and processes do not still exist (they do), and do not still dominate public discourse in many ways, but that the definition of what a journalist is, and what they do, is under increasing tension, and is beginning to crack and fragment as a result of that tension.

Journalistic privilege

In the Anglo-Saxon world, at least, the notion of journalistic privilege remains enshrined in law to some extent. This privilege essentially allows a journalist to offer a source confidentiality – that is, the journalist cannot be compelled to reveal the identity of the source, even by a court of law. This privilege is unique to a handful of professions: lawyers, religious confessors and journalists, and, although it is something most journalists will never need to test, remains an important part of the protections accorded to journalists.

There is no clear consensus within the legal frameworks of any of the Anglo-Saxon countries as to whether journalistic privilege extends to bloggers, social-media commentators or informal news organisations. A number of early rulings in various courts seemed to indicate that bloggers and informal journalists do have journalistic privilege, but, recently, that has changed.

Bloggers vs journalists

The debate around who is a journalist is most often framed as the conflict between 'bloggers' and 'journalists'. Although this is a somewhat dated dichotomy, it remains a useful benchmark of the debate, since to some extent it clarified the distinctions between formal and informal journalism.

The waters became muddier, however, as social media greatly expanded the range of opportunities for amateur journalists to publish information, and as news organisations began to move into this new, unregulated space. Increasingly, the distinction

Bloggers

Blog is an abbreviation of 'weblog', originally a log of daily life, information and material collected online, usually by an amateur. The word and practice have changed considerably, but 'blogger' is still used to refer to a casual or unprofessional online content producer, and contrasted with the 'professional' journalist.

between who is or is not a journalist is feeling irrelevant, at least to large parts of the population, but, given that there remain substantial privileges and obligations that accrue to journalists, it remains an unresolved tension.

The tension revolves around a number of areas – the legal rights of journalists, access and obligations.

Access

Access to sources is traditionally one of the ways by which a journalist's credibility and experience can be measured. Access can mean both the trust built up between a journalist and the elites within their beat, or patch (such as a long-trusted political reporter to whom no governmental doors are closed), or to the expertise and experience which gives the journalist the understanding of an issue or event which is needed to make sense of it for the audience.

Access can be a result of years of experience, but it can also be the result of a formal process of credentialing and verification. Despite the decreasing formality of the news sector, the erosion of the power and influence of formal news institutions, and the rise of informal and amateur news outlets and creators, elite structures within society often still rely on formal credentials from journalists before access is granted.

Courts, police officers, political and sporting events, and press conferences may all be off-limits to people deemed to be 'non-journalists', with the onus increasingly on the journalists to prove they are such (Niles, 2011). Having formal access can make it easier to be first with the news, but whether that matters is a separate question.

> ## Embargo
>
> An embargo is a formal request from an organisation to a news outlet to 'hold' a piece of information until a specific date or time. They are not legally binding, but breaking an embargo may damage your chances of further access to information.

> ## Chatham House rule
>
> The Chatham House rule says that any information discussed in a specific meeting or event may be used, provided no identification is given as to its provenance. Although it was devised by the Chatham House think-tank in London for its own meetings, the phrase and the rule are still widely used in any public discussion that should be considered 'off the record'.

Obligations

Official journalistic status does not only confer privileges, it carries obligations, ones with sometimes harsh penalties for breaking.

Embargoes

Information may be provided early to news organisations in order to give them time to prepare reports in advance. The agreement in an embargo is that they will not publish anything until after the embargo has passed. Information may be embargoed for a variety of reasons: companies wanting to wait until the stock exchange is closed, for example. An embargo is not legally binding, but it is a traditional mark of respect within the news industry that they are not broken.

Social media have damaged the embargo, to the point that public-relations experts advise clients not to request them, but to expect that information will be released to the public as soon as it has been released from the company (Kennedy, 2012). As one expert puts it: 'asking for a public embargo in the world of social media is like taking Kate Middleton into a room full of photographers and saying "don't shoot" ' (Oakes-Ash, 2011: 1).

However, for a journalist with privileged access, breaking an embargo can prove threatening to your access: you may find yourself cut off from further material from that source. Private-company embargoes are simply a matter of respect and trust – there is unlikely to be any legal ramification for breaking one. There are other forms of restrictions that journalists are expected, and sometimes compelled, to honour.

Elections

In Canada and France, among other countries, election results are released slowly, as the time for the closure of polling stations is different across time zones. It has always been the case in Canada that news organisations are forbidden from publishing the results of polls in the east of the country until the polling stations in the west are closed, so that rumours of preliminary results do not skew the voting that has not yet taken place. Before the advent of social media and the internet, the only organisations that were capable of breaking this restriction were broadcasters, and the threat of financial and legal sanctions on them was enough to have them keep the rule. However, the rule was never clearly articulated as one that prevented private citizens from discussing events. As the boundaries between private discussion and public journalism began to be eroded, these restrictions came under pressure. In the 2011 elections, social-media users were discussing results hours before polling stations closed in the west, using the hashtag #tweettheresults and fruit and flower-based coded language (Talaga and Fong, 2011).

In the French presidential election in 2012, the announcement of the winner was embargoed until 8 p.m., but users on Twitter and other social-media sites used coded language ('Netherlands' for eventual winner François Hollande) and the hashtag #radiolondres (a reference to the government in exile of Charles de Gaulle) to discuss the results before they were officially allowed to (Bounea, 2012).

Court reporting

Tweeting and other forms of reporting from court is another area where the law is having to rapidly confront the realities of technological change. In most democratic countries, access to the proceedings of court cases is the public's right, and courts are a prime source of stories for news organisations, especially local ones. In a high-profile case, interest can be international, and often courtrooms are packed with journalists giving play-by-play for their audiences (Morris, 2011). Again, traditionally, news organisations and their representatives are given special privileges to report on proceedings: although there is an assumption that they are aware of the requirements of contempt of court, and therefore can be trusted not to prejudice the outcome of the trial. The changing technology of journalism, as well as the changing definition of who is a journalist, has resulted in the legal systems having to revisit assumptions that go back more than 100 years.

In recent guidance issued by the Chief Justice of England and Wales, the right to tweet or use live, text-based communications was given to all 'representatives of the media', but not to the general public, since those representatives do 'not pose a danger of interference to the proper administration of justice in the individual case' (Lord Judge, 2011). The Chief Justice does not identify

Contempt of court

In the UK (and other countries with similar legal systems), contempt of court is an offence which carries stiff penalties. Contempt of court can be triggered by either disobeying a specific instruction from the court, or publishing information likely to prejudice a trial's outcome.

who constitutes a 'representative of the media', or what 'the media' is, which leaves the judgement open to interpretation by individual judges, and possibly to their own legal proceedings (Rozenberg, 2011).

In Canada, the legal system has swung the other way, and at least one trial has been closed to the general public because of the fear that unscrupulous journalists may publish material that will prejudice the trial. Accredited journalists were permitted to attend the Calgary trial of Dr Aubrey Levin, but only Canadian ones, who could be bound by Canadian law to honour restrictions on the publication of evidence. The issue in this case was that Levin is South African (and has a considerable history and notoriety in that country), and there would have been possibly more interest in the trial there than in Canada, but South African journalists could not in the view of Judge Bob Wilkins be trusted not to prejudice the trial, through publication of material on social media and the internet which could be accessible to the Canadian public and jury (Martin, 2011).

Aggregation, quoting, fair use and copyright

As the profession of journalism changes, the specific process of turning raw information into a news product has come under scrutiny, and the question of when data becomes journalism remains fundamental to the debate.

On a continuum in which raw information exists on the top, and formally presented packaged news exists on the bottom (analogous to the vertical axis of the matrix presented in Chapter 1), the question that arises is, at what point does the raw information become journalism, and therefore subject to the rights and restrictions that accrue to the news industry?

This continuum is sometimes expressed as the transition from raw data to curation, through aggregation and then to journalism. The technicalities of these processes are discussed in considerable detail in Part 1 of this book; the issue under question here is, when does information go from being information in its own right (and therefore something that can be claimed and owned), to being the source for another kind of information? This is more than simply an abstract question – it raises considerable concerns that touch on copyright, fair use and quoting.

Journalists have always made stories out of other people's words and information – from interviews to press conferences, to material published elsewhere, news is made up of second-hand material brought together in a formal structure (some news contains original, first-hand observation, but any perusal of a news product will show how rare that actually is). People are used to being quoted in the news – interviews, comments made in a public place, formal speeches and publications are all acceptable sources, and it is extremely rare for a quoted source to object to having their words used in the service of a news product. For most sources, the benefit of being quoted in the news is worth the negligible cost of making the material available: sources either have no particular financial attachment to the information given or, if they do, the publicity (or other rewards) afforded by the news machine is enough. In addition, conventional news practices and technological limitations also ensure that it was extremely

Fair use

Under copyright law, fair use allows for the quoting or excerpting of content for the purposes of commentary and critique. A book critic may quote a section of a book in order to illustrate a discussion; a review of an art show may reproduce an image from the show. How much can be used, and what, exactly, constitutes 'discussion' is open to interpretation.

rare (and usually unethical) for someone to appear in the news without being aware of being recorded or listened to.

As with everything else, technology has changed this in two ways – the possible financial benefits, and the potential invasion of privacy. New forms of news, aggregation and curation, especially, take content and words from publicly available material (from blogs, social media and other online material) and re-purpose it for their own benefit. Although the convention of the medium (the ethos of share and share alike runs pretty strongly through social networks) is that this is to be expected (and even encouraged), it can be a risk to re-use material in this way, especially if you represent a formal or commercial news organisation.

Users who object to having their material re-used by news organisations usually do so for one of two reasons: privacy or copyright. Privacy is extensively discussed in Chapter 8, so the focus will now be on copyright.

The Huffington Post is widely praised for its innovative news model – combining original reporting with blogs and comment (often from celebrities) and aggregated news content from other organisations. This is either a brilliant and innovative business model, or theft (or both) depending on who you are speaking to.

 But too often it [aggregation] amounts to taking words written by other people, packaging them on your own Web site and harvesting revenue that might otherwise be directed to the originators of the material. In Somalia this would be called piracy. In the mediasphere, it is a respected business model. (Bill Keller, New York Times (Keller, 2011))

This is only part of what can only be called a 'spat' that erupted between the New York Times and the Huffington Post in early 2012, but the fervour with which people leapt into the fray indicates that this is a contentious issue for people across the spectrum of journalistic practice.

Copyright law does not clarify what is fair use in terms of curation, and the ideal of only using material that is available through Creative Commons is unrealistic; there need to be guidelines on what fair use of other news organisations' content entails. A number of possibilities exist as to what would warrant fair curation, many of them built on the ideals of the copyleft movement.

Copyright and copyleft: theft and fair use

At its basis, the issue under discussion is the definition of copyright, and of journalism. Whether material posted on a social network belongs to the poster, the network proprietors or is in the public domain is a complex question, and although most people's eyes glaze over at the thought of having to read all those end-user licensing agreements, copyright is the primary mechanism protecting news organisations' content from theft, and is essential to understand.

Copyright law differs from country to country, but almost every country in the world is a signatory to the various international conventions on

Intellectual property

There are a range of intellectual-property rights that exist but the most applicable to technology and innovation are patents, copyright and design rights. They all refer to ownership rights of original creative thought. The problem with intellectual property is enforcement and proof. This is also discussed in Chapter 12.

copyright and intellectual property, and the basic principles remain the same. Copyright attaches to intellectual artefacts in two forms: moral rights and legal rights. The moral right of copyright is that which gives a person the right to be identified as the author or creator of a work, and is usually non-transferable. The legal right is the right to sell the work, copies of it, or derivative products, and that is transferable, or saleable. When a media product is created, the journalist usually sells that on to the publisher or broadcaster (explicitly in the case of a freelancer, implicitly for a staff reporter), and legal right is transferred to the new owner. Further rights, to syndication, to compilation, to translation and to the creation of new forms of the product may or may not be transferred with the legal right – read your contracts carefully.

Copyright

D.M. Berry's *Copy, Rip, Burn* (2008) is an excellent introduction to the politics of copyright and the copyleft movement. Every journalist needs an understanding of copyright law within their local context – a good local 'law for journalists' book should be on your shelf at all times.

Free and open source

The open-source software movement arose in response to the increasing commercialisation of software development in the 1970s and 1980s. There are two main aspects of the Free Software Movement – one is the creation of software that is free to use, the other is the creation of software that is 'open source', i.e. that can be edited and recompiled by users. Technically, open source refers only to software that is editable, that can be recompiled, but, in practice the phrase now tends to refer to anything that can be freely shared.

Copyright is a legal construct, and the law is not prescient: it can take a while for the law to catch up with technological advances. There is a fairly common belief within online communities that everything on the internet is fair game – given how long it has taken the law to catch up with the technology, people might be forgiven for believing that this is the case. The fact is, though, that copyright attaches to all created objects, whether it has been explicitly stated or not – the lack of a copyright declaration on a photograph does not mean it is in the public domain, and can be freely used. When in doubt as to the copyright status of an image, don't use it.

This is not to say that things aren't used, and abused, routinely, on the internet. It might have been common practice to take without credit, and reuse images, text and even whole stories on blogs and news sites, but, thanks to greater vigilance on the part of producers, and a greater awareness of the legal (and social) ramifications of using content without permission, this is changing.

As a formally constructed content-creating organisation or individual, whether you are the BBC or an independent blogger, copyright is important to observe: one lawsuit can destroy your business or career. More important, though, is the fact that if you create media content for a living, you need people to respect your copyright in order to pay the bills, and you can't expect your rights to be respected if you disrespect others'.

Creative Commons and copyleft

The copyleft movement was created in 2001 as an alternative to copyright. Building on the Gnu Public Licensing system of open-source and open-copyright software development, a set of licences and conventions were created by which users could share and limit the uses of their content without resorting to the proscribed mechanisms of copyright ownership. Creative Commons licences can be used by anyone, and allow creators to specify how their content can be used. By creating a standardised set of licences and restrictions, Creative Commons makes it easy for creators to control the ways in which their content is used while still making it available (Creative Commons, 2011).

Copyleft

At its simplest, the copyleft movement is a non-legalistic approach to the fair sharing and use of information and creative artefacts. The best-known example of copyleft is the Creative Commons organisation which creates a community of people sharing content under clear guidelines.

Creative Commons is not a single licence, but a series of licences that can be applied, giving and keeping certain rights. Users can select from the options to customise exactly which rights they retain, and which they are making available. As of version 3.0 of the CC licence (2011), the rights are:

Creative Commons

The Creative Commons is a co-operative organisation that allows anyone to use their guidelines and licences for their material. By creating a standard set of definitions and codes, Creative Commons makes it easy to find material you can use, and to protect it.

- Attribution (BY): the requirement that the creator be credited;
- ShareAlike (SA): the requirement that any works incorporating the original work be licensed under the same terms;
- NoDerivs (ND): no derivative works may be created, the work cannot be edited or altered in any way;
- Non-Commercial (NC): the work may not be used for commercial purposes;
- Public Domain (Ø): the work is fully in the public domain, and may be used, altered and redistributed without any restrictions.

To license a work under Creative Commons, users simply add the letters CC (or the Creative Commons logo), and the letters signifying the specific rights they wish to claim. A work such as a photograph with the letters CC BY–NC indicates that anyone may use the photograph provided attribution is given, and that the work is non-commercial (if you wish to use the photograph in a commercial product, you will need to negotiate directly with the photographer). The letters CC SA–ND indicate that the photograph can be used by anyone, provided the work is not altered in any way, and that the new work also be licensed under the same agreements. A full guide to using Creative Commons in your own work can be seen at: http://creativecommons.org/.

Creative Commons and the copyleft movement have succeeded not just because the idea is good, but because the licences have been adopted across the World Wide Web and social media, and have the power of the crowd behind them. Many social-media sites, including Flickr, Wikipedia and YouTube, embed Creative Commons licences directly within their systems, allowing users to easily mark their work with the licences, and others to find them.

Creative Commons can be an extremely useful way for media creators to find content they can use: Google offers the option to search for Creative Commons licensed material under its Advanced Search options, available at the bottom of the search page. By limiting your image or video search to files that are free to use, share, or alter, it is easy to find images or videos that can be used on your site.

Creative Commons, and its adoption by the social-media community, is another example of the ways in which the social-media landscape is changing the traditional producer/consumer relationship.

Even large commercial news organisations have adopted Creative Commons: in 2009 Al Jazeera began making some of their video footage available under the CC licence. Users could use, edit, redistribute and pass on to others, provided credit was given. Footage of the Arab Spring uprisings of 2011 and 2012, as well as of the blockade of Gaza, were made available to other broadcasters and the general public. In the view of Mohamad Nanabhey of Al Jazeera English, what they have lost in potential revenue, they have gained in increased audience and profile across the world: 'A large part of embracing free culture is accepting the fact that you are forsaking control in exchange for something greater – the empowerment of the creative community' (Creative Commons, 2011).

It is this empowerment that is so important in the modern world of media and social networks – the rigid requirements of the hierarchical relationships between producer and consumer have been replaced by the more fluid social relationships of the collaborative network. In this space, maintaining one's relationships is important, because one's status within the network, and one's ability to utilise it, depend on the respect with which one is viewed by the rest of the network. You cannot expect to gain from the sharing ethos of the network if you do not also contribute to it.

Fair curation

This brings us back to the question of curation. The Creative Commons licences don't fully encompass curation, and journalistic practice and fair use have always allowed for the quoting of content, which leaves the practices of curation and aggregation remaining somewhat unresolved. A number of people and organisations have been working on developing guidelines for fair curation, and although there is no clear consensus, they all have a few key ideas as their basis, and they all make the journalistic process more transparent than it currently is.

> # Curator's Code
>
> The Curator's Code is a proposed set of rules governing the use of ideas, links and content from other sources in the process of curation and aggregation. The site is at www.curatorscode.org/.

One of the proposed sets of guidelines is the Curator's Code (www.curatorscode.org/), which has as its main argument the importance of honouring and attributing 'discovery', the information or idea that led to a story, not just the information used in the process of creating the story. Interviewed by the New York Times, the creator of the code, Maria Popova, focused on the work that has gone into creating information, and the importance of respecting that work: 'Discovery of information is a form of intellectual labor,' she said. 'When we don't honor discovery, we are robbing somebody's time and labor. The Curator's Code is an attempt to solve some of that' (in Carr, 2012).

The Curator's Code has not been universally adopted or even universally accepted, as the response has been mixed, to say the least. Despite this, it raises some interesting questions about the obligations of journalists to those people whose information and ideas they use. For some, it is as simple as behaving yourself and treating others as you would be treated (Nolan, 2012); for others, the code's guidelines on full attribution are an unobtainable ideal, always coming up against the reluctance of commercial organisations to send traffic away from their sites (Arment, 2012).

It is hard at this point to judge whether the Curator's Code (or the even more newly proposed Council on Ethical Blogging and Aggregation) will have any staying power. In the world of the internet, sites, ideas, conventions and codes come and go like the tide. In the long term, though, sites are as likely to need others to link to them and source them as they are to need others to link to and source from, which takes us back to the basic rule of playground behaviour: treat others the way you would want to be treated yourself.

Conclusion

It would be impossible to write a chapter that permanently codifies exactly how journalists and media producers should behave, for all places and all time. What this chapter has done is to lay out some guidelines and considerations to keep in mind.

First and foremost: know the law for where you are, and what you are doing. Ignorance of the law is no excuse, and ignorance of any kind is inexcusable for a journalist.

Guard your copyright closely, and take care to guard that of others. Be respectful of people's property, and be aware that the crowd is all-knowing, and very powerful. You are only one node in this network, one person in the crowd, and everyone else deserves the same respect and consideration you would want for yourself.

 CASE STUDY > ## Cooks Source

Navigating the legal minefield of copyright, public domain, aggregation and curation can be difficult, and the temptation to simply ignore all of the rules and do what you want under the pressure of deadlines can be great. However, as one editor learned, the repercussions, and the revenge of the crowd, can be fatal. Cooks Source was a print (and Facebook) magazine containing recipes and cooking advice with limited distribution, primarily in the eastern United States.

In the 'Pumpkin Fest' issue in October 2010, the magazine reprinted an entire five-year-old blog post from cookery writer Monica Gaudio. Gaudio writes primarily about medieval cookery, and the post in question was a discussion of the evolution of apple pie, with two period recipes transcribed and updated. When Gaudio discovered that her article had been reprinted without her permission, she contacted the editor of the magazine, Judith Griggs, requesting an apology and a small donation to the Columbia School of Journalism in compensation. Briggs responded in almost textbook 'internet don't' fashion: 'But honestly Monica, the web is considered "public domain" and you should be happy we just didn't "lift" your whole article and put someone else's name on it! It happens a lot, clearly more than you are aware of, especially on college campuses, and the workplace.' (Griggs, in Mamatas, 2010).

Griggs then went on to critique Gaudio's writing, and suggest that Gaudio should pay Griggs for the editing and publicity gained by the reprinting of her article in the magazine. Gaudio responded by blogging about the incident, reprinting Griggs's email in full, and asking advice from her community on what to do. The outcry was massive, the campaign moved to Cooks Source's Facebook page, and the story was picked up by Salon.com, CNN, the Wall Street Journal and countless other media outlets. The Facebook page became 'the virtual stockade' (Williams, 2010) – lambasting Griggs and Cooks Source for stealing content, and for the aggressiveness of the response to Gaudio's request. The Facebook campaign soon coalesced around contacting Griggs's advertisers (her source of income), and collecting evidence of other instances of lifted material. Several other publishers and individuals contacted Cooks Source demanding compensation and apologies for the use of their material, and several advertising clients dropped their ads. By the middle of November, the magazine had closed (Gill, 2010).

The entire incident had taken two weeks: from Gaudio discovering the use of her material, to the closure of the magazine. The crowd works fast.

There are two issues here: one is the theft of copyrighted material, a practice which is prevalent online and offline, and the other is the aggressive 'you and what army' response from the editor. Plagiarism and theft are unethical, and can result in legal sanction; however, the cost of pursuing a legal resolution has often deterred victims, and it has been possible for unethical publications to proceed with impunity. It's clear that Cooks Source's business model was predicated at least in part on the use of unpaid-for material, under the supposition that nobody would know, care, or be able to respond to the theft of their words. The internet makes plagiarism easy – a quick Google and you can find anything you need – but it also makes finding out that you have been plagiarised easy, and social media make 'naming and shaming' the response of choice for injured parties.

What made this story so compelling, and predicated its international publicity, was Griggs's response. The bluntness of the email Griggs sent, the audacity of requesting compensation for her editing service, and the general rudeness meant that Griggs herself became an internet meme, her words reprinted, her identity spoofed and her magazine ridiculed around the internet. Griggs may have felt she was in the right (and she is at least correct in that plagiarism and theft are rife across the internet), but she did not understand the dynamics of the social space she worked within. Violating community values can destroy a publication; you can't expect the community to support you if you don't support the community in return.

Key reflections

- The social web is a public place, and it never forgets. It may be tempting to bend the rules, just this once, because you're under pressure, but the risk is massive – you may get away with it now, but it may come back to bite you.
- Your relationships within the web are important – the web is your source, your audience and your peer group. Treat everyone within it fairly, as you would want to be treated yourself.
- The law is slow, and may not have caught up with what is happening online. Obey the law, but be aware of new developments in social norms and expectations online.
- How do you protect your information from theft? How important is it to do so?
- As a start-up media company, how do you balance the need to be public with the need to protect your copyright?

TOOLKIT

Readings and resources

Creative Commons: (http://creativecommons.org/) holds a wealth of information about the copyleft movement, as well as links to resources of material that can be used under the CC licensing system.

Copy, Rip, Burn (2008): D.M. Berry's excellent introduction to the politics and philosophy of copyright and the copyleft movement.

David Carr of the New York Times: is active in questions of copyright and online codes of conduct. The *New York Times* maintains an archive of his work at http://topics.nytimes.com/top/reference/timestopics/people/c/david_carr/index.html and he tweets at @carr2n.

The Curator's Code: is available at www.curatorscode.org/ and the website also contains links to discussions and ideas in the area of attribution and copyright.

The BBC College of Journalism: maintains an archive of advice and ideas at www.bbc.co.uk/academy/collegeofjournalism/. The BBC's guidelines on copyright and fair dealing are available at www.bbc.co.uk/academy/collegeofjournalism/how-to/how-to-use-social-media/social-media-copyright-and-fair-dealing.

Part 4

THE NEW ECONOMICS OF JOURNALISM

>>Chapter 11<<

FREELANCING AND BUILDING YOUR BRAND

Overview

As journalists become more isolated yet empowered as unique entities of journalism, they grapple with how best to connect with audiences across multiple touch points. Questions of identity and branding need to be considered as boundaries become increasingly blurred: where does one role finish and another start? Journalists must be aware of how best to interpret notions of private and professional selves, making choices of how much of their personality to include in networked outputs. This chapter also explores opportunities and implications for working freelance.

Key concepts

- Commissions
- How much me?
- Identity
- Online conduct
- Pitching
- Reputation management
- Trust and credibility
- Working freelance

Springboard

- *Celebrate individualism*: understand where you fit in a wider web of connections and have faith that you are special, with plenty to offer. Despite being unpredictable, working as a freelancer could mean lots of open doors.
- *Be a participatory connector*: you need trust to work in a network and that comes from being there, and being transparent and honest about who you are and what you do. Don't be a parasite on the network; rather work on genuine connections.
- *Be transparent. Be detailed*: adding minutiae to your online presence can add value, but remember you are not in control of what gets amplified: the crowd is. You could be doing the equivalent of shouting from the rooftop naked – make sure your comments are worthy and appropriate.
- *Who are you?*: be clear on your own notion of private and professional. Make decisions on whether you need different personas for multiple identities or if you need to compromise or align with a news organisation. Visualising your audience helps. They make a big contribution to gauging what is socially appropriate to say in what is a very public space.
- *Identities are fluid*: presenting who you are happens in a constantly shifting cycle. Your identity is presented, compared, adjusted and compromised against a constellation of personal and professional forces. Be prepared to adapt to the backdrop of cultural, economic and political realities.

Introduction

The media industry is increasingly fluid as the potential for simultaneous communication on multi-devices on mass and interpersonal channels grows. To carve out a role and identity within this new media landscape, journalists must develop an expanded perspective on the interplay between different networks, and harness the enthusiasm for a new era in reporting.

In this constantly evolving matrix of media, journalists are more than one thing to more than one person. A foreign correspondent may file a piece to camera for consumption on a prime-time broadcast, act as a fixer for a fringe TV channel, write a blog under an alternative persona and use real-time updates to create a personally branded news wire. A paparazzo photographer may file celebrity gossip for a 'mainstream' magazine owned by a media tycoon but provide tip-offs for a celebrity blogger and images for a photo wire such as Big Pictures. A court reporter may be employed full time by the local newspaper but run a website on gardening and a Twitter feed on cookery. Filing to multiple outlets under multiple identities is par for the course as media fragment.

It is also increasingly apparent that to rely on a single printed portfolio to get a job would be foolhardy. Journalists are likely to work in an increasingly insecure job market, an inevitable consequence of a profession whose core model is in flux. The local newspaper – the traditional first foot on the ladder – has abandoned its trainee schemes and been hit harder than almost any other publishing genre by the economic recession and shifts in publishing trends. Even highly trained professionals are likely to spend significant periods working freelance, on short-term contracts or in other unstable positions.

One of the most complex questions from working across a fragmented media landscape is one of identity. Journalists find themselves with multiple roles and relationships, depending on their outputs and objectives. A reporter with a traditional working practice relied on a subset of trusted contacts and notions of identity drawn from title, authority within a newsroom, training, qualifications, superiors and colleagues – and the all-important press pass. But journalists may also find themselves working at the grassroots level, more closely connected to a larger range of audiences and sources.

Journalists working within (and outside) media organisations find themselves increasingly unable to define what they do in a single job title. They exist in an evolving collaboration with peers and users. Reporters – especially journalists starting out on their careers – need to recognise that the old roles of journalism don't always apply and that a top-down approach won't work. Against this social backdrop, the voice of the individual becomes clearer and identities blur. As discussed in Chapters 2 and 3, sources and outputs can be configured in diverse ways to frame work flows and identities. As a result, the word 'journalist' dissipates. There are lots of operating journalists but they may be bloggers, freelancers, broadcasters, podcasters, tweeters, YouTube commentators – or any combination of these.

Brand identity

There is a growing emphasis on personal branding and journalistic entrepreneurship within this landscape. We understand that brand is contentious, and it is not our intention to reduce journalists to a marketing phenomenon. We maintain, however, that brand identity is an important component of modern journalism practice, and reputation building: your stamp as a journalist. News correspondents are gaining authority and influence through social media and becoming 'network nodes', attracting significant audiences independent of their parent brands (Newman, 2011).

As such, it is important to understand what forces are at play as journalists engage directly

> # Grassroots journalism
>
> In Dan Gillmor's 2004 book of the same name he talks of journalism 'by the people for the people'. The concept of working at the grassroots level infers a journalist's ability to exist within a complex network. They must understand how the network and media ecology work to be a trusted part of it.

> By interacting and becoming known for a story at a personal level it means people come to you. [Social networks are] the fastest way you can interact with anyone. (Neal Mann, editor, in Cook, 2011b)

> Journalists serious about enlarging and maintaining a regular audience for their work might manipulate their products to incorporate SEO (search engine optimisation) techniques, audience management and traffic growth strategies. These alterations may not affect the ultimate quality of their work but they represent a growing consideration for journalists who seek to establish a personal brand. (Sivek, 2010)

> # Journalists as brands
>
> While controversial, referring to journalists as brands is a way of acknowledging that journalists are increasingly visible in their own right, with their own news outputs, identities, reputations and products. It is a notion of having an individual stamp or credible interpretation of journalism within the social space.

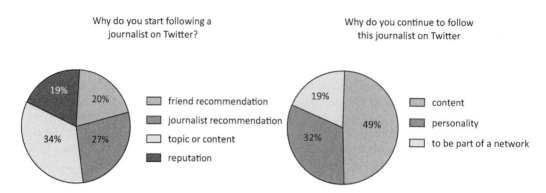

FIGURES 11.1 and 11.2   A survey of 100 followers of three journalists on Twitter. It found reputation and recommendations as the main reasons for beginning to follow a journalist. The majority said they continue to follow a journalist because of the content.

Presenting self

Zizi Papacharissi has worked extensively on the presentation of self in virtual life (2002, 2009, 2011). Wynn and Katz (1997) dismiss notions of alleged anonymity online and the ability to sustain a fragmented self. Garfinkel (2001) argues that privacy is now dead and that individuals exist in, and must cope with, a more transparent society. As Gilpin states, online interactions take place in a space that is 'neither distinctly professional nor distinctly personal' (in Papacharissi, 2011).

Managing identity online

Networking and joining in conversations helps people know about you. Respond to comments and treat social spaces as public spaces.

with audiences. As shown in Figure 11.1, a study of 100 followers of three journalists on Twitter found that specific content is not a strong reason why people begin to follow the journalist; it is the trappings of brand, recommendations and links that draw in audiences. But it is the content that keeps them. So a good brand may help an audience first connect with an individual journalist but it is the content that will keep them engaged (Cook, 2011).

Building a brand

As Tom Peters wrote in *The Brand Called You*, journalists have to develop a sense of 'Me Inc.' by understanding who they are and what they can deliver to audiences (Peters, 1997). In many countries, such as France, journalistic identity is still afforded via an official press pass, and many journalists construct a sense of their identity from a byline, their peers and superiors, a pay cheque or from being a staffer at a national newspaper or broadcaster. Being officially attached to a major news organisation simplifies questions of journalistic identity. Nowadays your calling card can also be about what you can learn, analyse, interpret, research and inform from the social world around you.

The process of constructing a professional identity is a complex one but it can evolve over time as you become more and more in tune with the network. Journalists should consider their interests and passions. Which news agendas do you follow and connect with? Most importantly, consider what makes you unique. Identify the qualities or characteristics that could make you distinctive from what is out there already, or what you could do more successfully. There will be subtle niches or skills that you can exploit and more than one style of project you can take on. Aim to have a portfolio of competences. Your brand of journalism will combine your objectives, the social ties you have and nurture, and the content you can output.

Professional identity

With myriad platforms on which reporters can interact with audiences, it is essential to have an idea of who you are and what you want to achieve. This will affect decisions about what you post online and the tone in which you write.

Establishing a niche means you can start developing an authoritative voice. Journalist Graham Holliday has proved this by becoming the 'go to' person in Rwanda. 'If the niche is geographic, then cover the oddest patch you can think of or cover the news in that patch in a way that leaves no stone unturned' (Holliday, 2010). Perhaps you add value through commentary and analysis. Your niche could be that you are simply the best person, and the best connected, for a particular topic. In every case, think positively about being the best you can be, showcasing your skills and vocalising what you do well.

Josh Halliday used social networking to showcase his journalistic abilities for a year before landing a job as the Guardian's trainee media and technology reporter in June 2010. 'Without wanting to sound too prescriptive, because we are not all self-aggrandising journodrones – the key is to map out interests, research the market and remember that what you publish online could quite easily make it before the eyes of a potential employer. It's a first step into the right circles without being pushy, obtrusive or unnaturally self-assertive.' (Halliday, 2011).

Journalists who can spot opportunities and develop personal brands can either reinforce a news organisation's status or launch independent projects. Brian Stelter started out anonymously launching TV Newser, which soon became required reading among industry insiders. His reporting was so compelling that he was hired by the New York Times. Michelle Leder started publishing information everyone else had missed at Footnoted.com which she went on to sell as a media product.

 Social media and blogs can elevate a reporter to the level where he no longer needs the news organisation. Eventually a reporter with a big enough web presence and social media savvy can start a news start-up like TechCrunch or start a blog. (Patrick Thornton, 2009)

Choosing a name

Focusing your attention onto yourself as a brand also requires domain names, usernames and avatars that are fit for purpose. Occupy the network with multiple accounts that best reflect what you can do. Make sure your best work is highly visible as are your contact details and

Avatar

An avatar or handle is an online representation of yourself, either with a graphic or username.

links to all your online profiles. People in the field should know who you are. Whether you choose a nickname for its attribute of being memorable or your real name to favour being more easily searchable, be prepared to register several accounts and stick to them. It's easier to pick a

> This open and collaborative future for journalism – I have tried the word 'mutualised' to describe something of the flavour of the relationship this new journalism has with our readers and sources and advertisers – is already looking different from the journalism that went before. (Alan Rusbridger, 2010)

username that says who you are, not who pays you. Choose one based on your own first or last names, initials or nickname, or make up some clever handle that you can keep even as your occupational circumstances change.

Freelancer and Guardian writer Sarah Hartley has multiple personas, one of which is @foodiesarah – born from a Twitter account that she started when she was experimenting as a writer on a food column at the Manchester Evening News. 'The foodiesarah was accidental but I am stuck with it now! My brand is as a trusted source and I have built a reputation for that. I have tried to experiment with different accounts, even dividing personal and professional, but I feel the minutiae of people's lives does help you paint a picture of someone, developing trust and a connection.' (Hartley, 2011).

Journalist in the North of England, Nigel Barlow, also credits social media for springboarding his career: 'I quickly realised that the movers and shakers of journalism and the people I needed to know were on social media so I started to make connections, leaving comments on other people's sites, creating blog rolls, attending events and experimenting. I got my first job because I cultivated the brand in Manchester that I was a media savvy, media social person.' (Barlow, in Cook, 2011b).

> One of the things that helps you as a journalist is that you are seen as an authority on a particular subject, because then people will come to you with ideas. And one of the ways that helps you become an authority and take ownership of a story is if you are doing more than the big exciting story but also doing the nitty gritty. (Robert Peston, journalist in Cook, 2011b)

Finding an audience

The internet enables anyone to broadcast and create content but it does not guarantee you an audience. To build and establish yourself as a journalist, you need to develop online representations of yourself and avoid being too prescriptive about what they are. A personal visibility campaign will ensure that you reach out to people. After all, the appeal of social networks is as a stage for self-presentation and social connections. Writing on a blog or microblog helps show potential commissioning editors or employers who you are and what you are about.

If you do work for a larger media organisation, the chances are your social-media posts will be amplified to a wider audience through operational systems of input and output flow. Many news organisations now employ community editors and coordinators who retweet or repost content in different streams across multi-outputs, all of which will grow your visibility. It is likely that content-management systems will become more and more advanced in terms of categorising and steering feeds. Robert Peston has built a respected brand from the beginnings of an internal-communication email at the BBC, promoting issues and the language of business. The business editor became the most-read blogger in the UK during the 2008 financial crisis, building a reputation as a repository of information that mattered.

'Go to' person

A 'go to' person refers to someone who has become the authority on a subject. Journalists increasingly want to be seen as this person online for certain topics or content.

Social media expert Neal Mann operates under @fieldproducer and has built up an influential network harnessing what he calls the 'peer-to-peer' internet. He promotes the need to add value and engage with an audience without being a gatekeeper, 'knowing who is important and how it ticks'. He says journalists need to build up a visible presence in real life and online, in a range of social networks to connect staff and people remotely. He also advocates using Twitter in part as a news wire, and says being a 'go to' person is a relevant way to be a journalist and that social media 'is just another broadcast platform'.

> ## PSB and brands
>
> Public service broadcasters have an even trickier balancing act to achieve between central editorial policy and the individual journalists. There are extensive sets of guidelines on the use of social media, steering journalists away from joining political groups and offering advice on tone.

Maintaining and protecting your reputation

Given the interlocking nature of social networks, any professional wanting to operate harmoniously in a network must be aware of the pitfalls. Ill-advised contributions to social media platforms or misrepresentations can cost reputations. The network can seem like a humbling place when you consider Dan Gillmor's assertion that 'my readers know more than I do' (Gillmor, 2004). Journalist Johann Hari, formerly at The Independent, learnt this the hard way when he was forced to apologise and re-train after he was accused by journalists and bloggers of using quotes taken from books and interviews, and passing them off as his own (Hari, 2011). The very fluidity and permanence of the internet mean you will be pulled up if something is wrong.

Working across social media is no different to any other form of live correspondence: apply the same checks and controls. Just as certain sides of your personality may not be appropriate in editorial conference or on air, you may 'have to adjust [your] behaviour to make it appropriate for a variety of different situations and audiences' (Papacharissi, 2011). Have a clear image in your mind of the audience, as it matters when you determine what is socially acceptable and appropriate to say. Ultimately, would you be unhappy if your comments went viral? Social and professional lives are now interlocked in a way they never were before. Journalists need to decide how to separate and integrate them.

Interacting and posting to the network can seem quite terrifying as journalists reconcile a relatively new sensation: loss of control. The network is in control, not you. The amplification that occurs with content in social spaces is not necessarily what journalists want but what the collective chooses to spread and bring to the fore. Lots of journalists are more comfortable with a production process that involves edits and checks. Dealing with constant feedback, comments, suggestions and pressures can leave bloggers and journalists feeling profoundly stressed (Faure, 2008).

Transparency is key to maintaining an online reputation. Outspoken columnist Rod Liddle was accused of allegedly posting racist and misogynist comments on a Millwall Online web forum under the username monkeymfc. While it was never clear exactly what effect the revelations had on his career, Liddle was not kept in the running for an editorship at the Independent (Greenslade, 2010a). Similarly, David Pogue came under criticism for not revealing potential conflicts of interest between his reporting as a technology writer for the New York Times and his authorship of manuals. Journalists wanting to act as independent elements must equally adopt an ethical transparency if they are to profit from 'portable brand equity' (Fry, 2009).

It can also be terrifying to engage with a network where all is not what it seems: people with false identities, trolls and hoaxes abound. American student Tom MacMaster caused outrage when his 'A Gay Girl in Damascus' blog turned out to be a hoax. Thousands of users, journalists and commentators believed the posts to represent the plight of Amina, a Syrian woman fighting oppression and tyranny, only to find out the passionate writings about crackdowns on the Arab Spring protests were fictional and being written from Edinburgh. Negotiating the uncertainty of the social media space is discussed further in Chapter 9.

Disclaimers

These statements are a way of indicating to audiences who is speaking and with what voice, authority and capacity. If you have an individual blog or microblog and use it as a separate output to employment elsewhere you can make that clear. They are used extensively to limit liability.

Your profile may also need to take others into consideration. Make it clear that views expressed are your own and use a disclaimer if it is appropriate to be clear who is speaking and with what authority. Remember, any contractual obligations about internal communications and privacy are likely to hold true in social media. No employer would want complaints voiced in inappropriate channels.

Injecting personality

In the process of building a stamp of identity, journalists find themselves asking the question 'how much me?' as the boundaries between personal and professional identity have become more fluid. Social media has strengthened the potential for individual journalists to act as personal portals for news, while also offering audiences insights into life behind the scenes or their personal lives.

There are a range of approaches. A more personal touch has helped journalists improve engagement with their audiences: individuals are 'often more effective than brands in social spaces because the currency of social media is people and because of the extra trust involved in receiving news or information from people you know' (Newman, 2011).

It is still a tough balancing act to know how much personal life to integrate into that identity. Knowing what a war correspondent had for breakfast may add value but a serious political correspondent discussing choosing his socks could undermine credibility. The most successful journalists have a clear sense of who they are and what they are trying to achieve, and how to develop a brand around these, yet protect their professional identity.

The issue is further complicated, as the very convergence of the internet means that identities and connections are constantly overlapping across social spheres. A journalist's identity could be rolled out to multiple audiences via myriad tools on multiple outputs. Automated updates from one profile can connect with another, while different profiles can create layers of identity which may not always be compatible.

Thus, some would argue it impossible to divide professional and private lives. Jason Mills, ITV News Web Development Editor, for example, states that broadcasters cannot segment their comments once you they've become professional public figures. Jemima Kiss, technology correspondent for the Guardian, blurs professional and personal in her regular Twitter updates, which include everything from the ups and downs of her home life, to her love of tennis and the core technology of the job. Kiss believes that a 'picture, a byline and some personal interaction help to break down the impersonal nature of electronic communication' (in Newman, 2009: 37).

Radio and television sports presenter George Riley asserts that social media are a useful additional touch point with the audience, where he is known under a university nickname, @georgeyboy. 'There are so many journalists on social media that you only stand out if you have something new or interesting to say. I include personal stuff because I don't mind poking fun at myself: it

> If you are a public figure and you are using a public forum then the two [personas] are too intermingled. You can have a licence within your professional work to make personal comments but you can't sustain separate identities because people know. It falls under the accountability of being on a broadcast medium like any other. In this way the only danger should be that something irrelevant is broadcast, not dangerous or fundamentally wrong. (Jason Mills, 2011)

is the same personality that comes through on the radio, the journalist on air. If you tell people about a cup of coffee no one cares, but if you do something funny – like I dropped my car keys in a post box – then they respond. You do have to remember that it is not real life' (Riley, 2011).

He also warns that social media give rise to new complexities. He is regularly asked to re-tweet messages, and has to constantly make decisions about interactivity and relationships on social platforms, blocking people if necessary and keeping Facebook private. 'Twitter is a blank wall on which you are inviting people to graffiti. People come up to me in the players' bar after they have chatted on Twitter and think they know you, but they don't' (Riley, 2011).

Laurie Penny, also known as 'Penny Red', is now known in wider circles than as a journalist for The New Statesman. She also lets personal ideas show, but without revealing too much of her actual personal life, bar the flaming red hair of her avatar. She finds a way to engage with an audience without letting it all hang out, leaving a reader feeling like they know her, without actually knowing too much about her personal life. She negotiates that line well – friendly, open, but not giving too much information.

> There's a whole realm of my activity over which they have no control. Social networking is more anarchic. When online content was introduced it was well-led and coherently developed but social media raises a wealth of compliance issues for regulators. (Jon Snow, Channel 4 news anchor, 2011)

Danah Boyd has examined social networks and how they complicate the boundary between professional and personal identity (Boyd and Ellison, 2008; Boyd, 2010). Aldridge rethinks the concept of professionalism as a set of values and identities mobilised as a form of self-discipline (Aldridge and Evetts, 2003) while others reference the distinction between brand and reputation (Ettenson and Knowles, 2008). Online personal branding also offers complexities when managing different audiences or influencing others (Cardon and Granjon, 2005; Labrecque et al., 2011; Hearn, 2008).

Out of the limelight

Not all journalists want to enter into a notion of brand – and are far more comfortable behind the scenes. Indeed, for many investigative journalists, discretion is everything. The trend towards celebrity correspondents may be exacerbated by a tendency highlighted by Andrew Currah to reward journalists for their 'clickstream' activity rather than their contribution to journalism as credible profession (Currah, 2009).

Critics have accused more brand-focused journalists of losing sight of true journalism. The Washington Post columnist Gene Weingarten wrote a scathing attack on the dangers of journalists being more interested in self-promotion than breaking news (Weingarten, 2011). It can also be time-consuming to focus on brand alignments and referral traffic, activities which, at first glance, seem to have very little to do with the core functionality of the profession.

Who is the boss, anyway?

As journalists increasingly carve out stronger identities and a social-media presence for themselves, news organisations that employ those journalists have a range of management issues to consider, not least to reflect the growing trend from a 'bulletin-led model to a correspondent-led model' (Bell, 2009; Bell and Barber, 2011). There is a clash of editorial culture between unregulated peer-to-peer social exchanges on networks, and the regulated, inspected and moderated organisations at the 'objective' end of the media landscape.

Many news organisations have already attempted to formulate guidance, rules and norms on social media policies. The New York Times advises against promoting political views on social-networking sites and counsels that journalists avoid suggesting bias while tweeting. There are many conflicts of interest, and policies need to be malleable enough so as to withstand the constantly shifting relationships within a network modelled on lucid technologies.

Many media ventures are as known by their individual journalists as they are their central brand. With so many journalists engaging across different platforms, individuals must be sensitive to editorial values, reputation and political bias. Previously, journalists were constrained, because the single output that was a broadcast or newspaper article would be edited and written in allegiance with the paper's editorial policy. But social media has changed all that, as multi-outputs inevitably bestow multiple opportunities to express different views. Guidelines are being rewritten, while training programmes are under way, yet there seems to be no uniform position on how news organisations or freelancers approach questions of identity.

Media organisations have realised that there is an element of risk when individual journalists strike up direct access to the audience, whether that be down to factual errors, embarrassment, defamation or libel. Journalists acting as independent elements of the production process act without the hierarchy of newsroom filters and checks that would previously have 'caught' mistakes or poor judgement calls. An incorrect alert sent out on the Canwest News Service wire in February 2010 of the apparent 'death' of Canadian folksinger Gordon Lightfoot is one such example (Faguy, 2010).

The immediacy and wide reach of the network mean an error can be amplified very easily. Financial Times blogger Gideon Rachman often posts to his blog on the move with no subediting or additional checks. 'Every now and then I've thought "oh no, that was a stupid thing to say" and I wish I'd taken more time – if it was a newspaper column I would have done' (Newman, 2011). More worryingly still, indiscretions or poor judgement calls can be life-threatening if locations or geotagging are used without due care and attention.

Yet the culture clash of spontaneous, networked connections and controlled editorial policies remains. Grzegorz Piechota, Head of Public Awareness & Social Campaigns for Gazeta Wyborcza, Poland, cites issues with managing a foreign correspondent whose attitude to the network is different from central editorial control. 'He is interested in pop culture and the combination in his feed of news and entertainment is not what we want' (Piechota, 2011).

Anchorman Jon Snow on Channel 4 News distinguishes between his followers on social platforms and his on-air audience. He cites a tension about who is in charge of his Twitter feed as management would like more editorial control. At the time of writing, his feed, which is largely free from personal minutiae, had more followers than that of the programme. His blog was managed by producers, who also manage the replies.

Intellectual property lawyers and legal experts are grappling with issues of corporate control of social media accounts. The question of who 'owns' followers when journalists, now working more prominently as individual brands, move from newsroom to newsroom is pivotal. Noah Kravitz and Phone Dog became embroiled in a complex legal battle over who owns Twitter followers (BBC News, 2011).

Former BBC News chief political correspondent Laura Kuenssberg brought the question to the fore when she moved to be the ITV business editor in 2011. She had built up 67,000 followers at the BBC, due in no small part to her coverage of a controversial general election. She said: 'For me, such talk of the BBC "losing" thousands of digital consumers as I "took" them with me as I moved to become @ITVLauraK was based on a misunderstanding of this new medium. Given my belief that those who tweet have minds of their own, the clamour over what would happen to @BBCLauraK, the corporation's first official journalist Twitter stream, took me rather by surprise. But, more importantly, what the fuss did demonstrate was how central online reporting has become to the work of journalists. No doubt, having started tweeting as an experiment two years ago during the party conference season, it became almost as important to me to break stories on Twitter as it did to get them on air on the BBC's rolling news channel.' (Kuenssberg, in Gunter, 2011a).

Working as a freelance

Facilitated by cheap publishing tools, open access to audiences and structural changes to the media market, working as a freelance (or freelancer) is becoming more tenable. Many journalists will never work full time in one media outlet, or perhaps even want to. In order to make the most of the multidimensional shifts in the profession, though, a measure of entrepreneurial acumen needs to be developed.

Freelancers

Freelancers work for more than one media outlet and are largely self-employed. Stringers are still freelance but they may work regularly for one media outlet, sometimes on a fixed-term contract.

The most important place to start is meeting people. Hook up with people from local newspapers, the wires, photographers, other freelancers – they know what is happening long before anyone else does. Find out where everyone hangs out, both online and off via tweetups and social media groups. Spend time tapping into the social networks and hubs. Network to get yourself known. Remember to use email and Skype as well as DMs on Twitter, @mentions and connections on LinkedIn or social-bookmarking sites.

Getting published in mainstream news outlets is a skill. Take notice of specific editions of newspapers or programmes: read, watch and listen to as much content as you can. Which channels are going for which angles? Which magazines want what type of pegs? What writing tone, style and voice are they after? It can take years to get really good at mapping the subtlety of how media outlets make themselves unique – and therefore how to produce content for them. You are aiming to get in the head of commissioners or producers: getting editors to trust you is half the battle. In terms of who to contact, look up details of the section editors or even deputies, certainly not the editor-in-chief.

Commissions

These are work orders. They are specific agreements from an editor for a journalist to work on a specified project or report. They can be treated as contracts of work.

The pitch

The pitch is when you promote a story idea to an editor, often to be commissioned. It should contain what the story is – the unique angle, what multimedia you can propose, why the issue is important and who the main contacts will be. Don't forget to promote why you are the right person to produce the piece.

The 'up-pitch'

This is a skill where you make one topic have multiple angles and multiple sales points. It is the way one pitch can become multiple commissions.

The pitch is the first main contact point you have with a potential commission: be very concise and precise. Getting a pitch accepted is trial and error. It can take years before work starts coming to you, so don't take it personally if you don't get a reply. It's your choice whether you send the same pitch to lots of outlets or focus lots of efforts on outlet-specific pieces. Either way, use the platforms available to you as broadcast channels of what you can do, your ideas and your drive.

Understand how to make one topic match different audiences and learn to pitch across multiple outlets. If you get one commission consider how to make more with it, known as an 'up-pitch'. One commission for a conservation story in Cambodia could be re-pitched as a travel piece in an outdoor-pursuits magazine, a travel section in a newspaper, a piece of video footage for a video outlet, photos for a sharing website, or a human-interest profile piece in a different locality. Consider your existence in a 360-degree network.

You also have to visualise yourself as a business by structuring the commissions you achieve. If you can work for one 'big player' then get them to underwrite trips by giving them your best work and working around them. Have a pen and paper, mobile phone or tablet by your bed for ideas. Keep clipping files and a portfolio – this could be a different blog which is 'you as the pitching journalist'. Use online platforms as a place to write and create even if no one wants to commission you yet.

Freelance journalists have a lot to learn from the targeted services that have been offered by foreign correspondents for several years. Rob Crilly has worked as a stringer for various British, American and Irish news organisations in Africa and advocates the need to be 'Mr Available': 'Working as a stringer is the ultimate meritocracy – no room for pedestrians. And if you work really hard, run things like a business you'll be set on the ride of your life. There's no re-writing press releases or being stuck on diary, like you would back home. You'll be kicking news in the nuts – and occasionally having it vomit on your shoes.' (Crilly, 2011).

In many ways the definition of a stringer lies in the output-payment mechanism: stringers are freelance journalists who are paid per unit of content they produce rather than being salaried or contracted. It means you are free to work for more than one outlet: more liberation and freedom of expression has to be weighed against the possible irregularity in income (which is inevitable at least for the first year) and a potentially gruelling series of pitch rejections until your reputation and unique selling point are better understood.

Conclusion

As the journalism network evolves, it is increasingly apparent that the jobs market will shift too. It is likely that journalists will work for more than one organisation, certainly over the course of a career. Even highly trained professionals may not want to be tied to one organisation or a prescriptive type of news output. What it means to be freelance will change: you may have one contracted employment but work on a blog or hyperlocal TV show at the same time. And with this, you are likely to have different relationships with audiences on different platforms.

This raises complex questions about identity and maintaining social media accounts or profiles. Journalists have to make informed decisions about how many identities to have and how best to manage them in a professional manner. How much of your personal life should be included in your professional 'spaces' online? To what extent should an employer have a say in the outputs you create or the comments you make online? Is it possible to run multiple personas while still maintaining transparency and authenticity? Journalists must carve out a new sense of who they are to whom in order to thrive.

Graham Holliday

Graham Holliday began his journalistic career in Hanoi in 1998 and went full-time freelance when he moved to Ho Chi Minh City in 2001. He currently runs kigaliwire.com and noodlepie.com, and writes for Reuters as their Rwandan correspondent. 'The most important element is that journalists are independent, have a decent reputation and a visible and active online presence. I find it very difficult to put myself in any particular pigeon hole. I am also working as Rwandan correspondent for Reuters, but, interestingly, the East Africa Bureau Chief first heard of me from Kigali Wire. In that sense the branding works: going somewhere or finding a niche, networking and making yourself very visible and very contactable does bring you work. That is why I call myself a freelance 'whatever I'm asked to do that sounds interesting'. It's a good position to be in but it is unpredictable and you have to be exceptionally flexible. The key is transparency, visibility, connections and being good at what you do.

'Working in this new environment, where you have to build up your reputation and relationships from the grassroots up, means running many different outputs and relating with different people in a way that makes sense to them. Kigali Wire is a news wire of links, blog posts, photography and original journalism produced from Kigali, Rwanda. Running the site in this way enables me to act like a newswire based around a niche, in this instance a geographic area. I can showcase my original photojournalism, interviews and reporting as well as bring in relevant news from other

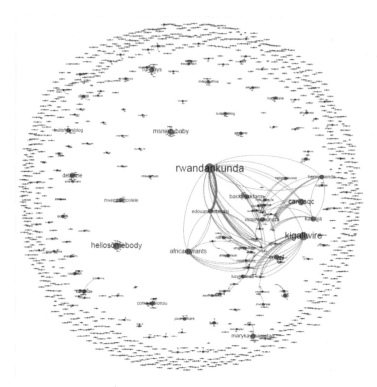

FIGURE 11.2 A social network node analysis shows how Kigali Wire connects the hub with other Rwandan sources.

sites that is relevant to this topic. It creates the best one-stop shop I can offer. I provide original insight and thoughts that people want to link to and discuss. Kigali Wire is my calling card in Rwanda. Reuters may supersede that, but I think it has given me a certain amount of credibility in the news sphere and in the digital publishing sphere.

I have generated income from Kigali Wire. I work as a photojournalist selling photographs to mainstream magazines such as ArikaPost in Germany, the BBC Focus magazine and a CNN slideshow. I have been invited to do talks for IREX in Rwanda and the Rwanda Project as well as doing some PR work and writing part-time for an NGO newsletter and for Current Intelligence. I am a foreign correspondent for a weekly subscription letter in the US and act as a fixer for other correspondents. If I know I am travelling to a certain area, I will think about multi-pitching so that one topic or trip can make more than one outcome.

I didn't really plan to choose different identities. They just evolved and they work for me. It made sense to separate Vietnam, journalism, media training and Rwanda. It works for me, for now; that's not to say I won't change my mind somewhere down the line. Some clients approach me about work purely through grahamholliday.co.uk and they have no idea I'm in Rwanda. To me, it's important they don't know I'm in Rwanda, as it may put them off employing me. And Rwanda will always be a temporary home. There's no need to put people off the scent, as I travel a lot for work. It's common for me to agree to a number of jobs in a two-week period across Europe. The fact I'm in Rwanda is not important to those people. However, it is vitally important to Reuters as they need that dateline and I can provide it. Kigali Wire plays into that.

To work as a journalist in this new sense of time, place and connectivity, there are certain tools that are a must: Twitter, RSS and social bookmarking. We all need a publishing outlet (blog), we all need to store research (social bookmarking), we all need to keep up-to-date with news (RSS, Twitter) and we all need to publish on the go from multiple devices (Twitter). You can use different accounts to store different types of information and create feeds from them to different sites and blogs. You can use specific tags to organise content and create collaborations with other journalists. The networking features are utterly priceless – where else can you follow such up-to-date thoughts, research and spot the latest trends? Just to say that I do believe Twitter has become an entirely new news platform. However, it's somewhat more fragile than previous newswires as it still does not have a solid business model. That said, what Twitter does is not going to disappear, even if Twitter goes under.'

Key reflections

- How much you? Reflect on how much of your personal life is already openly available online and where you consider the boundary to lie between your personal and professional identities. Do adventures in your personal life add value to your professional identity?
- Are journalists a brand?
- Does anyone ever 'own' followers and who chooses the audience? Is it wrong to force celebrity status on writers? Consider the parameters in deciding who does and does not get promoted as a personal brand by a news organisation.
- Who chooses the audience? What factors affect who the audience is, when and in what ways?
- Does the personality of a journalist have to be relevant to their role and professional identity? Consider the implications of journalists having more than one persona.

TOOLKIT

Tips and tools

Be the central station: social networks can drive attention your way. Twitter can start conversations; a public Facebook page can be a personal billboard pointing readers to your work and inviting them to talk back; photo-sharing sites give you room for the photos that didn't make your stories; professional networking sites such as LinkedIn let readers see behind your career; a branded blog provides a shop window for you and your work.

Online CV: tools to create an online portfolio or personal brand space are evolving all the time. Try Flavors.me, Cuttings.me or Pressfolios.com.

Share and share alike: as Chris Brogan points out, respect the network by promoting other people more than yourself and 'bring light to those people doing great work' (Brogan, 2011).

Every touch point counts: your behaviour will be noted, not just in the outward dissemination of content or the interaction with users online. The way you answer the phone, handle your voice mail, write your email signature and the way you reply to posts and comments all count.

Be where the party is: don't expect every interaction to occur on your playground. If networks, groups or conversations form away from your chosen platforms, blogs and wikis, interact with contacts there instead.

Dedicate time: the interactivity that can be created on social networks is well worth the investment but expect to be at your limits in terms of the capacity to process information.

Readings and resources

Kigali Back Wire: this blog by Graham Holliday is dedicated to explaining how a brand can be set up to cover a patch with explanatory notes on distribution: http://kigalibackwire.tumblr.com/post/185325006/distribution-process.

PayonTime: this is a UK-based resource bringing together advice and forums on the law: https://payontime.co.uk/.

Unions: America's Newspaper Guild and the National Union of Journalists offer a portal on expected rates, alerts, news and an advice index: http://newsguild.org/; www.londonfreelance.org/.

Find publications: sites such as Thepaperboy.com and Actualidad.com let you search stories and publications from around the world: www.thepaperboy.com/; http://actualidad.com/.

Brad Insight: this marketing and media intelligence company requires client login but brings together insights on all the major publishing houses: www1.bradinsight.com/.

Freelance job listings: there are a range of sites for journalism job listings and services such as journalismjobs.com, Gorkana, Holdthefrontpage.co.uk, *Guardian* Media, journalism.co.uk, writerfind.com, and Pigiste.org.

>>Chapter 12<<

BECOMING A MEDIA ENTREPRENEUR

Overview

Structural change in the media industry has opened up a range of opportunities for innovation. Media entrepreneurs have found ways to take their place in the new media ecology, whether it is as a hyperlocal or niche news site, an app, publication or a multimedia news platform. And this new era of innovation is not just about Silicon Valley: small teams around the globe are harnessing the capacity of social media to pool their talents and reinvent what it means to 'do' news. This chapter looks at some of the global considerations at play for launching, growing and sustaining a news product when the rules are still being written.

Key concepts

- Building teams
- Business plan
- Entrepreneurialism
- Innovation
- Investment
- Marketing
- Media management
- Organisational structure
- Start-ups
- Strategy

Springboard

- *Technology and innovation*: people often confuse these two terms. Advances in technology can deliver improved products and context. Innovation is about change.
- *Entrepreneurship is a personality trait*: it is about creating or identifying opportunities and having the passion, vision, skills, enthusiasm and know-how to make good ideas become a reality. Entrepreneurship drives innovation.
- *Embrace not replace*: if social media is about anything it is about collaboration, and Big Media are increasingly seeing tie-ups with media entrepreneurs in their strategic future.
- *Innovation is a process*: it is often a case of experimenting and finding a way forward as well as learning from failure.
- *The devil is in the details*: while it is very difficult to draw out a common 'success' gene for new sites or products, attention to detail is key. This may be attention to what audiences want, or identifying a service or interest that is not being served, or it could simply be seeing the same services differently.

Introduction

Today's media industry has a very different competitive landscape than that found in analogue media. Technology has lowered the barriers to entry, broadened the distribution to global audiences and democratised media production. A dazzling array of 'news' entities have sprung up, and variety abounds. Journalists are looking for ways to reinvent their careers. Many reporters are hoping to carve out niches in the digital space and launch their own ventures. New entry in media markets is higher than it is in many other industry sectors (Hoag, 2008).

Entrepreneurs

There are three different types of entrepreneur: a lifestyle entrepreneur wants to seek enough independence to earn a living, a growth entrepreneur wants to grow wealthy and be powerful, while an innovative entrepreneur tends to be driven by the desire to create or change something (Bessant and Tidd, 2008: 414).

Media entrepreneurs have flexed their muscles, creating all manner of new sites and services. Many have launched blogs or sites based on a niche topic or interest, to create digital communities such as FemaleFirst or TreeHugger. Others offer investigative reports such as @rretsurimages, MediaPart or Rue89. Some have created businesses based on news-production services: Storyful, Audioboo or CoverItLive. Others around user-generated content such as AgoraVox, Demotix or Citizenside.

This chapter recognises the valid place in the new media ecology for such media entities, which may exist in a more structured way than a freelance individual but are more independent and agile than larger media organisations. The vocabulary to describe such entities is lacking, as they can no longer be defined by their technical determinants. Their place in the media landscape will evolve according to their product development and their longevity, as well as their voice and intent. But their existence – and the increasing likelihood for journalists to work within, alongside or indeed launch, such an organisation – makes them a valid addition.

Of course entrepreneurship plays out in different stages of the business cycle from new ventures with lone entrepreneurs taking calculated risks, to 'intrapreneurs' – those people who act like an entrepreneur but are employed within an established organisation. This latest wave of media entrepreneurialism, however, seems to have more zest. Historically, media technologies took many years to go through the cycles of development, introduction, adoption and acceptance. Current media technologies are developing continually, often launching as unpolished products in beta stage. The rate of change has increased exponentially: it took the *New York Times* 50 years to achieve what Politico and TechCrunch have done in months. The grasp of Big Media can be easily rocked – take the *News of the World* closure or *Le Monde*'s bailout from bankrupcy as examples.

As such, the media ecology not only has space for new products and ideas but it positively feeds on them. Start-ups are constantly innovating and redefining how the content industry works and what services are on offer. This tectonic shift towards a more destabilised media ecology embraces all there is to celebrate about new and social media: the sense of fun, the power of conversations, welcoming criticism, sharing and collaboration, following and being followed and openness for all (Kaul, 2012).

Innovations are not happening 'on the horizon' but continually and collaboratively. There are individuals driving change, such as Deborah Estrin, the evangelist of crowd-intelligence and civic engagement, and Tom Coates, the man who predicted and celebrated the blog revolution. And there are cities: Stockholm is emerging with an entrepreneurial ecosystem led by pioneering ventures such as Skype, Bambuser and Spotify; Face.com's founder and CEO Gil Hirsch raised more than $5 billion in investment capital from a base in Tel Aviv. And there are plain good ideas: social games for stadium crowds; social sharing for ebooks; the creative audio platform SoundCloud. In this landscape, journalists need to be aware of how ideas and services move from the drawing board to target audiences, how they are managed, developed and grown. Navigating these waters requires a new blend of business, technical and journalistic skills.

First-mover advantage

Timing is important. Being first can be rewarded with significant market share or adoption, known as first-mover advantage. Fast-follower or second-mover advantage can mean you learn from the teething problems of others and sometimes benefit from others' mistakes.

Whether you are working for a company or you are out on your own, the rapidly changing media landscape means you have a chance to create the future you envision. This time of change is unprecedented in the history of media. And if you know a little something about the news business and have a good idea on how to do things differently, you already have what you need to get started. (Mark Briggs, author (Briggs, 2012: 3)).

Beta stage

In software, beta refers to the unpolished phase of a product's development when it is released for testing but may still have bugs or technical issues.

The long tail

Chris Anderson's theory explains how the digital marketplace has opened up possibilities for niche businesses in answer to users' demands for an 'uncategorisable sea of a million destinations' (2006: 2). It is this backdrop concept which fuels opportunities for start-ups and entrepreneurs.

Big Media: friend or foe?

In the last few decades, larger news organisations have mostly under-invested in research and development, and not expressed much interest in open innovation (Christensen, 1997; Picard, 2010; Lewis and Aitamurto, 2011). Innovation – which ultimately depends on risk-taking and failure – can harm big brands. Studies have found that more opportunities have opened up for media entrepreneurs as Big Media have often failed to meet the needs of the market, often hindered by red tape or bureaucracy. It may be easier to compete with larger corporations because the products are of poor or declining quality (Compaine and Hoag, 2012; Nicola and Neilsen, 2012) or where a 'purely marketing approach' to online opportunities has thwarted progress (Smyrnais and Bousquet, 2011).

BBC open source

Developers were invited to use various elements of the BBC site to shape innovative applications through the five-year Backstage open-source project. The call was to 'use our stuff to make your stuff' and people did, to the tune of over 500 prototypes (BBC Backstage, 2010).

Embrace risk

Entrepreneurs have to learn, somehow, to feel at ease with taking risks and failing. Only native business models to the new digital information ecosystem will reap the rewards of business innovation and succeed where legacy news companies did not (Thornburg, 2009; Briggs, 2012).

API

An API (application programming interface) is a mechanism that allows developers to create applications and content that bolt on to proprietary systems (such as an operating system). Open Application Programming Interface refers to the sets of technologies that enable websites to interact with each other. It has formed an integral part of distribution, as it allows programmers to move content from site to site.

Audioboo is one start-up that seized the opportunity to move on an idea when mainstream could not. As founder and CEO Mark Rock explains: 'In 2008 we were working with Channel 4 to do more recording with mobiles but the recession happened and it was clear they weren't going to launch so we thought we would develop it anyway. We put it in the app store and didn't think much more of it. But then loads of journalistic producers found usage for it: during the G20 protests and among BBC Radio 1 listeners. So the growth was quite serendipitous as we realised we were hitting a great market.' (2012).

Increasingly, however, social media are helping to break down a 'them and us' mentality between mainstream news organisations and start-ups, especially across Anglo-Saxon markets. Big Media are working in partnership with smaller news producers. The Guardian, the BBC, National Public Radio and the New York Times have all released application programming interfaces (APIs). There are also moves to increase collaboration: the New York Times teamed up with YouTube and the video-curation service Storyful to gather and share users' reflections on 9/11 and the meaning of the ten years that had passed since the attacks. One of the biggest benefits of this collaboration is the speeding up of internal and external product development.

These moves to increase collaboration can be a rich source of opportunity for the media entrepreneur under the umbrella of open innovation (Chesbrough, 2003; Bessant and Venables, 2010; Radcliffe, 2012).

It is the recognition that in a wired-up and social setting, much intellectual value can be drawn from the crowd, and how all companies can tap in to external knowledge rather than relying on internally generated ideas.

Getting started

It may seem overwhelming at first, with every author's blog offering advice about where and how to begin. Launching a start-up requires an innovative idea, hard work, good timing and plenty of luck. But there are certain steps that you need to consider, and continually revisit:

- Goals and ideas. At the outset, understand the difference between an idea that is interesting and one that will create a sustainable business. What is your product and how will it keep going?
- Identify an opportunity and a niche. Working out your market and competitor analysis will help. Who is the product aimed at and what makes it unique?
- Develop a business plan and revenue streams. Why and how will people use and pay for your service?
- Find resources: people, money and tech. What skills do you need from other team members or your founders?
- Product development. Consider how to move forward with the resources and niche that you have. How can you measure success and what are the major milestones?
- Build buzz. From early adopters to spreading the word, consider how you can best get people to love your product and run with it.

Finding an idea

Mark Little, founder and CEO of Storyful (a platform billed as the first news agency of the social-media age), started in journalism 20 years ago working as a TV anchor. He was drawn to

Follow my leader

Robin Klein, founder of The Accelerator Group, advocates following smart entrepreneurs rather than industry trends. 'Great people figure out the right direction,' he says. 'It's about working with founders, at times very intensively' (*Wired*, 2011).

Revenue streams

Revenue is the incoming money you make. A revenue stream is an activity that brings in money, such as advertising or sales.

Benchmarking

This is the process of systematically comparing products, services or processes to others on the market. It can be a rich source of innovative ideas.

Media entrepreneurs

Few academic studies have looked at the motivations of media entrepreneurs but they tend to be less risk-averse (Kihlstrom and Laffont, 1979; Knight, 2002) or may not perceive risk because they feel confident in their venture (Fiet, 1996). Entrepreneurial opportunity can be classed in three main ways: opportunity recognition, discovery and creation. These depend to what extent an obvious need has been identified through supply and demand, or if there is an entirely new opportunity (Sarasvathy et al., 2003).

Competitive advantages

These are all the aspects of your product, positioning or strategy which give you the upper hand over your competitors.

- Media entrepreneurs may be 'here today gone tomorrow' in what academics define as the 'wave of creative destruction'.
- Revenues and investments are more unstable.
- There is uncertainty and risk.
- The sheer volume of new products and services being created mean consumers are overwhelmed, and achieving adoption is tough.

- Gaps in services and products offered by Big Media open opportunities.
- Media entrepreneurs can replicate and produce high quality outputs cheaply and efficiently.
- Distribution is open to all.
- Small virtual teams can be mobilised globally.
- There are low or few barriers to entry.
- Start-ups can find opportunities to work with Big Media who are slower to innovate and change.
- Low production costs.
- The democratisation of resources online means less need for technical expertise.
- Geographic independence facilitated by online and mobile.

FIGURE 12.1 The balance for start-ups in the new-media ecology between potential gains and challenges.

managing a social-media product because of the changes in newsgathering: a freedom from cumbersome logistics, and the historic shift towards active audiences moderating an overabundance of information. He says, 'I looked around to see major problems coming with this. Firstly, how do you discover and filter the things you want, the valuable things; the second was verification; and then integration. How do we get social media integrated into the newsgathering process and then deliver stories to a much more active, social, mobile audience? So I looked around and thought: "What if you created a news agency from scratch that just built itself with social media in mind?" I went out and created something new. Every news event starts a community and if you start with that premise, everything else becomes a bit easier to work out. You find the wisdom in the community and you engage with it.' (Little, in #bbcsms).

> ## Unique selling proposition
>
> Originally coined by marketer Rosser Reeves, the USP has become associated with any factors that make your product or service unique.

For Storyful, the idea for a new media start-up came from personal experiences and wider reflections on changes in user behaviour. For Libération journalist Jean Quatremer, innovation came from within his organisation. His blog Coulisses de Bruxelles has become one of the most-followed sites on European politics. He cites: 'The idea for the blog was not mine: I didn't believe in it at the time because no one was interested in European ideas. I thought no one would care about a blog on Europe. I just presumed it would be dismissed as too technocratic, too bureaucratic, too boring, too hard. But it was completely the opposite and it gained readers around the world. Articles were a success because people were talking about them and people's opinions were being heard. It gave me notoriety and consolidated my post in Brussels: without it I would have lost this job for sure.' (Quatremer, 2012).

In both cases, media products were born because of astute recognition of the world at large, either by good luck or good management. But ideas and opportunities can be all around. Draw from your own experiences – is there a tool you need but can't find? Are there services that need improving or changes in technology? Can you think of a novel way of reconfiguring parts of a process? Almost anything can be a source of inspiration: a jolt or shock to the system, watching and learning from others, transferring one application to another setting, a change of rules, the Archimedes moment, feedback from users, deregulation or a change in users' behaviour (Mayer, 2006; Livingston, 2008; Anderson, 2009a).

> # Value proposition
>
> This term refers to what your business offers that no one else does. Define it, knowing your strengths, and then measure your competition against it.

Finding a niche

Getting started is all about finding an idea – and then proving its worth. You may spend a lot of time convincing other people to support you, and justifying why your idea is worth all the effort. So a basic understanding of marketing principles is helpful at this stage, as it is the management process responsible for identifying, anticipating and satisfying customer requirements (Chartered Institute of Marketing, 2012).

Recognising a niche in the media landscape and having the ability to fill that gap with a relevant, timely and innovative product has always been the secret to publishing success. Lonely Planet's Tony and Maureen Wheeler are living proof of that. They turned a coffee-table publishing idea into a multi-million-pound portfolio when they identified space in the travel-media market for accessible and practical guides. Even the man who wrote the purchase ledger when the brand was snapped up by BBC Worldwide, Nick Brett, says: 'There used to be a fairly straightforward career path in journalism but now there is much more scope for doing entrepreneurial journalism with desk-top publishing. The kitchen table or garage start-up is much more viable' (Brett, 2012).

Much of this relies heavily on understanding the unique selling point of your product, app, site, blog or forum. What makes it different or better from what is out there already? Whether you express your ideas in soundbites (Bessant and Tidd, 2008) or as a mantra (Kawasaki, 2004) or mission statement (Bedbury and Fenichell, 2002) sum it up so other people can easily latch on and spread the word.

A market analysis sets out your main competitors, and proves to what extent you have found a niche. Find out who are the movers and shakers in this patch and what their strengths and weaknesses are.

> # Positioning
>
> Part of target marketing is to understand where consumers see your product fitting in the market ecology. What are you offering in relation to the rest? It could be a better product that commands a premium, a free site that offers better content or a cheaper alternative to something that is already out there. Positioning is what you do for your customers.

If you want to write a blog then find out who else writes about the topics that interest you, which forums cover the same issues, who tweets, what trends, what other multimedia content there is around the web, in print podcasts or on TV.

Successful media entrepreneurs then prove demand by looking at the media market, dividing that market into segments and visualising where a new product could be positioned within it. Mark Soutar's launch of the free magazine Sport into the men's consumer market is a good example. Of all the initial conditions influencing the success of new ventures, the size of the target market has the most impact (Gao et al., 2010). All these elements make up your competitive advantages.

Identifying groups of users with sufficiently similar purchasing power so they can be targeted in a similar way is part of the marketing process. It is important because different groups have different needs, and social media may drive those groups in different ways. This is an inherently difficult task when it comes to start-ups because the product may be in beta, and is certainly going to evolve, but be specific: the most successful products target specific markets and then grow. Groups can be segmented in many ways: by what the product can do, how it will be used, where users will consume it, or by user beliefs and emotions. Much has been written about how best to understand readership and buyer personas (see for example Levinson et al., 2007; Scott, 2011).

Common approaches to understanding user needs include focus groups or surveys, latent needs analysis (to uncover unarticulated requirements), canvassing lead users especially across social media, drawing on industry experts, extrapolating trends and market experimentation. Test different interfaces, products and ideas on your focus groups.

The business plan

The business plan sets out what you need when and in what order to move forward. Managing a news product, you are likely to be working in fraught circumstances, often with a lot of uncertainty and guesswork. You may spend a lot of time convincing other people to support you, and justifying how durable the product is and how likely it is to succeed. Recognise that innovation, particularly in the new social-media ecology, is a moving target and a dynamic process.

Value chain

Business schools will often promote the value chain: how each company makes money by adding value to a product across its development.

The business plan can serve multiple purposes: it can be a document sent out to attract external funding, a formal agreement between partners or simply a means to help the entrepreneur see more clearly. It can help translate more abstract ideals into more explicit operational needs, and support decision-making or trade-offs when they come about. It's a good way to test if you can clearly communicate the concept to others. It should contain the story behind the idea, the vision, the market you are aiming it at, the competition, the financial plan and the exit route.

Non-disclosure agreements

A non-disclosure agreement is a legally binding document that records the terms under which you exchange secret information. It is especially useful for discussions with potential investors.

Use it to set out the value in your business. Once you have set out the niche and market analysis then add: why now? What trends will your product answer that you can see over the horizon? Think carefully about what the product does that is resourceful and adds value.

Ultimately, you need to set out how you are going to make it sustainable. For many journalists the public-service mission of their job has meant an aversion to dealing with money but that has to change.

Look at the revenue models available; see Chapter 13 for more. Set out the capital and revenue strategies, the sales forecasts, cash-flow calculations and any other financial-resource considerations. In some cases knowledge can be commercialised by licensing or selling the intellectual-property rights rather than the more difficult or specific route of developing the business and supporting the resources required.

There is a lot of research to be done and it's difficult to pinpoint why some media products have worked and others not. Remember Bebo, Kazaa, Plurk, Diaspora? These products were all once thought to be the next big thing, but all failed to gain traction. A careful diffusion among early adopters helps, as this influences the diffusion to the main market. Indeed, a positive response from early adopters can have more influence than any bells and whistles on the product itself. Trigger word of mouth within specialist communities, leverage your connections on sites like LinkedIn, increase the user base and collaborate with opinion leaders in what Briggs describes as 'socialising the process' (2012: 148). You may need to reposition the product before launching into your main market.

Set out the key risks or problems you anticipate. Porter's five forces were designed for business owners to consider their vulnerability. Consider how easy it would be for a competitor to enter the market. This is known as the barrier to entry. Have a clear strategy to deal with a fluid marketplace and protect your ideas where possible. Look into patents and intellectual property where appropriate to make sure you can recover the time and energy spent on your media ideas. Indeed, if it is a flop, how do you recover elements from it?

One of the early decisions to make is the business structure. Factors influencing the choice will be how much capital is needed to launch, what control or ownership will work best, the level of risk in case of failure, how large and how fast you intend to expand, what registration reporting and tax implications there are, what exit routes, and who is set to benefit? It's not uncommon to raise support early on by offering stock, instead of cash revenue. Muralist and graffiti artist David Choe, who painted the walls

Intellectual property

There is a range of intellectual-property rights that exist but the most applicable to technology and innovation are patents, copyright and design rights. They all refer to ownership rights of original creative thought. This is discussed more in Chapter 10.

Diffusion

Diffusion is the process by which an innovation is adopted by a social system or market segment and includes the rate and direction of change.

Porter's five forces

Named after Michael E. Porter, this model sets out five competitive forces that shape an industry's weaknesses and strengths. They focus on the competition, the potential of new entrants, the risks relating to suppliers, the influence of customers and the threat to your business of substitute products coming to market (Porter, 1979).

Company registrations

It is worth seeking financial advice about registering your start-up, as different business entities vary in complexity and liability, should the venture struggle. The most popular include: sole proprietorship, general partnerships, Limited Liability Partnerships (LLP), corporations, Limited Liability Corporation (LLC) or non-profit corporations, charities and foundations.

Innovation phases

Roy Rothwell has worked for many years pioneering models of innovation. His vision of the fifth generation of innovation is essentially the one we are in now, where rich and diverse networks exist, enabling linking and acceleration in innovation (adapted from Tidd et al., 2001).

of Facebook's first headquarters, got aproximately $200 million when the company was floated on the stock exchange after he agreed to take Facebook stock instead of cash for his original work (Duell and Gye, 2012).

Working with teams

A key part of launching a start-up is the team: who is involved and who you need (Kaplan and Warren, 2010). The dynamics of social media presented throughout this book mean that now, more than ever, networking will be important right across the innovation process. From finding opportunities with potential co-founders to pulling in resources, developing a product or diffusing it and then capturing the value in the end process, social media will form an integral part of your project management.

As such, you need to consider how to build a team. It is very rare for one person to have all the skills needed to manage a news product. Even those journalists who are outwardly a 'one-man band' will still need support on an ad hoc basis, but the resources you can afford to draw on may also be limited. Finnish food website Hellapoliisi is owned by Kati Jaakonen, who does all the content – recipes and photos – herself, yet she outsources all the technical maintenance, site design and development (Jaakonen, 2012).

The kinds of people you may need in your team are detailed in Figure 12.2. The team will change depending on the type of product you are trying to create and the resources available to fund people.

Last.fm and Spotify are great examples of businesses that tapped people in separate distinct networks at the same time. (Sherry Coutu, entrepreneur, 2012)

There are different types of team networks and levels of formality. You may rely on a friend to 'help out' but be careful if you are working on something sensitive or a prototype. You may pay a freelancer as a one-off or on a flexible contract, or crowdsource expertise either through virtual social networks, or searches on web databases. Attending regional clusters or best-practice clubs such as Hacks and Hackers or social-media cafes provide good contacts and networking opportunities. There are strategic alliances or consortiums, sector forums, multi-company innovation networks or geographical clusters such as those near San Jose, California, Gurgaon, India, and Shanghai, China. When you do meet people be clear about who you want to meet (press, lecturers, investors) and say clearly who you are so they remember.

Human-resource management

The recognition that people are not just 'workers' but rather assets incremental in achieving strategic goals began in the eighties. In the creative industries, its focus is on the value of talent products – the imagination, originality, skill and innovation of your team – rather than fixed non-emotional resources like computers (Foot and Hook, 2002; Bratton and Gold, 2007).

Much scholarly research has been dedicated to what makes an effective team. Focus on building high trust, choose competent team members, harness a collaborative climate, and make sure everyone has a unified commitment and common goals (Isaksen and Tidd, 2006).

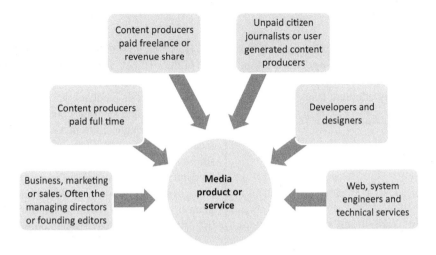

FIGURE 12.2   You will need an effective team to run a start-up. This graphic details some of the tasks and roles that may need to be filled.

You also have to be realistic about your limits, and expect long days. Political blogger Paul Staines, behind the Guido Fawkes blog, is a reporting operation where you 'can't spend a long time investigating a corporation across five continents' (in Gunter, 2011b). Markus Beckedahl typically works 12-hour days on Netzpolitic, a German blog set up in 2004 with around 20 contributors, all trusted friends. 'I try to devote as much time as possible to writing articles, but unfortunately things don't always work out like that. Sometimes I need to travel a great deal and at these times I can't attend to Netzpolitik properly. On average, about two-thirds of my working hours are allotted to doing content' (Beckedahl, 2012). Jonathan Lloyd, the founder and owner of Media Street Apps, a start-up business developing a web software application to run local websites, says: 'I like to structure it so that I'm publishing some content early in the morning so that people arriving at their desks can see a story. The rest of the morning I mostly do sales and marketing activities. In the afternoon I tend to be out and about seeing my local businesses and clients. In the evening I do development work' (Lloyd, 2012).

To be truly innovative it is essential that time is set aside continually for ideas and creativity (Briggs, 2009; Newmark, 2009; Spradlin, 2009). 'One good idea is not going to cut it. You need to have ideas coming your way. Demolish hierarchy because it works against creativity. You also have to let failure into the company. You have to screw things up to get things right' (Wilson, in Cook, 2011a).

Product life cycle

Sites will go through different phases and the management needed will change. The product life cycle describes the evolution from introduction, through growth to maturity and then decline (Levitt, 1965).

 I spend 15 hours a week on managing readers' comments alone. News does not stop when you go home for a true journalist. It is a permanent state and we are only at the beginning of nourishing the beast. It is a huge commitment. (Jean Quatremer, journalist, 2012)

Product development and marketing

At some point your product will need to go to market. How you do this – and get people on board – can be a critical part of a start-up. This is a fundamental building block of growing any media product. It requires attention to detail and a watchful eye – full time – on trends, searching, moving forward. Lead users or early adopters (those users or readers whose ideas or feedback is of particular value in developing and steering your product) become especially valuable. Entrepreneurialism in social media trades on three key currencies: relationships, accessibility and community. The product or content evolves organically, by listening and engaging to communities of interest. Growing your product is about understanding the equal importance of both features and communities.

As social media move from buzzword to strategic tool, there is no shortage of advice about how to use it for growing sites and marketing activity. Books, papers, blogs and magazine articles relentlessly tout the latest ideas about how to harness social media to extend brands and product awareness, build audiences and drive traffic. What are you trying to achieve and over what time scale? What resources can you afford and how will you measure the value in your social media activity?

The marketing mix

The 'seven Ps' form the basic principles of marketing first expressed by Edmund McCarthy: the right product, aimed at the right people, at the right price, promoted well, in the right place, with the right process and necessary physical evidence to show marketing has been a success (McCarthy and Perreault, 1984).

Adoption theories

Much study notably in the field of advertising has been given to how new products are taken up by users. Expect audiences to go through four main stages before they 'adopt' your site by either becoming a member or active user. These are: awareness of a product, interest in it, evaluation of it and then some kind of trial or experimentation.

The ABCDE of marketing

The marketing mix has come under scrutiny in a social era where the seven Ps of marketing become: Anyplace, Brand, Communication, Discovery and Experience to reflect the divergent and interactive ways people connect and find information online (Tapscott, 2009).

David Karp launched blogging platform Tumblr in private beta in 2006 'as something selfish, something that I wanted to use myself', but an integral understanding of his product and how people wanted to use it (as a site of self-expression rather than communication or authentication, as with Twitter and Facebook respectively) led to small changes that were pivotal in its growth. A reblog button introduced in 2007 (two years before RT functionality on Twitter) supercharged Tumblr user numbers – a direct response to the fact that 'users were hacking the network; they had no tools but were finding and drawing lines between each other'. Karp understood that his was a network built on content sharing (Cheshire, 2012).

To better understand the principles of growing media products in social spaces, compare marketing offline and online. Your strategies may include elements of both. The old rules of marketing focused on one-way messages: Big Media advertising, celebrity endorsement, sponsorships, special offers, leaflets or flyers, posters and billboards, cold calling, covermounts, product placement, advertorials and press releases. In social spaces, product awareness is more likely to grow based on multiway exchanges, listening to audiences, creating personalised experiences and increasing interactivity. In light of these shifts, there are a few themes to consider as part of the 'humanisation of business' (Joel, 2011) to create a more authentic awareness of your journalistic products and services:

- Give before you receive. It's essential to get out there – write articles or produce for more established sites and build up a strong reputation on other people's radars.
- Comment and respond. If you spend all your time posting and tweeting about your company, pushing out news and services, you'll probably have limited success. Use the 80/20 rule: add value to the community 80 per cent and take by promoting your own content 20 per cent of the time.
- Be where the audience are – and don't presume to know where that is. It's about fishing where the fish are (Zyman and Brott, 2003). Instead of rushing to join any and every social media community out there, opt for a slow and steady approach. Pick one or two communities that are important in your market and let your audience guide you on which social networks to be on.

Content spins off from advertising and back again. Your contact is direct with the reader, answering their questions, but you have to consider if topics highlight or spin off into new directions and go with it. (Craig McGinty, editor of ThisFrenchLife, 2012)

- Forge genuine relationships. Your success will rarely be reflected in the number of followers you have but rather in the quality of engagement. Having 10 million Twitter followers isn't as good as having 50,000 Twitter followers who interact with you, because social media is about 'the right audience – and the right audience is the one that wants to engage with you' (Speiser, in Behling, 2011).
- Be clear and simple. Use clear and decisive domain names, as these will often have to be communicated simply to advertisers, audiences and partners. A simple name that can become a verb (think 'Googling') has advantages.
- An open linking strategy shows that you are not taking without giving back in return, and avoid linking to dud or misleading sites.
- Make subscribing simple. Prime placement of both email and RSS options for subscribing will help build audiences.
- Social media create a direct-to-consumer model, so make sure you reward your loyal audience.
- Part of being truly open is to embrace appropriate elements of interactivity such as polls, ranking, or comments.
- Make multimedia work harder. Photo galleries and shared videos, podcasts or images are an excellent way of building 'social proof' and even more visibility online for your site.

Conclusion

There was much gloomy talk about the overall state of journalism at the turn of the new millenium. Job cuts and falling revenues made many in the industry fear for the changes that lay ahead. And many of those issues still exist today. However, journalists are increasingly flexing an entrepreneurial spirit: there is a passion, vision and enthusiasm for change both within larger news organisations and in smaller journalistic start-ups. Media entrepreneurs bring a relative buoyancy to the industry. Cheap publishing tools and a genuine passion for the trade come together to open up a range of exciting opportunities for journalists.

It is important to recognise the valid place in the new media ecology for start-ups, which may exist in a more independent and agile way than larger media organisations. There are opportunities opening up for collaboration between mainstream media and smaller startups in some economies. This can take many forms: a project by project basis, to act in some way as a research and development arm or to offer services that would be too costly or difficult to offer in-house.

As innovation continues to move the industry forward, there will be an ever greater range of sites, forums, services and tools which exist under the larger umbrella terms of newspapers, magazines or broadcasters. But their existence – and the increasing likelihood for journalists to work within, alongside or indeed launch, start-ups or innovative platforms – makes them a valid source of exploration in this book.

CASE STUDY > Citizenside

Citizenside's goal is to create the largest online community of amateur and independent reporters where everyone can share their vision of the news by uploading photos and videos. It was launched in France in 2005 and has 70,000 members in 150 countries, as former editor in chief Philip Trippenbach explained.

'It works as a press wire of images and video with citizen journalists able to earn a 65 per cent revenue share of content sold in the same country as the upload; 50 per cent if content is sold in a different country. It is made up of a 15-strong team of business development, editorial and technical staff, now registered as a limited company with Agence France-Press as a shareholder. Citizenside also offers direct sales to media outlets: exclusive video footage of the fashion guru John Galliano having a racist rant was sold to the Sun in 2011, earning the citizen reporter a substantial sum. Media outlets can subscribe to direct syndication of content on CitizensidePro.

'The inspiration for the site came after the London Tube bombings when iconic images from witnesses such as Adam Stacey made the rounds on the international press after being posted to Wikinews and Moblog.co.uk

'The site's main success has been in empowering citizens to earn money from their work. Like any social network, there is a long tail of activity among the users – a small group who is very active and then thousands who upload more rarely. The editorial team does a lot of work actively searching for images. They contact content producers on sites such as Twitter, Flickr and YouTube, inviting them to the site and to share their content.

'Citizenside has also learnt the importance of understanding what motivates people in a social landscape. People upload as a matter of course – most people are not motivated by money and we hadn't realised that at first. The site had been set up as a business to create uploading options with a commercial angle but people don't care about money mainly. The viral Twitpic content of the Hudson River plane crash proves that: he didn't want money; it was the 'holy shit' moment that there was a plane in the river. And for most people it is not even to show the world what has happened: it is to show their friends. That deeply ties into the potential for profitability.

'The business developers have put a lot of focus on motivation, feedback, loyalty and trust. To motivate the audience, Citizenside calls for witnesses with geo-targeting alerts, providing specifics about where news is occurring. There are points and levels of structure available, giving constant feedback to users including a reporter's rank report and status points, which gives people motivation to keep coming back, much like World of Warcraft social-status building. Citizenside has reporters of the month, and the potential to become a trusted member, operating much like a freelance stringer, where content can be posted pre-moderation.

'The introduction of game dynamics is a crucial part of the feedback circle. The process of participating and uploading is continually evolving and involves rewarding elements which improve the overall editorial quality of Citizenside as a product, such as commenting on images and uploads. This gives instant performance on how members are doing. Big brands like CNN and the BBC have huge news-gathering outlets and tremendous capacity technically but they are slow to move and have not yet captured the right ways to motivate audiences. Major news brands have an advantage because they have brand recognition and platforms that are sophisticated but they don't have the nimbleness of thinking or the speed and agility of a start-up.

'The challenge has come from the difficulty in securing content rights for something that has been widely shared already. Trying to maintain a rights' control situation in a landscape without rights control is very difficult. It is impossible to run a limited supply of copyrighted piece of media on the internet.

'It is extremely important to have the right technical team and move extremely fast. It is essential to turn operations round really quickly with new functionality and integration with other networks. Victory will go to a newcomer who can work with Big Media but develop a product that is good.'

Key reflections

- Look at what worked – and what no longer works – for old media. This knowledge will be the foundation of your new media enterprise.
- Think about how you would 'invent the web'. What are the features that make it innovative and truly different from legacy publishing?
- Critically analyse the last time a website or app made you stick around to discover more, and why that was.
- You have launched a new tool for aggregated news consumption. What are the key issues in getting it into mainstream use?
- Is there a built-in obsolescence in start-ups? To what extent must they continually evolve and collaborate to survive?

Readings and resources

Wired: Launched in 2009, Wired magazine has become a bit of a gospel among tech and start-up crowds wanting an edgy take on the industry: www.wired.co.uk. They also run a series of high-powered networking events.

Knight News Challenge is an international media innovation contest supporting transformational ideas that promote quality journalism, advance media innovation, engage communities and foster the arts: http://newschallenge.tumblr.com/.

SXSW Interactive is one of the highest profile events on the entrepreneurial tech calendar with plenty to sing and dance about in the media field. It's usually held in March: http://sxsw.com/.

Mark Briggs, author of *Journalism Next and Entrepreneurial Journalism*, has his finger on the pulse. Peter Drucker is also a key author in this field.

Innovation and Entrepreneurship (2008) by John Bessant and Joe Tidd crams a huge amount of theory as well as practical tips into one book.

Journals in international entrepreneurship, developmental entrepreneurship, strategic entrepreneurship, media management, media business studies, small business economics, and entrepreneurship theory and practice are a rich source of theoretical discussions.

Survival is Success maps journalistic online start-ups in Western Europe from the Reuters Institute for the Study of Journalism by Nicola Bruno and Rasmus Kleis Nielsen: http://reutersinstitute.politics.ox.ac.uk/publications/risj-challenges/survival-is-success.html.

Book resources: Tyler Cowen, *Create Your Own Economy: the Path to Prosperity in a Disordered World* (2009); Jonathan Law, Oxford's *A Dictionary of Business and Management* (2009); Jessica Livingston, *Founders at Work: Stories of Startups' Early Days* (2008).

Chasing Sustainability on the Net: International research on 69 journalistic pure players and their business models by Esa Sirkkunen and Clare Cook (2012) is available for download http://tampub.uta.fi/handle/10024/66378.

Websites: A range of discussion points and trends are presented on World Association of Newspapers and Newspaper Publishers (www.wan-ifra.org/), the worldwide magazine publishers association FIPP (http://fipp.com/) and the Professional Publishing Association (www.ppa.co.uk/).

Journalism schools are increasingly offering entrepreneurial modules and courses. Michael Rappa is creator of the open educational resource Digitalenterprise.org, Stanford runs the Entrepreneurship Corner, while the Centre for Entrepreneurship at Henley Business School offers a range of expert training.

>>Chapter 13<<

THE BUSINESS OF NETWORKED JOURNALISM

Overview

The social tools that have made media creation so ubiquitous have had a destructive effect on the business of journalism: audiences on traditional platforms are dwindling and alternative advertising revenues, once relied on for profitability, can no longer be guaranteed. This chapter explores the challenges facing commercial news outlets as they grapple for a sustainable business model, and how they are diversifying and experimenting with alternative payment methods. It summarises current thinking on where future profitability and funding may lie.

Key concepts

- Advertising
- Aggregation
- Business models
- Crowdsourcing
- Engagement
- Freemium
- Innovation
- Paywalls
- Revenue models
- Subscriptions

Springboard

- *Sustainability and profitability*: these two terms are often confused. Sustainability is about a product being able to maintain itself in whatever context its objectives dictate but profitability refers specifically to gross turnover being greater than net.
- *Quantity versus quality*: there has been much debate whether audiences are most valuable in socially networked environments in their quantity – generating the largest audiences possible – or in their quality, having fewer people but users who may be more loyal or engaged.
- *Know your audience*: what works for one audience on one platform won't work for another. If news organisations can work out readers' specific needs they can work on responding to and anticipating those needs.
- *Experiment and simplify*: this may be with the content and services on offer or by opening up alternative revenue streams. The most important thing, though, is to keep evolving.
- *Make paying simple*: in some ways there has been a delay in the potential to bring in revenues because of the sheer logistics of setting up payment methods. Users need to be offered easy and transparent ways to transact.

Introduction

The further into the networked environments we forge, the clearer it is that consumers have benefitted from technological advances in the digital age. They have more choices, speedier delivery of news and more platforms to choose from. As we have seen in preceeding chapters, new players have achieved impressive editorial results. But many, along with their more established news organisations, have yet to achieve financial stability.

There are many reasons for this. First, it's important to understand the foundations of traditional media business and how they turned large profits. The legacy model was built on advertising revenues, which required media companies to act as gatekeepers to information. It was a scarcity of supply that kept a stranglehold on advertisers. Before the global financial crisis but more than ten years after the spread of wide internet access, newspapers were very profitable businesses. In total, newspaper companies combined annual revenues of $49 billion in their best year: 2005 (Newspaper Association of America, 2012).

Newspapers moving online partially revoked the gatekeeping role. The culture of information-sharing on the web was already established by the time news organisations embraced it, and the new reality meant facing companies like Google, the era of free online content and what Jeff Jarvis

Revenue model

This is how you intend to make money. A revenue stream is an activity that brings in money, such as advertising or sales.

Business model

This is how you intend to continue making money. It combines revenue strategies with other elements of business planning.

refered to as the 'link economy' (Jarvis, 2008). When change came, it was difficult to see how far-reaching its impact would be. After all, change had come with the dawn of television, cable and satellite – and had been survived – many times before.

But this was different. To assume traditional mass media's monopoly over news production tools was sufficient for sustainable business models in an era of abundant news technologies was foolhardy. Social peer-produced media capable of supporting conversations, repurposing content and then redistributing it creates a landscape too complex for traditional media economics. Just as with production, the business of journalism is no longer in linear form.

We are now confronted with very real questions of how to finance and organise journalism for the social-media age. Media businesses are looking to be more innovative in what and whom they serve. Underlying all of this is a fundamental rethink of what it means to create value journalistically. Doing the same things in the same ways is unlikely to work in the future.

The legacy model

It's important to understand the legacy business model of mass media in order to identify opportunities for the future. Most other businesses are based on a simple formula: products or services for sale at a price. But commercial journalism has mainly been paid for indirectly. Sales revenue, either from cover price or subscription, has been only one part of meeting costs. The real money has come from advertising. For example, the global newspaper publishing market derives about 57 per cent of its revenues from advertising and about 43 per cent from newspaper sales (Organisation for Economic Co-operation and Development, 2010).

News content is the first commodity, as it is consumed by audiences who see value in it. The audiences themselves then become a second commodity, as they have value to advertisers who want to get a message seen and acted upon. So media companies can 'sell' their audiences to advertisers. This is known as 'dual product', a term coined by media business expert Robert G. Picard (1989).

Media organisations have perfected the art of segmenting that audience, in terms of demographics, social and economic standing and all manner of interests, so advertisers can accurately pitch products at them. The size of the audience is then calculated – circulation, readership, visits, listening and viewing figures – to determine a corresponding value of the audience.

> ## Dual product
>
> Journalism has mainly been paid for indirectly. While sales make up part of revenues, the largest proportion of money has come from advertising by 'selling' users to advertisers.

> ## Advertising
>
> Advertising is a paid form of communication intended to inform or persuade people to take action. It is a process based around audiences coming in contact with a message aimed at changing their consumer behaviour.

The most damaging misconception that still pervades the newspaper industry today is the belief that consumers used to pay for their news.
(Mark Briggs, author)

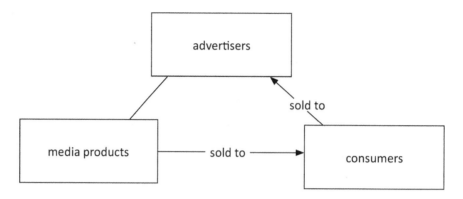

FIGURE 13.1 Much of traditional commercial journalism was founded on dual product: selling audiences to advertisers as well as the direct sale of a product.

Early attempts with digital

It was relatively easy to sell audiences to advertisers in the pre-digital world. So long as media owners could bundle together content, there were advertisers who wanted to get messages out to the mass audience. The model was based on news organisations selling advertising as if every page was turned or every minute of a broadcast watched. Advertisers had few alternatives to mass-media advertising and certainly nothing as powerful.

In the late 1990s there was plenty of enthusiasm about investing in online journalism. BBC Online officially launched in 1997; papers started to see classified advertising move online; market confidence in e-commerce spurred stock prices. But it was short lived. Within a few years, many had spent too much for too little return, gone bust or had no coherent business model.

The emergence of digital technologies disrupted the business model. Media organisations were slow to adapt to a new competitive landscape. They failed to push new lines of business or grapple with the unique capabilities of the medium. They were averse to change and resisted investing in an unproven medium, especially after the dotcom bust of 2001. Of course, there had been change before but never at this pace. Even relatively niche sites of amateur and freelance content such as Demotix topped 400,000 unique users, 1.3 million page views and 15,000 daily visitors in a month, just 3 years after launch.

Legacy media were also under siege from users. Instead of controlling the printing press, any man and his camera could record and upload content. In 2006, former PayPal employee Jawed Karim uploaded the first ever clip to YouTube. TIME magazine celebrated this shift with an iconic front-page ode to 'You' as the Person of the Year (*TIME*, 2006), while CNN and Fox News both launched their portals

 ## End of the offline

'Do we carry on regardless and follow the users? Do we retreat, as Richard Desmond did when he bought the Express Group and promptly closed its websites? Or do we press on even faster, in acknowledgement of the fact that you cannot de-invent the wheel?' (Emily Bell, academic and journalist, 2005)

for user-generated content. And access to these tools was exploding. Internet World Stats cite 361 million internet users in 2000, increasing to 939 million in 2005 and 2 billion in 2011 (Internet World Stats, 2011). This changing culture of engagement is a theme that comes up throughout the book.

Add to this a global recession in 2008–2009, the worst of the post-war period. News managers could not make anything more than a minimum investment in new expertise or technical staff. The impact was immediate and often severe for commercial news media organisations. The OECD's estimated change in total newspaper publishing revenues between 2007 and 2009 shows USA down 30 per cent, the UK down 21 per cent and Italy down 18 per cent (Organisation for Economic Co-operation and Development, 2009).

The problem of making money from a multi-player news landscape loomed large. News organisations around the world experimented as best they could. Aftonbladet was the first Swedish newspaper to go online and had success growing audiences and charging for content. Meanwhile, the New York Times tried putting top columnists behind a yearly fee paywall under the banner TimesSelect, but it was dropped after two years. The Guardian experimented with charging for an improved version of its email service The Wrap and advertising-free versions of content. But no sooner had news outlets grappled with online than tablets and mobiles opened up yet more change. One thing was clear: making a profit in a multi-dimensional landscape was going to be a lot easier said than done.

Rupert Murdoch's 'Digital Natives' speech to the American Society of Newspaper editors was seen as a tipping point. He expressed the 'peculiar challenge ... for us digital immigrants to apply a digital mindset to a new set of challenges' (Murdoch, 2005). It spurred a change in the attitude towards the web and the capacity for new ways of 'doing' news.

> ## Increase traffic but not profits
>
> ABC figures for April 2011 saw print circulation of the Guardian drop 12.5 per cent year-on-year to 262,937. Digital traffic was up 31 per cent, however, with 2.4 million unique users in April. Overall, turnover for the Guardian Media Group still dropped, from £221 million in 2009/2010 to £198 million in 2010/11 (Gunter, 2011c).

Why media need new business models

For most news executives it is the million-dollar question: why has a technology so empowering for the dissemination and creation of content not provided the same energy for companies to maintain and increase profits? There are several major issues:

- Consumers expect content to be free, especially breaking news.
- Advertising models do not translate directly to a networked media world.
- Social-media habits have changed the way we consume news.
- Disrupted distribution means media producers no longer own the process of news dissemination.
- Advertisers themselves have a different role and relationship with social media.
- The new media ecology has a new structure and costs.

Free content

News content is more popular than ever. Given that it can be consumed in a personalised, rebundled or on-demand way, more audiences are now being served. In October 2011, 11 per cent of US adults owned a tablet, with 53 per cent getting news as long articles and headlines every day (Project for Excellence in Journalism, 2011b). Hard-to-reach young users – who are especially coveted, as they represent audiences of the future, are more open to experimentation, and have more disposable income – are also consuming more content (Rideout et al., 2010).

> ## Audiences resist paying
>
> Among more than 2,000 online adults surveyed in a Harris Poll, 77 per cent said they wouldn't pay anything to read a newspaper's stories on the web (Whitney, 2010).

 Journalists and news enterprises seem genuinely shocked by the fact that large sections of the public are not willing to pay for news. (Robert G. Picard, in Levy and Neilsen, 2010)

Yet the first major battle in finding sustainable business models is the expectation among audiences that digital content should be free, as part of an open process for all. There may be more consumers of news but fewer of them are paying for it. Writing in the Wall Street Journal in 2009, author Chris Anderson said: 'Over the past decade, we have built a country-sized economy online where the default price is zero – nothing, nada, zip. Digital goods – from music and video to Wikipedia – can be produced and distributed at virtually no marginal cost, and so, by the laws of economics, price has gone the same way, to $0.00. For the Google Generation, the internet is the land of the free.' (Anderson, 2009b).

In effect, news organisations eroded one of the fundamental revenue streams that had propped up legacy media: direct sales. Having failed to charge for online content when their websites first went live, it was very difficult to retrospectively structure a business model or impose tariffs on customers accustomed to a free service. It is only relatively recently that online payment mechanisms even became reliable and secure enough to be viable.

Advertising models

Having missed an opportunity for revenues through direct sales, it became clear that advertising too would not be a simple way out. Advertising models that supported traditional media appear unable – for the most part – to do so in the digital age. Readers are worth less online. The fundamental of legacy platform advertising was scarcity of space. However, social and networked media offer an abundance of space so the rate that an advertiser is prepared to pay shrinks. Most attempts to shift business online fail as they trade 'old media dollars for new media pennies' (Nichols and McChesney, 2009).

Increased digital traffic has not compensated for drops in print readers, or resulted in proportional gains in advertising revenue. This isn't so surprising: newspapers have never made much money from news but have relied on cross-subsidising the core news production. They've made money from the special interest sections on topics such as cars, travel and food, where contextually targeted advertising is more effective and worth a premium. In effect, digital disrupts the old way of making profit from bundling content together and charging for the whole. Now, users want to consume exactly the 'bits' they want and are rarely prepared to pay for an entire product, if at all.

Unpredictable page views also mean there is a wide range of prices for advertising, with the highest rates being charged for the most desirable times, placements and audiences – leaving the rest worth almost nothing (Grueskin et al., 2011). Click-through rates are often low and metrics demarcating the performance of most advertising is still evolving. The other problem is that 79 per cent of US online news users said they never or hardly ever click on display ads, devaluing them even further (Purcell et al., 2010).

The worry is that social networks such as Facebook and LinkedIn have the power to further commoditise news organisations' general advertising rates because the services they offer to advertisers are so much more targeted. Social networks are valued highly on the back of the potential revenues from personal data collected from millions of users. Much of that data is about people's interests

Click-through rates

This metric quantifies the number of times consumers click on a link in order to access content. It can reflect the performance of advertising.

and likes, specifically highlighted in a click-by-click manner, making them streamlined competitors to the advertising service once dominated by media organisations. Any assistance in drilling through the multidimensional maze of social spaces, to reconnect adverts with audiences, proves lucrative.

Social-media habits

What works for one audience on one platform won't work for another – and this further disrupts the model of segmenting users and selling advertising to them. Where once audiences could be boxed and framed into clear segments or stereotypical groupings, they are now more fluid: using different networks and media outlets to serve a wide range of interests and objectives. Media experiences are much more peer-to-peer and anarchic. As such, advertising in the new media ecology requires a much fuller commitment to understanding audiences and shifting user behaviour.

Segmentation

A range of factors have historically been used to determine audience groupings, including social status, postcode, disposable income, education, career and family. These paint a picture of audiences to advertisers so they can accurately target products at them.

Most readers spend far less time looking at digital news content than they did traditional media. Online reading is ad hoc and sporadic, with readers getting their news from a variety of sources, allowing them to mix and match, and hop from one channel to another. Users may read the news at work during office hours when their attention is limited and there is increasing evidence to suggest mobile-only audiences. The younger generation especially graze or skim their way through news content. This has led to many news organisations chasing users' attention during their leisure time, when they are more likely to look at content and ads (see Chapter 3 on immersion in news production).

Disrupted distribution

Distribution in networked media takes content away from owned platforms – and with it the simplicity of generating revenue from quantifying the content in front of users. There is no clear methodology at present in terms of income generation from shared distribution.

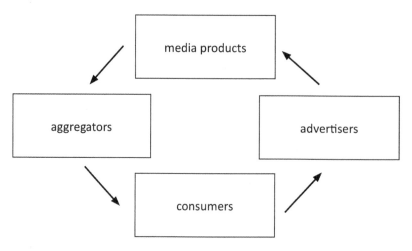

FIGURE 13.2 How aggregation disrupts the traditional dual-product model.

 We are just beginning to get glimmers of how it is going to work and it is this world where, if you can allow yourself to imagine the blurring of distinctions between the journalist and the reader and involve them more, and create a community around your journalistic core, you begin to see a new model. (Alan Rusbridger, editor (Institut für Medienpolitik, 2009))

Target market

A target audience is a segment of the public for whom products, events or services were created. This is the target market.

Aggregation confuses this yet further. It is complicated territory, as it disrupts the offline dual product model. Against a backdrop of newspaper closures and job losses, some demonise aggregation as theft and a copyright breach. The Huffington Post has fine-tuned its ability to aggregate in a way to justify a buy-out by AOL of $315 million, by bringing together headlines from other news producers, comments, and social media to intensely engaged audiences at marginal costs. Newser.com, co-founded by media critic Michael Wolff, has little in the way of original reporting yet has a stash of followers, which in turn can be valued in terms of revenue from advertisers.

There is a trade between those who have information and those who want it, and media organisations have a fluid place within that. This disintermediation (Katz, 1988; Bardoel et al., 2001) – cutting out the middle man – is made possible by the open and networked construct of the web.

Advertisers in social spaces

This 'opening up' of content distribution has affected advertisers in two main ways. First, journalism as a process, not a product, makes it susceptible to continual comment and modification. With traditional media advertising, the product and audience with which one was associating was always clear-cut. But now advertisers too are having to come to terms with being in an open social process.

Channel 4 learnt the hard way how social media interrupt the control of a media product. L'Oréal and Nestlé pulled out of advertising on Frankie Boyle's comedy show after a backlash over racist remarks. Carphone Warehouse withdrew sponsorship of *Big Brother* over the Shilpa Shetty race row that engulfed the UK show in 2007.

Second, many advertisers have a new scepticism of media organisations. Advertisers with big bucks to spend are carving out increasingly innovative campaigns, building direct relationships with their consumers and could, one day, cut out advertising in a media product entirely. They go direct to their target market on social platforms. For small-deal advertisers, they are only just making the foray into digital spaces themselves so are still a little wary about digital advertising and the statistics behind it. Media companies, especially some start-ups or local sites, have had to hand-hold and cajole advertisers into spending their money on online advertising.

Costs and competitors in the new media ecology

Legacy media found itself in an uncomfortable place against the backdrop of the 2007 recession. It was clear that round upon round of cost cutting might become a self-defeating strategy. Although essential for survival, cost-cutting measures such as using junior reporters, content farms or relying on press releases and advertorials affected the value of the product. The problem then was trying to make money from a weaker product in a drastically more competitive market.

Newspapers were left with very little money to finance the rapid business transformation needed to cope with the new digital competition. They were also bridled with legacy costs. In many cases the acquisitions and high fixed costs that were inherited from the boom years were proving to be a curse. To put this into context, roughly 50 per cent of the cost of producing a printed newspaper is in printing and distribution, with only about 15 per cent of total costs being editorial (Varian, 2010). Producers save a lot of money if the primary access to news is via the internet.

The other significant marker for change in journalism was the massive proliferation of news blogging and alternative sites this book has detailed throughout. The barrier to entry and development time from idea to market for start-ups was shorter, so competitors could imitate and adapt quickly. The divide between amateur and professional outputs was also increasingly put into focus, putting yet more pressure on the old way of doing media business. The new media-rich world allowed for experimentation and fragmentation on many different levels.

> # Direct relations
>
> There is much academic interest in the fields of marketing and PR and how companies and brands now communicate directly with their audiences, how public relations has gone truly public again and how today's consumers reject mass-market messaging (Scott 2011; Reinartz et al., 2004). Instead, Lucas Grindley and others propose zoning by interests or drilling towards niche and hyperlocal (Grindley, 2006).

> # Content farming
>
> This is an algorithm-based strategy that uses the number of hits to commission content. Content farms supply articles based on what is trending in order to maximise their impact against trending topics.

Marginal costs

In a perfectly competitive market, the long-term product price will be the marginal cost of production. Because of declining hosting and bandwidth costs, for most internet products the marginal cost today is practically zero, allowing products to be made available for free.

Barrier to entry

An organisation with low start-up costs or expertise is considered to have a low barrier to entry as there is little to block potential competitors from entering the market. First-mover advantage reflects the strengths a company can gain from having a head-start on its competitors.

Towards a successful business model

There has been much debate about digital and social media in terms of income generation: is it the source of the problem or the source of the solution? The new-media ecology requires a new way of thinking about audiences, one that somehow feasts on an abundance of information, and an abundance of players, rather than the advertising-supported scarcity of old.

Business strategies to cope with this new landscape currently fall into two main camps: pursuing quantity or quality. The quantity camp has an allegiance to the old way, in that it trades on bringing in revenues based on the largest audiences possible. Mass hits still command a premium. This is volume of traffic. Advertising attached to a viral video or a peak viewing slot are examples. There is still value in quantifying a large number of unique users.

The quality strategy can mean lots of different things. It is primarily about sourcing revenue based on added value. This added value may come from creating a niche in the content you produce, or a highly segmented audience, or offering a specific service that commands a premium. Or it may be quality through engagement. The quality over quantity suggests smaller cherry-picked audiences – but who may be worth more as they are more loyal and in tune with the content they are viewing.

Quantity: value in volume

There is a lot of money to be made from quantity when it comes to digital and online advertising. Dad Howard Davies-Carr can testify to it. His video clip of his one-year-old son Charlie biting his three-year-old brother's finger makes around £120,000 a year from accompanying ads as a YouTube Partner (Rollings, 2011). Lauren Luke has made an impressive make-up empire on the back of amateur how-to videos, also supported with advertising. In both cases it is the sheer quantity of views that advertisers are interested in, all be them largely general interest.

Classified sites such as Craigslist have also proved that quantity pays. There may not be a user-friendly interface, but the site makes multi-million-dollar sums by dominating the classifieds market with a collection of items for sale, jobs, relationships, services, rentals and products. It

Viral advertising

This technique focuses on the creation of advertisements with a high potential to be spread across social networking sites or by word of mouth. They aim to create a buzz around products or services. It relies on users spreading content among themselves.

was the dawn of sites such as this that sent shivers down media owners' spines as they realised classified advertising would move progressively online.

There is no doubt that the scope and range of advertising on the web, from video embeds to pop-ups and links, offers plenty of ways to reach audiences in ways that were never possible in static media products. Advertising space is sold by cost per thousand (CPM), cost per lead (CPA)

Dayparting

Complex studies are ongoing into a technique known as 'dayparting' to identify peak viewing times of digital content. It builds on the traditional notion of broadcast 'prime time' by drilling down to identify what types of content are popular when to whom.

and cost per click (CPC). Campaigns can also be negotiated for weekly or monthly space, combining a number of cross-platform strategies. Studies have consistently found advertising to be one of the staple ways of generating revenues for news producers online, with internet advertising enjoying a growing share of total advertising in most markets.

Quantity: value from traffic

In the pursuit of getting content in front of the largest audiences possible, search engines, aggregators and portals play an important part. Google sends about four billion clicks each month, or 100,000 per minute, to news publishers via Google News, web search and other services (Cohen, 2009). Each click is an opportunity for publishers to show ads, win loyal readers and register users. According to comScore, clicks from search engines – and therefore online revenue – account for 35–40 per cent of traffic to major US news sites (Salgado, 2010). The importance of portals such as Yahoo! and MSN as access points was seen in the fact that they accounted for 13 per cent of traffic to news websites in 2009 (Dougherty, 2009).

 If you want great food you pay for it. If you want great journalism you pay for it. We put information of super richness, politics economy and details. Therein lies the value of what we are selling. It is our information. It is our journalists. It is our skill. (Sabine Torres, founder and director Dijonscope, (2012))

Social networks such as Facebook and Twitter, while on the one hand blamed for undermining revenues in the long run, can drive more overall traffic to news sites through referrals. In March 2010, Hitwise reported that Facebook had become the largest news reader, sending even more traffic to news and media sites than the search engines (Hopkins, 2010). This realisation has led news organisations to fine-tune their own pushing strategies towards social networks (distribution is discussed further in Chapter 4).

Quality: engagement

It has become increasingly clear that to expect digital and social spaces to perform economically in the same way as their legacy platforms is foolhardy. Journalism producers have realised that pursuing quantity may not be the only – and certainly not always the best – way of generating revenues. As such, attention has also turned to quality: how to add value.

Much focus has been put on understanding audiences more fully. How they are influenced, how they behave in peer-to-peer environments, is vital to adapting an appropriate business

Engagement

This is a buzzword to imply an audience is loyal, interested or committed. It refers to the ability for content to hold a user's attention or to keep them within a site – valuable commodities in an advertiser's eyes.

model. This has prompted media owners to pursue engagement. Niche segmentation can provide more value to advertisers because they are 'stickier and more valuable than drive-by referrals' (Newman, 2011). In a 2011 study, several UK media companies noted a higher number of page views for traffic from social networks compared with search, with a higher tendency to sign-up for subscriptions. This backed up findings from Mashable.com, which showed Facebook and Twitter visitors spent 29 per cent longer and viewed 20 per cent more pages than visitors arriving from search engines (Newman, 2011).

Media managers have realised that to be rewarded with engaged audiences they must first show engagement towards that audience – involving users in the news business, listening to what they want and making them a valued part of it. News organisations are attempting a raft of initiatives to reconnect with audiences, from opening up newsrooms and newslists, as at the Guardian and the Atlantic Wire, for example, to running campaigns such as the Hull Daily Mail's apprenticeship campaign.

News organisations can build new audiences centred on specialised topics of interest. It's a logical reaction in many ways: if we can't make money from mass audiences then we will have to make them from niche. As such, there has been much experimentation towards drilling down to connect communities of interest. Hyperlocal – such as citizen-journalist site Backfence.com, or portal Västerbottens-Kuriren in Sweden – represents an attempt by news organisations to attract new sources of income by serving advertising to more targeted audiences.

Niche success can be built on high-end quality products offering robust services, not just online. Newsweek successfully repositioned itself in 2009 as a high-end magazine selling in-depth reportage. The Economist print edition bucked the trends of 2008 and 2009 with increased advertising and healthy circulations. It remains a highly valued product for highbrow analysis and critique.

Quality: make content worth paying for

Many digital platforms were, at first, treated as just another opportunity to publish existing content in a shovelware mentality, which was not conducive to a charging strategy. Regional publisher Johnston Press learnt the hard way when they were forced to quietly dismantle their paywalls at six local news sites. Users voted with their wallets that out-of-date, lacklustre web pages with little content were simply not worth spending money on (Greenslade, 2010b). The lesson: if media want to generate income by charging users to access content then there has to be some sort of added value.

Shovelware

Many newsrooms strapped for resources put content online without making it platform specific, or adding any value in terms of additional features, interactivity or multimedia. It is widely accepted to be ineffective in generating quality audiences.

Expecting to generate revenues by making consumers pay, however, relies on setting a pricing structure for content: a perplexing task in networked media. Publishers have approached this option in a variety of ways. Each relies on offering news as a service which justifies a fee. There are options to charge for content based on what that content is (exclusive analysis or long-form journalism can command a premium), where it is accessed (for example, a tablet or mobile version) or based on when the content is available (some users will pay to know news first).

Paywalls

This term is vilified by many as it has become associated with barriers, when it in fact just refers to the requirement of paying for content. In its purest application it does act as a block, however, as content is not available for consumption unless a payment has been made.

Rupert Murdoch erected the riskiest type of paywall around the websites of The Times and the Sunday Times in summer 2010 – by making content exclusively available to subscribers. By putting even general-interest news behind a paywall, there were many who hoped he was the vanguard of a cultural shift that would carve out a successful pricing strategy for all. But it is a tricky gamble. Some advertisers have simply abandoned the site because of the drop in the number of users. The Financial Times website

If there's no traffic on there, there's no point in advertising on there. (Rob Lynam, head of press trading at the media agency MEC (in Burrell, 2010))

has enjoyed some success charging for must-know information. The FT commands about $390 for an annual subscription to its website, many of which are bought by corporations, rather than individuals.

The most successful paywall implementation has been the Wall Street Journal: it now has more than a million paid subscribers, but it took ten years to get there. French publisher MediaPart has also demonstrated the potential for success: it launched after a six-month campaign to secure 10,000 paying subscribers. Its reputation for investigative journalism has enabled that figure to grow to 58,000. Dijonscope became Europe's first online regional website behind a subscription, removing advertising entirely from December 2011.

Quality: freemium payments

Many media organisations wanting to test the waters have instead opted for a metered model: identifying content or services that have perceived added value to certain users but allowing some content to remain free to all. This metered model combining free and premium has become known as 'freemium' (Lukin, 2006). It was espoused by Chris Anderson as a way of giving away abundance but charging for the scarcity. Payment thresholds can be set at different levels

Freemium

Combining payment structures that include some free content available to all and other content that is paid for is known as a 'freemium' model: derived from free and premium. It is also known as a metered model. Thresholds for payment can be based on a range of factors including exclusivity, timeliness, services or audiences.

Microsharing

This is licensed sharing of small chunks of content such as an article, picture or video. It is associated with micropayments which unbundle content to the lowest common unit of price.

and publishers can distinguish different services for different readers (basic versions of content are free but payment is required for top-end functionality) or how much of it is accessed (a certain number of page views are free before a fee is required).

Major players like the New York Times, the Daily Mail and the Independent are all experimenting with different pricing plans. In 2011, Canada's largest newspaper publisher, Postmedia Network, put up metered paywalls at all its 38 daily and community newspapers across the country. The Sun newspaper charges for breaking-news text messages. The downside, however, is that the majority of content behind paywalls is not open for sharing, which is a major consideration when the trend points to the power of social and digital media to distribute content.

Alternatives and diversifying

Diversification

Social-media and digital platforms have required media managers to not only enlarge and widen the scope for income generation around content but also expand their portfolio of businesses, services and competences.

For many media organisations, finding successful business models has been about combining or re-engineering existing revenue streams rather than developing entirely new ways of making money. Many have tried to draw on the best of both quantity and quality strategies. At first this centred on their core products. But, increasingly, media organisations have seized the opportunity of the social and new media ecology to widen not only the range and scope of their business, but also the revenue streams. The main categories of revenue are set out in the 'Tips and tools' section of this chapter.

Many media companies have attempted to expand their business portfolio. We are, after all, in an age of convergence that is commercial as well as technological. Wired magazine opened a pop-up store in New York City where it could sell gadgets and paraphernalia, just as the NME music magazine runs a ticket shop. Media owners have sought to generate revenues from being a physical as well as a virtual 'place to be'.

> We do [news:rewired] for commercial reasons but if the business was going under it would be the events that I would rescue. It is the events that add value to a business, an editorial business especially. (John Thompson, director, journalism.co.uk and news: rewired (2012))

Brand extensions can come in almost any form, from dating websites to classified listings to online coupons – all of which make sense for news organisations that already understand how to make sense of grouping audiences together around common interests. When it comes to diversifying, it's not always about people. It is the Bloomberg Professional terminals that have funnelled $6 billion – 80 per cent of revenues – into the finance and business news giant.

Aftonbladet is one of the biggest daily newspapers in the Nordic countries, which has been successful diversifying its business model to complement print and advertising revenues. A weight-loss club, run by experts, recruited 380,000 members paying $70 per year or $10 a month. They also moved into e-commerce by selling vuvuzelas during the 2010 World Cup. Revenues have been generated producing web TV and selling documentaries on a pay-per-view basis in collaboration with producers such as National Geographic and the BBC.

Many media companies have expanded the services they offer. China Files, for example, is an independent, multimedia news-agency based in Beijing. Its main products are journalistic content (in any format: breaking news, long-form stories, video and audio bulletins, interactive features) to which they have added supplementary services (press roundups, press office and social media consultancy). Italian news start-up Effecinque develops apps and multimedia content for the largest Italian news publications. F5 main products are web-native formats (social-media news gathering, live coverage, data-journalism projects) and now visual features (motion graphic videos, interactive infographics).

Others have turned to staging events as a way to bring in revenues. Finland's ArcticStartup and Journalism.co.uk in the UK have built communities promoting new digital, mobile and web-based businesses as well as offering services to journalism movers and shakers. Over half of ArcticStartup's revenue comes from conferences that they organise in the capital cities of the Nordic and Baltic regions, selling tickets and stands.

We have little doubt that where it finds itself in a crisis the business of journalism must first and foremost rescue itself if it is to be rescued. This calls for both managers (the business) and journalists (of journalism) to think more about the road ahead than lament what has been or what might have been lost. (Levy and Neilsen, 2010)

There are also technology specialists emerging. Blottr.com in the UK is a visible part of the rising citizen-journalism movement, but it makes most of its revenue by selling the technology that powers its own platform. Other media companies can buy Blottr's platform as a white-label product and use it as a content-management system to harness the possibilities of user-generated content and conversation. Similarly, Tweetminster makes its money by selling a licence to use their software while also selling curated and analysed content from the social web.

Many media professionals have generated revenues through consulting. Finnish-based Asymco soon discovered that his blog was stimulating demand for management consulting. He was commissioned for consultancy within three months of starting the blog and that is still the primary source of income. Douglas McLennan, the publisher of Artsjournal.com, did more than 60 talks and flew more than 200,000 miles in 2010. Half of the revenue based on ArtsJournal comes through these engagements.

Crowdfunding has been used effectively to generate revenues for several journalistic investigations via sites such as Kickstarter.com and Spot.Us, founded by David Cohn. 'We are trying to rethink the marketplace and see how you

Crowdfunding

This is a system where small payments or donations from a large number of people can generate revenues. These can be used to fund elements of journalism such as investigations or reports.

can get people to collaborate on investigations together.' David Cohn, founder, Spot.Us, (in Knight News Challenge, 2009). It is a system where small payments from a large community can generate enough revenue to fund a story or investigation, pitched by a reporter. Once it is published, the investors can get their money back. It is a crowdfunding initiative that supports J'aime L'info, developed by Rue89 and Le Spiil in France. The site hosts 130 community projects and websites with the principal aim of facilitating revenue from small reader donations. Crowdfunding is powered by micropayments, financial transactions involving a very small sum of money. It is a revenue model based on pay as you go.

Conclusion

Many news organisations, whether they are start-ups or more established producers of content, are struggling to find financial stability while embracing the culture of social media. For most news executives this is complex territory, and one which is constantly shifting as experimentation, trial and trends drive business options forward. There are many reasons for this, core questions need answering.

Consumers expect content to be free, especially breaking news. From the early years of putting content online for free, and being unsure how best to move forward with workable business models, producers set themselves up for a fall: there may now be more people consuming content but very few of them are prepared to pay. This may be changing.

Advertising models do not translate directly to a networked media world. They may have worked well offline, but in the fluidity of social media where units of content – and users – move freely around the web, advertising appears unable to support media (and certainly not exclusively). The sheer abundance of space drives the value of advertising space down.

Social-media habits have changed the way we consume news, and this has disrupted the 'old' way of segmenting users into categories and bundling them together. Disrupted distribution adds to this, as it means media producers no longer own the process of news dissemination. The way we move around the space opens up an entire new world in terms of monetisation.

As for the response, the new-media ecology requires a new way of thinking about audiences, one that somehow feasts on an abundance of information, and an abundance of players rather than the advertising-supported scarcity of old.

Business strategies to cope with this new landscape currently fall into two main camps: pursuing quantity or quality. The quantity camp has an allegiance to the old way in that it trades on bringing in revenues based on the largest audiences possible. Mass hits still command a premium. The quality strategy can mean lots of different things. It is primarily about sourcing revenue based on added value. This added value may come from creating a niche in the content you produce, or a highly segmented audience, or offering a specific service that commands a premium. Or it may be quality through engagement. The quality over quantity strategem suggests smaller cherry-picked audiences but who may be worth more, as they are more loyal and in tune with the content they are viewing.

> ## CASE STUDY > Piano Media

Piano Media has challenged the online media industry with an aggregated paywall concept, launched in May 2011. In the two test markets, Slovakia and Slovenia, readers paid a monthly subscription of €3.90 (Slovakia) and €4.89 (Slovenia), which enables access to the premium content of all participating online media, a total of 60 websites and 20 publishers. The innovation comes from pooling content from several different media organisations for one fee. The publishers receive a share of the revenue based on the traffic generated, while Piano Media keeps a commission. In the first month of the launch in Slovenia, a Central European country with a population of only two million people, Piano generated €26,000 for the participating publishers.

The concept is interesting for both customers and publishers. For customers, it is 'paywalls made ·easy', as they only have to pay a relatively small fee, small enough to remain an impulse purchase. They then get all the best cross-section of journalism services on offer. Publishers get 70 per cent of the total revenues from the paywall (the other 30 per cent is Piano Media's commission). The proportion they get changes, though, to keep an incentive to produce great content and journalism. A media producer would be rewarded with higher revenues if the subscription was instigated on their site, and if the user stays on their site for longer. Some content, including breaking news, remains free to access.

Jan Cifra, business developer of Piano Media, says cable TV-style bundling will prove a lucrative way for publishers to secure revenues on digital platforms. 'We did studies to look at usability of payment methods, as it has to be easy for people to pay. The pricing is critical. This is not pricing by cost, which is not very good business. We wanted spontaneous buying so as to make it as cheap as possible and go for the mass. We compared the price setting to what people buy daily: a drink in a bar and a cup of coffee. It is low enough that people even pay for access to the free stuff for the peace of mind that they can be spontaneous, or some people just pay by mistake.

They also understand that our goal is not to rip people off but that you need to pay for good journalism to survive online. It has proven to us that people are not against paying for content, just against messing around with lots of different payments to different people. One of our co-founders had tried a paywall and it was a disaster. Cable TV uses a bundle. They are more mature in this field, as there are more complex bundling options available, but the basic idea is the same. This is cable TV for publishing: one payment and then everything is much easier on the customer.

Publishers have to realise they are offering services not just content. We have 40 services from different publishers. People are not prepared to pay for breaking news; it is not exclusive. But they are willing to pay for long-form or opinion pieces from certain publishers, or for in-depth coverage from another. Some sites focus on video, or tomorrow's newspaper today. Some publishers are offering editions of the whole paper. Some have closed off comments unless you pay: some platforms are heavy on discussions and passionate about that. That is why we call them services. Each of the publishers has the freedom to offer services that no one else has. Customisation is key: publishers have to go above and beyond if you want people to pay. Fundamental for journalism online is that customers perceive it as a value service.'

Key reflections

- What potential and risks do paywalls offer for media businesses?
- Is it possible to put a value on importance? Can one piece of content be more important than another depending on who sees it, who has recommended it or who has created it? Does importance correspond to value?
- Does the future of media business models lie with quality or quantity?
- Is there a future for free? How far can crowdsourcing and micropayments make media sustainable?
- In what ways are aggregators and portals the 'frenemy' of media business models?

Tips and tools

Advertorial: advertisements in editorial form that appear to contain objectively produced content are known as paid editorial ads. While there are increasing ethical issues surrounding advertorial – see Nick Davies's *Flat Earth News* for more – they can be highly effective from the advertisers' point of view as they sit so closely to editorial content.

Affiliate: in a pay-per-action model, websites can host links to other stores and be paid. If a user clicks through, they are referred to the host site, where they can make a purchase. Amazon has been particularly successful with this, encouraging thousands of niche sites to host mini book stores from which potential buyers can navigate to the Amazon online store.

Behavioural targeting: when ads are served based on user behaviour, it is known as behavioural targeting. Here, a variety of online factors such as recent online purchases, searches and browsing history, as well as demographic details such as age or gender, are factored in.

Brokerage: brokers bring buyers and sellers together in a marketplace such as Amazon or eBay.

Classifieds: once the mainstay of local news, classifieds refer to any listings for small- to medium-sized companies. The classified section is primarily a destination point where readers locate to search for selected items or services, unlike display ads, which are often found next to editorial.

Contextual advertising: targeted ads appear based on the page's content after scanning the text of a webpage for keyword phrases. Then, the system returns specific, targeted ads based on the content people are viewing or users' interests.

Cost per click (CPC): advertisers pay a small amount whenever an advert is clicked on. Google Adwords works in this way.

Cost per thousand (CPM): they are often tied to editorial content and were the earliest type of adverts online, available as skyscrapers, banners, leaderboards and many more. Display spaces are priced to reflect the number of viewers and dimensions.

Crowdfunding: people pool small amounts of money together to support an appeal for money whether that be charitable, start-ups, political campaigns or for a cause.

Display advertising: image or graphics-based adverts that can highlight products, brands or offers. They are especially successful in periodicals where they can be perused at leisure.

E-commerce: this is electronic retail, so think of it as shops online. For any site where product recommendations fit, it can make sense that people are able to buy products via the site too.

Email advertising: this is direct marketing, which uses electronic mail or newsletters to communicate information. It relies on an accurate database, built up by organisations, or bought.

Floating ads: while pop-ups have become largely redundant now, as many users have pop-up blockers, floating ads work in a similar way, interrupting a user on their route to a site.

Freemium or metered models: this model allows publishers to combine free offerings with some services and content for which there is a charge.

Geotagging: any content that is served to a user based on their location has been tagged – and it can be effective in advertising to target users within a specific locality or region. It is especially lucrative for websites with global readers or mobile advertising.

Micropayments: these are financial transactions involving a very small sum of money. It is a revenue model based on pay as you go. Micropayments have worked well for Apple's iTunes.

Mobile advertising: with a range of mobile advertising options, from display ads, search ads, rich media, video and push notifications, the landscape can be complicated. Text message (SMS) adverts boast much higher click-through rates than other display ads.

Mobile applications: publishers are increasingly finding ways to package their content into convenient apps for use on mobiles or tablets. Revenues can come from direct sales; other apps are free to download, but you pay for more functionality.

Page impressions: each time an advert is displayed online it generates an impression. The more page views your site supplies, the more page impressions you have to inventory. You can charge the advertiser more, as they will get more page impressions for their advert.

Paywalls: the strategy of preventing open access to content until it is paid for either through subscription or a one-off fee.

Philanthropy: in the USA, Bay Citizen, Texas Tribune and MinnPost have all been buttressed with substantial beneficiary donations. ProPublica, the first all-digital news operation to be awarded a Pulitzer Prize, is funded by wealthy former banking chief executives Herbert and Marion Sandler.

Product placement: when actors or presenters mention, see or promote products – or brands are given a physical presence on set – this is known as product placement.

Proservices: several start-ups and digitally conceived media businesses offer a more sophisticated version of their product for a fee, often to mainstream news outlets or businesses.

Sales: media revenues can be generated by selling a product to a buyer. For example, coverprice refers to the price of a printed product.

Seed funding: these are the earliest funds necessary to start a business to sustain it for a period of development.

Selling data: money can be made selling user data – emails, addresses, browsing history, friends, credentials and preferences – and companies can build detailed databases on people. Facebook was forced to change the exposure of users' personal information, after an investigation showed that personal IDs were being transmitted to third parties via apps.

Subscription: users are charged a periodic fee to access a service. This model was a cornerstone of offline publishing business models but it has been given a new lease of life online with tiered options and options to mix and match.

Syndication: this involves making content available to a third party. In print it could be via a licence for news articles; on the web it could be where a feed of content could be sold to other sites (such as Tweetminster); and in broadcast it could be when programmes are sold outside of a network.

Unicast: these ads build on the TV commercial, as they offer a multimedia package that is clickable.

Venture capital: this finance is provided to early-stage, high-potential, high-risk start-ups, usually by owning equity in the company. It usually happens after seed funding.

Readings and resources

Columbia Journalism School: The Story So Far: What We Know About the Business of Digital Journalism is a timely report on media business models: www.cjr.org/the_business_of_digital_journalism/the_story_so_far_what_we_know.php (Grueskin et al., 2011).

Digital Natives Speech: this iconic address by Rupert Murdoch to the American Society of Editors summarises how media managers' attitudes would have to change: www.newscorp.com/news/news_247.html (Murdoch, 2005).

We the Media: examines the relationship between Big Media, or traditional publishers, and the new breed of bloggers, and is a must-read for media executives (Gillmor, 2004).

Funding Journalism in the Digital Age: this book by Jeff Kaye and Stephen Quinn (2010) offers a thorough insight into business models.

MondayNote: Frederick Filoux's blog presents key issues and developments in the debate for sustainable and profitable business models: www.mondaynote.com.

International studies: SubMoJour is a joint research project to create an emerging data archive of journalistic business models: www.submojour.net/.

The Changing Business of Journalism is published by Reuters and offers nuanced scrutiny of the threats and opportunities facing legacy news organisations across the world in countries as diverse as the United States, the United Kingdom, France, Germany, Finland, Brazil and India, as they transition to an increasingly convergent media landscape: (http://reutersinstitute.politics.ox.ac.uk/?id=560).

Wikinomics: How Mass Collaboration Changes Everything frames the problems in digital business (Tapscott, 2010).

Crowdsourcing: *Why the Power of the Crowd is Driving the Future of Business* is an interesting insight into the culture of social media as a driving economic force (Howe, 2009).

'The evolution of news and the internet' by the Organisation for Economic Co-operation and Development had a compelling message: 'The economic foundations of journalism have to be rethought' (2010): www.oecd.org/dataoecd/30/24/45559596.pdf.

Chris Anderson: ex-editor of *Wired* magazine and author of *Free: The Future of a Radical Price* (2009a) is well worth following.

Digital Journalism: this text by Janet Jones and Lee Salter (2012) is essential reading for a commercial awareness of the issues facing online journalism.

'Where else is the money?' by François Nel (2010), explores business models in the UK.

>>Chapter 14<<

CONCLUSION: NEWS IN A NEW MEDIA ECOLOGY

Overview

This book has laid out a comprehensive guide to the practice and principles of journalism in the age of social media. The practice has changed in many ways, but the fundamentals of journalism remain. Be honest, be open, listen to everyone and report fairly – those things haven't changed, but almost everything else has. This book has discussed the production, ethics and economics of journalism in the context of the more open, equal, and collaborative age of the internet. This final chapter will lays out a typology for understanding this new environment, and the new practices within it: the collaboration, the immediacy, the engagement with the audience. We hope in this chapter to re-orient thinking from the new media landscape's boundaries and features to a new media ecology, where platform is less important than relationships.

Key concepts

- Citizen journalism
- Freelance
- Intent
- Media landscape
- Network relationships
- Output
- Social media
- Sourcing
- Traditional media
- Voice

Introduction

Every year we stand in front of the new intake of journalism students and explain the landscape of the news environment as we see it. 'Here are the mainstream newspapers, grouped according to their political identity and their physical size. Here are the broadcast news outlets, and who owns what.' This is how we understood the media world, by physical output and ownership. The lecture gets more and more confusing each year, and the students more and more baffled – why do we call them 'broadsheets' when half of them are the same size as the 'tabloids'? Why does it matter what size it is when it's all the same on a tablet screen? Why is the New York Times a newspaper and CNN a broadcaster when online they have the same mix of video, audio, pictures and text?

It becomes clear when speaking to students who were born after the World Wide Web that we need a new way of thinking about the media landscape – one that goes beyond the technological determinism of 'newspaper' and 'television channel' and simple ideas of left and right politics, or target audiences divided by economic class and geography. The technological limitations on the media – the mechanism and scope of distribution – are no longer important. What remains important is what you are saying, and who you are saying it to.

The new media landscape: a matrix model

The macro level

The traditional way of defining news outlets was based on technological determinism – the medium was both the message and the mechanism of distribution. Organisations like the New York Times were the physical product: the 'Old Gray Lady' was a tangible grey and white collection of paper, or a building on Times Square. The measure of the organisation was its physical presence in the world.

In the new social and networked environment, output technology is no longer the determining factor of a news organisation, since it is a rare (and probably endangered) news organisation that is limited to one technological means of distribution. Traditional organisations are converging, using the same input to produce multiple outputs; new organisations are being created that do multiple things for multiple audiences. We can't identify these organisations by their physical product any more. Instead, we propose the measurement and determination of a news organisation or an individual journalist is based on three factors: the voice with which they communicate, their intent in communicating and their relative weight, or clout, within the news media landscape.

These three factors are plotted onto a two-dimensional matrix, with voice as the vertical axis, intent as the horizontal and influence or clout reflected by the size of the marker. This matrix is based on a subjective analysis of news organisations undertaken by the authors, but it is not intended as a definitive map of the landscape and all the players within it; rather, it is constructed as a challenge to existing models of the news media environment, and old ways of thinking about the news that make it difficult for researchers and theorists to grapple with the specific issues that this radically changed landscape has created.

Vertical axis: Voice

Traditionally, newsmaking is a process that takes events and turns them into recognisable news packages, using the 'third-person objective' voice of authority that we have come to associate with news. This voice is at the top of this axis. At the bottom of the axis is the loose, unedited, stream-of-consciousness voice of the personal blogger or tweeter, or the chaotic and unedited video footage taken by a participant in a protest. The amount of shaping, formatting and editing that goes into a story increases as you go up the axis, while the immediacy and rawness of the information decreases. Audience participation and inclusion also increases as you move down the axis, and traditional gatekeeping decreases.

At the top of this axis is the fully researched and written front-page story detailing exactly what had happened in Tahrir Square in Cairo, with comments and interviews with experts and bystanders carefully woven into a cohesive narrative.

Moving down this axis are the hourly bulletin updates from a reporter standing in the square, still formatted and structured in a predictable way – the journalist standing in front of the camera holding a microphone: 'I'm standing in Tahrir Square while all around me protesters shout slogans at the army. Earlier today the ministry of defence said ...' – the journalist is still acting as interpreter of events for the public, still working within defined formats and expected forms of address, although the material is live and unedited (albeit often rehearsed and prepared), and lacks the formal structure of the news package.

Even further down, you have the live blog feed of a news website, bringing inside information, comment from readers, twitter feeds and video uploads from people on the scene, and information

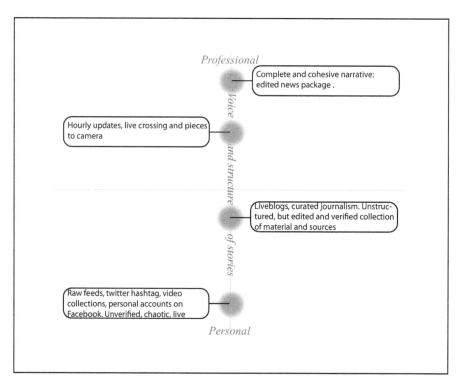

FIGURE 14.1   The vertical axis which measures the voice of the news outlet.

from other news sources together in a chaotic stream of information which no longer functions as a cohesive narrative or story, but which still retains some of the elements of journalistic practice: verification, mixing of sources and some consistency of expression.

At the very bottom of this axis you have the raw feed of events that appears when you search #tahrir on Twitter, or watch the raw uploaded videos on YouTube and pictures on Twitpic, Facebook or Flickr. At this level, the news is simply the outpouring of data and material of events, unedited, unverified and utterly raw.

Linked to this is the level of personal voice and opinion – as you move down the axis the news content becomes more personal, the traditional authoritative first-person voice is subsumed by the personal, subjective voice of the participant. This links it to Jay Rosen's call for journalists to move 'beyond objectivity', and into the personal in order to re-engage with the public (1993).

News products at the top of the axis have the traditionally closed gatekeeping approach, where professional journalists in the traditional sense construct the news product based only on their sources and research, and present a sealed and finite news product to a passive audience. As you move down the axis, the gates open, and the public are given more access to the news production process, more opportunities to participate and guide the news agenda. At the bottom of the axis, the distinction between journalist and audience has vanished completely: the gates have crumbled away.

The vertical axis also measures completeness and insularity of the news product. Traditional news products at the top of the axis strive to provide all the information and news one person could need. They were conceived as a single discrete product for each consumer, obviating the need for multiple sources of information. As you move down the axis, the news products become more divergent, incorporating multiple voices and channels, and creating an environment where, at the very bottom, one user would need to access hundreds of sources to provide an understanding of events.

From our perspective, the news landscape is moving down this axis, with a sinking centre of gravity currently located just above the middle line. Even the most traditional news organisations are including live blogs of events on their websites, incorporating amateur video into their feeds, and incorporating user comments and feedback in formal and informal ways.

Horizontal axis: intent

On the far right of this axis are the purely journalistic institutions – the BBC, CNN, the New York Times – that cover the events in Tahrir Square because they fulfil a traditional idea of what news is, and claim to do so in an 'objective' way: organisations that refer to 'President Mubarak' and 'protestors' in the most neutral way possible.

As one moves to the left along the axis, the news organisations that have stated social or political goals appear. A newspaper like the Guardian, with a clearly stated belief in social justice, sits more to the left. Their coverage of the same events would refer to Mubarak as a 'dictator' or 'despot', and the protestors as campaigners or activists. One's place on the axis is not a function of simple left–right politics, however: Egyptian state television, which holds an opposite belief to the Guardian, and would refer to the protesters in Tahrir Square as 'terrorists' or 'traitors', also sits to the left: it is the expression of bias or an underlying social or political goal that moves a news organisation from the right to the left. Highly commercialised media – such as Fox News and the British tabloids – are also here, because their journalistic goals are in tension with their commercial goals, and sometimes secondary to them.

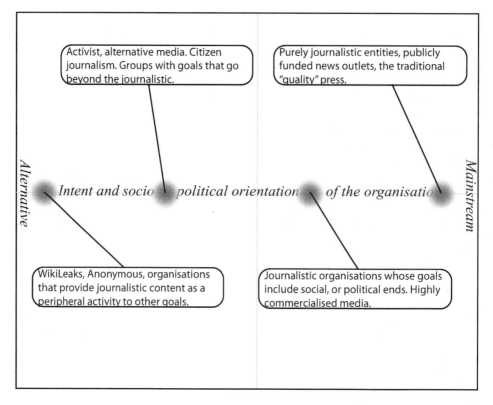

FIGURE 14.2   The horizontal axis which measures the intent of the news organisation, with the traditional, mainstream, commercial and industrial 'mass media' on the far right of the matrix. Moving towards the left, organisations' focus on news decreases, and other concerns – commercial gain, social change and political activism – creep in. On the far left are the organisations (and individuals) whose production of 'news' is entirely secondary, or even accidental, to their main goals. This is inherently a subjective measure, and we have placed the purely altruistic public news outlets (such as the BBC or NPR) on the right, representing the 'purest' form of news, and the commercial and industrial media to the left of that.

To the left of the centre line are organisations in which the journalistic goals are less important than the political or social goals. Groups like Indymedia, and related blogs such as Reportsfromtheegyptianuprising which describes itself as providing reports from Cairo 'in solidarity with the direct action of the people of Egypt against state repression' (Reportsfromtheegyptianuprising, 2011) are here.

On the very far left are organisations whose journalistic outputs are incidental to other goals. WikiLeaks's release of diplomatic cables relating to Egypt, and other documents are here: the goals are not simply journalistic, but include 'bring[ing] down administrations that rely on concealing reality from their own citizens' and 'the improvement of our common historical record and the support of the rights of all people to create new history'.

In this new media landscape, news outlets can find themselves competing with other forms of news, both from outlets that are setting up to directly compete with the news but have no traditional roots in the pre-internet news age, such as Global Voices online, or from people and organisations that have other goals than becoming a formal, commercial news organisation, such as 'zines, radical news outlets, activist groups online, and entities like Anonymous (and its parent 4chan) and WikiLeaks. News organisations to the right of the matrix may make use of information and content provided to organisations and entities to the left – bringing new ideas and audiences to their products.

Intent is measured from the formal news outlets that function within the expected and defined fourth estate role on the right, to the radical and activist organisations on the left.

News organisations on the right are those that are registered and subjected to what formal oversight is necessary within their specific national contexts; that exist in order to spread the news within defined parameters of the expected behaviour of news outlets. These are the organisations that have access to the parliamentary press gallery (or its equivalent), that have the protection of the courts to prevent the disclosure of sources, but may likewise be subject to regulations on content that would not necessarily apply to individuals. These are those outlets that are traditionally referred to as the 'mainstream' news, as well as those that have been specifically set up to compete with them.

Publicly funded news outlets (such as the BBC and the newer organisations like ProPublica) are on the farthest end of this axis, having goals that are primarily civic. State-supported media outlets move left along this axis, depending on the extent to which the preservation of the state overrides journalistic and civic goals. Commercial news outlets are slightly left of them, having their civic journalistic goals diluted by their commercial goals – highly commercialised media, those whose primary goal is financial, move even further left.

On the far left of this axis are the groups whose goals are not journalistic in nature, but which nevertheless participate in the same landscape as the news media by providing the same kinds of information in the same ways. WikiLeaks exists to the far left of this axis – an organisation that probably provided more raw news information than any other in 2010, but which nonetheless is not strictly journalistic in its goals or outputs (this runs counter to WikiLeaks's sometimes expressed intention of being a news organisation: however, since they do not in any way vet, edit, construct or package the information they have, it is our contention that they are not journalistic in nature). Also on the left of this axis are the news outlets produced by activist organisations or political parties, and the activities of informal groups such as Kuro5hin or Slashdot.org.

The complete matrix

Locations on the matrix are also represented by markers of differing size, representing the relative weight of the organisation within the field. Clout can be measured in a number of ways: the size of the enterprise, the size of the audience, the respect with which the organisation is viewed, the relative ranking of the organisation's website in Google, the multinational reach of its output, the size of its audience or the amount of money it generates. We have not attempted to measure the weight of organisations mathematically, or to represent them as scalable, but, as with the other aspects of the matrix, we have worked to create an admittedly subjective illustration of the environment.

This matrix is not intended as a comprehensive quantitative or mathematical model of the news environment: what we are proposing here is a fundamental shift in thinking as to what is important in the news media environment. By mapping news organisations on to this matrix we are making a statement about what we consider is important – the voice, and the intent of news organisations, and

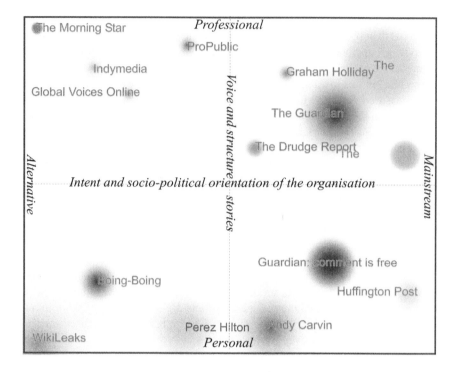

FIGURE 14.3 The completed matrix, with sample organisations mapped to it. Organisations are located on the matrix according to their intent and the dominant voice of their output. As news organisations grow and fragment, incorporating more convergent media, some organisations find themselves occupying multiple locations on the matrix – the *Guardian's* location is not the same as the *Guardian*-run Comment is Free site, the latter being further down the vertical axis, reflecting its greater volume of personal and subjective voice. Some applications and services, like Indymedia, or a microblogging site, rather than having a single dot on the matrix, would have a collection of very small interconnected dots.

to reopen debate about what constitutes a news organisation. The matrix is not so much a representation of the landscape as we see it, as a model for rethinking our perception of the landscape.

From landscape to ecosystem

A map shows location, but not connections. The matrices discussed above are an attempt to bring relationships into the picture. On the macro matrix, organisations are still identified as discrete entities, but the size of their marker, and the fuzziness of its boundary, indicate the impact of the organisation on its environment, and the extent to which it operates with open gates and collaborates with users.

This aspect of the matrix indicates the level of engagement and collaboration among organisations and individuals, and the extent to which they relate to each other. One of the fundamental arguments of this book is that news organisations (and individuals) can no longer work in isolation from their community and environment. The traditional uni-directional linear arrangement of information passing from source, to the journalist, to the audience can no longer work. Journalists

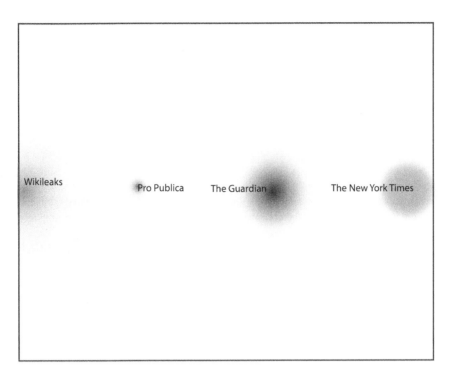

FIGURE 14.4 A sample of organisations, giving an indication of the level of engagement and openness the organisation adheres to. The *New York Times* has the least fuzzy boundary – as a traditional news organisation it limits access to trusted and vetted sources, and as a firewalled website and paid product it limits its access to audiences. Nonetheless, it has a large impact because of its reputation as a 'paper of record'. The *Guardian* has a much more diffuse boundary as it embraces collaborative and open journalism. It has a large impact because of its reputation and its open access online. ProPublica has a less fuzzy boundary again: despite its status as a non-profit, it relies on traditional news practices and makes little or no use of user-generated content or collaboration (except with other news organisations). WikiLeaks has the fuzziest boundary – it accepts (or did until 2011) almost any content and republishes it, making little to no editorial or journalistic impact on the content. It has a large impact because of the material it releases and it is widely used by other news organisations.

and news organisations must re-orient themselves towards the community – which contains sources, audiences and peers in a living ecosystem.

The micro level

As the traditional media landscape explodes and fragments, there is an additional factor that becomes more important: the individual journalist. In the traditional, technologically determined landscape, individual journalists were subsumed by their institutions, and their output was constrained by the conventions and technology of the organisation within which they worked. There was little or no need to discuss, or analyse the influence or role of individual players in this environment, except on the

rare occasions when an individual journalist gained celebrity status or had a reputation strong enough to attract attention back to the institute, such as Kate Adie or Christiane Amanpour. Even freelancers were largely attached to mainstream news organisations by way of payment or assignment briefs, albeit on a more ad hoc basis. Journalist was a simple descriptor, encapsulating the role and responsibilities of the job in one word, and needing only the clarification of 'print', 'radio' or 'television'.

In a social-media landscape, the voice of the individual becomes clearer. As we have seen, journalists working within (and outside) media organisations find themselves in direct contact with audiences, and with more options than ever as to where they source or output their work. They are increasingly unable to define what they do in a single sentence, although they know what they are doing, and are doing it well. They exist in an evolving web of connectivity, across sources and outputs. Neither the products journalists produce nor the resources on which they draw are fixed. As a result, the meaning of the word 'journalist' dissipates (Sivek, 2010). There are lots of people operating as journalists, but they may be bloggers, freelancers, tweeters, YouTube commentators or mainstream reporters – or any combination.

One way to frame a clearer understanding of a journalist's work is to compare the relationship between sources and output. How do you source the story, and how do you distribute it back to users? Do you produce a broadcast for a main channel news or do you produce blog posts and curated news feeds? We have attempted to visualise these relationships with a micro matrix. Again this matrix is not presented as a quantitative fixed analysis of the role or relationships of individual journalists. Rather, it is a visualisation of the considerations now presenting themselves to journalists on the social and networked news stage.

Sources and outputs

The micro matrix depicts the range of sources and outputs open to journalists now that social networks and traditional methods are both good resources on which to draw. The sources a journalist use are depicted on the bottom half of the matrix, the outputs on the top. Each journalist will decide on a relationship with sources and outputs for themselves – the rules have changed, and it is equally possible to succeed with a complex network of social media sources and outputs as with a paper contact book of senior politicians and a slot on the newsdesk of a quality daily paper.

Your identity as a journalist is determined not by your employer, but by how you navigate this space, and your relationships with the other people and organisations within the system. The bottom half of the micro matrix depicts the sourcing practices open to journalists, discussed in more detail in Chapter 2.

The horizontal line represents the social and public media landscape, and social-media sources and outputs both sit very close to, or on, the line. A journalist who works primarily within social networks, who sources material from the cloud and from the crowd, would occupy a wide shallow space along and just below this line. Reputation and identity for a journalist in this space comes from links, from followers and from name recognition within the network and the ecosystem. Figure 14.5 shows an example of this.

The bottom of the matrix, as far away from the horizontal line as possible, shows the deep, exclusive contacts that only an experienced journalist would have (and used to be accessible only to journalists with the big, mainstream, news outlets). Down here are the contacts with world leaders, best-selling musicians and heads of companies. Figure 14.6 demonstrates this.

These two extremes also incorporate a range of sources in between – as a journalist becomes better known and more experienced, more exclusive contacts and information will become known to them, and their sources will expand below the line.

The range of outputs (or the primary outputs – many journalists having multiple channels with which to communicate with their audience) are on the upper half of the matrix. The possibilities are near endless and changing all the time: it could be a mainstream broadcast, podcast bulletins, forum posts, one-off magazine features, microblogs, live blogs, curated feeds, or a blog post. The space directly above the horizontal line represents outputs that are largely informal, raw and unedited. Moving up the line, the outputs become more structured and packaged: more formal.

The space directly above the horizontal line represents outputs to the crowd which have mass penetration in large areas which are largely informal, raw and unedited. This space is dominated by instant activity in social networks. Moving up the vertical includes live tools and semi-edited production. Live reports and drafted updates occupy the middle space. As these products become more recognisably 'journalistic', more polished and packaged, they move up the line. At the very top are the most polished, curated and immersive packages. These different stages of content production are discussed in further detail in Chapter 3.

Networked journalism: Andy Carvin

Someone like Andy Carvin may not just produce output for mainstream channels. As they act within the network, they increasingly follow the rules of the cloud, sharing and collaborating – treating journalism as a process rather than a product. Here there will be more than one 'end point' (if any at

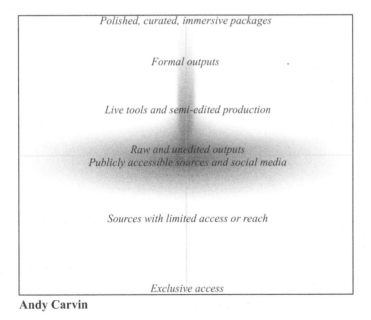

Andy Carvin

FIGURE 14.5 Shows networked journalist Andy Carvin, with his hundreds of linked, public sources. A reporter with a traditional working practice, relying on a subset of trusted contacts and traditional notions of expertise, draws his identity as a journalist from title and authority, training and qualifications, standing within a recognised organisation or demonstrable media business acumen. A networked journalist, however, draws his authority and identity from that bestowed on him from the crowd as a continually shifting phenomenon. Stories are sourced from a wide range of contacts often on digital platforms. Carvin finds and connects key people across social media in a way to add value in the journalistic storytelling process.

all) and the journalist uses informal or unedited outputs, which exist closer to the central horizontal, to connect and drive traffic. The widest and lowest sphere of outputs, along the horizontal, rests with social networks that have mass penetration in large areas such as Orkut, Facebook, Twitter and RenRen. Microblogs, socially disseminated photographs and unedited videos form part of output packages as much as formal content. His outputs may be to niche edited news products and streams which are accessed by large crowds and networks in a way to have made them seem 'normalised' such as @breakingnews, aggregated sites like the Drudge Report, or to heavily resourced but less traditional, alternate news outlets such as Al Jazeera.

Traditional journalism: Robert Fisk

Someone like Robert Fisk, who interviewed Osama bin Laden three times, is away from the horizontal line with a narrow source curve because he has exclusive access to otherwise elusive officials, contacts which have taken a long time to nurture and for whom the level of risk in them contacting a journalist – such as whistleblowers – is high. A major tip-off from an exclusive contact would be at the bottom of the vertical, symbolising the notion of journalist as gatekeeper (Shoemaker et al., 2001).

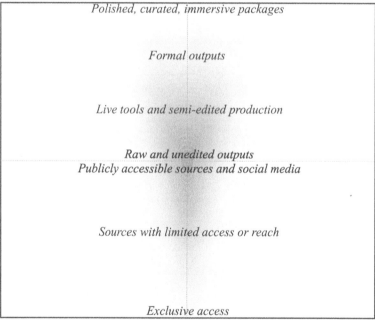

Robert Fisk - The Independent

FIGURE 14.6 Show that the *Independent*'s award-winning Middle East correspondent Robert Fisk has the contacts and clout to open doors. He embodies all the values of traditional journalism, with exclusive access and mainstream outputs. When Fisk speaks, government officials listen. The depth of penetration away from the horizontal line reflects how exclusive the contacts are and how specialist the working journalist's knowledge is.

The depth of the space below the line measures the accessibility of the sources to the general public – at the bottom are heads of state, corporate directors, film stars, pop musicians, people to whom the general public have limited access. Journalists who have access to these people trade on those sources as their unique selling point – this is the traditional measure of the success of a journalist's career, how good their contact book is. Robert Fisk has this access when he reports from Cairo, and he can get information that others can't via his contacts. Specialist journalists dedicate years cultivating contacts which can open doors and prove to be avenues of trusted communication, especially in times of crisis or when speed and accuracy are of the essence. The space he commands below the line is deep, but fairly narrow. He has few sources, but they are far below the surface which the public can access.

Fisk's outputs are represented by a tall curve above the line as the outputs are mainly polished, highly edited packages to mainstream news outlets. The depth of the space above the line measures output and the range of dissemination platforms to the general public. At the top, furthest away from the horizontal, are edited packages recognisable for branded mainstream media outlets that reach wide audiences. Here the notions of 'prime time' and 'front page news' still hold weight – very much the space in which Fisk operates. A journalist producing for mainstream prime-time broadcast is not only polished and well produced 'journalistic' content but it is also well trusted, verified and edited. These are increasingly interactive and immersive storytelling experiences. It remains to be a prime source of news for mass audiences. He produces trusted brand content and has a reputation for quality. His output presence on social-networking sites is rare, limited and sporadic hence a narrow occupancy of the space directly above the line.

The matrix graphic allows for a clearer representation of how individual journalists can occupy more than one space within this fragmented media ecology. It also frames our thinking in the book as a whole. Journalists need different skills as they move around the spaces depicted on the matrix. For sourcing stories, it is important for a journalist to understand the rules of engagement when sourcing content from the crowd, just as they need to know when trusted contacts may be the better way to source a story and how to go about finding them. Similarly, there's a vast scope of considerations in how best to tell and produce stories. There is a core toolkit of skills but also a range of unique and different production techniques for varying outputs. The fluidity across these spaces may also spark legal and ethical considerations – if the law or the state recognises 'journalist' as a specific class of person, with differing privileges and obligations to those of the general public, then who can be a journalist becomes a legal, as well as a personal, question. In terms of commercial interests, issues over professional and private brands, or prompt business opportunities as well as the need to understand media economics more fully rise to the surface.

Conclusion

This new understanding of the media landscape as an ecosystem – the new media ecology – underpins the whole of this book. That is not to say that the book has been an extended explication of the diagrams and examples in this chapter, or even a more detailed attempt to describe and analyse the matrices discussed here, but that the perspective on this new social, networked, collaborative community that this chapter illuminates is fundamental to everything we do as journalists and journalism trainers. This is the ecology of the new media environment.

GLOSSARY

ABCDE of marketing The *marketing mix* has come under scrutiny in a social era where the 'seven Ps' of marketing become: Anyplace, Brand, Communication, Discovery and Experience to reflect the divergent and interactive ways people connect and find information online (Tapscott, 2009). (Chapter 12)

Adoption theories Much study notably in the field of advertising has been given to how new products are taken up by users. Expect audiences to go through four main stages before they 'adopt' your site by either becoming a member or active user. These are: awareness of a product, interest in it, evaluation of it and then some kind of trial or experimentation. (Chapter 12)

Advertising Advertising is a paid form of communication intended to inform or persuade people to take action. It is a process based around audiences coming in contact with a message aimed at changing their consumer behaviour. (Chapter 13)

Aggrefilters These combine automated feeds with some editorial control. Adding a layer of human 'decision making' to aggregation is an added filter to make results more bespoke. (Chapter 5)

Aggregation Aggregation is a more or less automated collection of information, tweets, facts and reports from the web, collected into a single area. It differs from live blogging and curation in that the editorial input by the journalist is minimal. (Chapter 7)

Ambient journalism Much scholarly work has been dedicated to the changes in information discovery brought about through instant, online dissemination of content. Hermida (2010) suggests that these asynchronous, always-on systems are enabling citizens to construct a mental picture of events around them known as 'ambient journalism'. (Chapter 5)

Angles and pegs Topics like the Greek economic crisis have generated thousands of stories – the best ones have the most original or fresh angles. The angle of the story is your unique approach or 'take' on it. It's what makes your report original and interesting. The peg is why a story is being written or is relevant now. (Chapter 3)

API An API (application programming interface) is a mechanism that allows developers to create applications and content that bolt on to proprietary systems (such as an operating system). Open Application Programming Interface refers to the sets of technologies that enable websites to interact with each other. It has formed an integral part of distribution, as it allows programmers to move content from site to site. (Chapter 12)

Astroturfing Astroturfing refers to the process of trying to create the appearance of public support through the manipulation of social-media content and the media. Astroturfing is unethical, but common, and journalists should be careful of being sucked in by it. (Chapter 9)

Attribution Getting people's names and acknowledgements right is pivotal. Remember to clarify someone's title so that you can refer to them after first name mention as Mr, Dr, Mrs or Miss, etc., and check if sources want to be referred to as their real name or their avatar, such as @cecook (they may prefer the social recognition). (Chapter 3)

Avatar An avatar or handle is an online representation of yourself, either with a graphic or username. (Chapter 11)

Barrier to entry An organisation with low start-up costs or expertise is considered to have a low barrier to entry as there is little to block potential competitors from entering the market. First-mover advantage reflects the strengths a company can gain from having a head start on its competitors. (Chapter 13)

Benchmarking This is the process of systematically comparing products, services or processes to others on the market. It can be a rich source of innovative ideas. (Chapter 12)

Beta stage In software, beta refers to the unpolished phase of a product's development when it is released for testing but may still have bugs or technical issues. (Chapter 12)

Bloggers Blog is an abbreviation of 'weblog', originally a log of daily life, information and material collected online. The word and practice have changed considerably, but 'blogger' is still used to refer to a casual or unprofessional online content producer, and contrasted with the 'professional' journalist. (Chapter 10)

Blogging formats Moblogging is blogging from a mobile phone. Vlogging is where posts are made with videos, and podcasting is blogging using audio. Tumblelogs create a scrapbook of personal online experiences. (Chapter 3)

Blogosphere It is possible to communally refer to all blogs as the blogosphere to reflect the interconnections that exist between the various blogging communities. (Chapter 2)

Blogs Blog is an abbreviation of 'weblog', originally a log of daily life, information and material collected online. Blogs are made up of posts which include links and comments. The homepage of a blog will typically show the most recent post at the top. (Chapter 3)

Boolean logic English scholar George Boole left this formidable legacy: search operators. Most search engines accept + to mean and, – for remove, OR to expand a search and double quote marks to specify an exact phrase. Control + f finds on this page. (Chapter 2)

Breaking news Journalists refer to breaking news or the act of 'breaking' a story to refer to live information that interrupts the expected flow of news. (Chapter 2)

Business model This is how you intend to continue making money. It combines revenue strategies with other elements of business planning. (Chapter 13)

Chunking content Chunking is the technique used to produce stories in a non-linear way. It means splitting a story into specific chunks of material that each tackle a different aspect of the issue being covered (the 'who' as an image, the 'analysis' as a graphic, the 'where' as a map). It also serves to avoid long blocks of text. Stories are created by building units (sometimes known as modules) together: bullet points, side bars, break-outs, pull quotes, subheadings, images, maps, graphs, audio, comments, video – there are infinite possibilities. (Chapter 3)

Citizen journalism Citizen journalism as a term has been used to signify many different things and ideas over the last two decades. In its original form it was taken to refer to groups of citizens using the internet to report on events in their own communities, something the increasingly corporatised and commercialised press was failing to do. It has also been used to refer to people providing media content to other, more formal, outlets, such as the provision of video footage of events although this is more commonly distinguished as user-generated content. (Chapter 6)

Click-through rates This metric quantifies the number of times consumers click on a link in order to access content. It can reflect the performance of advertising. (Chapter 13)

Cloud Cloud-based applications are ones that store data on a central server, making them accessible to you from any internet connection as well as on multiple devices. This makes your contacts or files accessible even if you have lost your laptop or mobile phone. Consider Drop Box or Google Docs. (Chapters 2 and 12)

Comment ratings Allowing users to rate other participants' comments on a site is one of the simplest ways to both build community engagement and maintain some control of the discourse on the site. Rating systems vary from a simple up/down click, to more complex algorithms based on a sliding scale, and on the ratings of the users themselves. (Chapter 7)

Commissions These are work orders. They are specific agreements from an editor for a journalist to work on a specified project or report. They can be treated as contracts of work. (Chapter 11)

Competitive advantages These are all the aspects of your product, positioning or strategy which give you the upper hand over your competitors. (Chapter 12)

Contempt of court In the UK (and other countries with similar legal systems), contempt of court is an offence which carries stiff penalties. Contempt of court can be triggered by either disobeying a specific instruction from the court, or publishing information likely to prejudice a trial's outcome. (Chapter 10)

Content farming This is an algorithm-based strategy that uses the number of hits to commission content. Content farms supply articles based on what is trending in order to maximise their impact against trending topics. (Chapter 13)

Copyleft At its simplest, the copyleft movement is a non-legalistic approach to the fair sharing and use of information and creative artefacts. The best-known example of copyleft is the Creative Commons organisation which creates a community of people sharing content under clear guidelines. (Chapter 10)

Creative Commons The Creative Commons is a co-operative organisation that allows anyone to use their guidelines and licences for their material. By creating a standard set of definitions and codes, Creative Commons makes it easy to find material you can use, and to protect it. (Chapter 10)

Crowdfunding This is a system where small payments or donations from a large number of people can generate revenues. These can be used to fund elements of journalism such as investigations or reports. (Chapter 13)

Crowdsourcing Crowdsourcing refers to the practice of asking the public for input. This can be anything from soliciting pictures to asking for help in the reporting process. (Chapters 2 and 7)

Cues As well as an introduction, some stories have a lead in, either verbally as a cue or in text as a sell. For example: 'Voters throughout Europe are rebuking leaders who have promoted austerity measures. Will the new guard do any better? Our chief reporter has the details …' (Chapter 3)

Curation Curation is the process of gathering sources, interviews, comments and facts into a collection, and publishing it online as a finished product. Curation is a way for journalists to add value by adding context or filtering information. Curation is different from aggregation in that it contains at least some of the journalist's own voice, and cannot be automatically generated. (Chapters 2, 5, 7 and 10)

Curator's Code The Curator's Code is a proposed set of rules governing the use of ideas, links and content from other sources in the process of curation and aggregation. The site is at www.curatorscode.org/. (Chapter 10)

Data Data just means information, nothing more. In the common usage, however, it refers to large amounts of information, often numeric, which can be presented by use of graphs, maps and other illustrative means. (Chapter 4)

Data visualisation Visualisation is presenting the data in visual form, using colours, sizes and shapes to show change, relationships and comparisons. People respond better to numerical information when it is presented visually, but be careful of becoming too enamoured of the bells and whistles: focus on understanding. (Chapter 4)

Dayparting Complex studies, by MORI and OPA among others, are ongoing into a technique known as dayparting to identify peak viewing times of digital content. It builds on the traditional notion of broadcast 'prime time' by drilling down to identify what types of content are popular when and to whom. (Chapter 13)

Death knock, or 'pickup' Journalism often reports on death, and one of the tasks of a journalist covering a death is to visit the family and friends in search of quotes, pictures and other usable information. Visiting people at their most vulnerable is emotionally taxing for journalists, and requires a fine social sense, as well as nerves of steel. Every journalist remembers their first death knock, and although some find it a very rewarding task, many still find it harrowing (Cornies, 2010). (Chapter 8)

Diffusion Diffusion is the process by which an innovation is adopted by a social system or market segment and includes the rate and direction of change. (Chapter 12)

Disclaimers These statements are a way of indicating to audiences who is speaking and with what voice, authority and capacity. If you have an individual blog or microblog and use it as a separate output to employment elsewhere you can make that clear. They are used extensively to limit liability. (Chapter 11)

Disinformation Disinformation is the deliberate spreading of false information via the media. Journalists increasingly need to be on their guard for disinformation, especially any information or data that is provided anonymously. (Chapters 4 and 9)

Disintermediation There is a trade between those who have information and those who want it, and media organisations have a fluid place within that. This disintermediation (Katz, 1988; Bardoel et al., 2001) – cutting out the middle man – is made possible by the open and networked construct of the web. (Chapter 13)

Distribution How to get content in front of audiences has become more complicated, as content can be pushed, pulled and repurposed at almost every level of the production process. Distribution strategies play an integral part in rebooting journalism. (Chapter 5)

Diversification Social-media and digital platforms have required media managers to not only enlarge and widen the scope for income generation around content but also expand their portfolio of businesses, services and competences. (Chapter 13)

Dotcom bubble In the late 1990s there was plenty of enthusiasm about investing in online journalism. BBC Online launched in 1997; papers started to see classified advertising move online; market confidence in e-commerce spurred stock prices. But it was short lived. Within a few years, many had spent too much for too little return, gone bust or had no coherent business model. (Chapter 13)

Dual product Journalism has mainly been paid for indirectly. While sales make up part of revenues, the largest proportion of money has come from advertising by 'selling' users to advertisers. (Chapter 13)

Echo chamber This is when the same vocabulary is repeated in different story elements. It's bad practice for both a caption and sell to begin with 'the Eurozone crisis', for example. Story elements should be made to complement one another across platforms, not repeat themselves. (Chapter 3)

Embargo An embargo is a formal request from an organisation to a news outlet to 'hold' a piece of information until a specific date, or time. They are not legally binding, but breaking an embargo may damage your chances of further access to information. (Chapter 10)

Engagement This is a buzzword to imply an audience is loyal, interested or committed. It refers to the ability for content to hold a user's attention or to keep them within a site – valuable commodities in an advertiser's eyes. (Chapter 13)

Entrepreneurs There are three different types of entrepreneur: a lifestyle entrepreneur wants to seek enough independence to earn a living; a growth entrepreneur wants to grow wealthy and be powerful, while an innovative entrepreneur tends to be driven by the desire to create or change something (Bessant and Tidd, 2008: 414). (Chapter 12)

Facebook creeping 'Creeping' refers to the practice of looking through someone's social-media presence without their knowledge or permission, in pursuit of information. It is considered unethical and is against the terms of use of many social networks, but it is used by journalists in search of quotes, contacts or pictures (Riehl, 2011; Pugh, 2012). (Chapter 8)

Fair use Under copyright law, fair use allows for the quoting or excerpting of content for the purposes of commentary and critique. A book critic may quote a section of a book in order to illustrate a discussion; a review of an art show may reproduce an image from the show. How much can be used, and what, exactly, constitutes 'discussion', is open to interpretation. (Chapter 10)

First-mover advantage Timing is important. Being first can be rewarded with significant market share or adoption, known as first-mover advantage. Fast-follower or second-mover advantage can mean you learn from the teething problems of others and sometimes benefit from others' mistakes. (Chapter 12)

FOIA Freedom of Information Acts, or FOIAs, are any legislation that guarantees the legal right of access to government or corporate information – part of the stated democratic goal of transparency. Specific countries may use different titles for the legislation, but they are often referred to as FOIA, and in the USA at least, FOIA is now a verb – journalists talk about FOIAing a government institution. (Chapter 4)

Follow-ups Most stories have a basic trigger – the reason it is being reported now. The follow-up is the story that moves the issue on. Follow-ups can be dealt with in layers (see Chapter 3) and are often a development of story angles. They could involve diarying an event for future reference. (Chapter 2)

Freedom of Information This legislation, adopted by numerous countries, can bare a range of compelling, quirky and valuable stories: from Manchester United Football Club having to deal with a mice infestation, to convictions held by people applying to work with children. The potential as a source lies with the journalist's ability to know what would make a good story. (Chapters 2 and 7)

Freelancers Freelancers work for more than one media outlet and are largely self-employed. Stringers are still freelance but they may work regularly for one media outlet, sometimes on a fixed-term contract. (Chapter 11)

Freemium Combining payment structures that include some free content available to all and other content that is paid for is known as a freemium model: derived from free and premium. It is also known as a metered model. Thresholds for payment can be based on a range of factors including exclusivity, timeliness, services or audiences. (Chapter 13)

Frenemy Google is often dubbed the frenemy of news organisations: half friend and half enemy. Many media organisations are uncomfortable that Google can index and link with impunity yet they value the traffic it creates. (Chapter 13)

Friend recommendations In order to capitalise on the connections between friends for distributing content, media organisations have worked with major social networks either to bring apps onto their site, or take their content onto social networks. (Chapter 5)

Gamification This term refers to bringing elements of interactivity and game design mechanics into other disciplines to make them more engaging. It can incorporate everything from a simple quiz on current events, to elaborate scenarios in which the user role-plays a general, a president or other leader to try to solve a social, political or economic problem. (Chapters 2 and 4)

Gatekeeping The ways in which news organisations maintain control of the news agenda by deciding which stories will be published has been referred to as 'gatekeeping' since David White used the term in 1950. The image of the gates of news being guarded by journalists is an enduring one, and one that writers from Jane Singer to Axel Bruns to Mark Deuze have all invoked. (Chapter 7)

'Go to' person A 'go to' person refers to someone who has become the authority on a subject. Journalists increasingly want to be seen as this person online for certain topics or content. (Chapter 11)

Grassroots journalism Journalists exist within a network and must understand how it works to be a trusted part of it. The concept of working at the grassroots level refers to a journalist's ability to represent themselves and have others interact with them directly. (Chapter 11)

Hoax A hoax is a deliberate attempt to mislead someone, either for financial gain (although this could more rightly be called a 'con'), for attention, or as a prank. A hoax is more than a simple lie – it requires planning and the intent to mislead. (Chapter 9)

Hyperlinks Hyperlinks allow us to navigate around the web. There are two variables with links – the words highlighted and the destination content to which you link. The words you choose will become blue and underlined so choose them carefully to maximise scannability (and SEO – search engine optimisation) and to give an obvious indication of what the hyperlinked page contains. The link should add context and transparency, so consider who or what you need to credit, and what information the reader would find useful. (Chapter 3)

Incubators These bring innovators, experts and potential investors together, such as Le Camping or the New Factory. They usually offer start-ups efficient tools and channels to develop ideas and businesses. (Chapter 12)

Innovation phases Roy Rothwell has worked for many years pioneering models of innovation. His vision of the fifth generation of innovation is essentially the one we are in now, where rich and diverse networks exist, enabling linking and acceleration in innovation (adapted from Tidd et al., 2001). (Chapter 12)

Intellectual property There is a range of intellectual property rights that exist but the most applicable to technology and innovation are patents, copyright and design rights. They all refer to ownership rights of original creative thought. The problem with intellectual property is enforcement and proof. (Chapters 10 and 12)

Interactive media This includes products and services on digital computer-based systems that are open to be modified or respond to a user's actions. (Chapter 3)

Internet The internet is the infrastructure which connects computers around the world. The internet was originally designed to function as a robust communication network that would function well in times of war and disaster. Unlike other networks, such as broadcasting or telephone networks, it has no central hub that can be easily damaged. Instead, each node on the network connects to multiple other nodes, providing redundancy and meaning that even if nodes are destroyed, communication will continue to flow around the gaps. (Chapter 6)

Introductions In crowded social spaces, it is more important than ever to grab a reader's attention and hold on to them. A good introduction for news blurts out the main information and angle of the story as if you were telling a friend what has happened. (Chapter 3)

Journalistic privilege The privilege accorded to journalists allows them access to information and people in order to carry out the journalistic function of reportage. (Chapter 10)

Layering content The term 'layering' refers to the way stories can be built on the web. The story being read is the top layer, but each time a link is added it acts like another layer of content underneath. Understanding layering is key to social storytelling, as it acknowledges the user has different start points and needs, and the journalist has a wide range of content on which to draw. (Chapter 3)

Lists, circles, stacks The social-media version of a contacts book can have many forms: you can group people in circles, stacks or lists, depending on the network and platform. (Chapter 2)

Live blogging A live blog, at its simplest, is a record of an event, published live as it occurs. It is a written commentary online, the textual equivalent of a radio report. A single, automatically refreshing web page is created, with material added to a running narrative with a time stamp attached. It allows any user seeing the page to see the entire narrative, but with the latest material at the top. The journalist can then add to the page as events progress, incorporating material from other sites or news organisations, comments, links, audio and video. (Chapters 3 and 7)

Marginal costs In a perfectly competitive market, the long-term product price will be the marginal cost of production. Because of declining hosting and bandwidth costs, for most internet products the marginal cost today is practically zero, allowing products to be made available for free. (Chapter 13)

Marketing mix The 'seven Ps' form the basic principles of marketing first expressed by Edmund McCarthy in the 1960s: the right **p**roduct, aimed at the right **p**eople, at the right **p**rice, **p**romoted well, in the right **p**lace, with the right **p**rocess and necessary **p**hysical evidence to show marketing has been a success (McCarthy and Perreault, 1984). (Chapter 12)

Measuring success Audience and revenue figures are the primary measurements of success for digital media. (Chapter 12)

Metadata Metadata describes pieces of content in terms of what is 'behind the scenes'. The metadata of a picture may include its size or when it was created. The metadata of a news unit may include key words, tags, the author's name and its length. (Chapter 5)

Microsharing This is licensed sharing of small chunks of content such as an article, picture or video. It is associated with micropayments which unbundle content to the lowest common unit of price. (Chapter 13)

Motion tracking One of many interactive elements being used in broadcast news production. It allows tags as words or numbers to float against video footage to make content easier to understand and retain. (Chapter 3)

Narrative function The function of journalists is to tell stories and make sense of raw information. This is particularly evident in data journalism, where the difference between the raw information and the final story is clearly apparent. (Chapter 4)

New ecosystem Whether you are working for a company or you are out on your own, the rapidly changing media landscape means you have a chance to create the future you envision. This time of change is unprecedented in the history of media. And if you know a little something about the news business and have a good idea on how to do things differently, you already have what you need to get started (Briggs, 2012: 3). (Chapter 12)

News aggregators News aggregation scrapes available news content on the web and bundles it together. These services are becoming increasingly sophisticated and personalised. (Chapter 5)

News in brief A news in brief (NIB) is a story written in two to four paragraphs. A top is slightly longer. (Chapter 3)

Newslist and diaries The newslist, or diary, is the news organisation's plan of what they are working on, what stories are building, what the plan for the next edition will be, and it has traditionally been very jealously guarded. Increasingly, however, news organisations publicise their newslists online in order to solicit ideas, comments and sources prior to production. (Chapter 7)

Non-disclosure agreements A non-disclosure agreement is a legally binding document that records the terms under which you exchange secret information. It is especially useful for discussions with potential investors. (Chapter 12)

Objectivity Objectivity has often been held up as the ideal of journalistic practice – the completely disinterested and uninvolved commentator, presenting all sides of an argument 'without fear or favor' (Allan, 1999). More recent thinkers, influenced by postmodernism's contention that objective truth is an impossibility, maintain that objectivity is also an impossible goal. (Chapters 6 and 10)

On diary and off diary 'On diary' refers to any stories whose start point is scheduled (birthdays, anniversaries, press releases, embargoes, visits, strikes). 'Off diary' are stories that are sparked by unpredictable events (accidents, crime, crisis, reaction, comments). This includes observations or stories sparked by the journalist's news sense. (Chapter 2)

Open API Open Application Programming Interface refers to the sets of technologies that enable websites to interact with each other. It has formed an integral part of distribution, as it allows programmers to move content from site to site. (Chapter 5)

Open ethics Journalistic ethical codes have traditionally been set by elites within journalism, although there are increasing movements to creating ethics by social consensus, something described as 'open ethics' (Ward and Wasserman, 2010). (Chapter 8)

Participatory journalism In their 2011 book, Jane Singer and her co-authors coined the term 'participatory journalism' in order to cover the gap between professional journalists and the people who contribute to the news in ways that are increasingly visible in the end product. (Chapter 7)

Paywalls This term is vilified by many as it has become associated with barriers, when it in fact just refers to the requirement of paying for content. In its purest application it does act as a block, however, as content is not available for consumption unless a payment has been made. (Chapter 13)

Persistent identity The development of a mechanism to allow users a single persistent identity across websites probably dates to Microsoft's Passport (now Windows LiveId) which was launched in 1999 as a single sign-on service (SSO). Since then a number of competing services have arisen, including OpenId and Disqus. Although an SSO is convenient for users, it can create concerns about privacy and security. (Chapter 7)

Polling Polling usually refers to asking the electorate whom they will vote for, but in principle it simply means asking a range of people their opinions. Polling can be as formal as that conducted by professional organisations, or as informal as asking people at the bus stop what they think (a vox pop), or asking a question on a web site, social network or microblog feed. (Chapter 4)

Porter's five forces Named after Michael E. Porter, this model sets out five competitive forces that shape an industry's weaknesses and strengths. They focus on the competition, the potential of new entrants, the risks relating to suppliers, the influence of customers, and the threat to your business of substitute products coming to market (Porter, 1979). (Chapter 12)

Positioning Part of target marketing is to understand where consumers see your product fitting in the market ecology. What are you offering in relation to the rest? It could be a better product that commands a premium, a free site that offers better content or a cheaper alternative to something that is already out there. Positioning is what you do for your customers. (Chapter 12)

Press Complaints Commission (PCC) In the UK, the PCC is (at the time of writing) an industry body that polices the behaviour of the print press. It has no legal standing, but can require member newspapers to apologise or withdraw articles. Its Editors' Code of Conduct is considered to be the ethical standard by which UK newspapers operate. (Chapter 8)

Primary and secondary sources Primary sources are original reports or documents; secondary sources are those quoting, linking or commenting on something. Increasingly, journalists are expected to gather information in from other sources and synthesise or explain it to readers. This is seen as a tertiary source, as it offers a level of service. (Chapter 2)

Product life cycle Sites will go through different phases and the management needed will change. The product life cycle describes the evolution from introduction, through growth to maturity and then decline (Levitt, 1965). (Chapter 12)

Professional identity With myriad platforms on which reporters can interact with audiences, it is essential to have an idea of who you are and what you want to achieve. This will affect decisions about what you post online and the tone in which you write. (Chapter 11)

Public domain Public domain most commonly refers to the copyright status of an artefact (see Chapter 10), but it can also refer to material that is not private, i.e. that can be quoted or reproduced for journalistic purposes, and therefore roughly equivalent to 'on the record' in traditional journalistic parlance. (Chapter 8)

Public interest Public interest is a common journalistic defence against accusations of invasion of privacy, or even law-breaking. It's important to remember that what's interesting to the public is not necessarily in the public interest: public interest requires that the information be necessary for the public's continued participation in civic and political life.(Chapter 8)

QR codes Quick Response Codes are a two-dimensional matrix bar code that can be read by an appropriate app on smart phones. It allows users to access information such as web pages or special offers. They are used effectively to drive users between offline and online spaces. (Chapter 5)

Referral traffic A sophisticated range of metrics and analytical tools are being constantly developed to better understand how stories are distributed online – both at organisational level and through social media. Referral traffic maps where users have come from. (Chapter 5)

Revenue model This is how you intend to make money. See *revenue stream*. (Chapter 13)

Revenue streams Revenue is the incoming money you make. A revenue stream is an activity that brings in money, such as advertising or sales. (Chapter 12)

Rich media This is a term used to describe a broad range of digital interactive media. (Chapter 3)

RSS Really Simple Syndication is a way of publishing site updates via a feed. Subscribing to a feed allows you to receive those updates, rather than having to check sites manually. It is a fundamental building block of managing navigation of the web. (Chapter 2)

Search aggregation Content can easily be delivered to you, either on a home page or reader, via Really Simple Syndication so you automatically know when a site has been updated with something new. (Chapter 5)

Search engine optimisation This is done by content producers to make their site pages easy to find by search engines. There are hundreds of factors which affect performance – getting content to appear at the top of search results – but links, tags, key words and metadata within the HTML can help. (Chapter 5)

Search engines Search engines are good at looking through large sets of data and returning results based on key words. For publishers, making sure pages are well represented in searches is a fundamental building block of distribution. (Chapter 5)

Seeding This is a technique used to kick-start the viral dissemination of content. It counteracts the effects of a potential low pass-along rate between users, by using paid placements, syndication, sponsorships – or even just tapping into known hubs – to grow the initial number of users exposed to a piece of content. (Chapter 5)

Segmentation A range of factors have historically been used to determine audience groupings, including social status, postcode, disposable income, education, career and family. These paint a picture of audiences to advertisers so they can accurately target products at them. (Chapter 13)

Sentiment analysis Knowing how a follower feels about a brand or product can reveal more than a simple Like or Follow. Sentiment analysis focuses on the comments and suggestions left on social media, using the wording, tone, context and emotion to paint a full picture. (Chapter 5)

Shovelware Many newsrooms strapped for resources put content online without making it platform specific, or adding any value in terms of additional features, interactivity or multimedia. It is widely accepted to be ineffective in generating quality audiences. (Chapter 13)

Social bookmarking This is the way for you to organise and store all the information you read, socially. It acts like a favourites or bookmarks bar but, instead of being for an entire site, it lets you save individual web pages and share them. (Chapter 2)

Social Media Optimisation Content producers are increasingly sensitive to the performance of stories on social platforms. Optimising how content is shared and discovered across social media can increase a story's reach. (Chapter 5)

Social traffic This refers to the way social networks have contributed to someone finding or sharing your content. It comprises a range of analytics. (Chapter 3)

Spam Spam originally referred to unsolicited advertising emails, but now refers to any kind of content that is advertising-based and irrelevant to the original intent. Comment spam is increasingly a problem for any site which does not require registration to use, and even for those which do. (Chapter 7)

Start-ups This term is used loosely to describe fledgling businesses that are carving out new identities, products or services in the new media ecology. It incorporates the sense of entrepreneurialism required for any media unit to move beyond the drawing board. (Chapter 12)

Strategic objectives Usually mapping the three to five-year plans, these are goals that are general enough to then be broken down into attainable tasks. Those tasks may then be grouped together to steer decision-making and possibly who does what. (Chapter 12)

Syndication There are different types of syndication but most trade on how content produced by one organisation is made available to another. It could be individual programmes, articles or feeds. Tweetminster, for example, generate Twitter feeds relating to certain topics and syndicate them. (Chapter 5)

Tagging Tags are the metadata that describe, categorise and label content. When you click on a tag it will navigate you to all the content that has been filed under that term. A tag cloud is the list of tags commonly used on a site. You can also create alerts or RSS feeds on tag terms. (Chapter 3)

Target market A target audience is a segment of the public for whom products, events or services were created. This is the target market. (Chapter 13)

Threaded comments The simplest way to display comments on a story is to order them chronologically. However, creating a threaded conversation, in which responses to a specific comment are displayed linked to that comment, create more of a conversational dynamic, which in turn creates more engagement and discussion. Systems can also be set up to inform a user when someone responds to them directly, bringing them back to the site to contribute again. (Chapter 7)

Trolling This word, which has its origins in a fishing technique, refers to participants in an online community who seem to be there simply to create conflict and generate outrage. Trolls can drive initial traffic as people react to their presence with denouncements and outrage, but persistent trolling will also drive people away from a site. (Chapter 7)

Twitter jargon A post to Twitter is known as a tweet. RT is a re-posting of someone else's tweet. To direct a tweet to someone, you use the @mention functionality. A DM is a private message exchange between two people who follow each other. Following people means their updates will appear in your feed. (Chapter 3)

Two screeners The trend is increasingly for users to have more than one device in use at any one time (using a smart phone while watching a TV and surfing on a tablet). It is worth considering how this can be harnessed for better interaction. (Chapter 3)

Up-pitch This is a skill where you make one topic have multiple angles and multiple sales points. It is the way one pitch can become multiple commissions. (Chapter 11)

Upstream and downstream traffic Upstream refers to the incoming traffic to your site. If someone arrives from your site from a link on a blogroll, for example, that is upstream to you. Downstream is the traffic that is sent out from your site – if someone leaves your site by clicking on a link. Downstream was considered something to be avoided, as it meant users were leaving your site. But now it is a more commonly accepted part of web navigation. (Chapter 5)

Usability Usability refers to the ease with which your content can be consumed on different platforms. You may consider breaking up an article every few paragraphs with bolded up subheadings, bullet points or breakouts to make it easier to view on print, mobile phones, tablets or screens, for example. (Chapter 3)

User-generated content This somewhat clunky term is used to describe raw material, especially visual material, photographs and video, which has been produced by 'the public' and submitted to news organisations to be used in their content. It is distinct from citizen journalism in that it does not usually constitute a discrete news item, but is simply an element of one. (Chapter 7)

Value chain Business schools will often promote the value chain: how each company makes money by adding value to a product across its development. (Chapter 12)

Value proposition This business term refers to what your business offers that no one else does. Define it, knowing your strengths, and then measure your competition against it. (Chapter 12)

Verification Verification for a journalist involves not only checking facts, but also ensuring that people are who they say they are, that they could reasonably be expected to know the things they claim to know, and that all images and video are genuine. It is not a small task, but it is this that preserves the public trust in journalists. (Chapter 9)

Viral advertising This technique focuses on the creation of advertisements with a high potential to be spread across social-networking sites or by word of mouth. They aim to create a buzz around products or services. It relies on users spreading content among themselves. (Chapter 13)

Whistleblowers Whistleblowers are people who reveal (usually) criminal activity on the part of organisations to the government or the press. In many countries, whistleblowers are protected by the law, so even if they have broken copyright or contract law to make the information available they cannot be held liable if the information is in the public interest. However, this is not a judgement a journalist can make. If you are approached by a whistleblower, seek legal advice before proceeding. (Chapter 4)

Wikiwhat 'Wiki' is a Hawaiian word meaning quick, but in internet culture it is a kind of shorthand for an open-source, collaborative publishing project such as Wikipedia, the open-source encyclopaedia, WikiLeaks and WikiNews. A wiki can also refer to any site using an interlinked and collaborative structure, as exemplified by Wikipedia. (Chapter 6)

Wild track and actuality Wild track is the natural, ambient sound that can be good background noise for editing. Actuality is specific sounds or clips of speech. Both can add polish to a formal package. (Chapter 3)

REFERENCES

#bbcsms. 10:10 Technology & Innovation – YouTube, 2011. Available at: www.youtube.com/watch?v=0cNHq6rc-X8 (accessed 3 April 2013).

A dictionary of business and management, 5th ed. 2009., Oxford paperback reference. Oxford, England; New York: Oxford University Press.

Ahmad, A.N., 2010. Is Twitter a useful tool for journalists? *Journal of Media Practice*, 11(2), pp. 145–155.

Akalp, N., 2011. Social media for small businesses: 6 Effective Strategies. *Mashable*. Available at: http://mashable.com/2011/04/14/small-business-social-media-tips/ (accessed 13 April 2012).

Akinfemisoye, M.O., 2011. Untitled thesis. Master of Arts in Journalism. Coventry: Coventry University.

Aldridge, M. and Evetts, J., 2003. Rethinking the concept of professionalism: the case of journalism. The British Journal of Sociology 54, 547–564.

Allan, S., 1999. *News culture*, Buckingham; Philadelphia: Open University Press.

Allan, S., 2010. *News culture*, Maidenhead; New York: McGraw-Hill/Open University Press. Available at: http://site.ebrary.com/id/10404002 (accessed 3 February 2013).

Allan, S., Sonwalkar, P. and Carter, C., 2007. Bearing witness: citizen journalism and human rights issues. *Globalisation, Societies and Education*, 5(3), pp. 373–389.

Allan, S. and Thorsen, Einar, eds, 2009. *Citizen journalism: global perspectives*, New York: Peter Lang.

Alzner, B., 2012. What role does Facebook 'creeping' play in news coverage? The Canadian Journalism Project. Available at: http://j-source.ca/article/what-role-does-facebook-creeping-play-news-coverage (accessed 7 May 2012).

Amnesty International, 2011. Reports. Available at: www.amnesty.org/en/news-and-updates/report_abstract (accessed 24 August 2011).

Anderson, C., 2006. *The long tail: how endless choice is creating unlimited demand*, London: Business Books.

Anderson, C., 2009a. *Free: the future of a radical price*, New York: Hyperion.

Anderson, C., 2009b. The economics of giving it away. WSJ.com. Available at: http://online.wsj.com/article/SB123335678420235003.html (accessed 9 November 2011).

Andreessen, M., 2007. PMArchive. *PMArchive*. Available at: http://pmarchive.com/guide_to_startups_part4 (accessed 1 May 2012).

Applegate, C., 2011. Tweeting the killing of bin Laden: how a little geekery and I (maybe) helped break a story. qwghlm.co.uk. Available at: www.qwghlm.co.uk/2011/05/04/tweeting-the-killing-of-bin-laden/ (accessed 28 October 2011).

Arment, M., 2012. I'm not a 'curator'. Marco.org. Available at: www.marco.org/2012/03/12/not-a-curator (accessed 3 June 2012).

Armstrong, H., 2011. About. Dooce.com. Available at: http://dooce.com/about (accessed 29 April 2012).

Arscott, K., 2011. Rebecca Leighton innocent, who will the press smear next? Angry Mob. Available at: www.butireaditinthepaper.co.uk/2011/09/03/rebecca-leighton-innocent-who-will-the-press-smear-next/ (accessed 10 May 2012).

Atton, C., 2002. *Alternative media*, London; Thousand Oaks, CA: SAGE.

Atton, C., 2004. *An alternative internet*, Edinburgh: Edinburgh University Press.

Awad, I., 2006. Journalists and their sources. *Journalism Studies*, 7(6), pp. 922–939.

Bandurski, D., 2008. China's guerrilla war for the web. *Far Eastern Economic Review*. Available at: http://farectification.wordpress.com/2008/09/15/china%E2%80%99s-guerrilla-war-for-the-web/ (accessed 27 May 2012).

Bandurski, D., 2011. Under construction: new microblog controls. *China Media Project*. Available at: http://cmp. hku.hk/2011/12/16/17607/ (accessed 2 January 2012).

Banisar, D., 2006. *Freedom of Information around the World 2006*, Privacy International. Available at: www. privacyinternational.org/foi/foisurvey2006.pdf (accessed 10 July 2012).

Bardoel, J. and Deuze, M., 2001. Network journalism: converging competences of old and new media professionals. *Australian Journalism Review*, 23(2), pp. 91–103.

Barlow, J.P., 1994. The Economy of Ideas. *Wired Magazine*, 2(3). Available at: http://www.wired.com/wired/archive/2.03/economy.ideas_pr.html (accessed 4 September 2011).

Barnes, S.B., 2006. A privacy paradox: social networking in the United Stated. *First Monday*, 11(9). Available at: http://firstmonday.org/htbin/cgiwrap/bin/ojs/index.php/fm/article/view/3086/2589 (accessed 29 April 2012).

Bass, F.M., 1969. A new product growth for model consumer durables. *Management Science*, 15(5), pp. 215–227.

Battelle, J. and O'Reilly, T., 2004. Web 2.0 Conference The State of the Internet Industry. Available at: http://itc. conversationsnetwork.org/shows/detail270.html.

BBC, 2011. Editorial guidelines – guidance – social networking, microblogs and other third party websites: BBC use – guidance in full. *The BBC Editorial Guidelines*. Available at: www.bbc.co.uk/guidelines/editorial guidelines/page/guidance-blogs-bbc-full (accessed 6 April 2011).

BBC Backstage, 2010. *Open data and resources for the BBC*. Available at: http://backstage.bbc.co.uk/ (accessed 12 April 2012).

BBC College of Journalism, 2010a. *#pimpymyblog – Martin Stabe (FT)*, Available at: www.youtube.com/watch?v=_ILlwkpSHkQ&feature=player_embedded (accessed 26 October 2011).

BBC College of Journalism, 2010b. Authenticating UGC Emails. BBC College of Journalism. Available at: www.bbc.co.uk/journalism/skills/citizen-journalism/bbc-ugc-hub/authenticating-ugc-emails.shtml (accessed 31 December 2011).

BBC College of Journalism, 2010c. Hoax UGC image checks. BBC College of Journalism. Available at: www.bbc.co.uk/journalism/skills/citizen-journalism/bbc-ugc-hub/hoax-ugc-image-checks.shtml (accessed 31 December 2011).

BBC College of Journalism, 2012. Reporting averages, percentages and data. BBC College of Journalism. Available at: www.bbc.co.uk/academy/collegeofjournalism/how-to/how-to-report/reporting-averages-percentages-and-data (accessed 1 July 2012).

BBC News, (n.d.) Embedding video on external sites. BBC News. Available at: http://news.bbc.co.uk/1/hi/help/7895116.stm (accessed 28 October 2011).

BBC News, 2004. Gilligan quits over Hutton row in BBC news. BBC News. Available at: http://news.bbc. co.uk/1/hi/uk_politics/3446391.stm (accessed 9 July 2012).

BBC News, 2011. Rebecca Leighton: saline case nurse 'scared' to go out. BBC News. Available at: www.bbc. co.uk/news/uk-england-manchester-14984584 (accessed 10 May 2012).

Beaumont, C., 2009. New York plane crash: Twitter breaks the news, again. *Telegraph*. Available at: www. telegraph.co.uk/technology/twitter/4269765/New-York-plane-crash-Twitter-breaks-the-news-again.html (accessed 25 January 2012).

Beckedahl, M., 2012. Sustainable business models for journalism. Case study: netzpolitik.org (Germany). SubMoJour. Available at: www.submojour.net/archives/380/case-study-netzpolitik-org-germany/#more-380 (accessed 12 April 2012).

Beckett, C., 2008. It's 2013 – here's the news. Charlie Beckett's blog. Available at: http://blogs.lse.ac.uk/polis/2008/03/28/its-2013-heres-the-news/ (accessed 28 October 2011).

Beckett, C., 2010. *The value of networked journalism*, London: Polis; London School of Economics.

Bedbury, S. and Fenichell, S., 2002. *A new brand world: 8 principles for achieving brand leadership in the 21st century*, New York: Viking.

Behling, E., 2011. Social media strategy: data is everything. Emedia Vitals. Available at: www.emediavitals.com/content/social-media-data-everything (accessed 13 April 2012).

Bell, E., 2005. End of the offline? *British Journalism Review*, 16(1), pp. 41–45.

References

Bell, E., 2009. Lecture to Falmouth. Emily Bell's blog. Available at: http://publicserviceblog.wordpress.com/2009/05/08/lecture-to-falmouth/ (accessed 19 January 2012).

Bell, E. and Barber, E., Professorial Lecture Videos. *University College Falmouth*. Available at: www.falmouth.ac.uk/201/courses-7/investing-in-your-future-296/professorial-lecture-videos-2720.html (accessed 31 August 2011).

Benson, R., 2005. *Bourdieu and the journalistic field*, Cambridge; Malden, MA: Polity.

Bentley, D., 2012. Personal interview by Clare Cook.

Bergman, C., 2011. Crowdsourcing a live video interview via Twitter. *Lost Remote*. Available at: www.lostremote.com/2011/05/20/crowdsourcing-a-live-video-interview-via-twitter/ (accessed 30 May 2012).

Berry, D., 2008. *Journalism, ethics and society*, Aldershot: Ashgate.

Berry, D.M., 2008. *Copy, rip, burn: the politics of copyleft and open source*, London: Pluto.

Bessant, J.R. and Tidd, J., 2008. *Innovation and entrepreneurship*, Chichester; Hoboken, NJ: John Wiley.

Bessant, J.R. and Venables, T., 2010. *Creating wealth from knowledge: meeting the innovation challenge*, Cheltenham: Edward Elgar.

Bhargava, R., 2011. The 5 models of content curation. Web Pro News. Available at: www.webpronews.com/the-5-models-of-content-curation-2011-04 (accessed 14 April 2011).

Bichlbaum, A., Bonanno, M. and Engfehr, K., 2009. *The yes men fix the world*, HBO.

Binns, A., 2012. Don't Feed the Trolls. *Journalism Practice*, 6(4), pp. 547–562.

Blackhurst, C., 2012. Personal interview by Clare Cook.

Blanchard, B. and Wee, S.-L., 2011. China's effort to muzzle news of train crash sparks outcry. Reuters. Available at: www.reuters.com/article/2011/07/25/us-china-train-censorship-idUSTRE76O1IG20110725 (accessed 2 January 2012).

Blank, S., 2010. Why startups are agile and opportunistic – pivoting the business model. Steve Blank. Available at: http://steveblank.com/2010/04/12/why-startups-are-agile-and-opportunistic-%E2%80%93-pivoting-the-business-model/ (accessed 1 May 2012).

Blight, G. and Pulham, S., 2011. Arab spring: an interactive timeline of Middle East protests. *Guardian*. Available at: www.guardian.co.uk/world/interactive/2011/mar/22/middle-east-protest-interactive-timeline (accessed 4 September 2011).

Blog Preston, n.d. About Blog Preston. Available at: http://blogpreston.co.uk/about/ (accessed 4 January 2012).

Boeder, P., 2005. Habermas' heritage: the future of the public sphere in a network society. *First Monday*, 10(9). Available at: http://firstmonday.org/htbin/cgiwrap/bin/ojs/index.php/fm/article/view/1280/1200 (accessed 16 October 2011).

Böhringer, M. (2009). Really Social Syndication: A Conceptual View on Microblogging. Sprouts: Working Papers on Information Systems, 9(31). Available at http://sprouts.aisnet.org/9-31.

Bounea, M., 2012. The coded Twitter leaks that jumped the French election gun. *Guardian: Comment Is Free*. Available at: www.guardian.co.uk/commentisfree/2012/apr/24/coded-twitter-leaks-french-election?utm_source=feedburner&utm_medium=feed&utm_campaign=Feed%3A+theguardian%2Fmedia%2Frss+%28Media%29&utm_content=Google+Reader (accessed 24 May 2012).

Bourdieu, P., 1993. *The field of cultural production: essays on art and literature*, New York: Columbia University Press.

Bourdieu, P., 1998. *On television*, New York; New Press.

Bowman, S. and Willis, C., 2003. *We Media*, Media Center at the American Press Institute. Available at: www.hypergene.net/wemedia/weblog.php (accessed 30 October 2011).

Boyce, T., 2006. Journalism and expertise. *Journalism Studies*, 7(6), pp. 889–906.

Boyd, A., Stewart, P. and Alexander, R., 2008. *Broadcast journalism: techniques of radio and television news*, Amsterdam: Elsevier/Focal.

Boyd, D.M., 2010. Streams of content, limited attention: the flow of information through social media. *Educause Review*. Available at: www.educause.edu/EDUCAUSE+Review/EDUCAUSEReviewMagazineVolume45/StreamsofContentLimitedAttenti/213923 (accessed 21 May 2012).

References

Boyd, D.M., 2011. 'Real names' policies are an abuse of power. Apophenia. Available at: www.zephoria.org/thoughts/archives/2011/08/04/real-names.html (accessed 2 July 2012).

Boyd, D.M. and Ellison, Nicole B., 2008. Social network sites: definition, history, and scholarship. *Journal of Computer-Mediated Communication*, 13(1), pp. 210–230.

Boyd, D.M. and Hargittai, E., 2010. Facebook privacy settings: who cares? *First Monday*, 15(8). Available at: http://firstmonday.org/htbin/cgiwrap/bin/ojs/index.php/fm/article/view/3086/2589 (accessed 29 April 2012).

Bradshaw, P., 2007. A model for the 21st century newsroom: pt1 – the news diamond. Online Journalism Blog. Available at: http://onlinejournalismblog.com/2007/09/17/a-model-for-the-21st-century-newsroom-pt1-the-news-diamond/ (accessed 15 July 2010).

Bradshaw, P., 2010. Cooks source: what should Judith Griggs have done? Online Journalism Blog. Available at: http://onlinejournalismblog.com/2010/11/05/cooks-source-what-should-judith-griggs-have-done/ (accessed 18 June 2012).

Bradshaw, P., 2011. Newsgathering IS production IS distribution. Online Journalism Blog. Available at: http://onlinejournalismblog.posterous.com/cached-newsgathering-is-production-is-distrib (accessed 10 October 2011).

Bradshaw, P., 2012. How news consumption has changed from beats to a constant static. BBC College of Journalism. Available at: www.bbc.co.uk/journalism/blog/2012/04/peoples-news-consumptionhas-ch.shtml (accessed 21 May 2012).

Bradshaw, P. and Rohumaa, L., 2011. *The online journalism handbook: skills to survive and thrive in the digital age*, Harlow; New York: Longman.

Brand, S., 1987. *The Media Lab: inventing the future at MIT*, New York, N.Y.: Viking.

Bratton, J. and Gold, J., 2007. *Human resource management theory and practice*, New York: Palgrave.

Brett, N., 2012. Personal interview by Clare Cook.

Briggs, M., 2009. How to bring a startup culture into the newsroom. Journalism 2.0. Available at: www.journalism20.com/blog/2009/06/10/how-to-bring-a-startup-culture-into-the-newsroom/ (accessed 1 May 2012).

Briggs, M., 2010. JournalismNext: a practical guide to digital reporting and publishing. Washington, DC: CQ Press.

Briggs, M., 2012. *Entrepreneurial journalism: how to build what's next for news*, Los Angeles; Thousand Oaks, CA: CQ Press; Sage.

Brogan, C., 2011. Marketing versus connecting. Chris Brogan. Available at: www.chrisbrogan.com/marketing-versus-connecting/ (accessed 2 September 2011).

Brooke, H., 2011. *The silent state: secrets, surveillance and the myth of British democracy*, London: Random House.

Brooks, R., 2011. How social media helps journalists break news. Social Media Examiner. Available at: www.socialmediaexaminer.com/how-social-media-helps-journalists-break-news/ (accessed 11 June 2012).

Brown, J., 2005. No trial for soldier said to have faked Iraq torture photos escapes trial. *Independent,* 10 December.

Browne, M., 2012. Storyful's validation process. Storyful blog. Available at: http://blog.storyful.com/2012/04/24/inside-storyful-storyfuls-verification-process/ (accessed 26 May 2012).

Bruno, N., 2011. *Tweet first, verify later? How real-time information is changing the coverage of worldwide crisis events*, Oxford: Oxford University Press.

Bruns, A., 2005. *Gatewatching: collaborative online news production*, New York: P. Lang.

Bruns, A., 2011. Towards distributed citizen participation: lessons from WikiLeaks and the Queensland Floods. In *CeDEM11: Proceedings of the International Conference for E-Democracy and Open Government*. International Conference for E-Democracy and Open Government. Krems, Austria.

Bryant, M., 2012. Personal Interview by Clare Cook.

Burrell, I., 2010. Has Rupert Murdoch's paywall gamble paid off? *Independent*. Available at: www.independent.co.uk/news/media/online/has-rupert-murdochs-paywall-gamble-paid-off-2067907.html (accessed 24 June 2012).

Calhoun, C., 1993a. *Habermas and the public sphere*, Cambridge, MA; London: MIT Press.

References

Calhoun, C., 1993b. Introduction. In *Habermas and the public sphere*. Cambridge, MA; London: MIT Press.

Canavilhas, J., 2009. Online journalism blog. Online Journalism Blog. Available at: http://onlinejournalismblog. com/tag/joao-canavilhas/ (accessed 21 May 2012).

Cardon, D. and Granjon, F., 2005. Social networks and cultural practices. *Social Networks*, 27(4), pp. 301–315.

Carr, D., 2009. At South by Southwest in Austin, the messages are the media. *New York Times*. Available at: www.nytimes.com/2009/03/18/movies/18sxsw.html?_r=1 (accessed 29 May 2012).

Carr, D., 2012. A code of conduct for content aggregators. *New York Times*. Available at: www.nytimes. com/2012/03/12/business/media/guidelines-proposed-for-content-aggregation-online.html?_r=1 (accessed 24 May 2012).

Carvin, A., 2011. Israeli weapons in Libya? How @acarvin and his Twitter followers debunked sloppy journalism. Storify. Available at: http://storify.com/acarvin/how-to-debunk-a-geopolitical-rumor-with-your-twitt2 (accessed 27 May 2012).

Carvin, A., 2012. *Distant witness: social media, the Arab Spring and a journalism revolution*, New York, NY: CUNY Journalism Press.

Castells, M., 2000. *The rise of the network society*, 2nd edn, Oxford: Blackwell.

Channel 4 *Dispatches*, 2011. Could selling off Britain's assets cut the debt? *Channel 4 News*. Available at: www. channel4.com/news/could-selling-off-britains-assets-cut-the-debt? (accessed 15 October 2011).

Chartered Institute of Marketing, 2012. Definition of marketing. *Chartered Institute of Marketing*. Available at: www.cim.co.uk/resources/understandingmarket/definitionmkting.aspx (accessed 12 April 2012).

Chen, D.Q., 2011. *An exploration of social media sites and micro-blogs' influence on the mainstream media in China*. MA thesis, University of Central Lancashire.

Chervel, T., 2012. Sustainable business models for journalism – case study: Perlentaucher (Germany). SubMoJour. Available at: www.submojour.net/archives/394/case-study-perlentaucher-germany/ (accessed 12 April 2012).

Chesbrough, H.W., 2003. *Open innovation: the new imperative for creating and profiting from technology*, Boston, MA: Harvard Business School Press.

Cheshire, T., 2012. Tumbling on success: how Tumblr's David Karp built a £500 million empire. *Wired*. Available at: www.wired.co.uk/magazine/archive/2012/03/features/tumbling-on-success?page=all (accessed 13 April 2012).

China Internet Watch, 2011. *Whitepaper: China Internet Statistics*, Available at: www.chinainternetwatch.com/ whitepaper/china-internet-statistics/ (accessed 2 January 2012).

Christakis, N.A. and Fowler, J.H., 2009. *Connected: the amazing power of social networks and how they shape our lives*, London: HarperPress.

Christensen, C.M., 1997. *The innovator's dilemma: when new technologies cause great firms to fail*, Boston, MA: Harvard Business School Press.

CNN, n.d. iReport FAQ. *CNN*. Available at: http://ireport.cnn.com/faq.jspa (accessed 1 January 2012).

Cohen, J., 2009. FTC looks at the future of news. Google Public Policy Blog. Available at: http://google publicpolicy.blogspot.com/2009/12/ftc-looks-at-future-of-news.html (accessed 18 November 2011).

Coles, M., 2011. Pippa Middleton's arse: how newspapers optimise for the phrase without showing it to their readers. Malcolm Coles. Available at: www.malcolmcoles.co.uk/blog/pippa-middletons-arse-cheeky/ (accessed 25 October 2011).

Compaine, B. and Hoag, A., 2012. Factors supporting and hindering new entry in media markets: a study of media entrepreneurs. *International Journal on Media Management*, 14(1), pp. 27–49.

Cook, C., 2011a. Microsoft on launching new businesses: think big. Clare Cook Online. Available at: www. clarecookonline.co.uk/2011/09/microsoft-on-launching-new-businesses-think-big.html (accessed 13 April 2012).

Cook, C., 2011b. Tag me, tweet me: how journalists network brand and self management. In *Colloque Medias 011*. Aix-Marseille, France.

Cooper, G., 2012. Facing up to the ethical issues surrounding Facebook use. In R. L. Keeble, ed. *The Phone Hacking Scandal: Journalism on Trial*. London: Arima.

References

Cornies, L., 2010. Tips for reporters on dealing with grief-stricken families. *Doon Valley Journal*. Available at: www.larrycornies.com/2010/07/tips-for-reporters-on-dealing-with-grief-stricken-families/ (accessed 10 May 2012).

Courtney-Smith, N., 2011. Personal interview by Clare Cook.

Coutu, S., 2012. Your start up moment has come. *Wired Magazine*. May.

Cowen, T., 2009. Create your own economy: the path to prosperity in a disordered world. Dutton, New York.

Creative Commons, 2011. *The Power of Open*, Mountain View, CA.

Crilly, R., 2011. So you wanna be a stringer. South of West. Available at: http://robcrilly.wordpress.com/2009/11/19/so-you-wanna-be-a-stringer/ (accessed 22 August 2011).

Crowdsourcing, 2011. Citizen journalism: the *Guardian* crowdsourcing experiment on coverage of London riots. Crowdsourcing.org. Available at: www.crowdsourcing.org/editorial/citizen-journalism-the-guardian-crowd-sourcing-experiment-on-coverage-of-london-riots/5904 (accessed 2 January 2012).

Currah, A., 2009. *What's happening to our news*, Oxford: Reuters Institute for the Study of Journalism. Available at: http://reutersinstitute.politics.ox.ac.uk/fileadmin/documents/Publications/What_s_Happening_to_Our_News.pdf (accessed 31 August 2011).

Curran, J. and Gurevitch, M., 2005. *Mass media and society*, London; New York: Hodder Arnold.

Davies, N., 2008. Flat Earth news: an award-winning reporter exposes falsehood, distortion and propaganda in the global media. London: Chatto & Windus.

Davis, A., 2009. Journalist–source relations, mediated reflexivity and the politics of politics. *Journalism Studies*, 10(2), pp. 204–219.

Deuze, M., 2007. *Media work*, Cambridge: Polity.

Deuze, M., 2011. *Managing media work*, London: SAGE.

Doctorow, C., 2011. Google Plus forces us to discuss identity. *Guardian*. Available at: www.guardian.co.uk/technology/blog/2011/aug/30/google-plus-discuss-identity (accessed 27 December 2011).

Dougherty, H., 2009. Online news aggregators – friend or foe? Hitwise. Available at: www.experian.com/blogs/hitwise/2009/04/08/online-news-aggregators-friend-or-foe/ (accessed 19 June 2012).

Duell, M. and Gye, H., 2012. Facebook IPO: graffiti artist David Choe who painted first HQ set for bumper shares payday. *Daily Mail*. Available at: www.dailymail.co.uk/news/article-2095385/Facebook-IPO-Graffiti-artist-David-Choe-painted-HQ-set-bumper-shares-payday.html (accessed 11 April 2012).

Economist, The, 2011. The people formerly known as the audience. *The Economist*, 399(8741), pp. 9–12.

Ellison, N. B., Steinfield, C. and Lampe, C., 2011. Connection strategies: social capital implications of Facebook-enabled communication practices. *New Media & Society*, 13, pp. 873–892.

Eltringham, M., 2011a. The BBC UGC hub. BBC College of Journalism. Available at: www.bbc.co.uk/journalism/skills/citizen-journalism/citizen-journalism-guide/the-hub.shtml (accessed 29 December 2011).

Eltringham, M., 2011b. Social media: what's the difference between curation and journalism? BBC College of Journalism. Available at: www.bbc.co.uk/journalism/blog/2011/03/social-media-whats-the-differe.shtml (accessed 30 May 2012).

Ess, C., 2009. *Digital media ethics*, Cambridge: Polity.

Ettenson, R. and Knowles, J., 2008. Don't confuse reputation with brand. *Web of knowledge*. Available at: http://apps.webofknowledge.com/full_record.do?product=WOS&search_mode=GeneralSearch&qid=69&SID=X1h98fplOGGKA26e35L&page=2&doc=13 (accessed 2 December 2011).

Faguy, S., 2010. Lightfoot hoax leaves many questions. Fagstein. Available at: http://blog.fagstein.com/2010/02/18/lightfoot-death-hoax/ (accessed 31 August 2011).

Farber, D., 2008. Search arrives on Techmeme. CNet. Available at: http://news.cnet.com/8301-13953_3-9948848-80.html?tag=mncol;1n (accessed 26 October 2011).

Farhi, P., 2011. NPR's Andy Carvin, tweeting the Middle East. *Washington Post*. Available at: www.washingtonpost.com/lifestyle/style/npr-andy-carvin-tweeting-the-middle-east/2011/04/06/AFcSdhSD_story.html (accessed 30 May 2012).

Faure, G., 2008. Le stress mortel des blogueurs de fond. Rue89. Available at: http://www.rue89.com/et-pourtant/2008/04/13/le-stress-mortel-des-blogueurs-de-fond (accessed 9 December 2011).

References

Fiet, J.O., 1996. The informational basis of entrepreneurial discovery. *Small Business Economics*, 8(6), pp. 419–430.

Fleishman, G., 2000. Cartoon captures spirit of the internet. *New York Times*. Available at: www.nytimes.com/2000/12/14/technology/14DOGG.html?pagewanted=1&ei=5070&en=f0518aafeccf36fd &ex=1183089600 (accessed 3 July 2012).

Fletcher, K., 2007. Why blogs are an open door. *British Journalism Review*, 18(2), pp. 41–46.

Foot, M. and Hook, C., 2002. *Introducing human resource management*, Harlow: Financial Times/Prentice Hall.

Franklin, B. and Carlson, M., 2011. *Journalists, sources and credibility: new perspectives*, New York: Routledge.

Freedominfo, 2011. FreedomInfo. Available at: www.freedominfo.org/ (accessed 4 September 2011).

Friedland, L.A., 2010. Open source interview: the evolution of public journalism. In *Public journalism 2.0: the promise and reality of a citizen-engaged press*. New York: Routledge.

Friend, C. and Singer, J.B., 2007. *Online journalism ethics: traditions and transitions*, Armonk, NY; London: M.E. Sharpe.

Frost, C., 2012. Personal interview by Clare Cook.

Fry, J., 2009. An Industry of David Pogues. Reinventing the Newsroom. Available at: http://reinventingth-enewsroom.wordpress.com/2009/09/08/an-industry-of-david-pogues/ (accessed 30 January 2013).

Gallagher, R., 2008. Grazia issue to be produced in front of shoppers. *Press Gazette*. Available at: www.pressgazette.co.uk/story.asp?sectioncode=1&storycode=42280&c=1 (accessed 26 October 2011).

Galtung, J. and Ruge, M.H., 1965. The structure of foreign news. *Journal of Peace Research*, 2(1), pp. 64–91.

Gans, H.J., 2003. *Democracy and the news*, Oxford; New York: Oxford University Press.

Gans, H., 2004. *Deciding what's news: a study of CBS evening news, NBC nightly news, Newsweek, and Time*, Evanston, IL: Northwestern University Press.

Gao, J., Li, J., Cheng, Y., Shi, S., 2010. Impact of initial conditions on new venture success: a longitudinal study of new technology-based firms. *International Journal of Innovation Management*, 14, 41.

Garfinkel, S., 2001. *Database nation: the death of privacy in the 21st century*, Cambridge, MA: O'Reilly.

Garnham, N., 1993. The media and the public sphere. In C. Calhoun, ed. *Habermas and the public sphere*. Cambridge Mass, London: MIT Press.

Gaudin, S., 2011. Steve Jobs' death creates Twitter surge. Computerworld. Available at: www.computerworld.com/s/article/9220647/Steve_Jobs_death_creates_Twitter_surge (accessed 10 October 2011).

George Washington University, 2010. National survey finds majority of journalists now depend on social media for story research. George Washington University. Available at: www.gwu.edu/explore/mediaroom/news-releases/nationalsurveyfindsmajorityofjournalistsnowdependonsocialmediaforstoryresearch (accessed 23 June 2012).

Gerber, J., Lang, S. and Minnaar, I., 2010. Personal interview by Megan Knight.

Gill, K.E., 2010. Cooks Source magazine ignites copyright firestorm; magazine ceases publishing (with images, tweets). Storify. Available at: http://storify.com/kegill/cooks-source-magazine-ignites-copyright-firestorm (accessed 18 June 2012).

Gillmor, D., 2004. *We the media: grassroots journalism by the people, for the people*, 1st edn, Sebastopol, CA: O'Reilly.

Gillmor, D., 2010. *Mediactive*, [United States]: Dan Gillmor.

Global Integrity, 2011. Global Integrity. Available at: www.globalintegrity.org/ (accessed 4 September 2011).

Goldstein, M., 2006. The other beating. *Los Angeles Times*. Available at: www.latimes.com/la-tm-holiday-feb19,0,581354.story (accessed 18 December 2011).

Good, J., 2011. BBC News – resident parking permit costs increase across London. Inside Out. Available at: www.bbc.co.uk/news/uk-england-15881831 (accessed 25 January 2012).

Goodman, G., 2011. Social gaming: forget pointless points. Citizenside blog. Available at: http://blog.citizenside.com/en/2011/05/05/social-gaming-forget-pointless-points/ (accessed 26 May 2012).

Google, 2011a. Google Fusion Tables. Available at: www.google.com/fusiontables/Home (accessed 4 September 2011).

Google, 2011b. Google Maps. Available at: http://maps.google.com/ (accessed 4 September 2011).

Gosier, J., 2011. Queensland and the Ushahidi ecosystem. Ushahidi Blog. Available at: http://blog.ushahidi.com/index.php/2011/01/17/queensland-and-the-ushahidi-ecosystem/ (accessed 29 January 2012).

Gow, A., 2008. Why the deadline isn't 'Now'. Headlines and Deadlines. Available at: www.alisongow.com/2008/09/why-deadline-isnt-now.html (accessed 31 October 2011).

Gow, A., 2011. Your newspaper's BMDs column is now live on Twitter. Headlines and Deadlines. Available at: www.alisongow.com/2011/12/your-newspaper-bmds-column-is-now-live.html (accessed 29 May 2012).

Graham, P., 2009. Startups in 13 Sentences. Paul Graham. Available at: http://paulgraham.com/13sentences.html (accessed 1 May 2012).

Greenslade, R., 2005. Book review: confessions of a me man. *British Journalism Review*, 16(2), pp. 81–84.

Greenslade, Roy, 2010a. Rod Liddle no longer in running for *Independent* editor. *Guardian*. Available at: www.guardian.co.uk/media/greenslade/2010/feb/19/rod-liddle-independent (accessed 4 January 2012).

Greenslade, Roy, 2010b. The real lesson from Johnston Press paywall failure. *Guardian*. Available at: www.guardian.co.uk/media/greenslade/2010/apr/01/johnston-press-charging-for-content (accessed 19 June 2012).

Grindley, L., 2006. Zoning by Interest. Lucas Grindley's blog. Available at: www.lucasgrindley.com/2006/10/zoning_by_interest.html (accessed 22 November 2011).

Grueskin, B., Seave, A. and Graves, L., 2011. *The Story So Far What We Know About the Business of Digital Journalism*, New York: Columbia Journalism School/Tow Center for Digital Journalism.

Guardian, 2010. Journalist blogging and commenting guidelines. *Guardian*. Available at: www.guardian.co.uk/info/2010/oct/19/journalist-blogging-commenting-guidelines (accessed 7 May 2012).

Gunter, J., 2011a. @ITVLauraK: my Twitter followers don't belong to the BBC, ITV, or me. Journalism.co.uk. Available at: http://blogs.journalism.co.uk/editors/2011/09/01/itvlaurak-my-twitter-followers-dont-belong-to-the-bbc-itv-or-me/ (accessed 5 September 2011).

Gunter, J., 2011b. Be accessible, be realistic, Guido Fawkes advises small news outlets. Journalism.co.uk. Available at: http://blogs.journalism.co.uk/editors/2011/04/15/ijf11-be-accessible-be-realistic-guido-fawkes-advises-small-news-outlets/ (accessed 15 April 2011).

Gunter, J., 2011c. *Guardian* announces new 'digital-first' strategy amid losses. Journalism.co.uk. Available at: www.journalism.co.uk/news/guardian-announces-new-digital-first-strategy-amid-losses/s2/a544759/ (accessed 3 July 2012).

Guru-Murthy, K., 2011. Selling Off Britain. Guru blog. Available at: http://blogs.channel4.com/gurublog/selling-off-britain/848 (accessed 15 October 2011).

Habermas, J., 1989. *The structural transformation of the public sphere: an inquiry into a category of bourgeois society*, Cambridge, MA: MIT Press.

Hacks and Hackers, 2011. Hacks/Hackers. Available at: http://hackshackers.com/ (accessed 4 September 2011).

Hafner, K. & Markoff, J., 1991. *Cyberpunk: outlaws and hackers on the computer frontier*, New York: Simon & Schuster.

Halavais, A.M.C., 2009. *Search engine society*, Cambridge; Malden, MA: Polity.

Halliday, J., 2011. Personal branding is key for would-be journalists. Available at: http://www.bbc.co.uk/blogs/blogcollegeofjournalism/posts/personal_branding_for_would-be (accessed 30 January 2013).

Halliday, J., 2012. Sky News clamps down on Twitter use. *Guardian*. Available at: www.guardian.co.uk/media/2012/feb/07/sky-news-twitter-clampdown (accessed 7 May 2012).

Hamilton, M., 2011. Personal interview by Clare Cook.

Harcup, T., 2009. *Journalism: principles & practice*, 2nd edn, Los Angeles: SAGE.

Harcup, T. and O'Neill, D., 2001. What is news? Galtung and Ruge revisited. *Journalism Studies*, 2(2), pp. 261–280.

Hari, J., 2011. Johann Hari: a personal apology. *Independent*. Available at: www.independent.co.uk/opinion/commentators/johann-hari/johann-hari-a-personal-apology-2354679.html (accessed 4 January 2012).

References

Harner, D., 2011. College students miss the journalistic potential of social media/PBS. MediaShift. Available at: www.pbs.org/mediashift/2011/07/college-students-miss-the-journalistic-potential-of-social-media192.html (accessed 15 June 2012).

Harrison, J., 2010. User-generated content and gatekeeping at the BBC hub. *Journalism Studies*, 11(2), pp. 243–256.

Hartley, S., 2011. Personal interview by Clare Cook.

Hayes, J., 2009. *A shock to the system: journalism, government and the Freedom of Information Act 2000*, Reuters Institute for the Study of Journalism. Available at: http://reutersinstitute.politics.ox.ac.uk/fileadmin/documents/Publications/Hayes_A_Shock_to_the_System.pdf (accessed 2 January 2012).

Hearn, A., 2008. 'Meat, mask, burden': Probing the contours of the branded 'self'. *Journal of Consumer Culture*, 8, pp. 197–217.

Hennessy, B., 2006. *Writing feature articles*, 4th edn, Oxford; Burlington, MA: Focal Press.

Henry, L., 2011. Painful doubts about Amina/Composite. Bookmaniac. Available at: http://bookmaniac.org/painful-doubts-about-amina/ (accessed 27 May 2012).

Hermida, A., 2010. From TV to Twitter: How Ambient News Became Ambient Journalism. *M/C Journal*, 13(2).

Hermida, Alfred, 2011a. Mechanisms of participation. In *Participatory journalism guarding open gates at online newspapers*. Chichester, Malden, MA: Wiley-Blackwell.

Hermida, Alf, 2011b. REPORTR.NET: research shows benefits of open innovation for news. International Symposium on Online Journalism. Available at: http://online.journalism.utexas.edu/detail.php?story=356&year=2011 (accessed 27 February 2012).

Hermida, Alfred, 2012a. Sourcing the Arab Spring: a case study of Andy Carvin's sources during the Tunisian and Egyptian Revolutions. In International Symposium on Online Journalism. Austin, TX.

Hermida, Alfred, 2012b. Tweets and truth. *Journalism Practice*, pp. 1–10.

Hernandez, 2011. Directives from the Ministry of Truth: Wenzhou high-speed train crash. *China Digital Times*. Available at: http://chinadigitaltimes.net/2011/07/directives-from-the-ministry-of-truth-wenzhou-high-speed-train-crash/ (accessed 2 January 2012).

Herrman, S., 2010. BBC News linking policy. The Editors. Available at: www.bbc.co.uk/blogs/theeditors/2010/03/bbc_news_linking_policy.html (accessed 23 October 2011).

Hickman, L., 2001. Tracking down the tourist of death. *Guardian*, 30 November p. 4.

Hicks, W., 1998. *English for journalists*, London; New York: Routledge.

Hicks, W., Adams, S., Gilbert, H. and Holmes, T., 2008. *Writing for journalists*, London; New York: Routledge.

Hoag, A., 2008. Measuring media entrepreneurship. *International Journal on Media Management*, 10(2), pp. 74–80.

Hohmann, J., 2010–11. ASNE Ethics and Values Committee, 2011. *ASNE: 10 Best Practices for Social Media: Helpful guidelines for news organizations*, Reston, VA: American Society of News Editors.

Holliday, G., 2010. Publishing process – Kigali back wire. Kigali Wire. Available at: http://kigalibackwire.tumblr.com/post/185324727/publishing-process (accessed 13 April 2012).

Hopkins, H., 2010. Facebook largest news reader? Hitwise. Available at: www.experian.com/blogs/hitwise/2010/02/03/facebook-largest-news-reader/ (accessed 19 June 2012).

Howe, J., 2009. *Crowdsourcing: why the power of the crowd is driving the future of business*, New York: Three Rivers Press.

Hughes, N., 2011a. 600 Lines of Code, 748 Revisions = A Load of Bubbles | ScraperWiki Data Blog. Data Miner UK. Available at: http://blog.scraperwiki.com/2011/03/08/600-lines-of-code-748-revisions-a-load-of-bubbles/ (accessed 15 October 2011).

Hughes, N., 2011b. Data Miner UK. Available at: https://datamineruk.wordpress.com/ (accessed 24 August 2011).

Hulme, T., 2012. Start ups. *Wired*. May.

Ingram, M., 2011. The NYT tries to get its readers to 'level up'. GigaOM. Available at: http://gigaom.com/2011/12/02/the-nyt-tries-to-get-its-readers-to-level-up/ (accessed 29 December 2011).

References

Institut für Medienpolitik, 2009. Alan Rusbridger on the future of journalism, Available at: www.youtube.com/watch?v=Wra5rdLrWLw (accessed 16 November 2011).

Internet World Stats, 2011. World internet usage statistics news and world population stats. Internet World Stats. Available at: www.internetworldstats.com/stats.htm (accessed 15 November 2011).

Ireland, T., 2009. What have Martin Townsend and Paula Murray got to say for themselves? Bloggerheads. Available at: www.bloggerheads.com/archives/2009/03/martin_townsend/ (accessed 15 May 2012).

Isaksen, S.G. and Tidd, J., 2006. *Meeting the innovation challenge: leadership for transformation and growth*, Chichester; Hoboken, NJ: John Wiley.

Jaakonen, K., 2012. Sustainable Business Models for Journalism – Case study: Hellapoliisi (Finland). SubMoJour. Available at: www.submojour.net/archives/639/case-study-hellapoliisi-finland/#more-639 (accessed 12 April 2012).

Jackson, J., 2011. Zynga's secret to success: connecting casual friends. PC World Australia. Available at: www.pcworld.idg.com.au/article/376848/zynga_secret_success_connecting_casual_friends/ (accessed 23 June 2012).

Jan, F., 2011. Understanding the public sphere in a network society. Big Think. Available at: http://bigthink.com/ideas/40529?page=all (accessed 16 October 2011).

Jarvis, J., 2008. The imperatives of the link economy. Buzzmachine. Available at: http://buzzmachine.com/2008/07/28/the-imperatives-of-the-link-economy/ (accessed 19 June 2012).

Jarvis, J., 2009. Product v. process journalism: the myth of perfection v. beta culture. Buzzmachine. Available at: www.buzzmachine.com/2009/06/07/processjournalism/ (accessed 28 October 2011).

Jarvis, J., 2011. The article as luxury or byproduct. Buzzmachine. Available at: http://buzzmachine.com/2011/05/28/the-article-as-luxury-or-byproduct/ (accessed 24 May 2012).

Jempson, M. and Powell, W., 2012. Blame not the mobile phone, 'twas ever thus. In R.L. Keeble, ed. *The phone hacking scandal: journalism on trial*. London: Arima.

Jenkins, H., 2006a. *Convergence culture: where old and new media collide*, New York: New York University Press.

Jenkins, H., 2006b. *Fans, bloggers, and gamers: exploring participatory culture*, New York: New York University Press.

Jenkins, R., 2002. *Pierre Bourdieu*, rev. edn, London; New York: Routledge.

Joel, M., 2011. Humanization of business/six pixels of separation – marketing and communications insights. Twist Image. Available at: www.twistimage.com/tag/humanization-of-business (accessed 13 April 2012).

Johnston, M., 2012. DurhamRegion article: compassionate story gave snapshot of teen's life. Durham Region. Available at: www.durhamregion.com/opinion/columns/article/1301682--compassionate-story-gave-snapshot-of-teen-s-life (accessed 10 May 2012).

Jones, J. and Salter, L., 2012. *Digital journalism*. Los Angeles, Calif.; London: SAGE.

Jönsson, A.M. and Örnebring, H., 2011. User-generated content and the news. *Journalism Practice*, 5(2), pp. 127–144.

Kaplan, J.M. and Warren, A.C., 2010. *Patterns of entrepreneurship management*, Hoboken, NJ; Chichester: Wiley.

Karp, S., 2007. Journalism is now a continuous dynamic process, not a static product. *Publishing 2.0*. Available at: http://publishing2.com/2007/08/18/journalism-is-now-a-continuous-dynamic-process-not-a-static-product/ (accessed 28 October 2011).

Katz, E., 1988. Disintermediation: cutting out the middle man. Annenberg School for Communication. Available at: http://repository.upenn.edu/cgi/viewcontent.cgi?article=1165&context=asc_papers. (accessed 19 May 2012)

Katz, I., 2011. SXSW 2011: Andy Carvin – the man who tweeted the revolution. *Guardian*. Available at: www.guardian.co.uk/technology/2011/mar/14/andy-carvin-tunisia-libya-egypt-sxsw-2011 (accessed 27 May 2012).

Kaul, V., 2012. Changing paradigms of media landscape in the digital age. *Journal of Mass Communication and Journalism*, 2(2). Available at: www.omicsgroup.org/journals/2165-7912/2165-7912-2-110.digital/2165-7912-2-110.html (accessed 12 April 2012).

Kawasaki, G., 2004. *The Art of the Start*, London: Penguin Books.

References

Kaye, J. and Quinn, S., 2010. *Funding journalism in the digital age: business models, strategies, issues and trends*, New York: Peter Lang.

Keane, J., 1991. *The media and democracy*, Cambridge: Polity Press.

Keller, B., 2011. All the aggregation that's fit to aggregate. *New York Times*. Available at: www.nytimes.com/2011/03/13/magazine/mag-13lede-t.html?_r=2 (accessed 3 June 2012).

Kennedy, M., 2012. Why embargoes are dangerous in the age of social media. PRFuel. Available at: www.ereleases.com/prfuel/why-embargoes-are-dangerous-in-the-age-of-social-media/ (accessed 3 June 2012).

Kihlstrom, R. and Laffont, J.J., 1979. A general equilibrium theory of the firm based on risk aversion. *Journal of political economy*, 87(4), pp. 719–748.

Kim, E.-G. and Hamilton, J.W., 2006. Capitulation to capital? OhmyNews as alternative media. *Media, Culture & Society*, 28(4), pp. 541–560.

Kiss, J., 2011. Andy Carvin: the man who tweets revolutions. *Guardian*, 5 September, p. 31.

Knight, F.H., 2002. *Risk, uncertainty and profit*, Washington, DC: Beard Books.

Knight Foundation, 2012. Fantasy Election '12 Game – Knight Foundation. Available at: www.knightfoundation.org/grants/20115222/ (accessed 2 July 2012).

Knight, M., 2010. Blogging and citizen journalism. In N. Hyde-Clarke, ed. *The Citizen in Communication*. Cape Town: Juta.

Knight, M., 2012. Journalism as usual: the use of social media as a newsgathering tool in the coverage of the Iranian elections in 2009. *Journal of Media Practice*, 13(1), pp. 61–74.

Knight, M., 2013. The revolution will be Facebooked, broadcast and published. *Journal of African Media Studies*, in press.

Knight, M. and Cook, C. 2011. Beyond technological determinism: a model for understanding the new participatory networked news environment. *Conference proceedings MindTrek of the 15th International MindTrek conference: envisaging future media environment*. p. 249–53.

Knight News Challenge, 2009. David Cohn, Knight News Challenge winner, Available at: www.youtube.com/watch?v=PdpRmFHweBA (accessed 18 November 2011).

Kobie, N., 2010. Q&A: Conrad Wolfram on communicating with apps in Web 3.0. IT Pro. Available at: www.itpro.co.uk/621535/q-a-conrad-wolfram-on-communicating-with-apps-in-web-3-0 (accessed 31 October 2011).

Kperogi, F.A., 2010. Cooperation with the corporation? CNN and the hegemonic cooptation of citizen journalism through iReport.com. *New Media & Society*, 13(2), pp. 314–329.

Krums, J., 2009. There's a plane in the Hudson. I'm on the ferry going to pick ... on Twitpic. *@jkrums on Twitter*. Available at: http://twitpic.com/135xa (accessed 25 January 2012).

Kurpius, D.D., Metzgar, E.T. and Rowley, K.M., 2010. Sustaining hyperlocal media. *Journalism Studies*, 11, pp. 359–376.

Kuszewski, A., 2012. How to make your staff more creative. *Wired*. Available at: www.wired.co.uk/magazine/archive/2012/03/how-to/make-your-staff-more-creative (accessed 13 April 2012).

Labrecque, L.I., Markos, E. and Milne, G.R., 2011. Online personal branding: processes, challenges, and implications. *Journal of Interactive Marketing*, 25, pp. 37–50.

Lasica, J., 2009a. Associated Press's social media policy. Social Media Biz. Available at: www.socialmedia.biz/social-media-policies/associated-presss-social-media-policy/ (accessed 7 May 2012).

Lasica, J., 2009b. *New York Times'* social media policy. Social Media Biz. Available at: www.socialmedia.biz/social-media-policies/new-york-times-social-media-policy/ (accessed 7 May 2012).

Lasica, J., 2009c. *Wall Street Journal*'s social media policy. Social Media Biz. Available at: www.socialmedia.biz/social-media-policies/wall-street-journals-social-media-policy/ (accessed 7 May 2012).

Lasorsa, D.L., Lewis, S.C. and Holton, A.E., 2011. Normalizing Twitter. *Journalism Studies*, 13(1), pp.19–36.

Levinson, J.C., Livinson, J. and Livinson, A., 2007. *Guerrilla marketing: easy and inexpensive strategies for making big profits from your small business*, London: Piatkus.

Levitt, T., et al. 1965. Exploit the product life cycle, *Harvard Business Review*, 43, Nov-Dec, pp. 81–94.

References

Levy, D.A. and Neilsen, R.K., 2010. *The changing business of journalism and its implications for democracy*, Oxford: Reuters Institute for the Study of Journalism.

Lewis, S. and Aitamurto, T., 2011. Discussing open innovation and open source at the future of journalism 2011. Seth C. Lewis. Available at: http://sethlewis.org/2011/09/09/discussing-open-innovation-and-open-source-at-the-future-of-journalism-2011/ (accessed 12 April 2012).

Lewis, S., Kaufhold, K. and Lasorsa, D., 2010. Thinking about citizen journalism. *Journalism Practice*, 4(2), pp. 163–179.

Liebling, A.J., 1960. Do you belong in journalism. *The New Yorker*, 14 May, p. 105.

Life Magazine, 1963. Split-second sequence as the bullets struck. *Life*, 29 November, pp. 24–32.

Little, M., 2011. The human algorithm. Storyful blog. Available at: http://blog.storyful.com/2011/05/20/the-human-algorithm-2/ (accessed 26 May 2012).

Liverpool Echo, 2008. Police use Bluetooth to fight crime. Liverpool Echo. Available at: www.liverpool-echo.co.uk/liverpool-news/local-news/2008/06/17/police-use-bluetooth-to-fight-crime-100252-21087076/ (accessed 31 October 2011).

Livingston, J., 2008. *Founders at work: stories of startups' early days*, Berkeley, CA: Apress.

Lloyd, J., 2012. Sustainable business models for journalism – case study: Media Street Apps Limited (UK). SubMoJour. Available at: www.submojour.net/archives/784/case-study-media-street-apps-limited/ (accessed 13 April 2012).

Lo, P., 2011. #bbcsms: mainstream media, social media and emergencies. BBC College of Journalism. Available at: www.bbc.co.uk/journalism/blog/2011/05/bbcsms-mainstream-media-social.shtml (accessed 29 January 2012).

Lord Judge, 2011. *Practice guidance: the use of live text-based forms of communication (including Twitter) from court for the purposes of fair and accurate reporting*, Available at: www.judiciary.gov.uk/Resources/JCO/Documents/Guidance/ltbc-guidance-dec-2011.pdf. (accessed 4 June 2012)

Luft, O., 2007. AFP forges viral video distribution deal. Journalism.co.uk. Available at: www.journalism.co.uk/news/afp-forges-viral-video-distribution-deal/s2/a53439/ (accessed 10 October 2011).

Lukin, J., 2006. AVC: My favorite business model. *AVC*. Available at: www.avc.com/a_vc/2006/03/my_favorite_bus.html#c15324948 (accessed 19 June 12012).

Mackey, R., 2011. Sifting Syrian fact from fiction on state television, YouTube and the mystery of a gay girl in Damascus. The Lede – *New York Times*. Available at: http://thelede.blogs.nytimes.com/2011/06/08/sifting-syrian-fact-from-syrian-fiction/ (accessed 27 May 2012).

MacManus, R., 2010. Techmeme turns 5: interview with founder Gabe Rivera. Readwriteweb. Available at: www.readwriteweb.com/archives/techmeme_turns_5_interview_with_gabe_rivera.php (accessed 26 October 2011).

Macmillan, G., 2012. Hashtag power: Twitter numbers highlight success of C4's *Dispatches* #TicketScandal. The Wall Blog. Available at: http://wallblog.co.uk/2012/03/09/hashtags-power-twitter-numbers-highlight-success-of-c4%E2%80%99s-dispatches-ticketscandal/ (accessed 29 May 2012).

Mamatas, N., 2010. Copyright follies. Available at: http://nihilistic-kid.livejournal.com/1553538.html (accessed 18 June 2012).

Mandraud, I., 2011. Personal interview by Clare Cook.

Margulis, S.T., 2003. Privacy as a social issue and behavioral concept. *Journal of Social Issues*, 59(2), pp. 243–261.

Marks, P., 2011. One per cent: absurd rules make WSJ's new leak site a non-starter. *New Scientist*. Available at: www.newscientist.com/blogs/onepercent/2011/05/phone-hacking-publishers-leak.html (accessed 2 July 2012).

Marshall, S., 2011. How journalists can best use Facebook pages. Available at: http://blogs.journalism.co.uk/2011/07/01/jpod-in-depth-how-journalists-can-best-use-facebook-pages/ (accessed 23 June 2012).

Marshall, S., 2012. Campaign proposes 'number hygiene' rules for journalists. Journalism.co.uk. Available at: www.journalism.co.uk/news/getstats-12-number-hygiene-rules-journalists/s2/a547689/ (accessed 1 July 2012).

Martin, K., 2011. Public banned from doctor's sex hearing. Canoe.ca. Available at: http://cnews.canoe.ca/ CNEWS/Crime/2011/06/01/18223766.html (accessed 3 June 2012).

Mayer, M., 2006. Marissa Mayer, Google – nine lessons learned about creativity at Google. Stanford's Entrepreneurship Corner. Available at: http://ecorner.stanford.edu/authorMaterialInfo.html?mid=1554 (accessed 1 May 2012).

McAthy, R., 2011. #bbcsms: Use data to inform newsroom decisions, says panel. Journalism.co.uk. Available at: http://blogs.journalism.co.uk/tag/raju-narisetti/ (accessed 28 October 2011).

McAthy, R., 2012. How to: verify content from social media. Journalism.co.uk. Available at: www.journalism. co.uk/news-features/how-to-verify-content-from-social-media/s5/a548645/ (accessed 26 May 2012).

McCarthy, E.J. and Perreault, W.D., 1984. *Basic Marketing: a managerial approach*, Homewood, IL: Richard D. Irwin.

McGhee, G., 2010. Journalism in the age of data. Available at: http://datajournalism.stanford.edu/ (accessed 4 September 2011).

McGinty, C., 2012. Personal interview by Clare Cook.

McKane, A., 2006. *News writing*, London; Thousand Oaks, CA: SAGE.

McLuhan, M., 1964. *Understanding media: the extensions of man*, Corte Madera, CA: Gingko Press.

Merrill, J.C., 1997. *Journalism ethics: philosophical foundations for news media*, Boston; New York: Bedford/ St. Martin's.

Messner, M. and Distaso, M.W., 2008. The source cycle. *Journalism Studies*, 9(3), pp. 447–463.

Mills, J., 2011. Personal interview by Clare Cook.

Mirror, 2004. SORRY ... WE WERE HOAXED. *Mirror*. Available at: www.mirror.co.uk/news/uk-news/sorry-we-were-hoaxed-539838 (accessed 16 May 2012).

Mishra, G. and Bradshaw, P., 2010. The News Diamond reimagined as 'The Digital News Lifecycle'. Online Journalism Blog. Available at: http://onlinejournalismblog.com/2010/06/02/the-news-diamond-reimagined-as-the-digital-news-lifecycle/ (accessed 21 May 2012).

Moore, M., 2009. Facebook introduces 'memorial' pages to prevent alerts about dead members. *Telegraph*. Available at: www.telegraph.co.uk/technology/facebook/6445152/Facebook-introduces-memorial-pages-to-prevent-alerts-about-dead-members.html (accessed 10 May 2012).

Morgan, P., 2005. *The insider: the private diaries of a scandalous decade*, London: Ebury.

Morozov, E., 2011. *The net delusion: how not to liberate the world*, London: Allen Lane.

Morpork, 2011. The *Guardian* Newsblog and the death of journalism. *The Louse and the Flea*. Available at: http:// louseandflea.wordpress.com/2011/02/22/the-guardian-newsblog-and-the-death-of-journalism/ (accessed 30 December 2011).

Morris, S., 2011. How I tweeted the Vincent Tabak trial. *Guardian*. Available at: www.guardian.co.uk/uk/2011/ nov/02/vincent-tabak-trial-tweeted (accessed 4 June 2012).

Morris, S., Wells, M. and Blackstock, C., 2004. Arrests over *Mirror* photo hoax. *Guardian*. Available at: www. guardian.co.uk/media/2004/may/19/pressandpublishing.iraq?INTCMP=SRCH (accessed 16 May 2012).

Mortensen, M., 2011. When citizen photojournalism sets the news agenda: Neda Agha Soltan as a Web 2.0 icon of post-election unrest in Iran. *Global Media and Communication*, 7(1), pp. 4–16.

Murdoch, R., 2005. News Corporation speech by Rupert Murdoch to the American Society of Newspaper Editors. News Corporation. Available at: www.newscorp.com/news/news_247.html (accessed 15 November 2011).

Murray, A., 2011. Blog – #bbcsms: BBC processes for verifying social media content. BBC College of Journalism. Available at: http://www.bbc.co.uk/journalism/blog/2011/05/bbcsms-bbc-procedures-for-veri. shtml (accessed 18 May 2011).

Musser, J., 2007. What is a platform? Programmable web. Available at: http://blog.programmableweb. com/2007/09/19/what-is-a-platform/ (accessed 24 May 2012).

Nardelli, A., 2011. Journalists on Twitter: how do Britain's news organisations tweet? *Guardian*. Available at: www.guardian.co.uk/news/datablog/2011/apr/08/twitter-journalists-tweets?utm_source=feedburner&utm_

medium=feed&utm_campaign=Feed%3A+theguardian%2Fmedia%2Frss+%28Media%29&utm_content=Google+Reader (accessed 1 May 2011).

Nel, François, 2010. Where else is the money? *Journalism Practice*, 4(3), pp. 360–372.

Nel, François, 2011. Play it again: #socialden slides and links. Digital Editors Network. Available at: http://digitaleditorsnetwork.blogspot.com/2011/06/play-it-again-socialden-slides-and.html (accessed 31 October 2011).

New York Times, 2011a. Charting the American debt crisis – graphic. *New York Times*. Available at: www.nytimes.com/interactive/2011/07/28/us/charting-the-american-debt-crisis.html (accessed 4 September 2011).

New York Times, 2011b. Mapping America: Every City, Every Block. Available at: http://projects.nytimes.com/census/2010/explorer (accessed 4 September 2011).

Newman, N., 2009. *The rise of social media*, Oxford: Reuters Institute for the Study of Journalism. Available at: www.oxforduniversitystores.co.uk/browse/extra_info.asp?modid=1&prodid=869&deptid=89&compid=1&prodvarid=0&catid=65 (accessed 31 August 2011).

Newman, N., 2011. *Mainstream media and the distribution of news in the age of social media*, Oxford: Reuters Institute for the study of Journalism. Available at: https://www.oxforduniversitystores.co.uk/browse/extra_info.asp?modid=1&prodid=869&deptid=89&compid=1&prodvarid=0&catid=65 (accessed 31 August 2011).

Newmark, C., 2009. The acceptance of failure as a spur to innovation. *Huffington Post*. Available at: www.huffingtonpost.com/craig-newmark/the-acceptance-of-failure_b_231348.html (accessed 1 May 2012).

Newspaper Association of America, 2012. Annual (All Categories). *Advertising Annual Expenditures*. Available at: www.naa.org/Trends-and-Numbers/Advertising-Expenditures/Annual-All-Categories.aspx (accessed 19 June 2012).

Newton, J. and Duncan, S., 2012. Hacking into tragedy: exploring the ethics of death reporting in the social media age. In R. L. Keeble, ed. *The phone hacking scandal: journalism on trial.* London: Arima.

Nichols, J. and McChesney, R.W., 2009. The death and life of great American newspapers. *The Nations*. Available at: www.thenation.com/article/death-and-life-great-american-newspapers (accessed 18 June 2012).

Nicola, B. and Neilsen, R.K., 2012. *Survival is success*, Oxford: Reuters Institute for the Study of Journalism.

Nieman Lab, 2011. Pushing to the future of journalism. Nieman Lab. Available at: www.niemanlab.org/tag/data-journalism/ (accessed 4 September 2011).

Niles, R., 2007. A journalist's guide to crowdsourcing. OJR: The Online Journalism Review. Available at: www.ojr.org/ojr/stories/070731niles/ (accessed 6 January 2011).

Niles, R., 2011. What's the point of media credentials? OJR: The Online Journalism Review. Available at: www.ojr.org/ojr/people/robert/201111/2034/ (accessed 4 December 2011).

Nip, J., 2009. Citizen Journalism in China. In S. Allan, ed. *Citizen journalism: global perspectives*. New York: Peter Lang.

Nolan, H., 2012. We don't need no stinking seal of approval from the blog police. Gawker.com. Available at: http://gawker.com/5892453/we-dont-need-no-stinking-seal-of-approval-from-the-blog-police (accessed 3 June 2012).

O'Sullivan, J. and Heinonen, A., 2008. Old values, new media. *Journalism Practice*, 2(3), pp. 357–371.

Oakes-Ash, R., 2011. How social media killed the embargo. PitchIt2Me. Available at: http://pitchit2me.wordpress.com/2011/07/06/how-social-media-killed-the-embargo/ (accessed 3 June 2012).

Office for National Statistics, 2011. Home: UK National Statistics Publication Hub. Office for National Statistics. Available at: www.statistics.gov.uk/hub/index.html (accessed 24 August 2011).

Organisation for Economic Co-operation and Development, 2009. OECD examines the future of news and the Internet: estimated newspaper publishing market decline in OECD countries 2007–2009. OECD. Available at: www.oecd.org/document/48/0,3343,en_2649_33703_45449136_1_1_1_1,00.html (accessed 19 June 2012).

Organisation for Economic Co-operation and Development, 2010. The evolution of news and the internet, OECD. Available at: www.oecd.org/dataoecd/30/24/45559596.pdf. (accessed 19 June 2012)

Osofsky, J., 2010. Making news and entertainment more social in 2011. Facebook developer blog. Available at: http://developers.facebook.com/blog/post/443/ (accessed 27 October 2011).

References

Ostrow, A., 2011. Facebook now has 800 million users. Mashable. Available at: http://mashable.com/2011/09/22/facebook-800-million-users/ (accessed 31 October 2011).

Outing, S., 2005. Taking tsunami coverage into their own hands. Poynter Institute. Available at: www.poynter.org/uncategorized/29330/taking-tsunami-coverage-into-their-own-hands/ (accessed 27 December 2011).

Oxfam, 2011. Resources and publications. Oxfam.org. Available at: www.oxfam.org.uk/resources/ (accessed 24 August 2011).

OxIs, 2011. Highlights from the OxIS 2011 Report launch. Oxford Internet Surveys. Available at: http://microsites.oii.ox.ac.uk/oxis/blog/2011/highlights-oxis-2011-report-launch (accessed 19 January 2012).

Papacharissi, Z., 2002. The virtual sphere: the internet as a public sphere. *New Media & Society*, 4(1), pp. 9–27.

Papacharissi, Z., 2009. The virtual geographies of social networks: a comparative analysis of Facebook, LinkedIn and ASmallWorld. *New Media & Society*, 11(1–2), pp. 199–220.

Papacharissi, Zizi, 2011. *A networked self: identity, community and culture on social network sites*, New York: Routledge.

Pape, S. and Featherstone, S., 2006. *Feature writing a practical introduction*, London; Thousand Oaks, CA: SAGE Publications.

Pavlik, J.V., 1999. New media and news: implications for the future of journalism. *New Media & Society*, 1(1), pp. 54–59.

Pavlik, J., 2001. *Journalism and new media*, New York: Columbia University Press.

Peters, T., 1997. The brand called you. Fast Company. Available at: www.fastcompany.com/magazine/10/brandyou.html?page=0,0 (accessed 30 August 2011).

Phillips, A., 2006. *Good writing for journalists: narrative, style, structure*, London; Thousand Oaks, CA: SAGE Publications.

Phillips, W., 2012. *The house that Fox built: anonymous, spectacle and cycles of amplification*. PhD thesis. Eugene, OR: University of Oregon. Available at: https://scholarsbank.uoregon.edu/xmlui/handle/1794/12204?show=full. (accessed 15 May 2012)

Picard, R., 1989. *Media economics: concepts and issues*, London: SAGE Publications.

Picard, R., 2010. A business perspective on challenges facing journalism. In David Levy and Rasmus Kleis Nielsen (eds) *The changing business of journalism and its implications for democracy*, Oxford: Reuters Institute for the Study of Journalism, pp. 17–24.

Pickard, M., 2010. Open door: the *Guardian*'s head of digital engagement on ... the rules of participation. *Guardian*. Available at: www.guardian.co.uk/commentisfree/2010/nov/01/digital-engagement-rules-of-participation (accessed 7 May 2012).

Pickard, M., 2011. Personal interview by Clare Cook.

Pickard, M. and Catt, D., 2011. *Robots, editors, strangers and friends*. Presented at Future Everything, Manchester.

Piechota, G., 2011. Personal interview with Clare Cook.

Poell, T. and Borra, E., 2011. Twitter, YouTube, and Flickr as platforms of alternative journalism: The social media account of the 2010 Toronto G20 protests. *Journalism*, 13(6), pp. 695–713.

Polymuche, 2011. Interview of Tom McMaster AKA Amina Arraf (a gay girl in Damaskus). Daily Motion. Available at: www.dailymotion.com/video/xjaq0d_interview-of-tom-mcmaster-aka-amina-arraf-a-gay-girl-in-damaskus_news (accessed 27 May 2012).

Ponsford, D., 2011. Mail Online hits new record with 79m unique browsers. *Press Gazette*. Available at: www.pressgazette.co.uk/story.asp?sectioncode=1&storycode=48335 (accessed 2 July 2012).

Poor, N., 2005. Mechanisms of an online public sphere: the website slashdot. *Journal of Computer-Mediated Communication*, 10(2), article 4. Available from: http://jcmc.indiana.edu/vol10/issue2/poor.html. (accessed 10 July 2012)

Porter, M.E., 1979. How competitive forces shape strategy. *Harvard Business Review*, (Issue: 79208).

Poynter Institute, 2011. Hacks/Hackers. Poynter Institute. Available at: www.poynter.org/tag/hackshackers/ (accessed 4 September 2011).

Press Complaints Commission, 2009. 2009 statistics and case studies. Press Complaints Commission. Available at: www.pcc.org.uk/review09/2009_statistics/case_studies.php (accessed 6 May 2012).

Project for Excellence in Journalism, 2011a. Navigating news online. Project for Excellence in Journalism. Available at: www.journalism.org/analysis_report/navigating_news_online (accessed 23 January 2012).

Project for Excellence in Journalism, 2011b. The tablet revolution. Project for Excellence in Journalism. Available at: www.journalism.org/analysis_report/tablet (accessed 19 June 2012).

ProPublica, 2011. Tools & data. ProPublica. Available at: www.propublica.org/tools/ (accessed 4 September 2011).

ProPublica, 2012. About us. ProPublica. Available at: www.propublica.org/about/ (accessed 1 January 2012).

Pugh, A., 2012. Is Facebook 'plundering' the new phone-hacking? *Press Gazette*. Available at: www.pressgazette.co.uk/story.asp?sectioncode=1&storycode=48789&c=1 (accessed 12 March 2012).

Purcell, K., Rainie, L., Mitchell, A., Rosenstiel, T., Olmstead, K., 2010. *Understanding the participatory news consumer: how internet and cell phone users have turned news into a social experience.* Pew Research Centre.

Quandt, T., 2008. (No) News on the World Wide Web. *Journalism Studies*, 9(5), pp. 717–738.

Quatremer, J., 2012. Personal interview by Clare Cook.

Quinn, S., 1998. Newsgathering and the internet. In M. Breen, ed. *Journalism: theory and practice*. Paddington, NSW: Macleay Press.

Quinn, S. and Lamble, S., 2007. *Online newsgathering: research and reporting for journalism*, Oxford: Focal.

Radcliffe, D., 2012. *Here and now UK hyperlocal media today*, Nesta. Available at: http://www.nesta.org.uk/areas_of_work/creative_economy/destination_local/assets/features/here_and_now_uk_hyperlocal_media_today. (accessed 10 July 2012)

Randall, D., 2011. *The universal journalist*, London; New York: Pluto Press.

Reinartz, W., Krafft, M. and Hoyer, W.D., 2004. The customer relationship management process: its measurement and impact on performance. *Journal of Marketing Research*, 41(3), pp. 293–305.

Reportsfromtheegyptianuprising, 2011. Available at: http://reportsfromtheegyptianuprising.wordpress.com/ (accessed 4 January 2012).

Rideout, V.J., Foehr, U.G. and Roberts, D.F., 2010. *Generation M2 media in the lives of 8 to 18 year olds*, Kaiser Family Foundation. Available at: www.kff.org/entmedia/upload/8010.pdf. (accessed 10 July 2012)

Riehl, M., 2011. Is lifting condolences off Facebook too easy? *Kings Journalism Review*. Available at: http://kjr.kingsjournalism.com/?p=3321 (accessed 7 May 2012).

Riley, G., 2011. Personal interview by Clare Cook.

Roberts, D., 2011. The *Guardian* is opening up its newslists so you can help us make news. *Guardian*. Available at: www.guardian.co.uk/media/2011/oct/09/the-guardian-newslists-opening-up (accessed 31 December 2011).

Robinson, J., 2010. Facebook generates 10% of Mail Online's UK traffic. *Guardian*. Available at: www.guardian.co.uk/media/2010/nov/15/mail-online-uk-traffic-facebook (accessed 25 October 2011).

Rock, M., 2012. Personal interview by Clare Cook.

Rogers, S., 2011a. England riots: suspects mapped and poverty mapped. *Guardian*. Available at: www.guardian.co.uk/news/datablog/interactive/2011/aug/16/riots-poverty-map (accessed 4 September 2011).

Rogers, S., 2011b. *Facts are sacred: the power of data*, London: Guardian Books.

Rogers, S., 2011c. Wikileaks Iraq war logs: every death mapped. *Guardian*. Available at: www.guardian.co.uk/world/datablog/interactive/2010/oct/23/wikileaks-iraq-deaths-map (accessed 2 January 2012).

Rogers, S., Sedghi, A. and Evans, L., 2011. UK riots: every verified incident – interactive map. *Guardian*. Available at: www.guardian.co.uk/news/datablog/interactive/2011/aug/09/uk-riots-incident-map (accessed 4 September 2011).

Rollings, G., 2011. Brits making money from home-made YouTube videos. *Sun*. Available at: www.thesun.co.uk/sol/homepage/features/3935617/Brits-making-money-from-home-made-YouTube-videos.html (accessed 19 June 2012).

Rosen, J., 1993. Beyond objectivity. *Nieman Reports*, 47(4), pp. 48–53.

Rosen, J., 2006. The people formerly known as the audience. Pressthink. Available at: http://archive.pressthink.org/2006/06/27/ppl_frmr.html (accessed 24 June 2012).

References

Rosenberry, J. and St John III, B., 2010. *Public journalism 2.0: the promise and reality of a citizen-engaged press*, New York: Routledge.

Royal Statistical Society, 2012. Campaigning to make Britain better with numbers and statistics. Getstats. Available at: www.getstats.org.uk/ (accessed 1 July 2012).

Rozenberg, J., 2011. Judges will decide who can tweet from court. *Guardian*. Available at: www.guardian.co.uk/law/2011/dec/14/judges-decide-who-tweets-from-court?utm_source=feedburner&utm_medium=feed&utm_campaign=Feed%3A+theguardian%2Fmedia%2Frss+%28Media%29&utm_content=Google+Reader (accessed 22 December 2011).

Rusbridger, A., 2010. The splintering of the fourth estate. *Guardian*. Available at: www.guardian.co.uk/commentisfree/2010/nov/19/open-collaborative-future-journalism (accessed 23 June 2012).

Saklofske, J., 2011. Using 4chan.org to challenge the status quo illusion of media stability. In *MIT7 unstable platforms: the promise and peril of transition*. Cambridge, MA: MIT.

Salgado, R., 2010. March 2010. Google Public Policy Blog. Available at: http://googlepublicpolicy.blogspot.co.uk/2010_03_01_archive.html (accessed 19 June 2012).

Sarasvathy, S.D., Dew, N., Velamuri, S.R., Venkataraman, S., 2003. Three views of entrepreneurial opportunity. In Z.J. Acs and D.B. Audretsch, eds. *Handbook of entrepreneurship research*. New York: Springer-Verlag, pp. 141–160. Available at: www.springerlink.com/index/10.1007/0-387-24519-7_7 (accessed 27 March 2012).

Scenable, 2012. What is a platform, anyway? The Scenable Platform for Local Community. Available at: https://scenable.com/blog/what-is-a-platform-anyway/ (accessed 24 May 2012).

Schudson, M., 2008. *Why democracies need an unlovable press*, Cambridge: Polity.

Scott, D.M., 2011. *The new rules of marketing & PR: how to use social media, online video, mobile applications, blogs, news releases, and viral marketing to reach buyers directly*, Hoboken, NJ: John Wiley & Sons.

ScraperWiki, 2011. Refine, reuse and request data. ScraperWiki. Available at: https://scraperwiki.com/ (accessed 4 September 2011).

Seamark, M., 2011. Jeremy Clarkson injunction: *Top Gear* star lifts the gag on ex-wife Alex Hall. *Daily Mail*. Available at: www.dailymail.co.uk/news/article-2053800/Jeremy-Clarkson-injunction-Top-Gear-star-lifts-gag-ex-wife-Alex-Hall.html (accessed 3 July 2012).

Shaw, A., 2011. Explore sources: a new feature to 'show our work'. ProPublica. Available at: www.propublica.org/nerds/item/explore-sources-a-new-feature-to-show-our-work (accessed 1 January 2012).

Shaw, D., 2008. Wikipedia in the newsroom. *American Journalism Review*, 30(1), pp. 40–45.

Shirky, C., 2008. Clay Shirky on information overload versus filter failure. Available at: http://blip.tv/web2expo/web-2-0-expo-ny-clay-shirky-shirky-com-it-s-not-information-overload-it-s-filter-failure-1283699 (accessed 29 May 2012).

Shoemaker, P.J., Eichholz, M., Kim, E., Wrigley, B., 2001. Individual and routine forces in gatekeeping. *Journalism & mass communication quarterly*, 78, pp. 233–246.

Sigal, L., 1973. *Reporters and officials: the organization and politics of newsmaking*, Lexington Mass.: D. C. Heath.

Silverman, C., 2012. 8 must-reads detail how to verify information in real-time, from social media, users. Poynter Institute. Available at: www.poynter.org/latest-news/regret-the-error/171713/8-must-reads-that-detail-how-to-verify-content-from-twitter-other-social-media/ (accessed 29 April 2012).

Simpson, A., 2007. Amanda Knox wrote stories about rape. *Telegraph*. Available at: www.telegraph.co.uk/news/uknews/1568639/Amanda-Knox-wrote-stories-about-rape.html (accessed 10 May 2012).

Singer, J. and Ashman, I., 2009. "Comment Is Free, but Facts Are Sacred": User-generated Content and Ethical Constructs at the Guardian. *Journal of Mass Media Ethics*, 24(1), pp. 3–21.

Singer, J.B., Hermida, A., Domingo, D., Heinonen, A., Paulussen, S., Quandt, T., Reich, Z. and Vujnovic, M., 2011. *Participatory journalism guarding open gates at online newspapers*, Hoboken, NJ: John Wiley & Sons. Available at: www.msvu.ca:2048/login?url=www.msvu.eblib.com/patron/FullRecord.aspx?p=700654 (accessed 10 July 2012).

Sissons, H., 2006. *Practical journalism: how to write news*, 1st edn, London; Thousand Oaks, CA: SAGE Publications.

References

Sivek, S.C., 2010. Social Media Under Social Control: Regulating Social Media and the Future of Socialization. *Electronic News*, 4(3), pp. 146–164.

Sky News, 2010. Who should I vote for? Sky News. Available at: http://news.sky.com/home/election/vote (accessed 2 July 2012).

Smith, H., 2012. Greek election: live Q&A. *Guardian*. Available at: www.guardian.co.uk/world/2012/may/03/greece-elections (accessed 24 June 2012).

Smyrnais, N. and Bousquet, F., 2011. The development of local online journalism in South-Western France: the case of La Dépêche du Midi. In ECREA Journalism Studies Section and 26th International Conference of Communication (CICOM). University of Navarra, Pamplona.

Snow, J., 2011. Personal interview by Clare Cook.

Socialbakers.com, 2012. Facebook Statistics by country. Available at: www.socialbakers.com/facebook-statistics/ (accessed 29 April 2012).

Society of Professional Journalists, 1996. Code of Ethics. SPJ.org. Available at: www.spj.org/ethicscode.asp (accessed 3 July 2012).

Sonderman, J., 2011a. *New York Times* overhauls comment system, grants privileges to trusted readers. Poynter Institute. Available at: www.poynter.org/latest-news/media-lab/social-media/154615/new-york-times-over-hauls-comment-system-grants-privileges-to-trusted-readers/ (accessed 29 December 2011).

Sonderman, J., 2011b. *New York Times* plans new social networking, comment features for fall launch. Poynter Institute. Available at: www.poynter.org/latest-news/media-lab/social-media/141868/new-york-times-plans-new-social-networking-comment-features-for-fall-launch/ (accessed 29 December 2011).

Sonderman, J., 2011c. Why the *New York Times* replaced its Twitter 'cyborg' with people this week. Poynter Institute. Available at: www.poynter.org/latest-news/media-lab/social-media/133431/new-york-times-tries-human-powered-tweeting-to-see-if-users-value-the-interaction/ (accessed 26 October 2011).

Spradlin, D., 2009. Building an innovation culture. *Business Week*. Available at: www.businessweek.com/media-center/podcasts/innovation/innovation_06_10_09.htm (accessed 1 May 2012).

St Clears Times, 2010. This is South Wales/councillors' plea to halt 74 homes/St clears ... Slideshare.net. Available at: www.slideshare.net/sanclertimes/this-is-south-wales-councillors-plea-to-halt-74-homes-st-clears-town-council-assembly-planning (accessed 26 October 2011).

Stashko, J., 2012. Personal interview by Clare Cook.

Steger, I., 2011. Photos of Syrian-American blogger called into question. *Wall Street Journal* blogs. Available at: http://blogs.wsj.com/dispatch/2011/06/08/photos-of-syrian-american-blogger-called-into-question/ (accessed 27 May 2012).

Stoll, C., 1989. *The cuckoo's egg : tracking a spy through the maze of computer espionage*, New York: Doubleday.

Stray, J., 2011. Wikileaks Iraq: how to visualise the text. *Guardian*. Available at: www.guardian.co.uk/news/datablog/2010/dec/16/wikileaks-iraq-visualisation (accessed 2 January 2012).

Tableau, 2011. Free Data Visualization Software. Tableau Public. Available at: http://www.tableausoftware.com/public (accessed 4 September 2011).

Talaga, T. and Fong, P., 2011. Social media users flout election reporting laws. *Star*. Available at: www.thestar.com/news/canada/politics/article/984433--social-media-users-flout-election-reporting-laws (accessed 4 July 2012).

Talbot, D., 2011. A social-media decoder. Technology Review. Available at: www.technologyreview.com/computing/38910/?p1=A1 (accessed 31 October 2011).

Tapscott, D., 2009. *Grown up digital: how the net generation is changing your world*, New York: McGraw-Hill.

Tapscott, D., 2010. *Wikinomics: how mass collaboration changes everything*, expanded edn, New York: Portfolio Penguin.

Tarbox, K., 2001. *Katie.com: my story*, New York: Penguin.

The Editors, 2011. Cyberpunked: Journal of Science, Technology, & Society. Available at: http://www.cyberpunked.org/ (accessed 4 September 2011).

The Guardian et al., 2011. *Reading the Riots: Investigating England's summer of disorder*, London: The Guardian.

Thompson, J., 2012. Personal interview by Clare Cook.

Thornburg, R., 2009. The future of news: the one tool your newsroom needs right now: a failure form. Ryan Thornburg. Available at: http://ryanthornburg.com/2009/06/10/the-one-tool-your-newsroom-needs-right-now-a-failure-form/ (accessed 1 May 2012).

Thornton, P., 2009. Pushing the practice of beat reporting – part 9. Beatblogging.org. Available at: http://beatblogging.org/page/9/ (accessed 11 July 2012).

Thorsen, E., 2008. Journalistic objectivity redefined? Wikinews and the neutral point of view. *New Media & Society*, 10(6), pp. 935–954.

Tidd, J., Bessant, J. R and Pavitt, K., 2001. *Managing innovation: integrating technological, market and organizational change*, Chichester; New York: John Wiley.

TIME, 2006. *TIME* magazine cover: person of the year: you. *TIME*, 25 December. Available at: www.time.com/time/covers/0,16641,20061225,00.html (accessed 2 January 2012).

Torres, S., 2012. Personal interview by Clare Cook.

Trippenbach, P., 2011. News rewired 2011. Available at: www.slideshare.net/trippenbach/news-rewired-oct-2011 (accessed 9 July 2012).

Tryhorn, C. and O'Carroll, L., 2004. Morgan sacked from *Daily Mirror*. *Guardian*. Available at: www.guardian.co.uk/media/2004/may/14/pressandpublishing.iraqandthemedia (accessed 16 May 2012).

Tsotsis, A., 2011. Twitter for newsrooms!? Twitter *is* a newsroom. Techcrunch. Available at: http://techcrunch.com/2011/06/27/pilcrow/ (accessed 29 May 2012).

Turkle, S., 1995. *Life on the screen: identity in the age of the Internet*, New York: Simon & Schuster.

Turner, Nick, 2012. Personal interview by Clare Cook.

Twitter Developers, J., 2012. Jake Tapper. Twitter Developer's Blog. Available at: https://dev.twitter.com/media/newsrooms/report (accessed 9 July 2012).

United Nations, 2011a. The Universal Declaration of Human Rights. UN.Org. Available at: www.un.org/en/documents/udhr/ (accessed 12 March 2012).

United Nations, 2011b. UN data. Available at: http://data.un.org/Default.aspx (accessed 24 August 2011).

van Dijk, J., 2006. *The network society. Social aspects of new media*, London: SAGE.

Varian, H., 2010. Newspaper economics, online and offline. Scribd.com. Available at: www.scribd.com/doc/28470293/Newspaper-economics-Online-and-Offline-03-13-2010-Hal-Varian-FTC-Preso-Revised (accessed 19 June 2012).

Vena, J., 2011. Justin Bieber guest editing *Vanity Fair*'s Facebook page. MTV. Available at: www.mtv.com/news/articles/1655606/justin-bieber-vanity-fair-facebook.jhtml (accessed 27 October 2011).

Viegas, F.B., 2005. Bloggers' expectations of privacy and accountability: an initial survey. *Journal of Computer-Mediated Communication*, 10(3). Available at: http://jcmc.indiana.edu/vol10/issue3/viegas.html (accessed 29 April 2012).

Voget, A. and Selbach, J., 2006. The effect of outgoing links on your web site. Free SEO News. Available at: www.free-seo-news.com/newsletter220.htm#facts (accessed 23 October 2011).

Vowl, A., 2009. The enemies of reason: a new low for the Express. Enemies of Reason. Available at: http://enemiesofreason.blogspot.co.uk/2009/03/new-low-for-express.html?showComment=1236771240000#c7536308361711223560 (accessed 15 May 2012).

Ward, S.J.A. & Wasserman, H., 2010. Towards an Open Ethics: Implications of New Media Platforms for Global Ethics Discourse. *Journal of Mass Media Ethics*, 25(4), pp. 275–292.

Wardle, C. and Williams, A., 2010. Beyond user-generated content: a production study examining the ways in which UGC is used at the BBC. *Media, Culture & Society*, 32(5), pp. 781–799.

Wattenberg, L., 2011. Baby name wizard. NameVoyager. Available at: www.babynamewizard.com/voyager# (accessed 4 September 2011).

Weinberger, D., 2007. *Everything is miscellaneous: the power of the new digital disorder*, New York: Henry Holt & Company.

Weingarten, G., 2011. How branding is ruining journalism. *Washington Post*. Available at: www.washingtonpost.com/lifestyle/magazine/2011/06/07/AGBegthH_story.html (accessed 30 August 2011).

Wells, M., 2011. How live blogging has transformed journalism. *Guardian*. Available at: www.guardian.co.uk/media/2011/mar/28/live-blogging-transforms-journalism (accessed 30 December 2011).

White House, 2011. Open for questions: the president's speech on the Middle East and North Africa. White House. Available at: www.whitehouse.gov/photos-and-video/video/2011/05/19/open-questions-president-s-speech-middle-east-and-north-africa (accessed 30 May 2012).

Whitehouse, G., 2010. Newsgathering and Privacy: Expanding Ethics Codes to Reflect Change in the Digital Media Age. *Journal of Mass Media Ethics*, 25(4), pp. 310–327.

Whitney, L., 2010. Poll: most won't pay to read newspapers online. CNet. Available at: http://news.cnet.com/8301-1023_3-10433893-93.html (accessed 3 July 2012).

WikiLeaks, 2011. Available at: http://wikileaks.org/ (accessed 4 September 2011).

Wikinews, 2011. Mission statement – Wikinews, the free news source. Wikileaks. Available at: http://en.wikinews.org/wiki/Wikinews:Mission_statement (accessed 1 January 2012).

Williams, B.A. and Delli Carpini, M.X., 2000. Unchained reaction: the collapse of media gatekeeping and the Clinton–Lewinsky scandal. *Journalism*, 1(1), pp. 61–85.

Williams, M.E., 2010. Cooks Source: the Internet roasts a plagiarist – internet cultures Salon.com. Available at: www.salon.com/2010/11/05/cooks_source_internet_revenge/ (accessed 18 June 2012).

Wired, 2011. 2nd annual *Wired* 100: Positions 29–11, *Wired* UK. Available at: www.wired.co.uk/magazine/archive/2011/06/the-wired-100/the-wired-100-29-11?page=all (accessed 20 February 2012).

Woodward, B., 2005. How Mark Felt became 'Deep Throat'. *Washington Post*. Available at: www.washingtonpost.com/wp-dyn/content/article/2005/06/01/AR2005060102124.html (accessed 30 May 2012).

Wynn, E. and Katz, J.E., 1997. Hyperbole over cyberspace: self-presentation and social boundaries in internet home pages and discourse. *The Information Society*, 13(4), pp. 297–327.

Zelizer, B. and Allan, S., 2003. *Journalism after September 11*, London; New York: Routledge.

Zyman, S. and Brott, A.A., 2003. *The end of advertising as we know it*, Chichester: Wiley.

INDEX

Notes: **Bold** indicates figures, *italic* indicates boxes and quotes

Index